MY NINE YEARS AS GOVERNOR
of the
TERRITORY OF NEW MEXICO
1897–1906

MY NINE YEARS AS GOVERNOR
of the
TERRITORY OF NEW MEXICO
1897–1906

Facsimile of Original 1940 Edition
by
Miguel Antonio Otero
Former Governor of New Mexico

New Foreword
by
Ray John de Aragón

SANTA FE

New Material © 2007 by Sunstone Press. All Rights Reserved.

No part of this book may be reproduced in any form or by any electronic or mechanical means including information storage and retrieval systems without permission in writing from the publisher, except by a reviewer who may quote brief passages in a review.

Sunstone books may be purchased for educational, business, or sales promotional use. For information please write: Special Markets Department, Sunstone Press, P.O. Box 2321, Santa Fe, New Mexico 87504-2321.

Library of Congress Cataloging-in-Publication Data

Otero, Miguel Antonio, 1859-1944.
  My nine years as governor of the territory of New Mexico, 1897-1906 : facsimile of original 1940 edition / by Miguel Antonio Otero ; new foreword by Ray John de Aragón.
       p. cm. -- (Southwest heritage series)
    Includes index.
    ISBN: 0-86534-556-2 (softcover : alk. paper)
   1. Otero, Miguel Antonio, 1859-1944. 2. Governors--New Mexico--Biography. 3. New Mexico--History--1848- 4. New Mexico--Politics and government--1848-1950. I. Title.

F801.O89A3 2007
978.9'04092--dc22
[B]
                              2006053548

WWW.SUNSTONEPRESS.COM
SUNSTONE PRESS / POST OFFICE BOX 2321 / SANTA FE, NM 87504-2321 /USA
(505) 988-4418 / ORDERS ONLY (800) 243-5644 / FAX (505) 988-1025

The Southwest Heritage Series is dedicated to Jody Ellis and Marcia Muth Miller, the founders of Sunstone Press, whose original purpose and vision continues to inspire and motivate our publications.

CONTENTS

THE SOUTHWEST HERITAGE SERIES / I

FOREWORD TO THIS EDITION / II

FACSIMILE OF 1940 EDITION / III

I

THE SOUTHWEST HERITAGE SERIES

The history of the United States is written in hundreds of regional histories and literary works. Those letters, essays, memoirs, biographies and even collections of fiction are often first-hand accounts by people who wanted to memorialize an event, a person or simply record for posterity the concerns and issues of the times. Many of these accounts have been lost, destroyed or overlooked. Some are in private or public collections but deemed to be in too fragile condition to permit handling by contemporary readers and researchers.

However, now with the application of twenty-first century technology, nineteenth and twentieth century material can be reprinted and made accessible to the general public. These early writings are the DNA of our history and culture and are essential to understanding the present in terms of the past.

The Southwest Heritage Series is a form of literary preservation. Heritage by definition implies legacy and these early works are our legacy from those who have gone before us. To properly present and preserve that legacy, no changes in style or contents have been made. The material reprinted stands on its own as it first appeared. The point of view is that of the author and the era in which he or she lived. We would not expect photographs of people from the past to be re-imaged with modern clothes, hair styles and backgrounds. We should not, therefore, expect their ideas and personal philosophies to reflect our modern concepts.

Remember, reading their words and sharing their thoughts is a passport back into understanding how the past was shaped and how it influenced today's world.

Our hope is that new access to these older books will provide readers with a challenging and exciting experience.

II

FOREWORD TO THIS EDITION

By Ray John de Aragón

Miguel Antonio Otero was not only an author and popular territorial governor of New Mexico from 1897-1906, he was also a major presence in the rough and tumble days of New Mexico politics and Wild West turmoil.

He once stood up against the infamous Santa Fe Ring which was a shifty group of land grabbers and speculators who were stealing Spanish and Indian land grants throughout New Mexico. Otero had inherited a ranch of nearly a million acres from his father and the Ring was trying to lay claim to a portion of it by expanding the boundaries of an old Spanish land grant they had swindled. Otero, along with an armed group of his companions, chased off the Ring's men when they tried to squat on the land. The Santa Fe County sheriff arrested Miguel Otero and threw him in the Santa Fe jail until a group of Hispanic cowboys from Las Vegas busted him out. The rapid pace of this exciting episode would be reflective of this daring governor's career. He even claimed he had broken bread with the notorious outlaw Billy the Kid.

Miguel A. Otero was born on October 17, 1859, in St. Louis, Missouri. His father, who bore the same name, and who was born in Valencia, New Mexico in 1829, had built up a stellar career in the East. He was noted variously as a college professor of Latin and Greek, an attorney for the law firm of Trusten Polk in St. Louis, as a successful merchant on the Santa Fe Trail, as a bank president, and railroad president. The elder Otero also served as a delegate to the Congress for the New Mexico Territory and was appointed Secretary of the Territory by President Abraham Lincoln.

Young Miguel Antonio Otero, Jr. was brought up in a family of wealth and influence, but he also experienced the hardships of growing up in a household that was always on the move. His family's sojourns took him from one town to another across Missouri, Kansas,

Colorado, and New Mexico. At one point Miguel Antonio was left at a boarding school, the likes of which he compared to Dickens' *Oliver Twist*. Needless to say, he escaped with a couple of companions but they were turned in to the law after purchasing a train ticket to New Mexico. They were given a choice of going to jail, or returning to the boarding school. They opted for a return to the school and were severely punished. He later wrote that it would have been much better to have spent time in jail than to have been back at the school.

During Miguel A. Otero's travels and frequent stopovers in Wild Western towns he came into contact with notorious outlaws like Clay Allison and popular lawmen such as Wild Bill Hickok, Pat Garrett, Elfego Baca, and other well known figures including Doc Holliday, William F. Cody ("Buffalo Bill"), General George A. Custer, and frontiersman Christopher "Kit" Carson. In fact, Miguel Antonio was such an adventurous soul that he always sought out, or was in close contact with, anyone making headlines during the turbulent era he lived in. He even published a short lived newspaper called the *Otero Optic*, which eventually became the *Las Vegas Daily Optic*.

The family finally settled permanently in Las Vegas, New Mexico in 1879. Miguel A. Otero worked for his father's mercantile business, Otero, Sellers and Co., and he also helped his father establish the San Miguel National Bank and the first telephone company in New Mexico. Otero's father was busy paving the way for a railroad system through New Mexico while he, in turn, began an illustrious career in politics as Las Vegas City Clerk, San Miguel County probate clerk, county clerk, and recorder, and district court clerk. Then in 1892 President William McKinley appointed Miguel Antonio Otero as governor of the New Mexico territory where he served until 1906.

Miguel A. Otero rightly distinguished himself as a political leader in New Mexico where he raised a family and lived out his life as a champion of the people, but he is also highly recognized for his career as an author. He published his legendary *My Life on the Frontier, 1864-1882*, in 1935, followed by *The Real Billy the Kid: With New Light on the Lincoln County War* in 1936, *My Life on the Frontier, 1882-1897* in 1939, and *My Nine Years as Governor of the Territory of New Mexico, 1897-1906* in 1940.

These books are filled with the raw power and intrigue of the Wild West written by one who lived it. One would expect no less from such a vibrant personality who filled the pages of his monumental history with the passionate memories of an exciting era.

III

FACSIMILE OF 1940 EDITION

My Nine Years As Governor
of the
Territory of New Mexico
1897-1906

By
MIGUEL ANTONIO OTERO

Foreword by
MARION DARGAN
Editor

1940

THE UNIVERSITY OF NEW MEXICO PRESS
ALBUQUERQUE, N. M.

Copyright, 1940 by
MIGUEL A. OTERO
All rights reserved

THE UNIVERSITY OF NEW MEXICO PRESS
ALBUQUERQUE, N. M.

Dedicated to
WILLIAM McKINLEY
President of the United States

With Love and Affection
IN MEMORY
of the kind consideration shown me by him throughout
my term of office as Governor of New Mexico
to which he appointed me
WITHOUT SOLICITATION OR RECOMMENDATION
of others but solely upon his own
judgment and responsibility

FOREWORD

There was a wild scramble for office among the politicians of New Mexico in the spring of 1897. President McKinley had scarcely taken over the reins of government when he found himself confronted with the knotty problem of deciding between nineteen or twenty candidates for the governorship of that distant territory. Perplexed at first by the charges filed against likely individuals, he finally hit upon the happy idea of passing over these and appointing a young leader of the territory whom he knew personally and in whom he had great confidence. Thus it happened that Miguel Antonio Otero—a member of one of the leading Spanish families of New Mexico—suddenly arrived at a high position he had not sought. Possessed of unusual ability as an administrator, financier, and politician, the young business man had the satisfaction of seeing the territory prosper along almost every line during the next nine years. A man of strong will and determination, he had enemies as well as friends—all of which adds excitement and interest to the story. Train robbers and politicians, congressmen and chorus girls all play their part in the narrative which describes dinners at the Waldorf-Astoria and receptions at the White House, as well as political rallies and fishing trips in the territory.

Former Governor Otero has already published *My Life on the Frontier* in two fascinating volumes. Now a man of 80 years of age, he has given us an interesting account of the ups and downs of a territorial governor at the turn of the century. Equipped with a retentive memory and many documentary sources, he has added much information to our knowledge of a period somewhat neglected by historians who have never been able to resist the fascination of the early Spanish days. And if the present narrative does not please all of those readers who have some recollection of territorial days in New Mexico, perhaps it may stir some of them to take pen in hand and set forth the story from other points of view.

MARION DARGAN.

CONTENTS

Page

Chapter I
I Become Governor of the Territory of New Mexico 1

Chapter II
Saving the Waters of the Rio Grande for New Mexico 28

Chapter III
New Mexico Proves Her Loyalty 35

Chapter IV
I Join in the Victory Celebrations 54

Chapter V
Locating the Territorial Capital Permanently .. 67

Chapter VI
The Territorial Legislative Assembly 74

Chapter VII
Criminals and Convicts 90

Chapter VIII
The Folsom Train Robberies 111

Chapter IX
I Take a Hand in Territorial Politics 132

Chapter X
I Am Reappointed in Spite of My Political Enemies 142

Chapter XI
My Second Inaugural 162

Chapter XII
My Relations with President McKinley 170

Chapter XIII
I Triumph Over My Enemies Again 179

Chapter XIV
Answers to the Charges Against Me 188

Chapter XV
My Part in the Movement for Statehood 199

Contents *(Continued)*

	Page
Chapter XVI Bull Andrews Goes to Congress	223
Chapter XVII I Remove the Hubbells	240
Chapter XVIII Social Life in Old Santa Fe	249
Chapter XIX Here and There in the Territory	264
Chapter XX Moody Merrill	282
Chapter XXI I Visit the States	286
Chapter XXII The Louisiana Purchase Exposition	304
Chapter XXIII Theodore Roosevelt as I Knew Him	314
Chapter XXIV I Wind Up My Administration	332
Appendix	343
Index	397

Chapter I

I BECOME GOVERNOR OF THE TERRITORY OF NEW MEXICO

ON JUNE 2, 1897, I was appointed by President William McKinley as governor of the territory of New Mexico. Nineteen or twenty candidates had been fighting desperately for the office for some weeks, but I was not among them. In fact, although I was in Washington at the time, the appointment came to me most unexpectedly. This was, without doubt, due to an acquaintance with the President which had resulted from a casual meeting five years previously during the Republican national convention at Minneapolis, Minnesota, in June, 1892. Although I had no idea of it at the time, this chance acquaintance with the Ohio statesman developed into a lasting friendship which I shall always look back upon as one of the most cherished possessions of my whole life. It exercised a decisive influence upon my future, and it was undoubtedly this friendship with William McKinley which made my political career.

The fact that my appointment as governor was due solely to the President's friendship for me was put beyond doubt by the testimony at the time, of one who stood very close to him. It was at a luncheon given by me to Honorable John Addison Porter at the old Chamberlain restaurant in Washington, D. C. Mr. Porter was private secretary to President McKinley. During the luncheon he said:

> Governor Otero, there is one thing I think you ought to know in connection with your appointment. The other day, while in conversation with the President, he remarked, "I hope Governor Otero will thoroughly understand that he is in nowise under any obligation to anyone, other than myself, for his appointment as governor of New Mexico. I chose him on my own judgment from among the large number of candidates and without even a suggestion from anybody. I greatly admire the young man and believe he will make good, and, having selected him myself, I intend to watch his course in the management of that important territory. I am convinced he is honest, fearless, and capable."

Mr. Porter added:

> The President, I know, would feel hurt if, by any chance, you thought somebody else had anything to do with your appointment aside from himself. Now, govern yourself accordingly.

The fact that the President regarded mine as a personal appointment was confirmed by him some months later, when he consulted me regarding the judicial appointments for New Mexico. I shall discuss this fully later in this chapter.

So quickly did the Associated Press spread the news of my appointment that on the very day it was made I received two hundred and fifty telegrams and letters of congratulation. I took them all to the White House and showed them to President McKinley. After reading them, he seemed greatly pleased. He remarked: "The people seem to approve my selection for governor of the territory." I took great pleasure in his conviction that he had found the right man for the job, and also in the many messages from my friends. One letter, which I cherished especially, was from my lifelong friend, John S. Clark, with whom I had been associated for some years in Las Vegas. I quote in full in Appendix, p. 343.

My appointment was hailed by some of the newspapers of the territory as marking the end of the political career of Thomas B. Catron, would-be Republican boss of New Mexico for twenty years. If Max Frost, the influential editor of the *Santa Fe New Mexican,* and General E. L. Bartlett, felt any chagrin at my appointment, at any rate they lost no time in rallying to my support, as the following telegram indicates:

East Las Vegas, N. M., June 4th, 1897.

Hon. M. A. Otero,
National Hotel,
Washington, D. C.

> Reliable information from Santa Fe to effect that Frost and Bartlett wired Senator Shoup to hasten confirmation. Catron very sore. I go to Santa Fe tonight. Will keep you advised.
>
> (Signed) John S. Clark.

Two days later I received a third message from Clark, as follows:

East Las Vegas, N. M., June 6th, 1897.

Hon. M. A. Otero,
National Hotel,
Washington, D. C.

Important to have new judges. Secure Parker's appointment before leaving, if possible.

(Signed) John S. Clark, John R. McFie.

I received many other such messages before I left Washington. Apparently, my political friends in New Mexico were giving the governorship very little thought. They seemed to think that I was simply acting as their agent in Washington, and could order the President of the United States to dish out appointments according to their wishes. Naturally I wished to assist my friends all in my power, but, at the same time, I had to tread very softly and watch my step. Being on the ground, I knew what was best, and I was abiding my time, and not making a nuisance of myself. I made haste slowly.

As soon as my appointment had been confirmed by the Senate and the President had handed me my commission, I left for Santa Fe. Here I was inaugurated, at noon on June 14, as the fifteenth civil governor of the territory of New Mexico, the oath of office being administered by Associate Justice Napoleon B. Laughlin, judge of the first judicial district of New Mexico. This ceremony, which was more fully described in the last chapter of volume two of *My Life on the Frontier,* took place on a platform erected by the committee on arrangements at the eastern end of the Old Palace.

It was not until August 5 that I moved my family over from Las Vegas to make Santa Fe our home. We made the seventy-five mile trip in the private car of Mr. J. E. Hurley, of the Atchison, Topeka and Santa Fe railroad. Mrs. Otero; her father, Judge Lafayette Emmett, formerly of Minneapolis, Minnesota; Miguel, Junior; and I made up the party.

Four days before this, the citizens of Las Vegas gave us a farewell banquet and reception at the Montezuma Hotel at the Las Vegas Hot Springs. The *Las Vegas Examiner* described the grand affair as follows:

> The farewell reception, concert, banquet, and ball given Gov. M. A. Otero and his estimable wife last night at the Montezuma hotel, was a fitting testimonial of the high esteem in which they are held by the people of Las Vegas. Mr. and Mrs. Otero are both favorites, and the large number present last night fully attested their popularity. Promptly at the appointed time the special train of four coaches left Las Vegas for the Hot Springs, arriving there at 9:00 o'clock. Mr. and Mrs. Otero cordially received the guests in the reception room of the hotel, receiving the congratulations of the many who attended. After the exchange of greetings the band played a march, and large assemblage formed in line for a grand march in the ball room. The governor and Mrs. W. E. Gortner led the grand march, Mrs. Otero and W. E. Gortner following. The ball room was brilliantly illuminated by the light of numerous electric lamps, and was artistically decorated with draperies and festoons of the national colors, which, together with the fair ladies in elegant attire, and their gallant knights, made it a lovely picture long to be remembered. The happy couples tripped the light fantastic toe until midnight, when the doors of the beautiful dining room were thrown open and the banquet was announced. The Las Vegas band was at its best, and under the able leadership of Prof. Hand, delighted the guests with excellent music and pleasing selections, playing in the reception room during the banquet.
>
> Hon. Frank Springer, in a short toast, proposed the governor's health, which was replied to by Governor Otero in an appropriate speech.
>
> The entire affair was a pleasant one in all its appointments, and will be a memorable occasion to all who were present.
>
> The first train came to Las Vegas at 1 a. m., some of the guests returning at that hour, and those who remained for more dancing did not get home until after 5 o'clock this morning.

About a month after my inauguration, I returned to Washington in accordance with President McKinley's request, as he wished to consult me regarding other appointments to be made in the territory, it having been arranged that I was to return to Washington as soon as the newly appointed secretary, George H. Wallace, had arrived in Santa Fe and had qualified. I went to Raton to meet him and accompany him to Santa Fe as I had many things to tell him before my departure for Washington. We reached Santa Fe on July 10th and Mr. Wallace took his oath of office immediately before Judge Napoleon B. Laughlin. Having some private business in Las Vegas I left Santa Fe for that place on the same night and left the territory for Washington on July 12th, 1897, and on my arrival there had several meetings with the President and the secretary of the interior. On July 22, I had a conference with the President regarding the appointment of United States marshal and collector of internal revenue. Mr. Solomon Luna, of Valencia County, one of the leading Spanish-American citizens of the territory and the Republican national committeeman for New Mexico, was a candidate for United States marshal. Mr. Luna was in Washington at the time and I took him to the executive mansion with me and introduced him to the President and we had quite a talk. The President, as usual, was very kind. In regard to the position of United States marshal, he said he had partially agreed with Senator Hanna to appoint the brother of Senator Joseph B. Foraker, of Ohio, but nothing was final. Turning to me the President said, "Governor Otero take Mr. Luna with you and see Senator Foraker and whatever you three agree to I will carry out." So Luna and I drove over to the capitol and I walked into the Senate and asked Senator Foraker to come out with me. I introduced him to Mr. Luna. At once Senator Foraker said: "Governor Otero, I am glad you and Mr. Luna are here, and, if it is your wish, I will withdraw the name of my brother, Creighton M. Foraker, and join in the endorsement of Mr. Luna for the position." He had scarcely finished when Luna spoke up and said, "No, senator, I certainly appreciate what you say, but under no circumstances will I permit you to do so. I will be the one to withdraw, and what is more I will gladly do it and join with you and Senator Hanna in recommending your brother for the appointment." Luna was awfully pleased with Senator Foraker's willingness to withdraw his brother's name and tears were in his eyes. I asked the senator if he could get away for a few moments and drive with us to the executive mansion and see the President, so we could settle the matter at once and he said, "Yes." So we all drove up and saw President McKinley, and the whole matter was amicably settled in a very few minutes, and the President made the appointment at once.

When the others left, I remained behind and the President and I took up the matter of the appointment of the collector of internal revenue. McKinley immediately said: "Governor, I wish to appoint my old Irish friend, Morrison, to that office, and I wish you to endorse him." Of course I did as the President wished, and Alexander L. Morrison, of Santa Fe, received the office. Having arrived in America just in time to take part in the war with Mexico, Morrison had gotten his first glimpse of New Mexico as a soldier. He had been in the territory for some years prior to 1897, having held important federal offices under the last two Republican administrations. Morrison was a good official, and kept the post to which McKinley appointed him until his resignation, in May, 1905.

Morrison's appointment having been agreed upon, we then took under consideration the position which Morrison had held under President Harrison. I nominated the man of my choice, explaining that he was the father-in-law of Solomon Luna. The President readily consented and gave me a note to the secretary of the interior which said: "Appoint Manuel Rito Otero as Register of the U. S. Land Office at Santa Fe, with or without endorsements." I then took my leave and met my friends at the Arlington, where we felt that we had earned a good Scotch horse's neck. After driving Senator Foraker back to the Capitol, we then went to the department of the interior where I delivered the note from the President. Secretary Bliss ordered the appointment at once, and Luna and I went away, greatly pleased at the work we had done that day.

As the President was not ready to take up the appointment of the judges for New Mexico at this time, he suggested that I return to Washington early in December. Accordingly I took the train west, and arrived in Las Vegas on August 1.

As early as the week of my inauguration, Mr. Catron had gone to Washington with the announced intention of working for the judicial appointments for the territory. He gave out that his friend, Stephen B. Elkins, would go with him to see the President, "to see that the right men were appointed." However, the shrewd senator from West Virginia knew his way around pretty well and declined to exert himself in this matter. He told his former law partner in Santa Fe: "McKinley will only appoint judges in New Mexico who are endorsed by Governor Otero. I suggest that you see Otero." Elkins well knew that neither Senator Hanna nor the President had any use for Catron. I knew this, too, but even so, I wired friends in Washington of the latter's departure for that point. The result was that a few days later I received a telegram from Mr. Porter, the President's private secretary, asking me to come to Washington as the President wished to see me. Accordingly, I left Santa Fe the following Sunday.

However, the President did not take up these appointments for some months. When he finally got around to them, he gave me a striking confirmation of the fact that he regarded my own appointment as one made by him personally. At the same time, he showed clearly that he expected to give me his hearty support in the administration of the territory which he had entrusted to me.

My family accompanied me on this second trip. We left home on November 22. On my arrival, the President asked me to call at the executive mansion on the following Friday, which was cabinet day. I was a little late, and as I entered the doorkeeper said, "Governor Otero, the President wants you at once in the cabinet room." I hurried upstairs and was ushered into the room by the doorkeeper. As I entered, the President left his chair at the head of the long table and came toward me, putting his arm around my shoulders, and said: "Gentlemen, I sent for Governor Otero of New Mexico, for I want you all to know him. He is my governor, the youngest and best governor in the United States. Should he want anything in your departments, I want you to treat him with the same consideration that I do, here in the executive office." I then shook hands with each member. The President then spoke to the attorney general, Hon. Joseph McKenna, saying, "Mr. Attorney General, the governor is here to help us select five judges for the Supreme Court of New Mexico, and I would like for you to come over tomorrow morning at ten o'clock, or, if you prefer, put it off until next Monday morning, at the same hour, and we three will go over the applications on file." It was arranged to meet on Monday morning, so we were all there on time. There were a great many applicants, some of whom I had never heard of. I noticed that the attorney general seemed to favor some more than others, but the President submitted each to me, asking if I had any objections. I objected to all of them, and finally the President said, "Well, governor, tell us whom you want, I understand there are five appointments and some of my friends want me to give them some of these territorial appointments for the bench. Now, how many do you want?" I said, "I think I ought to have three, a majority of the court, as you appointed me governor of the territory, and it is very important that I know just who the judges are to be." The President laughingly remarked, "Well, you will allow me two and keep three for yourself, is that it?" I said, "That is for you to say, but I would feel more secure in my position, if I could name three." The President agreed with me, and asked me to name them, which I did, namely: For chief justice and judge of the fourth judicial district, William J. Mills; for judge of the first judicial district, John R. McFie; for judge of the third judicial district, Frank W. Parker. All three were residents of New Mexico. The President asked about each one, and

I told him frankly. Objection was raised to William J. Mills that he was a Democrat and a resident of Connecticut. I laughingly remarked that Mr. Mills had been chairman of the Gold-Democrats of Connecticut, who were responsible for giving McKinley and Hobart a majority of 54,000 at the last election in that state, and further, that Mr. Mills had left the Democratic Party for good, and was now a full-fledged Republican, and I would vouch for him as such in the future. The President agreed with me, and said he wanted to recognize some of the Gold-Democrats. At the request of the President, I then called on Senators Hawley and Platt, of Connecticut. Both of them endorsed Mills, provided he received his appointment as a resident of New Mexico. I agreed to this but, through an error on the part of the appointment clerk, Mills' name was sent to the Senate as a resident of Connecticut. The two senators from that state immediately objected, and the President had the clerk make the necessary correction. Considerable objections were raised as to the McFie appointment, and Delegate Ferguson went to the White House and made an earnest appeal to the President to withdraw his name. When the matter came up in the Senate, I was forced to make a special trip to Washington to appear before the committee in his behalf. Fortunately, I succeeded in having all objections withdrawn. In the case of Frank W. Parker no objections were raised, so all three of my selections were duly confirmed. Neither scandals nor complaints were ever raised against any of these three judges during their tenure of office, but, unfortunately, this could not be said about the two judges appointed by the President to the second and fifth districts. In fact, these two judges were almost continually under fire, and many changes were found necessary in those two districts.

Even while I was in Washington at the express summons of the President, rumors were rife in New Mexico. Schemers who would have been glad to put something over on the people of the territory themselves were unwilling to believe that I was making a prolonged stay in Washington simply to make sure of the appointment of honest and capable men. The following telegram speaks for itself:

Las Vegas, N. M., December 10th, 1897.

M. A. Otero,
Hotel Wellington,
Washington, D. C.

Denver Washington dispatches state you are pushing appointments of judges favorable to bond funding in New Mexico with Jefferson Raynolds as Commissioner. Very sensational. What is your desire as to local papers? This emanates from Santa Fe, or Lewis C. Fort who is now in Washington.

(Signed) John S. Clark.

To the above telegram I answered as follows:

Washington, D. C., December 11th, 1897.

John S. Clark,
East Las Vegas, New Mexico.

Not responsible for lies concocted in Santa Fe by gang of vilifiers. Outrageously false. Your telegram first intimation. Simply vaporings of monumental egotism enjoyed by combination. Know nothing of the charge and care less. Everything is satisfactory here so do not worry. Their position is well known here.

(Signed) M. A. Otero.

When I left for Santa Fe, the judiciary was finally settled, and everything seemed to be moving along in fine shape. I do not believe any man ever took over an office with brighter prospects, or under more favorable circumstances than I. However, as often happens in politics, the seeds of venom, malice, and personal spite were sown by a gang of unscrupulous freebooters whose one aim was to injure. Disappointed Republican bosses scarcely waited until the ink was dry on my oath of office, before they began their villainous attempts to misrepresent and malign me in Washington.

In territorial days, many offices which are now elective were filled by appointment by the governor. Besides important territorial officials, these included the offices of district attorney for the various counties, and the membership of a dozen or more boards, a number of which controlled various territorial institutions. When a new county was created, the governor appointed the first officials for the county. Naturally, much of my time was taken up with the eternal problem of choosing the right man for the right place. A complete record of my administration would list many appointments made by me; however, consideration for the reader has decided me to mention only a few.

My first appointment was made on June 21, when I appointed Mr. H. B. Hersey, of Santa Fe, to be adjutant general, and fixed his bond at seven thousand dollars. Later Mr. Hersey and I took up the matter of appointments to my staff. My first order was that no one would be considered unless he would order, immediately, two uniforms, one full-dress and one fatigue. I then appointed Hon. Venceslao Jaramillo, of Rio Arriba County, as colonel and aide-de-camp, and he proved to be the youngest colonel in the United States. Mr. Harry Whigham, of Colfax County; Mr. E. Goodwin Austen, of San Miguel County; and Mr. E. W. Dobson, of Bernalillo County; were also appointed to the same position and rank. Dr. William R. Tipton, of San Miguel County, was appointed as colonel and surgeon-general; while Mr. Ralph E. Twitchell, of Santa Fe County, who later achieved some distinction as a writer on the history of New Mexico, became colonel and judge-advocate. Commissions were sent to each with a request that they secure uniforms before the date set for the opening of the Albuquerque fair. All of which they did.

However, I had more important things to think about than getting my staff appointed and dressed up for the fair. Before I could make many important appointments, I had to fire a number of officials whom I had inherited from the preceding administration. In order to understand how this came to be the case, we must recall some shady politics which had been pulled off several months before I came into office.

Territorial politics were often turbulent, in the old days, and the session of the thirty-second legislative assembly had been no exception in that respect. That, of course, was the winter before I became governor, but I was in Santa Fe at the time.

The organization of the assembly proved difficult, the Democrats and Republicans having about the same strength in each house. A bi-partisan committee drew up an agreement by which the offices and jobs were to be split equally between the two parties. Hon. Antonio Joseph was then elected president of the council, while Hon. William H. H. Llewellyn was elected speaker of the house. Herbert B. Holt, of Dona Ana County, became clerk of the council, and W. C. Reid clerk of the house. The council was a remarkable body of men. Albert B. Fall and George Curry, both of whom were destined for high honors in future years, were both members. So was Charlie Spiess, sometime law partner of T. B. Catron. It was at this session of the assembly—and many will remember the incident—that Senator Fall left the Democratic side of the council and walked over to the Republican side and slapped Senator Spiess in the face. The Santa Fe leader took it without a whimper.

However, far more notorious and more significant was the way in which a number of members of the assembly sought to put themselves upon the payroll for the next two years. When Governor Thornton resigned, in April, 1897, the secretary of the territory, Lorion Miller, became acting governor. Miller, who had been the one chiefly responsible for the Democrats "stealing the legislature" early in 1895, and who was on very bad terms with Thornton, was an able politician. The council, knowing that a Republican governor would be appointed, played individual politics—"every man for himself and the devil take the hindmost." Accordingly Miller sent in a batch of appointments, some of them Republicans, with the understanding that all of them would be confirmed by the council. The most important of these officials were as follows: Albert B. Fall, Democrat, to be solicitor general (attorney-general) ; Samuel Eldodt, Democrat, to be territorial treasurer; Marcelino Garcia, Democrat, to be territorial auditor; Col. E. H. Bergmann Democrat, to be superintendent of the penitentiary; Placido Sandoval, Republican, to be superintendent of public instruction; William E. Martin, Republican, to be coal oil inspector.

There were also district attorneys and numerous other appointments. Needless to say, many of them were members of the legislature, and all were duly confirmed for a two-year term. I knew all along that something like this was likely to happen. Placido Sandoval, who represented San Miguel County in the council, was a Republican, but he was very much under the influence of Felix Martinez, a prominent Democrat from our county. I did everything in my power to keep Sandoval straight, but, unfortunately, he was not built that way; so he finally slipped over to the Democratic side, in spite of all I could say or do. I had a long talk with him at the southwest corner of the plaza, in which I pointed out that McKinley's election meant that a Republican governor would soon be appointed for New Mexico. I told him that, if he remained loyal to the party, I would see the new governor, and do all I could for him in the way of an appointment. But that, if he sold out to the Democrats for the office he was seeking, I would surely see the new governor and do all in my power to see that he was removed. I could plainly see that the temptation offered by Martinez was too much for him. He accepted the appointment and went along with the Democrats.

The coup planned by the acting governor aroused great indignation in the territory. At the time of the adjournment of the legislature, along with others who had watched what had happened, I felt that, whoever might be the new governor, it would be our duty to ask him to remove every one of these appointees. However, I had no idea that I would be the one who would be called upon to take this action.

After I became governor, the talk on the street was to the effect that I was too cautious a politician to remove territorial officials without just cause, but that I would be "dead safe" in removing Lorion Miller's unconstitutional district attorneys. The *Dona Ana County Republican* demanded that every member of the last legislature who held a territorial office should be removed and especially the so-called Republican members who had been guilty of making the swap. The *Las Vegas Daily Optic* said, editorially:

> Governor Otero's first duty to the honest people of the territory is to remove from office those councilmen who sold out in the recent legislature, sparing neither Republicans nor Democrats. Begin with ex-Councilman William E. Martin, who holds the office of coal oil inspector, by virtue of attending Republican caucuses and reporting the proceedings to the Democrats; let ex-Councilman Placido Sandoval follow next, the man whom both parties were compelled to buy. After these two gentlemen are properly disposed of, let Fall, Finical, and the rest of them follow. This will do more to purify politics in New Mexico, than any other thing ever attempted.

All of the important territorial offices having been distributed before I became governor, I was, at first, without a legal adviser whom I could consult freely. Politicians were pulling in all directions, but I made up my mind to "make haste slowly" and to follow my own judgment in most matters. However, just before I left for Washington, in July, 1897, Judge Henry L. Waldo came to tell me that A. B. Fall had been to see him, and said that he knew that Governor Otero would like to appoint his own solicitor general, and that, if the governor would write him a nice letter asking for his resignation, he would be glad to accommodate him. Moreover, he authorized Judge Waldo to give me this message. Judge Waldo and I talked over the matter for some little time, and we finally decided that the best procedure would be for me to write the letter, and for Judge Waldo to hand it to Mr. Fall, personally. The latter should then write out his resignation and sign it, and hand it to my friend. Accordingly Judge Waldo saw Fall and gave him my letter. On reading it, however, Fall put it in his pocket, saying "This is just what I want and I shall keep it, but I will not give in my resignation." Judge Waldo was a man of very few words and he became quite angry, saying, "No, sir, you will do nothing of the sort, and if you refuse to give your resignation as promised me, give me back that letter at once." Fall handed back the letter and the judge brought it to me, with a full report as to what had occurred. The letter was as follows:

Santa Fe, New Mexico, June 23rd, 1897.

Hon. A. B. Fall, Solicitor-General of New Mexico,
Las Cruces, N. M.

My dear Mr. Fall:

Since entering upon the duties of my office I have found it almost a necessity for me to have some close personal and political friend to consult and advise with. The office of solicitor-general, as you know, is one involving the most confidential relations between the executive and its incumbent, and while in every other respect one holding that position may be well qualified, like yourself, the fact of differences of political views and affiliations would make it desirable for me to have a change.

I desire to express to you my personal esteem and entire confidence in you, in all of your official relations.

I need not suggest to you that it would be very agreeable to me, in view of what I have said, to have your resignation, and I sincerely trust that with your knowledge of public affairs, you can see your way clear to tender the same to me at an early date.

Very respectfully,
(Signed) M. A. Otero,
Governor of New Mexico.

Under the circumstances, there was only one thing to do and I did it. I appointed E. L. Bartlett, solicitor-general, vice Albert B. Fall, removed. Fall had not paid much attention to the office, anyway, but left it to his assistant, William H. Pope. Like his superior, the latter later became an ardent Republican. He went out to the Philippines, where he became a judge under Governor William Howard Taft. When Taft became President, he appointed Judge Pope chief justice of the territory of New Mexico. Just after I had removed Fall, Pope took it upon himself to advise the territorial auditor, Marcelino Garcia, not to recognize my appointment of Bartlett as solicitor-general, but to issue his warrants for payment of salary to Fall. I immediately sent word to Garcia that if he followed Pope's advice there would soon be a vacancy for me to fill in the auditor's office. Fall's removal was followed by all kinds of threats. One was that he would take the matter up in Washington, but he never did. He did the proper thing: he stayed removed. I liked Judge Fall and we became the best of friends, and when I had the opportunity I appointed him a captain of the First Territorial United States Volunteer Infantry, and he made good. We were always good friends during the balance of my terms as governor and I was particularly fond of Mrs. Fall, Alex, and Jouett.

Whatever doubts I may have entertained as to the constitutionality of my action in removing these officials were dissipated by a decision handed down by the United States Supreme Court as to the power of the President, or a governor, to remove an official before the expiration of his term. The precise point determined was that "the provision of law is one of limitation, and not of grant, and that, although the commission runs for four years, the effect is merely to fix the utmost time an incumbent may remain in office, without entitling him to hold against the power of the President or governor to remove. The power of removal is held to be in the President or governor, and may be exercised whenever, in his discretion, he considers that the public good demands a change, and this, although the term has been fixed by the statute creating the office." In reporting this case the *Las Vegas Daily Optic* remarked:

> This decision practically reverses the decisions of the New Mexico supreme court in like cases, and leaves Governor Otero free to act in the matter of removal of the appointees of his predecessor. Here is the opportunity to turn down such dirty deals as the confirmations made by the last legislature.

My Nine Years as Governor 17

Edward L. Bartlett, whom I appointed solicitor-general in Fall's place, was a down Easterner from Maine, but he had picked up a knowledge of the West in Kansas and learned to practice law. Like many other leaders in territorial days, he had come to New Mexico along with the railroad. Bartlett was a good lawyer and dependable official, as well as a fine fellow and good after-dinner speaker. He was my right hand man at all times, and was the only one who ever helped me in writing my messages to the legislature and my speeches.

Regarding the rest of Lorion Miller's appointments, shortly after my inauguration I sent for Placido Sandoval and reminded him of the conversation we had had a few months before. He remembered it very well. I told him that I had seen the new governor, and that he agreed with me perfectly, consequently I was requesting his resignation as superintendent of public instruction. I added that if it was not delivered to me at once I would feel it my duty to remove him. He handed in his resignation but became one of my bitterest enemies in San Miguel County. W. E. Martin also resigned as coal oil inspector, by request, but was to work with me amicably later. I appointed Hon. Manuel C. De Baca superintendent of public instruction and John Clark coal oil inspector. I had no serious objections to Samuel Eldodt as treasurer, to Marcelino Garcia as auditor, or to Col. E. H. Bergmann as superintendent of the penitentiary. Accordingly, I allowed these three officials to retain their respective offices for the full term of two years.

Naturally I was pleased that I was able to appoint my friend Clark to a lucrative position. His home town and mine seemed to approve the appointment, as the following telegram from Las Vegas shows:

> The appointment of John S. Clark as coal oil inspector ... is welcome news to every citizen of Las Vegas. No man has done more for the Republican Party of San Miguel County than Mr. Clark and no man is more esteemed for his personal qualities than he. The duties of the office to which

he has been appointed will be discharged in most conscientious and able manner.

Shortly after Chief Justice Mills, Judge Parker, and Judge McFie had qualified, they all agreed that, since they owed their appointments solely to me, it would be the nice thing for them to allow me to name their clerks. Of course, I accepted their offer. The chief justice laughingly suggested that he would like to appoint Clark Carr as his clerk, but for me to do as I liked. Jose L. Lopez, Manuel C. De Baca, and Secundino Romero were the candidates. After several meetings, I decided to recommend the last named, which I did and Judge Mills appointed him. As for Judge McFie's clerk, I had made a solemn promise to Mrs. A. M. Bergere, sister of Solomon Luna, that I would recommend her husband. She was a beautiful woman and was anxious to live in Santa Fe during my administration, as she was a particular friend of Mrs. Otero and realized that she would have a splendid time at the territorial capital. When it became known that I intended to recommend Bergere, Solomon Luna came to Santa Fe to see me. He entered a strong protest against the appointment, saying: "I have always taken care of the family of my sister by giving her husband a position in Valencia County. I know them well and will tell you that, if you bring them to Santa Fe, you will regret it all your life." However, I laughed at him and said: "I have promised Eloisa and I intend to make my promise good." Accordingly I spoke to Judge McFie, and he readily made the appointment, and the Bergere family moved to Santa Fe, where their hospitable home became quite a musical center. Bergere, who was of Italian ancestry, was a musical prodigy who had given public recitals in London, as a youth. He was a man of great charm, was well educated, and proved an efficient clerk, as well as an ardent Republican. Furthermore, he was an outstanding New Mexican gentleman for over half a century.

As I had no real candidate for the clerkship in Judge

Parker's district, and the judge and I were very good friends, I quietly asked him whom he wanted. He replied: "If it is left to me, I will name my friend, James P. Mitchell." Accordingly I recommended Mitchell and the judge appointed him.

Speaking of my appointments, the *New Mexican* for March 16, 1898, said:

> The *New Mexican* is in receipt of many letters from various portions of the territory, highly commending the course of Governor Otero in the recent territorial appointments. The voice of the people is heard in favor of Governor Otero's action. It is well.

While I always acted independently in public office, I was much gratified at the attitude of the territorial press, since the newspapers throughout the territory greatly praised my administration, expressed their confidence in me at the outset, and later praised what I had accomplished. Shortly after I came into office, the *Lordsburg Liberal* said:

> If Governor Otero does not run the territory all right it will not be because he lacks advice. Enough of that useful article has been tendered him to run three territories forty years. Notwithstanding all the *Liberal* has faith to believe that he will pull through all right and prove that he is in fact, as well as in name, governor of New Mexico.

About the same time, my home town paper, the *Las Vegas Optic,* made the following forecast:

> The success of the administration of Governor Otero will depend largely upon the course adopted and pursued by him in those matters which have made the administration of his predecessors a prominent feature.
>
> It may be truthfully said that Governor Thornton endeavored in every way possible to faithfully administer the duties of his office, particularly in the suppression and punishment of crime. It is also true that while this was the end in view, there has always been a lurking suspicion that sinister motives of personal and political aggrandizement have been controlling factors in carrying out this policy. The retiring governor has given some indications in his official conduct that situations might arise which would become embarrassing.
>
> Be this as it may, the *Optic* feels safe in predicting that Governor Otero will carry out to the end any policy which strikes at crime and its perpetrators, and that the administration of this office during the next four years will show an executive whose straight-forward, manly manner will be a decisive bar to attacks of the kind made upon the retiring governor and his policies.

There will be no weak-kneed, temporizing, vacillating occupant of the gubernatorial office; no waking dreamer; no political star gazer; no demagogic comet finder; no political "poseur" longing for the appearance of a planet to serve as his guiding star to greater office.

There will be a governor of the people and for the people, and when the time arrives for change, the verdict will be, "well done, good and faithful servant."

Las Vegas has ample cause for self congratulation in witnessing one of its prominent citizens thus honored by the Republican party. Never before in its history as a city has it been in position to feel certain that her particular wants and necessities will not be slighted. It is true we have had representatives in the legislature, but political bosses and personal preferments have so warped their efforts in behalf of this community that we have profited little.

Governor Otero's well known familiarity with men and conditions, his knowledge of those methods which control party policies, together with his well known loyalty to home interests, as well as his personal worth and integrity of character, are a sufficient guaranty that in his administration of his office no one community will profit at the expense of another, if he can prevent it.

Party or personal interest will not control his actions to the disadvantage of any section of this territory. HE WILL BE GOVERNOR OF NEW MEXICO.

No governor of New Mexico has ever started in under so favorable auspices—so far as kindly feelings from all are concerned—as has Governor M. A. Otero.

It is gratifying to note that the appointment of Governor Otero gives satisfaction all over the territory.

Not all of the press comment was favorable, however. Thus the *Independente,* a weekly Spanish paper also published in Las Vegas, came out with an article entitled "The Coming Storm," saying that I intended to ignore all of the old Republicans, the Pereas, the Lunas, the Chaves, the Romeros, etc. There was not a word of truth in the article, which was published for the sole purpose of creating trouble in the Republican Party. On the other hand, the *Deming Headlight,* a Democratic paper not overly favorable to Republicans, said in February, 1898:

From the many complimentary notices which Governor Otero is continually receiving in the territorial press, we think the young governor is making many friends regardless of party.

Individuals and mass meetings, as well as the territorial newspapers, expressed themselves as strongly in favor of my administration. Thus a Cripple Creek dispatch to the *Denver Republican,* in 1898, said:

> Hon. F. A. Reynolds of Socorro, New Mexico, is in the city looking up some business matters, and incidently talking about the wealth that lies hidden in the hills and gulches of the territory that lies to the south of Colorado. When President McKinley appointed Mr. Otero governor he made no mistake. That gentleman thoroughly understands the needs of the territory and is perfectly familiar with its resources. He is an American in the best sense and his ideas for the advancement of the land in which he has lived since his birth will quickly be felt.

Upon my arrival home again, after my second trip, I discovered that a rebellion against my authority was already brewing. Accordingly, I lost little time in showing that I intended to be the governor of the territory. This determination cost me many a fight, but I came off victor in all of them. This first scrap was with George H. Wallace. The latter was formerly from Massillon, Ohio, and had been one of the leading candidates for the governorship of New Mexico for some weeks before my appointment was even thought of. When the President decided to make me governor, he gave Mr. Wallace the office of secretary of the territory upon the urgent request of both Jefferson Raynolds and myself, and against his own judgment. Playing second fiddle, however, did not satisfy that ambitious gentleman. Having been placed in charge as acting governor while I was absent in Washington, he immediately proceeded to take advantage of his opportunities. He "started the ball a-rolling" by complaining to all who would listen that President McKinley felt he *had* to recognize the "Mexicans" by appointing Otero as governor, but that he had "appointed me as secretary, to watch over him and keep him straight." The gentleman from Ohio added that he was to keep the President fully advised, and at the proper time, the latter would "find a way to dispose of Otero and place me in the chair." Such an infamous lie made him at once eligible to membership in the free booters gang, and consolation gatherings of the faithful took place nightly in the secretary's office, or some other hospitable rendezvous on the plaza where the hopeful schemers might safely congregate and exchange their views on "what is best" for the "good of the order."

A few days after I returned to Santa Fe, my friend, J. Wallace Raynolds, resigned his position as chief clerk in the office of Secretary Wallace on account of the wonderful lies—told by his chief—which he was forced to hear. Raynolds came over to my office and told me about the plotting while I was away, and of the numerous secret meetings being held at the secretary's office.

My predecessor, William T. Thornton, had resigned the governorship on April 3, and gone to Mexico on some mining business. He got back to Santa Fe on June 22, after nearly a three months' absence from the territory. While he was a Democrat, we were always on good terms. He immediately came over to congratulate me, and we had a pleasant visit. Before leaving he said that he had some chairs and other furniture at his house which really belonged to the governor's office, and that he would send them over; which he did after my second trip to Washington. When they arrived, and were being placed in the hallway between my office and that of the secretary, the latter walked out and told the man to bring the chairs into his office, saying to him: "I am the custodian, and I want those chairs." I was near the door and heard what he had to say. I told the man to put the chairs in my office, which he did. Raynolds was in my office and I asked him to go over to the secretary's office. Major Llewellyn and some others who had heard these lying stories also dropped in by my invitation. When the stage was all set, I joined them in the secretary's office, and gave Mr. Wallace a piece of my mind which he never forgot. He was a perfect Uriah Heep, a boastful hypocrite, if there ever was one. When I walked in, he arose from his chair and with a sweeping bow, said "Your Excellency." I did not let him go any further in his salutation, but said: "Let up on that, I want no more 'Your Excellency' from you, just address me as 'Governor' hereafter. I am here to tell you that I have been hearing of all your damn lies about me, and your supposed guardianship, and if it were not for your feeble asthmatic condition, I'd take you by that little goatee, and slap your face good and plenty. Now, I want you to either deny those statements which have been told to me, and admit that they are all manufactured lies, or affirm them here in the presence of all these gentlemen." He choked up with asthma, and between sobs, admitted he was a liar, and that his stories were pure and unadulterated lies, and asked my forgiveness. On my next visit to Washington I told the President of this meeting and what was said. He asked if I wanted him to remove Wallace as secretary, and I said "No, Mr. President, you did not want to appoint him in the first place, but Jeff Raynolds and I begged you to appoint him. I do not anticipate any more trouble with him, and as I wanted him, I can stand him until his term expires." Wallace, however, died before his term expired.

Many of my enemies were constantly writing letters and sending lying affidavits against me to Washington. However, George H. Wallace, as far as I knew, took no part in this malicious propaganda. I think I caught him in time. Unfortunately, however, the others were not so easily beaten, and were to fight me without mercy and with great determination and bitterness for nine years. I shall pay my respects to them later in this book. In speaking of them, as well as of all other matters connected with my administration, it is my purpose to confine my writings to actual facts and to adhere strictly to the truth, to call a spade a spade, to hew to the line, allowing the chips to fall where they may.

Naturally the administration of any political unit, no matter whether a state or a territory, depends not only upon its head, but also upon the character and ability of the men who fill the other offices. Consequently, during my first months in office, I was much concerned regarding the kind of men who would be appointed to the federal offices in the territory. It is a notorious fact that the territories had suffered much in the past at the hands of disgraceful carpetbaggers sent out from the East who knew little law and still less about the problems of the West. Of course, the Republican Party had pledged itself to the principle of "home rule for the territories," and McKinley had announced that he would be guided by this principle in making his appointments. However, anything can happen in politics. As a matter of fact, George H. Wallace, who had been appointed secretary of the territory, was a newcomer in New Mexico, and could scarcely be regarded as a bonafide resident.

A month or two after we had taken up our residence in Santa Fe, quite a large number of Indian governors called to pay their respects to the new governor. Each one had an interpreter, but none of them could speak a word of English. Some of them had to interpret through three different interpreters before it reached me, but I got along nicely. Many of them had black ebony canes with silver heads, all engraved. These canes were presented to them by President Abraham Lincoln, and were used in each pueblo as a sign of authority, and passed from one governor to another. It was rather an amusing gathering, and the Indian governors seemed to enjoy it as much as I did. I gave each of them a couple of cigars and, after the visit, took them all to my home where they met Mrs. Otero and were served with chocolate and cake.

I was greatly pleased on hearing from the Galisteo precinct, in Santa Fe County, that at a mass meeting held there on March 14th, 1898, the citizens, Republicans and Democrats alike, passed an unanimous vote, expressing their high regard for my administration, as follows:

> We, the Republicans and Democrats of this precinct, think highly of Governor Otero, and desire to say: that now New Mexico has the right man in the executive chair, a man who is not afraid to do right.

Of course, I felt extremely well pleased at the unsolicited

My Nine Years as Governor 25

compliment paid me by my friends, without regard to politics.

I shall close this chapter with an original poem written by a warm personal friend.

ODE TO THE GOVERNOR

Respects, Miguel A. Otero, let me greet you
With a hearty welcome, not as one of
Those who fought you to the bitter end, and
Now come fawning to thy feet and swear their
Love undying; swear they always hoped to
See thy smiling face adorn the Palace
Which has honored been so long in Santa Fe,
And which in turn will honor thee with
All its wealth of reminiscence.

                                Hear my
Song of welcome for a moment and be
Sure an honest wish for thy success goes
With this crude effusion from the heart of
One who loves the sunlit land, the chosen
Land of Montezuma.

                       What a chance is
Thine to do a lasting favor to this
Boss-cursed, priest-ridden land of ours, and by
A course directed clear of all the dark
And shady elements within our midst
(To whom, thank God, you owe no favors), do
Full honor to the manhood which I know
Is in thee, which stoops not to traffic with
The cursed gang which runs the old machine.
The ones who fought thee most will gladly spread
Their mantles now and carpet every plank
Thy feet must travel if thou wilt but let
Them thus subserve thee, but, be sure that when
The time is near its close, and thou must leave
The oaken chair, no matter how thy course
May honor it, they all will strive to give
*A parting kick and lusty boost to start
Thee down the hill of dark oblivion.*

Wealth have we for those who would attain it,
Health for those whose pallid faces hunger
For a taste of mountain air, and crave the
Golden sunshine which, with jewels, tips the

Mountain peaks and bathes the valleys at their
Feet with floods of liquid gold and amber
Cheering our beloved land—New Mexico.

Oh, take thy inspiration from the sun,
Which cheers us all, and, standing on the peak
Where thou art placed and may retain thyself,
Disdain to beckon to the foul and
Mud-bespattered host, whose company you ne'er
Can have and proudly hold thy present place
Of honor, but whose bad companionship
Can only be thy lot by thy descent
Adown the slimy canyon where they love
To reveal and would feign seduce from thee
Thy manhood, which our hope is and our trust.

Be true, and not a fairer glow shall tint
The cheek of sun-kissed peaches in the vale
Of old Mesilla than shall grave thy brow
And beautify thy memory, if thou
Wilt only faithful prove and lead us on
To that success we merit. 'Til no head
Shall pose so proudly, none such garlands wear.

As this of our own brunette belle, the fond
And loving daughter of our Uncle Sam,
New Mexico, God bless her!
                              Sparkles bright
The silv'ry ribbon of the Rio Grande
Which stretches from the snow-clad mountains of
The North, and bears our kindest wishes to
The belle upon whose breast the lone star shines.
Oh! Bear in mind, the river which brings wealth
To that fair vale, where señoritas, dark-
Eyed maidens, pluck the purple clusters from
The vineyards, emblematic scenes of that
Rich stream of silver, which our mines shall yield,
When Mammon loses grip upon the soul
Of labor, and his manacles of gold
Are broken. Be thou true to us. Desert
Us not, in this our day of struggle for
Our rights. Our country needs the silver stream,
Our boundless fields of carbon fain would coax
The flow, that stream which life again would give
To trade, and make her pulses bound once more
Within her arteries; as doth the Mora.
The silv'ry orb brings inspiration to

My Nine Years as Governor 27

The drooping heart, and to the tongue brings words
Of sweetness, which revive the fainting soul.
Success and honor thy power is
To weave in wreaths about that name, which in
The past has been bedecked with both.

                                                    The friend,
Who pens these lines will ask no favors at
Thy hand, but, this, that thou wilt favor all,
By keeping clean thy hands, thy heart, and day
By day, exert thy noblest energies
Toward the common good, the building up
Of fair New Mexico.
                                                            H. W. L.

Santa Fe, N. M., June 12th, 1897.

Chapter II
SAVING THE WATERS OF THE RIO GRANDE FOR NEW MEXICO

As NEW MEXICO was only a territory, the welfare of her people was very dependent on policies decided upon in the national capital, where there was often little understanding of the problems of a semi-arid country. Such being the case, it was clearly my duty to act as a watchdog and see to it that no damage was done to my people because of ignorance of the West on the part of Eastern congressmen and senators and the selfishness of those who were nearer home.

One of the greatest dangers which threatened New Mexico during my administration was the proposition to prevent the construction of storage and irrigation systems along the Rio Grande within the territory and to grant to the Republic of Mexico joint control with the United States of these waters. Such a proposal, if carried out, would have effectually blocked the development of the territory. Yet, for several years, legislation to bring this about was being considered favorably by Congress, and a treaty was pending with Mexico. The most enlightened of our citizens were fully aware of the vast possibilities of irrigation on a large scale, and an English syndicate, headed by Dr. Nathan Boyd and having a capital of several million dollars, had begun the construction of a huge dam at Elephant Butte on the Rio Grande, about 150 miles north of El Paso. This large undertaking aroused the jealousy of a group of land speculators, residing in El Paso, Texas, and Ciudad Juarez, Mexico, and having large interests on both sides of the international boundary. They, accordingly, began to scheme in the hope of putting an end to the construction work at Elephant Butte and promoting instead the building of an international dam and reservoir a few miles above El Paso.

Since they knew how to pull the wires, these land speculators were quite successful in stopping the work already begun in New Mexico. The United States government instituted a suit against the Rio Grande Dam and Irrigation Company. Some lumbermen had floated logs down the Rio Grande during the spring floods, hence the American government set up the impossible claim that the Rio Grande was a navigable stream. The case first came into court in the Third Judicial District, with Justice Gideon D. Bantz presiding. Justice Bantz held that the Rio Grande above El Paso was not a navigable stream, as contended by the government; that its waters were local waters and hence, by authority of Congress, were under local control; and that their diversion was not in violation of any law of the United States, or any treaty.

This was only a temporary victory, however, as the decision was later reversed and the United States Supreme Court solemnly decided that the Rio Grande was a navigable stream. Meanwhile, I had entered the fight. The matter had claimed my attention during the first week I was in office. Needless to say, I was bitterly opposed to putting the dam —an international dam—at El Paso, where it could not possibly do New Mexico any good. During my first trip to Washington after my inauguration, I took up the matter with the President, who instantly took my part. He arranged a meeting between John Sherman, secretary of state, and myself, at which it was agreed that I should write a letter to the secretary, setting forth all the facts in my possession. (Appendix, p. 344.)

With my letter I enclosed a copy of Justice Bantz's opinion. Although Spanish blood flowed in my veins, I did not propose to truckle to Mexico or any other foreign country. At the time this protest was made the *Santa Fe New Mexican* highly commended the stand I was taking. An editorial said:

> The Elephant Butte reservoir proposition will have a staunch friend in Governor Otero. In common with the citizens of the territory cognizant of the situation he believes that the great work ought to go forward to a successful consummation, and he is accordingly preparing for a stubborn contest to that end.

Which was quite true. We carried on the fight along two fronts—working up sentiment in the territory against the international dam and then getting in some good licks in Washington. The first was easy, since considerable excitement and indignation had been aroused in New Mexico when Congressman John S. Stevens first introduced his bill in Congress to prevent the people of New Mexico from using the waters of the Rio Grande. Stevens, who lived in El Paso, was very unpopular with the people of our territory. Nor was he liked by his constituents in his home town. This was as it should be. A congressman who was doing the bidding of a small clique of speculators in order to hurt a whole people could not hope to stand well with the people at large.

In order that the people of the territory might make an effective protest against the Stevens Bill, I called a convention which met in Albuquerque on May 15, 1900. About 150 delegates, including the most prominent men from every county in the territory, assembled in the Commercial Club building. The sentiment of these citizens is shown by the resolutions which they adopted unanimously by a standing vote. (Appendix, p. 347.)

In accordance with these resolutions I immediately appointed the following committee to go to Washington and protest against the enactment of the Stephens Bill: Frank Springer, Thomas B. Catron, S. B. Newcomb, H. B. Fergusson, William H. H. Llewellyn, W. A. Hawkins, C. B. Eddy, O. N. Marron, A. B. Fall, S. Burkhart, A. A. Freeman, Thomas S. Hubbell.

The day following the convention, I returned to Santa Fe with a severe cold, but with the feeling that I had put in a good day. The railroads were kind enough to give me a free pass for each member of the committee to and from the city of Washington, and the appropriate committees of the House and the Senate promised to give us hearings. Meanwhile, Senator Culberson, of Texas, introduced a bill in the Senate which was similar to the Stephens Bill, so that it seemed extremely likely that Congress might do something injurious to the best interest of New Mexico. Accordingly, by the second week in January, 1901, I was in the national capital, accompanied by a strong delegation. Usually our dealings were with the committee on territories of one or both houses of Congress, but at this time—since we were fighting a proposed treaty—we appeared before sub-committees of the committees on foreign relations. My speech before the Senate committee may be found in Appendix, p. 349.

By no means did all of our work consist in making speeches before committees. Much was done through personal work with members of Congress. Just after I finished my argument before the Senate committee, the committee took a recess. I lingered around in order to tell some of the bitter Democrats what was on my mind. As soon as I found three or four in a group I walked up to them and said:

> I hope, should you gentlemen recommend the passage of this bill, that you will amend it, so as to provide that you yourselves go out to New Mexico to enforce it. Do not permit innocent United States marshals to attempt to enforce it, for our people will resent the enforcement of this bill to the very limit, and if any injury is inflicted let those who are responsible for its passage suffer, and not officers who are forced to perform their duties.

My Democratic hearers responded with a laugh. They realized that, while I was making an earnest fight for the rights of my territory, I had a sense of humor. Nor was I afraid to beard the lion in his den, but conferred with several leaders who were fighting for the treaty. Brigadier-General Anson Mills, U. S. A., retired, was the head of the powerful and well organized group behind this whole proposition. General Mills was in Washington, using his great influence with both the war department and Congress in order to have the treaty approved and signed. It was thought that he had everything arranged. The speculators in El Paso and Ciudad Juarez had no idea that failure was possible, as no opposition to the treaty had developed until I appeared on the scene. Even then, they regarded this as of slight importance.

I had a lengthy conference with General Mills, who became greatly incensed, and showed considerable temper, even to the extent of offering threats against me, but, fortunately, I had had many experiences with arrogant army officers in the past, and did not even shudder.

General Mills was a great personal friend of General H. B. Freeman, U. S. Army, and an uncle of my wife, and he endeavored to have General Freeman intercede for him, but I explained the situation fully to General Freeman. While he agreed with the position I had taken, he, nevertheless, wished to favor his old friend and army associate. General Mills became very hostile towards me, for what he termed "gross interference on my part."

My talk with Senator Culberson was more pleasant. He promised that no further action would be taken in the matter under consideration without first advising me, so that I might come to Washington myself or send a delegation to represent New Mexico. This was exactly what I wanted. I thanked the senator and invited him to join me in a visit to Shoemaker's on upper Pennsylvania Avenue, which invitation he accepted. We walked by the Supreme Court room and Judge David J. Brewer joined us. The three of us took a carriage and drove to Shoemaker's where we took a table in a secluded corner in the rear and enjoyed a most pleasant afternoon. Judge Brewer was from Leavenworth, Kansas, and a warm friend of my father. Naturally we "renewed assurances" as the judge had frequently visited our home in Leavenworth, years past when I was a very small lad. We never referred to politics nor international dams, as our visit was of the most social nature.

My Nine Years as Governor

That same night I took the train for Santa Fe, as the territorial legislature would convene in a few days and I had considerable work to do on my message to the joint session.

While I prefer to discuss the international dam business independently from irrelevent matters, the reader will, of course, understand—life being so full of many different things—that I gave a good deal of my attention while in Washington to other matters. This is shown by the following Washington dispatch which appeared in the *Santa Fe New Mexican,* January 24, 1901:

> Governor Otero has made his second trip to Washington, about 8,000 miles altogether, at heavy expense and no little discomfort, in behalf of the interests of New Mexico, both trips being made within one month. But with the results he attained he feels well repaid for the time, trouble, and expense incurred by him. He put in good work for statehood, though, owing to other important business, the statehood bill will not be reached until the long session. On the subject of reservoir construction and irrigation, Governor Otero did telling work, also on the Las Vegas and Albuquerque land grant matters, also the infamous *Culberson and Stephens Bill.*
>
> When Governor Otero reached the Senate committee room to make an address in opposition to the Culberson-Stephens Bill, and also the Senate committee which was holding a special session on the grants, one of his senator friends took him to one side and asked: "Governor, there is a matter here on which I have been waiting to hear from you. Do you want to have that Albuquerque land bill blocked?" The governor answered: "No, I have come to speak in favor of its passage as soon as possible." The Senator replied: "All right, but if you wanted it blocked, I would have blocked it for you, but if you want it passed we will see to it that it passes all right."
>
> Governor Otero has many warm friends both in the Senate and in the House. He was the guest of honor at a dinner given by Senator and Mrs. Stevan B. Elkins a few evenings ago.
>
> Governor Otero has practically defeated the *Culberson-Stephens Bill,* in the face of a big lobby under General Anson Mills who is entertaining lavishly in favor of it.

The *New Mexican* was right. I had taken the whole matter up directly with the President, and he stood squarely behind me after I had explained the scheme fully and he had read my letter to the secretary of state. Furthermore, I had brought the opposition to the treaty within the territory to a focus by calling for a convention, and had then driven the matter home to Congress by bringing a delegation to Washington to fight the powerful lobby on the ground. I was, without a doubt, the immediate cause for the defeat of the treaty. I was very proud of the part I had played, and have always felt that it was the greatest achievement of my life. President McKinley was also greatly pleased with my conduct in this whole affair, as it convinced him of my honesty and sincere desire to protect the interests of the territory of New Mexico and those of the United States as a whole. Nor have the historians been slow to recognize the important part which I had in the defeat of the treaty. Thus Ralph E. Twitchell, in *The Leading Facts of New Mexican History* (Vol. II, pp. 527-529), says:

> The protest made by New Mexico's executive had great force and in a large measure prevented the construction of the dam at a point (a short distance above El Paso), resulting afterward in the adoption of the Elephant Butte project by the government reclamation service, and the delivery of a limited amount of water from the Rio Grande to the lands lying within the valley of the Rio Grande, in the vicinity of Ciudad Juarez, in the state of Chihuahua.

Chapter III

NEW MEXICO PROVES HER LOYALTY

THE PRINCIPAL event of national importance which occurred during my administration was the Spanish-American war. Those who were on the inside of affairs could probably see war coming by the time President McKinley had come into office and had placed me in charge in New Mexico. However, as long as the United States enjoyed peace with other nations, and did not seem on the brink of becoming embroiled with our near neighbor to the south, the Republic of Mexico, we did not pay a great amount of attention to foreign affairs out in the territory. Consequently, the outbreak of hostilities was probably more of a surprise to the people of New Mexico than it was to people in the East who were accustomed to read their metropolitan newspaper every morning at breakfast. But when war came, our people were ready to do their share of the fighting, and more—even though many of them were proud of their Spanish blood.

I had been governor less than nine months when an event occurred which claimed the attention of American citizens everywhere. The entry in my chronicle reads as follows:

February 16th, 1898. Great excitement throughout the nation on account of the blowing up of the United States Battleship Maine, at Havana, Cuba, by the Spaniards, at 9:40 p. m. o'clock last night, February 15, 1898. Reports indicate that about 300 of our sailors were drowned. Details and particulars harrowing in the extreme. Still a fearful mystery.

About a week later I received the following inquiry from the *New York World:*

New York, Feb. 25th, '98.
Governor Miguel A. Otero, Santa Fe, N. M.:

What in your view would be the duty of the President should court of inquiry find destruction of *Maine* due to Spanish treachery? Should we not exact freedom for Cuba, rather than money indemnity? How many men could your territory furnish, 30 days, upon call of President? Kindly telegraph answer *New York World* at our expense. *The World.*

To which telegram I sent the following answer:

Santa Fe, N. M., Feb. 26th, 1898.

The World, New York City.

As I believe most thoroughly in the patriotism, prudence, and caution of President McKinley, I would not venture to offer any suggestions as to what ought to be done. President McKinley knows better than anyone what his duty is, and will do it. If it shall be found that the destruction of the *Maine* was due to Spanish treachery, the transfer of all Spain's West Indian possessions direct to the United States would not be sufficient atonement for the outrage; and our government would be fully justified in deferring all negotiations concerning it until after merited chastisement is inflicted; but if Spanish authorities are blameless, and the destruction was not merely accidental, then this country could not in honor, demand more than compensation for the lives of the gallant men so sacrificed and for the property destroyed. While the people would like to see Cuba free, I do not see that the question of her independence is necessarily involved in the settlement of this difficulty. In case of war, or any call of the President for troops, New Mexico will furnish, as she did during the war of the rebellion, more men in proportion to her population, than any state or territory in the Union; a large majority of her soldiers are Spanish-speaking and are as loyal to this country as any New England troops; they will rally round the stars and stripes, and fight as hard for this government as any soldiers of the United States, and may be counted and relied upon to make good the above prediction.

(Signed) Miguel A. Otero, Governor of New Mexico.

In response to another inquiry, I wired the *World,* on March 28, expressing confidence in "the masterly manner" in which the President was handling the crisis, and adding: "In anticipation of war, the New Mexico National Guard, in many localities, are drilling night and day."

Reports that a portion of the people of New Mexico sympathized with Spain aroused great indignation in the territory. A call for a public meeting to refute these slanders was signed by fourteen prominent citizens—seven of whom were of Spanish descent—and was distributed throughout Sante Fe County. The result was a large gathering of patriotic people at the court house the day after the declaration of war. Many speeches were made in English and in Spanish. I was called upon for the first speech, and was followed by Judge A. L. Morrison, Chief Justice William J. Mills, Hon. Thomas B. Catron, and many others. Hon. Amado Chaves read the resolutions which were adopted unanimously by a standing vote. He also made a speech in which he pointed out that I was not the first member of my family to carry on the government of the territory during war times. Mr. Chaves said:

> The natives of New Mexico, who received commissions during the late war to serve with the volunteers of the territory of New Mexico, received them with the signature of Miguel Antonio Otero, as secretary of the territory, and that it was a matter of special gratification to the native population, especially that, in these critical times, there was another Miguel Antonio Otero as chief executive, and to look after their interests, a worthy son of an illustrious father, and that he felt sure that many of the pages of the future history of New Mexico would be inscribed with the acts of his administration and that the honor would not be for himself alone, but for all the people of the territory, especially to those of Spanish descent.
>
> During the late war, the elder Otero rendered very valuable services to the government, and to its people. On various occasions numbers of prominent men were arrested by the confederate troops and would have been tried by drum-head court martial and shot, had it not been that Miguel Antonio Otero, at the risk of his own life, went to the confederate camps and by his efforts saved the lives of people who are still living today. Miguel Antonio Otero, father of the present governor, came from an old and illustrious Spanish lineage. His ancestors, on his mother's side, first became distinguished in the olden times in the year 1160, when one of the kings of Spain, Don Alfonso Enriquez, in recognition of their services, gave them as a gift one of the most valuable cities of the kingdom to hold it for themselves and, from that time, dates the coat of arms of his family.
>
> The people of New Mexico should feel very grateful to President William McKinley for the appointment of Governor Miguel Antonio Otero. His whole heart is devoted to the welfare of the people of the territory, and it is believed that his administration will be the most successful this territory has ever had.

The people expressed their sentiments during the crisis not only in oratory and historical reminiscences, but also in poetry. Thus the following poem by Sam Cary Meek, of Socorro, was dedicated to me by the author on the same day the meeting in Santa Fe was held:

WE ARE COMING, GOVERNOR OTERO!

> We are coming, Governor Otero, yea, we're coming on the run
> For we've heard the proclamation, that hostilities have begun,
> Between this glorious nation and the monarchy of Spain
> On behalf of bleeding Cuba, and our battleship, the Maine.

> Likewise our noble seamen, who perished in the waves
> Of old Havana's harbor! and found their watery graves,
> So we're coming, Governor Otero, ten thousand men or more
> Of New Mexico's patriotic sons; to sail for Cuba's shore,
> To help chastise a nation of murderers serene
> Of women and of children, though governed by a Queen.
> Lost to every sense of charity, who neither virgins fair
> Escape their brutish passions: Will God His vengeance spare?
> Let patriots from the east and west, and from the north and south,
> Make them dance to deadly music, from out the cannon's mouth,
> And give the Cubans liberty; baptized in patriot's blood.
> To bequeath to their posterity; a birthright born of God.

Naturally, most of the "he-men" of the territory cared nothing for words. If there was to be any fighting, they craved action. Long before the declaration of war, offers of military service in case of hostilities poured in. Many of these came from leading citizens and officers of the New Mexico National Guard. After a thorough survey of the military resources of the territory, I telegraphed the secretary of war as follows:

> In case of hostilities, New Mexico tenders you a full regiment of cavalry, 95 per cent Spanish-speaking, who will respond immediately on first call, and go where ordered. Can send more regiments if desired. It occurs to me that our volunteers would be very desirable in a Spanish-speaking country.
>
> Miguel A. Otero, Governor of New Mexico.

To which the following answer was received:

> Governor Miguel A. Otero, Santa Fe, New Mexico
> Washington, D. C. April 8th, 1898.
>
> Your telegram offering regiment of Spanish-speaking cavalry received. Many thanks. Will communicate with you later.
>
> R. A. Alger, Secretary of War.

The war feeling throughout New Mexico was very strong. Taos offered five hundred men, all native citizens of the territory. About the third week in April, I issued orders through the adjutant-general, instructing all military companies of the National Guard to recruit to full strength. Volunteers from all parts of the territory poured in, requesting that their services be offered to the government for

My Nine Years as Governor 39

active military duty. Since all regular troops had been removed from New Mexico, our border left unprotected and in danger of lawless raids and Indian uprisings, I wired Hon. R. A. Alger, the secretary of war, on April 22, recommending that Fort Bayard and Fort Wingate be garrisoned with New Mexico volunteers at once. I added:

> Our volunteers are excellent horsemen, first-class marksmen, and are all accustomed to hardships of camp life, and a large proportion speak both Spanish and English. They will be ready on short notice and are anxiously awaiting orders to go wherever sent.

War was declared on April 25. On that day I telegraphed the President:

> Should my services be required in the field, I tender the same to you in any position you may see fit to place me. New Mexico volunteers will fight in the front ranks with the soldiers of any sections of our country for the preservation of the flag.

He replied: "Many thanks, but I prefer that you perform your duty by remaining in New Mexico as governor."

On April 23, President McKinley issued a proclamation calling for 125,000 volunteers to serve two years. On the day war was declared, I received a telegram from Secretary Alger asking what aid New Mexico could give in recruiting men for a regiment of western cowboys to be commanded by Leonard Wood as colonel and Theodore Roosevelt as lieutenant-colonel. I offered to send two squadrons, but was informed that the quota for the territory would be 340 men. I immediately communicated with every ranch and town in New Mexico. Offers for enlistment came in by the hundreds, each one being acknowledged through the *Santa Fe New Mexican*. Besides having the territorial militia to start with, we were literally swamped with applications. I selected Santa Fe as the rendezvous for the troops, and my choice was approved by the secretary of war.

The *New Mexican* also approved this decision. An editorial in the issue for April 28, 1898, said:

Governor Otero selects Santa Fe. Santa Fe is certainly under great and lasting obligations to Governor Otero. He stands by the capital manfully and courageously and his stand is successful. The last instance in point is the fact that he secured the location of the rendezvous for New Mexico's volunteers for this city. This should never be forgotten and must not be forgotten.

The *New Mexican* continued by saying:

Governor Otero is taking hold of military matters like one to the manner born. The New Mexico contingent of volunteers will be creditable, alike to the United States Army and to the territory. As a war governor, the present executive of this territory is all right.

I appreciated the kind words of the *New Mexican* all the more because a small number of "knockers" were declaring that I was interfering in military matters too much. Of course, they overlooked the fact that, until the volunteers were mustered and sworn into the service of the United States, the governor as commander-in-chief of the territorial forces was in absolute charge. The delegate to Congress had nothing to do with military matters. Even some of the officers of the Territorial National Guard, stationed in Albuquerque, Las Vegas, and Las Cruces, took it upon themselves to criticize my acts, and thus were in danger of being courtmartialed.

Captain Charles L. Cooper, U. S. A., was assigned by the department of war, as the mustering officer for the regiment, and he examined and selected the men. He was a fast worker, and on occasion examined 129 men in twenty-four hours. He was well pleased with the rapidity with which things were accomplished. He said:

Governor Otero, as a war governor, is certainly a success. When one considers the great distance men have to travel in New Mexico and the time required to communicate with the many places, having no telegraphic connections with the outside world, the recruiting of the four troops of picked men in five days shows great work.

Captain Cooper carried on his work without interference from me. However, one day early in April, he came to my office and said that he wished to examine two volunteers there in my presence, because there were some questions which he wished me to decide. I consented, and the captain brought in Mr. W. E. Dame, a former speaker of the house of representatives of the territory. Captain Cooper informed me that he was inclined to reject the applicant because of a hernia which might be expected to interfere with his riding a horse. Mr. Dame assured him that he could ride as well as any man and wished to appeal to me to have the objection waived. I knew Dame quite well and was satisfied that his statement was correct and that he would make a valuable soldier. Accordingly I asked the captain to pass him, and this he did. Dame was made a sergeant in his troop, and was soon promoted to lieutenant. He made good, became a warm personal friend of Colonel Roosevelt, and as a captain in the 34th Infantry rendered valuable service in the Philippines. I always felt proud of my action in his behalf.

The other volunteer was Mr. W. K. Etter, who was, at that time, chief clerk in the office of Colonel J. E. Hurley, division superintendent of the Atchison, Topeka and Santa Fe railroad at Las Vegas. The latter appealed to me to have Etter turned down by the muster officer on account of defective eye sight. However, Colonel Hurley wrote:

> The real truth regarding Etter is that I cannot spare him from my office force as he is too valuable a man for me to lose, and one who would be very difficult to replace.

Feeling that I could not refuse a request made by my colonel, I suggested to Captain Cooper that he make the examination in my office, and I saw to it that he paid particular attention to the applicant's eyesight. Mr. Etter, who had come to Santa Fe to volunteer, was very much disappointed and returned to Las Vegas greatly disheartened. However, as the years went by, I watched his rapid advancement with the railroad with great satisfaction, knowing that I was the one responsible for his not going to Cuba, where he might have stopped a Spanish bullet.

The first four companies raised in New Mexico—made up partly of the territorial militia and partly of volunteers—were mustered into the military service of the United States as the First Volunteer Cavalry, but they were popularly known as "Rough Riders." According to orders from the war department, all of the other officers, besides the colonel and lieutenant-colonel, were to come from the vicinity where the troops were raised. Accordingly I organized the squadron as follows:

Captain Frederick Muller, Lieutenants Griffin and Coleman as Troop E.

Captain Maximiliano Luna, Lieutenants Weakley and Keyes as Troop F.

Captain W. H. H. Llewellyn, Lieutenants Green and Leahy as Troop G.

Captain George Curry, Lieutenants Kelly and Ballard as Troop H.

There was absolutely no politics involved in the appointment of these officers. I did what I considered best for the interests of the United States, the territory of New Mexico, and the enlisted men, regardless of what my political enemies might say or think.

New Mexico's squadron having been completed, the four troops went into camp at Santa Fe as a body. On the motion of Captain Maximiliano Luna, the camp was given the name of "Camp Otero." In replying to the unanimous vote of the men, Major H. B. Hersey said:

> It is certain that no governor has labored more assiduously in the loyal effort of providing volunteers for the purpose of defending the nation's honor, than New Mexico's chief executive, Miguel A. Otero, and no more appropriate name could be bestowed on this camp than that of "Camp Otero."

Official duties prevented my being present on this occasion, but Col. Ralph E. Twitchell, a member of my staff, thanked the assemblage in my behalf. Three cheers and a tiger were then given for me, and the ceremony was concluded while the band played "Three Cheers for the Red, White, and Blue."

On May 6, New Mexico's full quota of thirteen commissioned officers and 340 enlisted men were sworn and mustered into the military service of the United States. I felt at the time—and I have not changed my mind since—that they would compare most favorably with any similar body of men in the army. The next day the addition of Major James A. Massie, assistant surgeon, and of two stewards, increased the number to fourteen officers and 342 enlisted men. The entire squadron marched to the depot to take the train for San Antonio, Texas.

All business was suspended in the city and a large parade of men, women, and children marched to the depot to say goodbye. Flowers, cakes, nuts, candy, sandwiches, and useful trinkets were in evidence everywhere. Mothers, sisters, sweethearts, and well wishers shed tears, but the boys all appeared happy, just as though they were going to some picnic. Before leaving they were all lined up to listen to a few remarks by Hon. T. B. Catron and myself. The first section of the train left Santa Fe at 5:20 p. m., and the second section ten minutes later. I accompanied the troops as far as Raton, returning on a special arranged for me and my staff by Colonel Hurley.

Five days after our troops left Santa Fe, I received the following telegram from Col. Leonard Wood in camp near San Antonio:

New Mexico's troops arrived this morning, and I find them a splendid body of men. Am delighted with them.

Three days later Colonel Wood wrote me as follows:

In Camp near San Antonio, Texas, May 14th, 1898.
Hon. M. A. Otero, Governor of New Mexico,
My dear Governor:
I have the honor to acknowledge the receipt of your letter of May 6th, 1898, and would state in explanation of my delay in replying, that I have been overrun with work and busy from early morning till late at night attend-

ing to the purchase of horses and the receiving and issuing of supplies, etc.

It gives me great pleasure to say that I am very much pleased with the New Mexico contingent and feel sure that they will do most excellent service. We are rapidly getting the men into shape and in a very few days will be able to take the field. I heartily concur in your remarks concerning Major Hersey and the officers generally. I trust that before we leave here we shall have the pleasure of being inspected by you.

Thanking you very much for your great courtesy and kindness and for the personal attention which you have given to the selection of your quota,

I have the honor to be,

Very respectfully yours,

(Signed) Leonard Wood, Col. 1st Reg. U. S. Vol. Cav.

Before the Rough Riders entrained for Cuba, I made a significant announcement. This was: "A volunteer soldier does not forfeit any civil office he may be holding when he enlists."

About the same time the women and children of the territory found a way to show their patriotism and their interest in our boys. They raised $253 and purchased a beautiful silk flag which was presented to the battalion at San Antonio, Major Hersey making the presentation. After the war, Major Fritz Muller delivered it to the adjutant-general of New Mexico, and it was placed in the territorial archives.

In allotting the original quota for the territory, the secretary of war had added: "Want every man a picked man." Evidently Colonel Wood was really pleased with the showing made by our men, as he telegraphed several times for fifty, seventy-five, or one hundred additional volunteers to bring the four troops up to their maximum strength. His first requests came direct from San Antonio, whereas they should have come to me through the war department. After some delay, the proper word was received from Washington, and Captain Cooper, who had received instructions similar to mine, went to work examining the men.

On June 28, I received another telegram from Colonel Wood, urging that one hundred volunteers, which he had previously requested, be sent at once. New Mexico had already furnished the Rough Riders with more than 450 men, and they were still calling for more. However, on July 1, Captain Cooper reported to me that the one hundred men had been examined and accepted. I immediately got in touch with the railroad officials, and in less than four hours the men were on their way in special cars. They were sent to Savannah, Georgia, where they embarked for Cuba. It took quick, decisive work to get this detachment off in time, but it was done in fine shape. Altogether New Mexico furnished over six hundred men and officers for the famous Rough Rider regiment.

The first engagements with the Spaniards served to increase the martial spirit in the territory. The news that Admiral Dewey had defeated the enemy at Manila aroused the fighting spirit of every true American, men and women alike. My desk was piled high with telegrams and letters from citizens in all parts of the territory who wished to offer their services. Every train brought men anxious to volunteer, and my office was crowded from morning until night. In May, the Negro citizens of the territory offered to organize a full company of either cavalry or infantry, and other groups showed a similar patriotism and desire to get at the enemy.

Early in the summer, the President issued a second call for volunteers. On June 24th, I received orders from the war department to enlist 424 men and fifteen officers for an infantry regiment to be known as the First Territorial Regiment. Captain D. D. Mitchell of the 15th Infantry, U. S. A., reported to Santa Fe as the mustering officer, and the work went forward rapidly. Myron H. McCord, governor of Arizona, was appointed by President McKinley as colonel of the regiment. This appointment was a great surprise to Governor McCord, and he did everything in his power to get out of it, even coming to Santa Fe to ask my assistance. He remained as my guest for three days while I got in touch with the war department and the secretary of the interior. I finally received a confidential telegram which convinced me that nothing could be done in the matter. McCord was greatly disappointed, but returned to Arizona and sent in his resignation as governor, which was immediately accepted. During his stay in Santa Fe I became convinced that he knew very little about military matters, consequently I hesitated to place my men under his care unless some competent United States Army officer was appointed lieutenant-colonel. I accordingly took up the matter with the war department, and they authorized me to select and appoint a lieutenant-colonel. I accordingly named Captain Mitchell, and with the approval of the war department he became lieutenant-colonel in the Arizona-Oklahoma-New Mexico and Indian Territory United States Volunteer Infantry.

As soon as it had become known that a call had been made for a battalion of infantry for this regiment, requests for commissions as officers began to pour in. Within a few days I received more than two hundred applications. As the call allowed me only fifteen officers, I had plenty from whom to choose, and many suffered disappointment.

New Mexico furnished four companies to this regiment, E, F, G, and H, under the following commissioned officers: Company E, Captain John Borrodaile; first lieutenant, L. H. Chamberlain; second lieutenant, Louis A. McCrea. Company F: Captain, W. C. Reid; first lieutenant, W. O. Morrison; second lieutenant, A. Luntzel. Company G: Captain, William Stover; first lieutenant, John Catron; second lieutenant, J. P. S. Mennet. Company H: Captain, Albert B. Fall; first lieutenant, C. G. Cruickshank; second lieutenant, N. E. Bailey. New Mexico was allowed to name a major for the regiment, and I appointed my brother, Page B. Otero, promoting him from the rank of first lieutenant. Dr. H. M. Smith was appointed assistant surgeon.

The appointment of Albert B. Fall as captain of Company H was made under rather unusual circumstances. On

July 18th, Adjutant-General Whiteman and other officers went to Las Cruces with me to swear in the officers and men of this company, which was the last one. Many of the men were opposed to my appointing Captain Eugene Van Patten to command the company, as he was getting old. I finally compromised by promoting him to be a lieutenant-colonel in the national guard, at the same time accepting his resignation as captain of the Las Cruces company. The principle Republicans of Dona Ana County held a meeting that night and asked me to appoint Fall to the vacant post. I saw through the proposition at once: they thought this an excellent opportunity to get rid of the leading Democrat in the county. I did not give them much encouragement, although I knew Fall to be an excellent soldier. I was making my headquarters at the home of Hon. Numa Reymond, his family having turned the home entirely over to me. A Swiss by birth, my host had come to New Mexico before the Civil War, and made a fortune through the stage coaches which carried the mail through New Mexico, Colorado, and Kansas. Judge Fall was on very bad terms with him, so he declined to enter the Reymond home. However, he called on me several times, and we talked in front of the house. Without consulting anyone, I then called a meeting of the Republican leaders. After each of them had spoken, I finally said: "Gentlemen, I have listened attentively to all of your reasons why Judge Fall should be appointed captain. Now, if you will put your request in writing, I shall be glad to give it my consideration."

Mr. John H. Riley then wrote out the following paper, which all present signed:

Las Cruces, N. M., July 16th, 1898.

Governor Miguel A. Otero,
Las Cruces, N. M.

Governor:

The undersigned taxpayers of the County of Dona Ana, beg leave to say that in view of existing conditions in this county and in southern New Mexico, the reasons therefore we have presented personally to you; we deem it our duty and do hereby request you to appoint Judge A. B. Fall, of Las Cruces, as Captain of Company D of the Infantry Battalion now being organized in New Mexico.

We believe Judge Fall will be a courageous officer and thoroughly qualified for the position.

> Numa Reymond
> F. H. Bascom
> J. R. McFie
> Jacinto Armijo
> Jno. H. Riley
> P. F. Garrett
> Martin Lohman

On receiving this communication, I put it in my pocket, saying that I would decide the question later. After they all had left, I saw Judge Fall on the street, where I joined him. Without saying a word, I took out one of my visiting cards and wrote on the back as follows:

> Adjutant-General W. H. Whiteman: I have just appointed Albert B. Fall as Captain of Company H, administer to him the oath of office and turn the company over to him. His commission will be issued when I return to Santa Fe. (Signed) Miguel A. Otero, Governor of New Mexico.

When I showed what I had written to the judge, he took off his hat and jumped for joy. He said: "Governor, give it to me." When he had the card, he ran every step of the way to the camp near the courthouse where the company was drilling.

Captain Fall made good and became one of the most popular officers in the regiment. One of the conditions made by the Republican leaders, who had urged his appointment, was that he was never to return to New Mexico. I declined to accept this, and said frankly: "Any man who holds a commission from me is at liberty to return to the territory whenever he likes. I would not appoint a man whom I thought unfit to reside in New Mexico."

It was fortunate for me that I had the foresight to require these prominent Republicans to put their request in writing, and that I kept the document. Several years later, when Captain Fall had returned to Dona Ana County, and

My Nine Years as Governor

was taking an active part in politics, Judge McFie came into my office and gave me a severe scolding for having made a Democrat a captain. He said that the appointment was a great mistake, and that he had been bitterly opposed to it at the time.

"Judge," I said, "I have always been of the opinion that you favored the appointment at the time."

"No, indeed," he replied. "I remember quite well that I warned you against it at the time."

I asked him if he was quite sure on that point, and he answered, "Yes." Ringing for my secretary, I asked her to bring me all the papers in the Company H enlistments. Having found what I wanted, I asked the judge if he had not signed a document recommending Fall's appointment.

"Never, never," he replied.

Well, judge, kindly read this little document. It may refresh your memory."

I then handed him the paper. When he had read it, his eyes flickered like an electric spark. Heaving a sigh, he frankly admitted that he had forgotten all about the circumstances, and was glad that I had the papers on him. Blushing, he walked out of my office, perfectly subdued. However, before he left, I had the satisfaction of telling him that the reason I had his group put their request in writing was because I was sure that some of them would repudiate their action and blame me for the appointment.

The New Mexico Battalion of the First Territorial Regiment was organized at Las Vegas and went into camp there. The officers and men of the various companies had been mustered into the United States service at different times and places. I was present on these occasions when other duties allowed. After the battalion was complete, it was transferred to a camp at old Fort Whipple, in Arizona, where it was joined by the contingent from that territory. On August 18th, while the boys were there, a handsome flag was presented to our battalion by the citizens of New Mexico. After two months in Arizona, these troops were transferred to Lexington, Kentucky, where the regiment was completed by volunteers from Oklahoma and the Indian Territory. These western boys had high hopes of getting to the front, but the end of the war found them in a Georgia camp.

However, even to those of us who remained at home, the war was both exciting and stimulating. I was very proud of the fact that, in proportion to her population, New Mexico had furnished more volunteers for the war, per capita, than any other state or territory in the United States. The territorial press reflected this pride in our achievements from time to time. Thus, on July 22, the *Raton Range* had this to say:

> This territory has promptly and loyally responded to the demands of the national government for soldiers during the present conflict with Spain. The quality of the men furnished is of the highest character as has been attested by all the general officers who have commanded New Mexico troops. Governor Otero has diligently and intelligently devoted himself to this feature of his administration and merits great credit for the successful manner all requirements of the war department have been more than filled.

Frequently the part which I had played in establishing the fine military record of the territory received greater emphasis. Thus my friend, E. S. Stover, a former lieutenant-governor of Kansas who had located in Old Albuquerque in 1877, contributed the following letter to the press:

> To the *Albuquerque Citizen*: With the departure last evening of Captain Fall's company for Whipple, the last of New Mexico's quota under the second call of the President for volunteers has been completed, and we are to be congratulated that the work of organization has been so prompt, efficient, so particularly and thoroughly performed.
>
> To Governor Otero is due the honor and credit of this most excellent work, for from the beginning to the close he has given it his most earnest, undivided attention, and personally superintended the organization of every company, and gave each his hearty godspeed on its departure.
>
> The work has not been performed in a merely perfunctory manner, but he has thrown into it an enthusiasm that has imbued whole communities and every member of the organization.
>
> He had an opportunity to reward many of his personal friends and to make political capital in the appointment of officers, but with the credit of

the service, honor of the territory and interest of the men solely in view, he has performed his duties, we believe, in such a manner to be equaled by but few executives in the whole Union, and certainly excelled by none.

War is a great science. In no other war has science and skill over mere unskilled force shown more conspicuously; therefore, in selecting trained scientific officers to command his troops, Governor Otero has not only held the best interests of his men in view, but the glory and honor of the whole commonwealth.

The imperishable honor and renown already won by our gallant troops on the stormy fields of battle prove conclusively the wisdom and patriotism of Governor Otero in the organization of his troops, and should opportunity occur the latter organizations will but add additional honor to him, the territory, and the whole United States. Honor to whom honor is due.

(Signed) E. S. Stover.

The first death among the troops belonging to the New Mexico Squadron was that of Private Irad Cochran, of Las Vegas, who died at San Antonio, Texas. He was buried on May 30, Decoration Day, in the Las Vegas cemetery, with Rev. George T. Gould officiating as chaplain. I was invited to speak at the memorial services and funeral. Several companies of the New Mexico National Guard, under Col. R. C. Rankin, and many officers accompanied the remains to the cemetery, as well as numerous friends in carriages, on horseback, and walking. Irad had been a very popular young man in Las Vegas, as was evidenced by the large funeral and floral tributes from friends.

The glorious record which the New Mexico troops made at the front is a part of the history of the war, and hardly needs to be retold here. Hence I shall conclude this chapter by referring briefly to a few of the many messages which I received from the front.

On June 16, I received a telegram from Tampa, Florida, advising me that the Rough Riders would arrive near Santiago, Cuba, late today or tomorrow, and were expected to go into an immediate engagement with the Spanish soldiers at the point of landing.

On June 25, a telegram announced that the Rough Riders were receiving their first baptism of blood on the soil of Cuba. As soon as the news had begun to circulate through the territory, I began receiving telegrams and visits from anxious mothers and relatives. Of course, I was unable to answer their many inquiries. However, I telegraphed the war department, asking for a list of casualties, if any, among the New Mexico squadron.

In July I received a letter from Cuba which read:

> The New Mexico Troops of the Rough Riders are all doing most excellent service in front of Santiago de Cuba. These three troops are commanded by Captain Luna, of Los Lunas; Captain Llewellyn, of Las Cruces; and Captain Muller, of Santa Fe. This fact should be remembered by the people of New Mexico in the days to come. These officers and men are bravely and gallantly upholding the good name and fame of their territory in front of the enemy, amongst death, carnage, and destruction. All honor to them.

In the same month I received a splendid letter from Captain Llewellyn, who wrote from Santiago. Among other things he said:

> Those young fellows from Santa Fe: William C. Schnepple, Ralph McFie, Arthur Hudson, Will Hogle and others, whose names I have forgotten, are making most excellent soldiers. They are brave, obedient and "Muy Vivo," on the field of battle as well as in camp. They are alright.
>
> The Rough Riders have been in the front ever since landing. They are strictly in it and are now classed as veterans. Rather a funny story was overheard between a 10th Cavalry-man (Negro Regiment) and a volunteer belonging to the 71st New York regiment, a few days ago. The 10th Cavalryman said: "I tell you what, mister, dem 'Rough Riders' are de best fighters in the army, and any one who says anything against dem, has the 10th Cavalry to fight."

One of the companies furnished by New Mexico for the Rough Riders failed to get into the fighting in Cuba. This was Troop H, commanded by Captain George Curry. When the regiment was boarding a transport for Cuba, Colonel Wood had announced that only three troops from the territory would be allowed to go. It is said that Captain Luna and Captain Curry flipped coins to see which would be the third troop, and that Curry lost. George was to show his fighting qualities in the Philippines later, and was to be rewarded by President Roosevelt by his appointment as

My Nine Years as Governor

governor of New Mexico. However, years afterwards, the boys who were lucky enough to get to Cuba in the summer of 1898 laughingly said: "We left George in Tampa to take care of the mules!"

I did what I could to get Troop H into the fighting, but the Spaniards defeated me by calling for an armistice too soon. Evidently the boys appreciated what I did, as Captain Curry wrote, in August, to a friend in Santa Fe: "Tell Governor Otero that every officer and enlisted man in the troops who were left here appreciate his efforts to get us to the front, and will never forget him for his kindness."

Chapter IV

I JOIN IN THE VICTORY CELEBRATIONS

HAVING BEEN active in organizing some of the troops who helped to win the war, when it was all over, I was, naturally, present on several occasions when honor was done to our fighting men of the army and the navy who had fought their way to victory.

I shall never forget the naval parade of the victorious fleet as it steamed up the Hudson River on its return from Cuba. It was August 18, 1898—only a few short months after we had been straining every nerve to send our soldiers to the front. I happened to be in Washington on territorial business. Having completed the most urgent matters which had taken me east, I went to New York to see the fleet come in. Besides, I planned to visit Camp Wykoff, at Montauk Point on Long Island, to meet the Rough Riders on their return to the United States.

On the train to New York I met up with several members of President McKinley's cabinet. One of these, C. N. Bliss, the secretary of the interior, asked me if I would like to join the party on board the government boat which was going out to meet the fleet. Naturally, I replied that it would be a great pleasure, so he gave me a note to the captain. Of course, I felt it a great honor, not only for myself but also for New Mexico, that its chief executive was so nicely recognized, particularly as it was well known that thousands of applications from prominent men and women had been denied. I left the Waldorf-Astoria early Saturday morning and reported promptly at the dock where the boat was tied, and handed my note to the captain who received me most cordially. On going aboard I found Abner McKinley, the President's brother; Charles G. Dawes and his brother; a Mr. Leland, the owner of the Windsor Hotel where President McKinley always stopped on his visits to

New York; and a few other personal friends of the President. By common consent we elected Abner McKinley commodore on the trip. We had a fine dinner together, along with a few bottles of champagne which tasted very nice, as the small boat was rolling considerably and we were all feeling a little uncertain. The wine was just what we needed, our dizziness disappeared, and we were soon out on deck. The boat, which was one of the fastest on the river, went down toward Tomkinsville and met the victorious fleet steaming up the Hudson. We turned and came up alongside the flagship. The steps were lowered and "Commodore" McKinley mounted them to welcome the admiral in the name of the President. Our boat continued alongside the flagship all the way up the river.

As the fleet steamed slowly up the river, there were hundreds of vessels of all sizes by the side of the fleet or in the rear, and every whistle on the boats, or near the shore within a mile or two, were blowing for dear life, while the officers stood at their posts. The seamen were never so happy in their lives as now, when they stood on the decks of the battleships, dressed in their best bibs and tuckers.

As Grant's tomb came into view, the roar of the salutes from the guns on the warships on the placid waters of the Hudson mingled with similar sounds from the cannon on land. As the procession reached the tomb, our boat made the curve at the head of all the warships, and was closely followed by the *New York* and the fleet and hundreds of other boats. The roar of cannon, the noise of whistles, the waving of handkerchiefs, and cheers of probably two millions of people on the New York and New Jersey shores were continuous from their first appearance until they faded from view. Never was there such a demonstration of warm welcome in the United States.

The next morning, after breakfast, I took the train for Montauk Point, Long Island. On the train were General Joe Wheeler and his son, a young cavalry lieutenant, just out of West Point; and General H. F. Kneeland, judge advocate general on the staff of Governor Black of New York, who accompanied General Wheeler. I did not meet them on the train as they were in another car, but I quickly recognized the general as we all stepped out on the depot platform. A troop of cavalry, composed of members of each troop from the New Mexico Squadron of the Roosevelt Rough Riders, was lined up at the end of the platform, all mounted and under command of Capt. Frederick Muller, of Troop E. There was also a government ambulance with four mules, the entire escort being under command of Major H. B. Hersey, of the Rough Riders. Every one of the large crowd on the platform thought the escort was intended for General Wheeler and his party and, as Major Hersey was walking up the platform towards me, he met General Wheeler and saluted. The general asked him why the escort and ambulance were there, and Major Hersey said: "We are here to meet Governor Otero, of New Mexico." General Wheeler then asked to be introduced to me. I was just behind the general and heard every word of the conversation and, of course, stepped up and shook hands with Major Hersey, who turned and introduced me to General Wheeler. The general was very cordial and told me that after he had graduated at West Point he was sent out to New Mexico, and that his best friend in that territory was my father, Don Miguel A. Otero. Seeing that there was no conveyance for the general and his party, I asked him to accompany us, which he did, as well as General Kneeland and the general's son. They were going to the camp of the Third Cavalry which adjoined the Rough Riders, so after ordering the Third Cavalry band to join us, we all started for the Rough Riders' camp. The headquarters tent was beautifully decorated with flags and flowers. In front of the tent was proudly floating the now historic battle flag of the Rough Riders, with nine holes from Spanish bullets through it. There was also nearby the beautiful silk banner, inscribed "New Mexico Squadron, First United States Volunteer Cavalry—war with Spain, presented by citizens of New Mexico."

When we reached headquarters, Major Hersey said that Colonel Roosevelt had ordered him to put me in command of the regiment while I was visiting at the camp. Of course, I appreciated this additional honor very much. Major Hersey announced that lunch was ready in the officers' dining room, and I invited General Wheeler, his son, and General Kneeland to join me, which they did. Before going over, on Major Hersey's suggestion, we all entered the tent and took a nice Scotch highball which the major had arranged for my visit. After lunch I had one of the buglers sound the call for the New Mexico Squadron to fall in. I then spoke to them in a short address of welcome and walked down the line, shaking hands with each of the troopers. I asked them if they had anything they wanted me to do for them and they said: "Yes, Governor! Now that the war is over we want to be mustered out of the service, as we are wanted at home."

I promised them I would go back to Washington at once and see the President and ask him to issue the order, if it possibly could be done. The troopers then gave three rousing cheers for me. When they broke ranks, many came over to see me, and asked if I would deliver some messages back home and, of course, I promised them I would.

All during the afternoon the crack band of the Third Cavalry played beautiful pieces, and we all greatly appreciated the treat given us by General Wheeler. One very sad occurrence took place on the following day: General Wheeler's son, whom every one greatly admired, was drowned while swimming in the ocean near the camp. It was a dreadful blow to the general. It was so sudden, none of us realized what had happened. I telegraphed the general from New York, as soon as I heard the awful news.

Before leaving the camp, I appointed six officers from

the New Mexico Squadron to act as aides to me during my stay in New York, and I took them with me and put them up at the Waldorf-Astoria Hotel and, believe me, I simply owned New York City. We all had the time of our young lives. The following day we all went to the Presbyterian Hospital to visit Major Llewellyn who was quite sick with fever. I never saw anyone so glad to see us as was the major, who fairly beamed and called in his nurses to meet us. I saw the doctor and the head nurse and told them to see that their patient got the best of care and to spare nothing in the way of comforts. When we were about to go, the major burst into tears and begged us not to leave him.

As I had promised, I stopped in Washington and called on the President to urge that the Rough Riders be permitted to leave the service as early as possible. My request was reinforced by an urgent telegram to the same effect from Colonel Theodore Roosevelt. The President sent for the secretary of war, and the order was issued at once, while I was there. McKinley then turned in his chair and said: "Now, Governor, what else can I do for you?" I smiled and thanked him for all he had done, and, as I was leaving for Santa Fe that same evening, I bade him a hearty good-bye. I went at once to the hotel and telegraphed the good news to Major Hersey, and asked him to tell the boys.

I arrived in Chicago on the morning of the 26th of August and stopped there one day at the Auditorium Hotel. In the afternoon, I met Admiral W. S. Schley and Mrs. Schley and they invited me to dine with them, which I did. Later we attended the opera, in a box-party. I certainly enjoyed the evening, as I found both the Admiral and Mrs. Schley to be salt of the earth. At about that time there was considerable talk about the Sampson and Schley controversy, growing out of the naval battle with the Spanish fleet at Santiago. While the court of inquiry found in favor of Admiral Sampson, I believe the American people as a whole

My Nine Years as Governor

sided with Admiral Schley. I left for New Mexico the next day and arrived in Santa Fe on August 29th, 1898.

General Wheeler was a peerless cavalryman. A few days after my meeting with him at Camp Wikoff, I was shown a copy of a letter from him addressed to his cavalry division. It was a wonderful tribute to his men. As one-half of the Rough Riders had been organized in New Mexico under my direction, I cannot but believe that this striking tribute by a great soldier reflects additional credit on the territory of New Mexico during my administration as governor. I believe that my readers will enjoy it.

Headquarters Cavalry Division
Camp Wikoff, L. I.
Sept. 7th, 1898.

To the Officers and Soldiers
of the Cavalry Division,
Army of Santiago:

The duties for which the troops comprising the Cavalry Division were brought together have been accomplished.

On June 14th, we sailed from Tampa, Florida, to encounter in the sickly season the diseases of the tropical Island of Cuba, and to face the historic legions of Spain in positions chosen by them and which for years they had been strengthening by every contrivance and art known to the skillful military engineers of Europe.

On the 23rd, one squadron each of the First and Tenth Regular Cavalry and two squadrons of the *First Volunteer Cavalry,* in all 964 men and officers, landed on Cuban soil. These troops marched on foot fourteen miles, and early in the morning of the 24th attacked and defeated double their number of regular Spanish soldiers under command of Lieutenant-General Linares. Eagerly and cheerfully you pushed onward, and on July 1st forded San Juan River and gallantly swept over San Juan Hill, driving the enemy from its crest. Without a moment's halt you formed, alligning the division upon the First Infantry Division under General Kent, and, together with these troops, you bravely charged and carried the formidable entrenchments of Fort San Juan. The entire force which fought and won this great victory was less than seven thousand men.

The astonished enemy, though still protected by the strong works to which he had made his retreat, was so stunned by your determined valor that his only thought was to devise the quickest means of saving himself from further battle.

The great Spanish fleet hastily sought escape from the harbor and was destroyed by our matchless Navy.

After seizing the fortifications of San Juan Ridge, you, in the darkness of night, strongly entrenched the position your valor had won. Reinforced by Bates' Brigade on your left and Lawton's Division on your right, you continued the combat until the Spanish Army of Santiago Province succumbed to the superb prowess and courage of American Arms. Peace promptly followed, and you return to receive the plaudits of seventy millions of people.

The valor displayed by you was not without sacrifice, 18 per cent, or nearly one in five, of the Cavalry Division fell on the field, either killed or wounded. We mourn the loss of these heroic dead, and a grateful country will always revere their memory.

Whatever may be my fate, wherever my steps may lead, my heart will always burn with increasing admiration for your courage in action, your fortitude under privation and your constant devotion to duty in its highest sense, whether in battle, in bivouac or upon the march.

(Signed) Joseph Wheeler,
Major General U. S. V.
Commanding.

I was present on several occasions when the Rough Riders of the territory or of the whole regiment got together for a reunion. However, one of these affairs stands out most vividly in my memory. This was quite an elaborate banquet at the Palace Hotel in Santa Fe on February 11th, 1899. It was given in my honor by the officers of the New Mexico Squadron, and I was presented with a beautiful gold medal. Major William H. H. Llewellyn had been selected to make the presentation speech, and he did it with eloquence and grace. The major looked very handsome in a striking new uniform. As he approached me with the medal in his hand, I arose to meet him while everybody listened intently. His words are quoted in the Appendix, p. 352.

Naturally, I was greatly overcome at this expression of confidence and affection from the representatives of the volunteers as expressed by Major Llewellyn, and after he had pinned the medal on my coat, I responded in the manner shown in the Appendix, p. 354.

During the banquet the following telegram was received and read:

Albany, New York, Feb. 10th, 1899.
Governor Miguel A. Otero,
Santa Fe, N. M.

Permit me to join in with the officers of the New Mexico Squadron in presenting your medal. New Mexico furnished half the Rough Riders, so that to you, more than any other one man, we owe the getting up of the regiment. I am prouder of having been its colonel than of anything else in my life and I want to join in thanks and congratulations to you.

Theodore Roosevelt.

One of the most interesting of the "victory celebrations" which I attended was the first reunion of the Rough Riders. After much discussion, it had finally been decided to hold it in Las Vegas, in June, 1899. The date was inconvenient for me, as I had to shorten a trip to Washington so as to get back to New Mexico in plenty of time to aid in the necessary preparations. My family came to Las Vegas to meet me, and went with me as far as Lamy. Here they took the train for Santa Fe, while I proceeded to Albuquerque, as I had received a telegram calling me there. As soon as I had attended to some important business matters, I doubled back on the next train going to Santa Fe. I did not arrive until 11 p. m., thus missing a pleasant serenade by the regimental band which had called at the executive mansion earlier in the evening. Mrs. Otero, however, acknowledged the compliment with her usual tact and hospitality.

At the depot in Las Vegas I had been met by a committee of citizens who informed me that the city was booming the Rough Riders' reunion and that five thousand dollars had already been subscribed toward their entertainment. Colonel Hurley also came down to see me, and I arranged with him to have a special train from Santa Fe to Las Vegas for the reunion.

The day after my arrival I issued a proclamation, setting aside Saturday, June 24, as "Rough Riders' Day." Four days before the appointed date, my family and I went to Las Vegas to be the guests of Mr. and Mrs. Joshua S. Raynolds during the reunion week. When the big day arrived, possibly five hundred people from Santa Fe alone came over on the special which left the ancient city at 6:30 a. m. and started back on the return trip at 10:30 p. m.

The thing which I remember best about this reunion was the unfavorable impression which I received of the man who was to follow my beloved McKinley in the White House. Colonel Roosevelt, who was governor of New York at the time, arrived with Mr. Paul Morton, vice-president of the Santa Fe Railroad, in the latter's private car. Governor N. O. Murphy, of Arizona, and Governor Alva Adams, of Colorado, also attended the reunion. I headed a delegation of citizens to go to Wagon Mound to meet the train having Governor Roosevelt on board. Both trains arrived at Wagon Mound about the same time. Mr. Martinez, of Wagon Mound, had a large number of school children dressed in white and carrying bouquets and small United States flags to meet the colonel of the Rough Riders. They sang some patriotic songs, when the colonel greeted them with a few remarks each presented him with a bouquet of fresh flowers and shook hands with him. Our committee entered Mr. Morton's car and we proceeded to Las Vegas. Before reaching Watrous, Governor Roosevelt retired to his drawing-room and soon appeared in his Rough Rider's uniform, calling attention to the polka dot handkerchief around his neck. He walked out to the rear platform of the car and wished to be left alone, so he might receive all the attention from the gatherings at the small stations where the train passed. He continued to pose on the rear platform entirely alone. If any one was so bold as to walk out on the rear platform, the colonel ordered him back in the car. He held this unique position until we reached Las Vegas just before noon. He at once mingled with the Rough Riders and took a select bunch into the room reserved for him. He would not allow any man to enter, but bell-boys carried many trays loaded with drinks to the room. Several photographers from eastern papers were there and appealed to me to get Governor Roosevelt out on the roof of the pòrch together with the other three governors, Murphy, Adams, and myself. I well knew that Colonel Roosevelt would not miss a picture, so I had one of the bell-boys tell him about the wish of the photographer representing the Collier magazine. He came out in a hurry and as the photographer was placing the four governors, Colonel Roosevelt turned around in a very contemptuous attitude and ordered Murphy, Adams, and me off the roof. He shouted: "They want my picture, not yours." We all left, and the Hero (?) "alone in Cuba," had several pictures taken in different positions. Having finished with Roosevelt, the photographer then asked the three rejected governors if we would step down in front of the hotel and allow him to take our pictures. We consented, and he posed us just as the parade was about to start. Roosevelt and Llewellyn were looking on from the side. Just as the photographer was about to snap his kodak, they jumped forward and pushed the crowd in front of us and the picture was lost. It was rather an ungentlemanly trick, and those who saw it remarked: "That was simply a damn dirty trick." The parade started and ended at the fair grounds, where Frank Springer made a speech, presenting Governor Roosevelt with a gold medal and the cowboys gave several exhibitions of riding, racing, and lariat throwing, but a hard rain soon stopped the amusement and we all returned to the city.

That afternoon, Colonel Roosevelt was introduced by Lieutenant-Colonel Alexander Brodie to the crowd of Rough Riders, citizens, and newspaper men in the Tamme Opera House. After stating that he had never been in the territory before, Roosevelt concluded by saying: "If New Mexico wants to be a state, you can count me in, and I will go to Washington to speak for you or do anything you wish." This fine promise was greeted with tremendous applause. Time was to show, however, that his enthusiasm vanished when the speaker found himself in a key position where he could have carried out his pledge if he had wished.

After this brief speech, a resolution was unanimously adopted electing me an honorary member of the Rough

Riders' Association. Colonel Roosevelt then presented me with a copper regimental medal, remarking that I was the only honorary member of the association who was not in Cuba during the war. He added: "His active work in organizing the regiment won him this honor, and we congratulate and welcome him within our association." In accepting the medal, I made the following short speech which was received with cheers from all the Rough Riders present:

Mr. President, Members of the Rough Riders' Association,
   Ladies and Gentlemen:
   Article I of the federal Constitution provides that "no person holding an office of profit or trust under the United States shall accept any title of nobility," and if we were within the United States, instead of a territory (which has no recognized rights in the Union) I might hesitate to accept the title, which you have seen fit to confer upon me, for, next to having been an actual Rough Rider, my being considered worthy to be elected an honorary member of that association, is an honor which falls little, if any, short of the prohibited title.
   I am proud of this honor; I am proud of the badge of the regiment; I am proud of the medal presented to me by the New Mexico Squadron; I am proud of the fact that from this territory were mustered into service one-half of the men who, a year ago, gained for themselves and the American volunteer undying fame, and made the name "Rough Rider" synonymous with victory and glory. I am proud to meet and welcome to New Mexico that gallant officer and gentleman, Governor Theodore Roosevelt, whose abiding confidence in Americanism, and particularly in the Western American, whose insistent energy and zeal resulted in the organization of that body, and whose patience, endurance, and courage made its achievements, during its brief existence, a brilliant series of victories; knowing but few of the men when the regiment was assembled at Tampa, in sixty days he had won the admiration and personal affection of every officer and man of the organization; that he reciprocated this feeling and loved his men is shown in his history of the regiment, and also by the fact that he has taken the time from his pressing duties as governor of the Empire State to make the long journey here during the heat of summer, solely to meet his comrades and assist in keeping alive the memories of the regiment. Honor to Governor Roosevelt; love and affection to Teddy Roosevelt, colonel of the Rough Riders. The regiment is gone; it can never be again; of others like it, there will doubtless be many, should occasion arise, but the idea and fruition could come but once; all others must be imitations. While the regiment is gone, as are the old guard of Waterloo and the light brigade of Balaklava, this association remains to keep its memory and its history alive forever; and when those whom I see around me now, who a year ago were in the din and shock of the first battle in the war with Spain, have joined those comrades who gave their

My Nine Years as Governor

lives that June day under their country's flag, may this association still live, recruited from the children of the regiment, not only to commemorate the deeds of their sires, but to keep warm the fires of patriotism and nourish the love of country and devotion to its flag, which has ever marked the true American.

At this point Colonel Roosevelt introduced Mr. H. H. Kohlsaat, of the *Chicago Times-Herald,* and Mr. Lafe Young, of Iowa.

The following toast was taken from Mr. Paul A. F. Walter's suggestion for a Fourth of July Toast:

> TO OUR LEADERS
> Lift the goblet for a toast
> To the leaders—our boast!
> To McKinley lift them high,
> To Otero drain them dry,
> To all victors o'er the foe,
> Honor by New Mexico!

After the war, most of the officers and men whom New Mexico had sent to the front returned to the territory to take part in the ordinary affairs of peace. Some, like Major Llewellyn and Fritz Muller, were more or less active in politics, and will be mentioned in later chapters of this narrative. George Curry found his way to the Philippines and and was absent from New Mexico during the remainder of my term as governor. Lieutenant Maximiliano Luna dabbled a little in territorial politics on his return home. Having been defeated for the nomination for delegate to Congress in 1898, he soon returned to the army and was sent out to the Philippines. On November 18, 1899, I received a telegram from the war department announcing that General Henry W. Lawton had just cabled that Lieutenant Luna had been drowned while crossing the Agno river on horseback. It thus became my painful duty to notify his grandmother, Doña Isabel B. de Luna, and his aunt, Mrs. A. M. Bergere, both of whom resided in Santa Fe. This was the second time that Max Luna had been reported killed, and we all hoped that this second report might prove false like the first. However, we all were to suffer disappointment. The body was never recovered.

Luna came of a good family, and was one of the most promising young men in the territory. Accordingly I appointed a committee to design and have made a suitable bust of him. This now stands in the capitol building.

Chapter V

LOCATING THE TERRITORIAL CAPITAL PERMANENTLY

WHILE Santa Fe has been the capital of New Mexico since the seventeenth century, there has been considerable agitation over moving. Most of the states have changed the location of their capital once or twice in the course of time, and many argued that we should follow their example. The coming of the railroads had created new towns and cities, and greatly increased the population of other old ones. When the Atchison, Topeka and Santa Fe Railroad was built in the 1880's, the engineers decided that it would be too expensive to go by Santa Fe with its elevation of 6,947 feet, hence they followed a route direct from Glorieta Pass to Albuquerque, which is about 2,000 feet lower. While a branch line had been built from Lamy to Santa Fe, the ancient city was the only capital in the country not on the main line of a railroad. For a while in the 1880's, there was a question as to whether Albuquerque or Socorro would become the chief commercial center of New Mexico. Energetic citizens of both towns urged that the capital should be located in a more central part of the territory. Citizens of southern New Mexico favored this contention.

However, the native people of New Mexico are conservative by nature, and clung to the traditional capital. The citizens of Santa Fe, especially the business men and the church authorities, were strongly opposed to making a change. T. B. Catron, a member of the territorial council, undertook to settle the question once and for all by securing the enactment of a law authorizing the erection of a substantial and imposing capitol building in Santa Fe. He succeeded in getting the law passed, though there were many charges of corruption in connection with the passage of the bill. Don Diego Archuleta, of Rio Arriba County, was carried to the house of representatives, although he was quite ill with pneumonia at the time. His vote saved the bill, but he died as a result of this exposure a few days later. By 1886 the building, which had been completed at a cost of about $250,000, was in use, but the question was still unsettled. The agitation continued, becoming so bitter that an incendiary set fire to the building, doubtless with the idea of throwing the question wide open. However, criminals can't think straight, and the only thing which this firebug succeeded in doing was in destroying a building which the property owners of the territory were still paying for, as well as a number of valuable records and public documents which could not be replaced. This crime, which took place on May 12, 1892, aroused great indignation throughout the territory.

Nevertheless, there was renewed talk of moving the capital. It was not until February 5, 1895, that the legislature established a capitol rebuilding board to supervise the construction of a new building in Santa Fe on the same site as the old one. Bonds were voted to the amount of $75,000. However, no buyers could be found, since the depression was still on and the amount of these bonds exceeded the limit imposed by Congress on the indebtedness of the territory. It was not until January 5, 1897, that Congress passed an act validating the bonds and making it possible for us to go ahead. Even then the bonds were not sold until the middle of May.

As I came into office in June, 1897, about a month after the bonds were actually sold, I naturally had a good deal to do with the rebuilding of the capitol. However, the removal of the capital was still being agitated, and who could be sure that there would be no more fires? Besides, I had a hunch that where Catron had failed in settling the question, I might succeed. My idea was to get Congress to pass an act locating the capital of the territory permanently in Santa Fe. Convinced that this was the only way to settle the question, I took up the matter with Hon. Harvey Fergusson, our delegate to Congress at the time, and persuaded him to introduce the act which became known as "H. R. 4066." I also went to Washington in December, and appeared before the committee on territories of the House and Senate and argued for the proposition. I also saw President McKinley and explained the matter to him and the annoyance, uncertainty, and corruption caused by one "Capital Removing Bill" after another. The President promised to see that the matter was pushed and he did.

The report of the House committee before which I appeared summed up the need for the act as follows:

> Ten or twelve years ago an agitation was begun on the part of the people of Albuquerque to have the capital removed from Santa Fe to the city of Albuquerque by vote of the legislature. The agitation over this question has grown bitter, though every succeeding legislature has refused to change the capital from its present location. The contest has degenerated until it is used as a means of trading, and the best people of the territory of New Mexico think that it is the best interest of the territory that this contest should cease and that Congress should fix Santa Fe as the capital.

The report also included the following letter:

Hon. W. S. Knox,
Chairman Committee on the Territories,
House of Representatives, Washington, D. C.

> Sir: Hon. H. B. Fergusson, Delegate to Congress from New Mexico, requests me to write you briefly my views regarding HR 4066, "that the city of Santa Fe, in the county of Santa Fe and territory of New Mexico, shall be, and remain the seat of government of the territory of New Mexico."
>
> I most heartily unite with Mr. Fergusson in urging the early passage of this bill. Santa Fe has always been the capital of the territory, and should be, and, if left to a vote of the people, would remain so, by a large majority.
>
> I regret to say, that for years past, almost every legislature has had "Capital Removal Bill" introduced, which very much disturbs the business interests of the territory, and has been the means of forcing legislation on the territory that otherwise would not have been considered.
> Very respectfully,
> (Signed) Miguel A. Otero,
> Governor of New Mexico.

The Senate committee evidently thought that my letter

summed up the matter satisfactorily, as it was incorporated in a report made by Senator George Shoup, of Idaho, on February 11, 1898. But, then, the senator was always a good friend of mine.

During the debate in the House, which had taken place about two weeks before this, Congressman Albert Hopkins, of Illinois, seemed rather suspicious of the bill, and asked why it was necessary to have legislation on the subject. In answering his objections Delegate Fergusson emphasized the fact that I strongly favored the bill. On being assured that I came from another part of the territory, and had no business interests or property in Santa Fe, Mr. Hopkins was apparently finally convinced that the bill was "not a land deal job," so it was passed without further opposition.

On March 14, I received a telegram from Washington advising me that the bill had passed the Senate. Of course, I knew that the President would sign it when it reached him. It was pleasing to think that we had heard the last of the "Capital Removing Bill," and that future legislators would have to find something else with which to amuse themselves and to use as a club. There was much joy in Santa Fe, where I received many congratulations over my success in originating the idea. At my suggestion a number of telegrams were sent to Mr. Fergusson for introducing the bill and pushing it through Congress.

Due to delay in converting the bonds, authorized by the law of 1895, into money, little was accomplished toward the building of the capitol for over two years. However, public spirited citizens of Santa Fe had advanced money to clear away the debris of the old ruins and prepare the site for construction as soon as the cash was in hand.

Although the bonds, authorized under the law of 1895, carried 5 per cent interest, the territory realized only about eighty two cents on the dollar. Still, the board hoped to keep within the appropriation as the law anticipated certain savings in labor and material. It provided that the labor of convicts at the penitentiary should be utilized, and that the same institution should furnish brick, lime, and other material.

When I entered upon my duties as governor, the capitol rebuilding board was just starting to work on the new building. This board served for five years without any compensation whatever. The members even paid expenses incurred in attending meetings, although two of them lived many miles from Santa Fe.

Many difficulties were encountered in the work. The penitentiary did furnish some excellent stone cutters, but all of the other skilled laborers had to be imported at great expense. The convict labor, which it was expected would be free, actually cost more than $7,000. The stone, with which it was expected that the building would be constructed, could not be found, as the quarry had become exhausted. Furthermore, prices of building material were constantly rising. Consequently, in 1899, the thirty-third legislative assembly authorized a second series of bonds to the amount of $60,000. While these bonds carried only 4 per cent interest, they were sold for $1.03 on the dollar. The board was able to stay within these two appropriations, and even turned a small surplus over to the capitol custodian committee, who used it to beautify the grounds.

The board as well as the architects, Messrs. I. H. and W. M. Rapp, of East Las Vegas, deserve great credit for this achievement. However, I do not believe they would have been so successful in keeping down expenses without my coöperation. During my first years in office, I made a number of trips to Chicago on business of the board. Frequently the board would wire me when I was in Washington to stop in the Windy City on my way home. I even visited the stone quarry in Indiana to pass on material to be used for the pillars of the building. In Chicago I personally selected the furniture for the executive office and made numerous other purchases for the board. My greatest service, however, was in persuading railroad officials to cut down the freight charges on shipments from Indiana and Chicago. Thus in June, 1899, Mr. I. H. Rapp called at my office and stated that my efforts and influence with the railroad companies had saved the territory $2,500 in freight charges. This, of course, was very cheerful news to me.

On completion, the building was a massive structure of the modern classical style which reflected great credit on the taste and skill of its architects. It was dedicated with great ceremony on June 4, 1900. The weather was perfect, and the streets of Santa Fe were crowded with people. Many of the buildings were decorated with flags, bunting, and evergreens. I stood in the reviewing stand on the west side of the building, while the colorful parade passed by. Beside me stood Archbishop Bourgade and Chief Justice Mills, as well as the members of my staff, who were in full dress uniforms. On entering the building, we proceeded to the hall of the house of representatives, where, after an invocation by the archbishop, a brief oration was delivered by the chief justice. Hon. Francisco A. Manzanares, president of the capitol rebuilding board, then with a few appropriate words delivered the keys of the building to me. I was greeted with great enthusiasm and was frequently interrupted by applause as I proceeded. (Appendix, p. 357.)

At the close of my speech, Secretary Wallace, who was ex-officio the head of the capitol custodian committee, formally accepted the building in a few well directed remarks.

The oration of the day was then delivered by Ex-Governor L. Bradford Prince. When he had finished, the Rev. Father J. L. Gay pronounced the benediction. Amidst music and joyful exchange of congratulations among the people, the audience dispersed.

That evening at twilight, the Las Vegas band gave a concert in the plaza, and its music was highly praised. At 8:30 p. m. both bands were playing at the capitol. The large building was richly illuminated, over five hundred electric lights throwing a blaze of glory everywhere. Surrounded by my staff in full dress military uniforms, I took my stand at the west end of the corridor on the second floor beneath the folds of a huge American flag. Here I stood for an hour and held a public reception, which was attended by a great throng constantly going and coming. More than seven hundred people greeted me and then inspected the building during the hour. Many ladies and gentlemen were in full dress.

Capter VI

THE TERRITORIAL LEGISLATIVE ASSEMBLY

SHOULD I take the trouble to record the doings of the various territorial legislatures which met, deliberated, and adjourned during my administration, most of my readers would probably skip this whole chapter. However, I shall attempt to give a few sidelights on the type of men who helped to make the laws for the territory in those days. And I shall indicate the kind of recommendations I made to these lawmakers, and shall point out a few things I accomplished, with or without their aid.

One of the very best of these legislators was William B. Walton, a Democrat from Grant County. He never allowed politics to enter into his work and was always anxious to assist in the passage of good laws for the territory. I always wished we had more men like Walton.

Another valuable member of the house of representatives was Pedro Sanchez, of Taos. He was a highly educated man, possessed considerable wealth, and was always known as "the friend of the poor." Another member at that time was John R. Guyer, of Union County. He was always hard-up and borrowed money from everyone in the legislature who was supposed to be gullible. On one occasion he had selected Don Pedro for his next victim and looked for him all morning without finding him. A member from Santa Fe County met Don Pedro in my office and informed him that Mr. Guyer had been looking for him. At once Don Pedro suspected that Guyer wished to borrow money, so he hit upon a plan to frustrate him. Seeing Guyer standing across the street, he hurried out and called to him. Guyer came over to greet him, and Don Pedro told him that he had been looking for him all morning, that he was greatly in need of fifty dollars and wished him to lend it to him for one month, when he would repay it with interest. Guyer assured Don

Pedro that he would be glad to let him have the money but, unfortunately, he was broke and was looking for a loan himself, but had passed up Don Pedro as a man without means. Soon Don Pedro returned to my office shaking with laughter and with a bright twinkle in his eye. He said: "I saw Guyer first." Don Pedro Sanchez was about five feet six inches in height and weighed nearly two hundred and fifty pounds. He had a very large head and always wore a derby hat and a military cape. He was a strong Republican and a thorough politician.

Naturally, the territorial legislature always included some who should have been left at home to mind their own business, since they thought more of it than of the public welfare, anyway. Of these, Thomas B. Catron, who was usually a member of the council from Santa Fe County, took first rank. He was a brainy man and one of the ablest lawyers in the territory, but was thoroughly selfish. Since he fought me throughout my entire administration, it was natural that he should regard a session of the legislature as an opportunity to oppose me. It was rather amusing to me to note how, throughout the session, he would oppose everything I advocated, including every recommendation in my message and all my appointments. However, this did not bother me in the slightest degree, as Catron was a notorious kicker. I was especially amused at his tactics during the session of the thirty-third legislative assembly. I knew that he was greatly disappointed over my message, as he hoped that it would leave some gaps and cause much adverse criticism. As a matter of fact, the message was well received by the people and press throughout the territory.

Another member, whom we could have gotten along without very well, was Benjamin M. Read, also of Santa Fe County. He was speaker of the house of representatives during the thirty-fourth assembly. He was also a member of the board of trustees for the deaf and dumb asylum at Santa Fe and was the secretary of the board. The general appropriation for the upkeep of the asylum was small. However, Mr. Read sponsored a bill to pay himself as secretary a salary of $1,800 a year. The asylum could not afford it, and I told Mr. Read that I would not approve the bill. He became very mad. The appropriation bill for the asylum was passed and put into his hands. However, on the last day of the session he declined to sign it, so the asylum was compelled to close for two years. His act was not only inhuman and uncharitable, but scurrilous, mean, and contemptible. However, what could one expect from a man who wrote a history of New Mexico and left my father out of the book simply because I declined to pay him $300 to put him in? The idea of ignoring a citizen who had been New Mexico's delegate to Congress for three terms, and attorney-general, and secretary of the territory as well, as though he were not a part of the history of New Mexico! Read demanded the same sum of money in my own case. Because I refused to pay, he left out any mention of my administration as governor of the territory, although I served for nine years as such. He also questioned the record of the old bell brought to this country by Francisco Vasquez de Coronado—simply because it belonged to me, and I had refused to donate $600 to his *supposed* history of New Mexico.

The thirty-third legislative assembly was the first one during my administration. It was to convene on the third Monday in January, 1899. I had returned from a trip to the East only a few days before this. In fact, I had such a short time in which to get ready for the legislature that I put a notice on the door of my office: "No admittance. Am busy writing message."

After the burning of the capitol, in 1892, arrangements had been made for the legislative assembly to meet in one of the buildings of St. Michael's College. This served the purpose very nicely. In addition to two large halls, where the council and house met, there were committee rooms, a governor's room, just to the rear of the council chamber, and the secretary's room adjoining.

When the thirty-third legislature convened, Col. J. Francisco Chaves, of Valencia County, was chosen president of the council, and Hon. Maximiliano Luna, of the same county, as speaker of the house. On Monday, January 16, I was notified by a joint committee of the house and senate that the two bodies would have a joint session at 10:30 that morning to hear the governor's message. Accordingly at that time, Mr. Chaves introduced me to the assembly and I delivered my message in person. I include it in the Appendix since it throws much light on the economic condition of the territory at the beginning of my administration and shows the way in which I handled the problem of territorial finances. (Appendix, p. 359.)

During this assembly, Senator Catron fought bitterly every one of my appointments. However, all were duly confirmed by the council except that of Jefferson Raynolds to be territorial treasurer. Mr. Raynolds was my particular, personal friend, and Catron succeeded in holding up the confirmation of his appointment. The office in question was still held by Samuel Eldodt, a Democrat who had been appointed by Lorion Miller. I had permitted him to serve out his full term, as I regarded him as a personal friend. Besides, he had told William B. Childers to tell me that he would resign after the adjournment of the legislature, thus leaving a vacancy in the office for me to fill. Relying on this promise, I felt perfectly secure. I sent in Mr. Raynold's name three times, but it was rejected twice. The last time, they simply held the appointment, without acting upon it, until adjournment. Senator Catron had been in consultation with Mr. Eldodt, and had informed that gentleman that I could not remove him from the office, and that, if I did, he would take his case and defend him without cost. Consequently, much to the surprise of Childers and myself, Mr. Eldodt refused to resign as he had promised, and placed his case in the hands of Senator Catron. I tendered a vacation appointment to Mr. Raynolds, but he declined to accept it, as he did not want to be bothered with litigation. I knew that the only way Catron could proceed was by applying to the solicitor general for a writ of *quo warranto*. On hearing that General Bartlett had already told Catron that he would give him the writ if he asked for it, I sent for him and asked if this were true. He answered "yes," and went on to explain that it was customary to grant the writ at the request of an attorney. I then told him frankly without mincing a word that he must refuse to grant the writ in this case, that I did not propose to furnish ammunition to the enemy in his efforts to defeat my plans. Bartlett, of course, carried out my instructions, and Catron was left high and dry without his writ, so his promise to Eldodt was never fulfilled. Having removed the latter by executive order, I appointed Mr. J. H. Vaughn, of Santa Fe, territorial treasurer, and he qualified at once and took over the office.

As this was the first legislative session after I became governor, I was constantly looking out for pitfalls. I knew that Senator Catron would do anything to get me into trouble, so I watched his moves carefully and was always on my guard. Some queer things happened during this assembly. On the last day of the session Senator Catron was fearful that I would not approve a bill in which he was greatly interested. He knew Senator Richardson was a personal friend of mine and that the latter was interested in a bill which had passed the house, but had not been acted upon by the council. He called Mr. Richardson into one of the committee rooms and asked him if he would do him a great favor by taking his bill into my office and asking me to approve it. He promised that if he would do so, he, in turn, would call up Senator Richardson's bill and personally see that it was passed. Mr. Richardson said:

> I voted for your bill, Mr. Catron, and I see no objection to the governor signing it, and I believe he will do so when it reaches him. So I have no

objections to taking it to Governor Otero and asking him to sign it, and it will be an additional pleasure to me, to have you interest yourself in seeing that my bill is reached and passed.

Senator Catron assured him that he would do so, and handed Senator Richardson his bill which had been passed by both houses and duly signed, enrolled, and engrossed. Senator Richardson brought it to me and told me of Senator Catron's fears. We both laughed, and I signed the bill, which I would have done had it reached me in the usual way. I gave it to my messenger and had him take it to the secretary's office for filing, and when he returned with the secretary's receipt, I allowed Mr. Richardson to take the receipt to show to Senator Catron, which he did and immediately returned it to my office. I should have told Mr. Richardson that I would sign the Catron bill, after he, Catron, had delivered the goods, as it was a case of "fighting the devil with fire." As soon as Senator Catron saw the receipt, he arose from his seat and moved that the council adjourn *sine die*. His motion passed. Senator Richardson was heartbroken and cried when denouncing Senator Catron for his action, and Mr. Catron simply laughed, for he was pleased at securing an adjournment without advising the governor's office, as was the usual procedure, so the governor might, in turn, advise the council that his desk was clear. But men who stoop to such methods do not always succeed in their plans. I fully recognized his attempt to belittle the governor's office, but it was his system. Many of the senators did not realize what had been done, until it was all over, and they came to my office the next day to apologize, but I only laughed. As I had not been advised by the council of the completing of the legislative work by that body, I dismissed all thought from my mind regarding that branch of the legislature. Speaker Max Luna of the house did the gentlemanly act by sending a committee from the house to notify me, as was the usual custom, so I closed nicely with the house. Early the next morning, the chairman of the enrolled and engrossed bills committee, came to my office with an armful of bills which had been passed, enrolled, and engrossed. I simply declined to take them, telling him, "The legislature has adjourned, and so have I." He was thunderstruck. He went to the secretary's office, where Mr. Catron happened to be, and told them of what I said. Mr. Catron was greatly surprised and told the secretary, "It has always been customary for the governor to receive bills for several days after the legislature had adjourned and I wish you would go in and tell him, as I am greatly interested in some of the bills." The secretary came in and told me, and I answered him, as follows: "You tell Mr. Catron for me, that it may have been the custom with other governors, but that custom does not prevail with this governor." I never received the bills and they died.

Money to pay the legislative expenses for the sixty days is furnished the territory from Washington, and there is no way for the governor to call a special session, so it may be seen at a glance that the most important bill is the *appropriation bill*. Without it the territory is at a standstill. I had no idea at this time of there being the slightest doubt about the passage of an appropriation bill. The bill had to be in my hands before the adjournment of either house. The bill, which had been introduced in the house, had been acted upon and passed and sent to the council, but in some mysterious manner it was lost. The house was forced to take one of the printed bills and make alterations in pencil or ink, and this crudely drawn bill was sent to the council and additional amendments were added in pencil and finally signed by the president and clerk of the council and returned to the house for the speaker and clerk to sign. When this dangerous bill had been completed, it was carried to my office by someone unknown to me and placed on the window sill with other papers. I gave no receipt for it and notified both the council and the house that the bill had not reached me. Later, one of my clerks in looking around the room discovered it on the window sill. I barely had time to sign it before the council adjourned. It was a close call, and for several hours I was greatly worried about the appropriation. To this day, I do not know who brought the bill in and laid it on the window sill, certainly no friend of mine.

Just before adjournment, both the council and the house passed the following resolution by a rising vote:

BE IT RESOLVED, That to his Excellency Miguel A. Otero, governor of the territory, be expressed our sincere esteem and respect commanded by his untiring devotion to duty, his energy in the interest and for the welfare of the territory, his unflinching fidelity to the great trust reposed in him, and his example of strict uprightness and integrity in office. That we believe his purposes and ideals to be high, and have every confidence in his earnest resolve to elevate and advance the territory of New Mexico in all things.

When the resolution was being read in the council, Senator Catron left his seat and remained out in the hall until after the vote, saying, as he walked out, "I'll be damned if I vote for the damn little son of a bitch." Everybody laughed. His was the only vote in both houses which showed his personal venom, and being absent, the vote in both houses was unanimous.

In spite of his hostile attitude toward me at all times, Mr. Catron never caused me the least alarm. I did not fear him or any of his clique. He was a man of considerable determination, and openly declared that he would fight me to the bitter end and by any means. The line was drawn squarely, and both of us knew where we stood and what to expect. He was always the aggressor, but I was always prepared to meet his despicable thrusts. His attacks were so continuous and unyielding that I was compelled to make several unnecessary trips to Washington, at great expense, to explain his trumped up charges. Of course, he hurt me financially, as these trips were expensive, but that was all he ever succeeded in doing to injure me. So persistent was Mr. Catron in his efforts to dislodge me from the governorship, that frequently I found myself almost regretting that I had interfered at the time the miners from San Pedro wished to kidnap him and take him down to the mines. However, I knew this would have meant certain death, and I was not as heartless as he has shown himself to be against me.

There was nothing especially outstanding about the thirty-fourth legislative assembly, which met in January, 1901. I had just gotten back from Washington, and there was the usual rush in getting my message ready. Ten days before the end of the session I sent a second message, calling special attention to the recommendations which I had made in the first one. The *New Mexican* for March 12, 1901, commented on my relations with this legislature, as follows:

> Those critics who have asserted that Governor Otero dominates the legislature in every minute respect, and that whatever he asks is a command to the legislators, and whatever the legislature does, meets his unqualified approval, were taught a lesson by the veto message sent in yesterday by Governor Otero, and the passing over the governor's head by the council of the bill vetoed. Governor Otero has backbone and the legislature possesses independence, although both endeavor to work together in harmony. Governor Otero places the responsibility for omissions in legislation where it belongs.

About a week later the *New Mexican* commented on my appointments, as follows:

> An analysis of the appointments made by Governor Otero on Saturday and confirmed by the council shows them to be first class in every respect. The men appointed are not only respected citizens of the territory, but they are especially fitted for the work to which they have been assigned. Only credit can come to Governor Otero and to the territory of New Mexico by appointments made with so much forethought and wisdom.

Two or three of the territorial newspapers were very critical of my administration. The *New Mexican* for April 2 paid its respects to one of these "yellow journals," as follows:

> The *Las Vegas Optic* slings mud at Governor Otero and his administration daily. Truth cuts no figure in this matter with the *Optic* or its correspondents.
>
> The mud slinger here at Santa Fe, who, of course, works for so much per column, and cares not for truth nor veracity, among other false charges, recently accused Governor Otero of having signed a bill which passed both

houses, giving the probate judges of the territory increased salary. This is a lie. The fact is that the bill came to the governor during the closing of the session of the recent assembly, and he killed it by putting it into his pocket.

Another charge by this despicable gang is that many bills were passed increasing county salaries. This is absolutely untrue. There was but one increase of salary of county officials made, and that only for superintendent of public schools of the counties of Bernalillo and San Miguel, and this was pushed through by the delegation from those counties which numbered four councilmen and a half dozen representatives. An amendment granting this increase of salary was tacked to what is known as Council Bill No. 23, the Springer school bill, and was accepted by its introducer, Mr. Springer. This was done in order to insure the passage of the bill, after Governor Otero had already removed a very objectionable feature in the original bill, and which Mr. Springer was willing to accept, and which was insisted upon by *Mr. Frank Hubbell,* the school superintendent of Bernalillo County, and had he succeeded in passing it the governor would have vetoed the bill. The bill contained many good and wholesome provisions greatly desired by the educators of the territory.

This mud slinging does not hurt Governor Otero, but it does hurt the territory, but this latter phase of the question cuts no ice with a penny-a-liner who gets up the lying truck, nor with the paper that is low enough to publish it.

Even Governor Otero's enemies must admit that, in appointing the county officials of Luna County, he made an excellent and discriminating choice. The citizens selected for the various county offices are all of good standing and reputation in the county, and accept office not so much for the money that there is in it, as for the ambition to give the new county of Luna a business administration.

The Santa Fe correspondent of the *Las Vegas Optic* admits that he lied in accusing Governor Otero of signing the bill passed by the thirty-fourth legislative assembly increasing the salary of probate judges—Ergo, he has lied in a good many other instances. Once a liar, always a liar, is the correct rule in this case.

The thirty-fifth legislative assembly, which convened in January, 1903, stands out conspicuously in my memory. I had learned the ropes by that time, and we had a good session. The recommendations which I made in my message were well received, as is shown by the following editorial from the *New Mexican* for January 20:

> Governor Otero's message to the legislature is a well thought-out and well written document, comprehensive in its scope and yet concise in its recommendations. A service of over five years as governor of this great territory has made him well acquainted with its progress and its needs. The

suggestions contained in his message are not the inspiration of a moment but the result of deep study and careful deliberation. The brief review of financial and educational conditions are but the relations of facts which show that Governor Otero's administration has been the most prosperous, the most progressive, and the most successful that New Mexico has thus far enjoyed.

The striking recommendations are, for the creation of the offices of traveling auditor, insurance commissioner, irrigation commissioner and for an appropriation for free text books for the public schools. These recommendations are all in line with growth and true advancement, the legislature will undoubtedly heed them, for they are born of need. Splendid as is the status of territorial finances, just as unsettled and deplorable is the condition of the finances of many counties, the lack of system in the making of assessments and the collection of taxes, and these the creation of the office of traveling auditor will remedy and that speedily.

Most commonwealths have an insurance commissioner or insurance department and the insurance business transacted in New Mexico is of such great volume and so vital to the people that it should have separate and thorough supervision as a matter of protection to the people who annually spend many thousand dollars for insurance for their homes or as a protection to their family in case of sickness or death.

As necessary as are a traveling auditor and an insurance commissioner to New Mexico, just as necessary is an irrigation engineer. In irrigation lies New Mexico's future. Thus far, with the exception of three or four large systems, irrigation is still in a primitive condition in New Mexico and the irrigation laws need a thorough revision.

The fourth important recommendation, that for free text books, for the public school children, shows that Governor Otero has the welfare of popular education at heart. Free text books are necessary to general free public education. It takes away the last excuse for failure to give every child a public school education. It is the first step toward making the public school system of New Mexico the equal to that of any other commonwealth of the Union.

There are other important recommendations in Governor Otero's message, such as for the amplification of the powers of the territorial board of equalization, the codification of the school laws, the building of a reform school and a territorial orphan's home, the enactment of a good roads law, the passage of a local option law, and many other suggestions which the legislature will do well to take notice of and to act upon.

The thirty-fifth legislative assembly will undoubtedly legislate along the lines suggested in the message and that will make this session a notable one in the history of New Mexico. It probably will be, at least it should be, the last territorial legislative session and its task is to complete the groundwork for the future state of New Mexico. It can do no better in accomplishing this task than by giving heed to the suggestions and the recommendations made by Governor Otero, a wise, liberal, and progressive executive, to whom the welfare and the growth of New Mexico are close to heart and mind at all times, and who has made a study of conditions in the territory and knows that it is not theorizing, but dealing with facts that are the need of the hour.

On January 21st, the *New Mexican* said:

Governor Otero's recommendations that a local option law for the territory be enacted by the assembly, meets with the approval of many right thinking people. A good local option law, thoroughly enforced, is much better for the well being of the people than the Sunday closing law enforced only in parts and in sections of the territory. In this respect, what is sauce for one should be sauce for the other.

The comments upon Governor Otero's message by the press as well as by the people are uniformly commendatory. That is as it should be, for the message was written from a standpoint of the greatest good to the people of New Mexico.

The resolution, passed by the house this week without a dissenting vote in praise of Governor Otero's administration, was timely and well merited. It is now a matter of history that the representatives of the people of New Mexico, including Republicans and Democrats, unanimously endorsed the acts of the administration of Governor Miguel A. Otero from the day that he assumed the high office of chief executive of New Mexico. The dwindling opposition and personal haters and slanderers of the governor have now not even a shadow to stand upon.

On January 30, 1903, the *New Mexican* had this to say:

Governor Otero on yesterday afternoon very promptly vetoed Council Joint Resolution No. 6, appropriating about $4,500 for the payment of the legislative employees, which appropriation was to come out of the territorial treasury. Under the federal statutes this duty became incumbent upon the governor and he carried out the law as he found it in the statutes of the United States. The council passed the resolution over the governor's veto, which reads as follows:

VETO MESSAGE NO. 1

"January 29, 1903.

"To the President and Legislative Council of the Thirty-fifth Legislative Assembly of New Mexico:

"Gentlemen: I herewith return to your body, being the house in which it originated, Council Joint Resolution No. 6, providing for the payment of employees and contingent expenses of the legislature, without my approval.

"My objections to this resolution are that it diverts from the territorial treasury a large amount of money which has been collected under appropriations made for specific purposes by the previous legislature, which should not be changed from those purposes unless the necessity is great and an emergency exists. This is not shown in the resolution, nor are the objects for which the money is sought to be appropriated stated in any except the most vague and general terms, from which it is impossible for me or the taxpayers to know to what objects the expenditure of so large a sum of money is to be devoted. It is only proper that the executive should be informed by the terms of the resolution or act submitted to him for approval of the purpose of such legisla-

tion, in order that he may know whether he is authorized by the law to approve the same; the treasurer of the territory is also entitled to such information, in order that he may not exceed his power, and the taxpayers who have contributed this money should be definitely informed of its disposition. *Therefore,* I feel unable to place the executive approval upon this act.
Very respectfully,
(Signed) Miguel A. Otero, Governor of New Mexico."

The council could not very well do less as it believed that the business of the present session of the thirty-fifth legislative assembly could not be transacted as promptly and speedily as the public interests demanded without more help than is allowed by the United States. That the appropriations for employees for territorial legislative assemblies are too niggardly and too small is a well known fact; on the other hand, Governor Otero is deserving of high commendation for the stand he has taken. He is sworn to execute the law and he did so. This seems to be a case in which there is much to be said for both sides.

It was the thirty-fifth legislative assembly which passed the infamous Hawkins Bill over my veto—only to have it annulled by Congress. I regarded the bill—"An act establishing the law and procedure in certain cases"—as one of the most vicious and unnecessary acts ever enacted by any legislature in the United States. I vetoed it on March 11, and sent it back to the house, but on the motion of R. L. Baca, of Santa Fe County, it was passed over my veto. The bill took its name from the member of the council who introduced it: Mr. W. A. Hawkins of Alamogordo, an attorney for the El Paso and Southwestern Railroad. Its nature is indicated by the following comment from the *New Mexican* for March 12:

Governor Otero has vetoed House Bill No. 155, relating to damage suits, but it was passed over his veto. The bill is not of general interest except to some railroads running through New Mexico. It provides in a few words that suits for damages sustained in New Mexico must be brought in the courts of this territory by the injured or aggrieved party. In the matter of damage suits brought, for instance, in Texas or Colorado against railroad companies, the latter universally and uniformly get it where "Katie wears the necklace." In New Mexico a better and more friendly feeling towards railroads seem to obtain, and juries are either more friendly disposed towards the railroads, or more easily handled by railroad attorneys. Therefore, some of the roads favored the enactment of House Bill No. 155. The governor vetoed it upon the grounds that it was extraordinary and unnecessary legislation; that there was no precedent for it in states or other territories and changed the usual practice of the courts in this territory; also that it was intended to operate as a mandamus not only to compel persons to bring suits in this territory, but also to restrain the exercise of jurisdiction of courts in surrounding states and territories. The governor, in the opinion of this paper was right in his veto. The legislature overruled it by a very heavy majority, eleven to one in the council and twenty-one to three in the house. Whether the law will stand the test of the courts is problematical, but test cases will no doubt soon arise and then the matter will be determined.

My veto message may be found in the Appendix, p. 366.

This bill caused great agitation throughout the territory. Labor, and especially the railroad trainmen, were strongly against it. Every lawyer in the territory, except some interested railroad attorneys and some interested railroad politicians, wrote me complimentary letters on my courage in vetoing the bill. What the few selfish attorneys wanted was for me to quietly approve the bill and permit them to carry on their illegal and nefarious methods without opposition, and this I declined to do. Mr. Spiess was the only member of the council who voted to sustain my veto, but he spoiled it all by laughingly admitting that, had his vote been needed, he would have voted with the others to pass the bill over my veto.

I wrote many letters to Washington and especially to the committee on territories, sending them copies of the Hawkins Bill and giving them the facts about the iniquitous bill. Finally, while I was on a trip to California, I happened to meet Congressman B. P. Birdsall, of Iowa, and we became good friends. I told him all about the Hawkins Bill and he promised to take it up when he returned to Congress, and he did, and finally succeeded in having the bill killed by Congress.

At the time I vetoed the bill, W. A. Hawkins became a deadly enemy of mine and used every possible method to injure me with the railroads, but my good friend, Judge Henry L. Waldo, stood behind me firmly. He told me I was right in vetoing the bill, and that it was such bills and methods which would hurt the railroads in New Mexico.

In the history of the territory of New Mexico this bill was the second one to have been annulled by Congress. The other was a bill known as the "Jesuit School Bill." This bill incorporated the Jesuit Fathers of New Mexico and gave them the right to establish educational institutions anywhere in the territory and to own property which should be free from taxation forever. The bill was passed on January 11, 1878, by a legislature composed almost entirely of Spanish-Americans. Governor Samuel B. Axtell vetoed it, and after it was passed over his veto, it was annulled by Congress February 4, 1879. I am proud to think that I vetoed the Hawkins Bill, and that I rendered substantial aid in having Congress annul it. Probably Governor Axtell felt the same way about the notorious bill he vetoed.

The most important piece of constructive legislation passed by the thirty-fifth assembly was the creation of the office of traveling auditor for the territory. I was gratified that this recommendation of mine had been carried out, and have always felt that this change was one of the best things I ever accomplished. The need for such an official and the good work which was being done was shown by the report which the first holder of this office, Charles V. Safford, made to me some six months later. Many of the counties were in a terrible condition, especially in the office of several county treasurers, who were defaulters in rather large amounts. I instructed the auditor to give them a short time to settle up their shortage as shown by him, and should they fail, the same would be reported to the next grand jury through the offices of the district attorneys in the different counties of the territory. The defaults were mostly due to a careless system of bookkeeping, which had prevailed for years, and were not malicious in many cases. Hence, I decided to give them all a chance to settle up before having the district attorneys present the case to the grand jury. It had a good effect on all county and territorial officials handling county and territorial funds, and finally they made good. Bernalillo, San Miguel, Rio Arriba, and Socorro counties were in bad shape, but a few removals from office and some threats brought them to their senses. I was particularly anxious to get the money, for the territory needed it, so I told the auditor to use his best judgment in many of the difficult cases, and in this manner he was able to recover thousands of dollars due. My action was very popular in most instances; however, many old politicians did not like the new order of things, and I, naturally, made enemies in that class, and they became splendid "affidavit men" as in the case of Placido Sandoval, of San Miguel County.

The thirty-sixth legislative assembly was the last one during my administration. It convened on January 16, 1905, and organized by electing my old friend, Honorable John S. Clark, as president of the council, and Honorable Carl A. Dalies, as speaker of the house. The message, which I delivered to the joint session, contained the recommendations enumerated in the Appendix (p. 367).

Naturally, the assembly did not carry out all of my recommendations. Furthermore, I vetoed some measures that were passed, as the following item from the *New Mexican* for February 8 shows:

> Governor Otero vetoes Council Bill No. 44. It has probably never happened before, that after a legislature has passed a measure unanimously in both houses and the executive has vetoed it, that the veto was sustained unanimously in both houses without a single dissent. It must be very gratifying to Governor Otero.
> It was Governor Otero who discovered the graft that was hidden in the bill and he promptly vetoed it. Well done, Governor Otero.

Chapter VII
CRIMINALS AND CONVICTS

OUTLAWS, TRAIN robbers, and other desperadoes furnish a rather picturesque element in the West of fiction and the scenario. However, in real life they gave the southwestern territories a reputation for crime and violence and insecurity of life and property which greatly retarded the coming of both immigration and capital. My predecessor in office, Governor W. T. Thornton, fully realized that New Mexico would have to be made a safe place in which to live before there could be much progress. Consequently, he took particular pains to suppress crime and disorder during the four years in which he administered the territory. When his term of office was about to expire, it was significant that he did not resign until after the four men charged with the murder of Frank Chaves, sheriff of Santa Fe County, had been hanged, in spite of the desperate efforts of T. B. Catron to save them. It was not until he wound up this infamous Borrego case, that Thornton willingly turned from public life to his business interests.

Not that he left a clear docket, by any means. In fact, among the cases which hung over to my administration was one of the most baffling crimes in the history of New Mexico. This was the murder of Colonel Albert J. Fountain and his little son, which occurred on February 1, 1896—over a year before Thornton's resignation.

Colonel Fountain was very prominent in New Mexico and had had a wonderful career. He was born on Staten Island, New York, in 1838. He had traveled around the world, finally going from Canton, China, to Sacramento, California. When the filibustering activities of William A. Walker put Nicaragua in the limelight in the 1850's, Fountain had gone to that troubled spot as a newspaper correspondent. Here he was arrested by Walker and sentenced to be shot. However, he disguised himself as a woman and escaped. Making his way back to San Francisco, he had studied law and had been admitted to the bar. When the Civil War broke out, he enlisted and became a second lieutenant of the First California Volunteer Infantry. He marched across the desert under General Carleton and was later commissioned a captain of volunteer cavalry. During the war, he was married at La Mesilla, New Mexico, to Miss Mariana Perez y Ovante, a member of a very prominent Mexican family. After the war, he went to El Paso, Texas. In 1875, he returned to New Mexico and took part in the campaign against Victorio. Ten years later, as a colonel of the First New Mexico Cavalry, he fought against the Apache chief, Geronimo.

He served as a member of the legislative assembly of New Mexico and was elected speaker of the house during the twenty-eighth assembly. In 1889, Colonel Fountain was appointed assistant United States attorney by President Harrison. Later, he was made special counsel to aid the New Mexico Live Stock Association in the prosecution of cattle thieves. Fountain was absolutely fearless, was very attentive to duty, and had much to do with driving "rustlers" out of southern New Mexico.

Colonel Fountain and his wife had twelve children. The colonel and his youngest son, Henry, who was only eight years old, were returning from Lincoln, where the former had been attending court, to their home in Las Cruces, when they disappeared at a point known as the Chalk Hills adjoining the White Sands. Apparently they were murdered there by cattle rustlers, although the bodies were never found, and no one was ever convicted of the crime.

This infamous murder had not been forgotten when I became governor, sixteen months later, and there was considerable talk as to what would be my attitude toward the matter. I, accordingly, made an announcement to the territorial press that I would do everything in my power to bring the assassins of Colonel Fountain and his son to justice.

On April 6, 1898, I appointed T. B. Catron to assist District Attorney John D. Bryan and William B. Childers in the prosecution of the men charged with the murders of Colonel Fountain and his son. Two days before this I had received a telegram from Las Cruces, advising me that indictments for murder or accessory to murder had been found by the grand jury in the case. I was also informed that Sheriff Pat Garrett had arrested two men, Carr and McNew, under warrants issued by the court, and that a posse had been dispatched to Dog Canyon to arrest Oliver Lee and James Gilliland. However, these two defied arrest for some time. Three months later, while trying to perform his duty, Garrett and his deputy, a Mr. Kearney, were fired upon by Lee and Gilliland at the ranch of the former in Dog Canyon. Kearney was badly wounded and later died. Unable to make the arrest, the sheriff returned to Las Cruces, while Lee and Gilliland made their escape. However, I later sent requisitions for their arrests to the governor of Texas and the governor of Chihuahua, Mexico. The result was that Oliver Lee was returned to Las Cruces where he was tried for the murder of Colonel Fountain. However, there being no *corpus delecti,* it was impossible to convict him.

It was with the hope of getting some evidence in this case that Pat Garrett and I visited the penitentiary at Yuma, Arizona. Mrs. Otero and Miguel, Junior, and I had gone to Los Angeles for a little vacation. My friend, N. O. Murphy, governor of Arizona, told me that I might go to Yuma and talk with a life prisoner in the penitentiary, by the name of Johnson, about the Fountain case. Murphy, furthermore, told me that if I wanted this man pardoned, he would pardon him.

Johnson declined to testify in Garrett's presence, so I asked Pat to leave the room, which he did. I immediately asked Johnson why he had refused to testify before the sheriff. He replied, "Garrett is in with the bunch, and if he heard what I am going to tell you, he would report it, and my life would not be worth much." I told him I thought he was mistaken, but he would not give in. He said, "I was with the party at some mining camp called Zunol, or some such name." He gave several names of those present which I later communicated to Pat Garrett. He went on to say, "They had a lookout who came in and reported that Fountain was on his way home and had stopped at Tularosa to rest. They hurriedly sent three men on horseback from the camp to where the road passes just north of the White Sands. [He mentioned these men by name.] Later, some of us got on our horses and rode down to the White Sands. I was one of them and took notes where the bodies were buried. I can take you right to the spot, but I would not go with Garrett; besides, I would want my full pardon before I would go with anyone." I told him that would be impossible, but that if he would go with men and an escort, and locate the bodies, I would send him to any place or any country, with sufficient funds to last him. The Masonic lodges were to furnish the money, but I did not tell him this. I was very emphatic that he would have to locate the bodies before I could ask Governor Murphy for his pardon. He insisted upon getting the pardon first, so I broke off the interview, feeling that nothing could be done. I waited awhile for Pat, who wanted to see some other men in the penitentiary, then we went down to the hotel and had dinner together. Pat returned to El Paso while I took the train back to Los Angeles where Mrs. Otero and Miguel, Junior, were waiting for me.

The territorial press and the people generally, irrespective of party, strongly approved of the efforts of my administration to bring the murderers of Colonel Fountain to justice. My only regret was that we were not successful.

Black Jack Ketchum and several other members of his

gang were brought to justice during my administration, but I shall describe the activities and final fate of these notorious train robbers in the next chapter.

An attempted crime early in my administration interested me greatly, since it was apparently nothing less than a conspiracy to poison me. A few days prior to the adjournment of the thirty-third legislative assembly, Colonel E. H. Bergmann, superintendent of the territorial penitentiary, called at my office in a state of great excitement, and asked my secretary for a private interview with me, as he wished to relate something he thought would be of great interest to me. I told my private secretary to admit him.

The colonel began his story by telling me that there was a terrible conspiracy going on in the peniteniary, which had been revealed to him by one of the convicts, and which concerned me personally and very seriously, as the conspiracy was arranged to kill me. Of course, this statement naturally interested me very much, and I asked him to proceed with his story.

At this point, Colonel Bergmann produced a small package which he opened on my desk. It contained several notes written in cipher with a lead pencil, and translations attached to each, also several bones from a chicken's leg. The latter were clean and cut smoothly at each end with paper stuck in for stoppers. Colonel Bergmann said these bones contained strychnine, and the convict had told him the gang he was working with lived in Newton County, Missouri, near Neosho, and he gave me several names of those in collusion with him, some having signed these cipher notes. These notes indicated that Thomas B. Catron had been to Neosho and had arranged with them to have me poisoned. Colonel Bergmann further stated that the convict told him he had purposely committed a crime so he might go to the penitentiary where he could do his poisoning without being suspected. The plan was for him to watch his opportunity when

I was invited there for a meal, at which time the strychnine was to be placed in the food I was to eat.

I read all the translations attached to the cipher notes, and told Colonel Bergmann to leave them and the chicken bones containing the poison with me. As he was preparing to leave, I told him I would go out to the penitentiary at four o'clock, and for him to have the convict in his office, as I wished to see him and ascertain from him just what the plot was all about, and how it all started. Colonel Bergmann seemed to be pleased at having me make the trip. After he left my office, I sent for the district attorney, Robert C. Gortner, and showed him the notes and chicken bones. He became greatly interested when I told him the story. I asked him to treat all I had told him in strict confidence, as we had to work cautiously for the time being. He promised to do so. I then told him I intended to visit the penitentiary that afternoon, and wanted him to accompany me. Gortner promised to meet me at my office at a quarter to four, so we both left for lunch. He was there at the agreed time and, together, we drove out to the penitentiary.

On our arrival, we found Colonel Bergmann and the convict together in the office. The convict was a man about five feet, ten inches in height, rather slim and quite pale. He at once impressed me as being a very weak specimen of humanity, cowardly and cringing, very nervous and watchful. He had a bad look out of his eyes, so I scrutinized him very closely. He must have noticed my attitude for his very first words were that he had reformed and wanted me to know that his sole desire now was to protect me from the men who wanted to have me killed. I told him to tell me his story from beginning to end, and in doing so, I wanted him to tell me the whole truth. He began by saying, "Tom Catron is a very bad man. He wanted to have you killed by our gang, and that was what brought me here to the penitentiary, as I was expected to do the dirty work for him."

I kept the translation and handed him one of the cipher

notes, and to my astonishment he read it, and it was like the translation I held in my hand. I listened very attentively to all he had to say. He finally finished his story by saying, "There is a man right here in Santa Fe, a go-between, who is constantly in touch with Tom Catron, and it is through him the strychnine was passed in to me."

Gortner and I left the penitentiary and drove to my office where we discussed all the different angles connected with the interview. Of one point we were certain, and that was that both Colonel Bergmann and the convict thought we were intensely interested and, of course, we wanted them to think so. However, as a matter of fact, neither Gortner nor I were very much impressed with all we heard and, finally, I decided to send Bob over to see Mr. Catron and have him come to my office, but I cautioned him not to reveal anything to Mr. Catron until he came over to my office, as I wished to be the first to tell him what we had learned. When they arrived, I did not "beat around the bush." I told Mr. Catron plainly that I had heard he was in a conspiracy to have me killed. I could see that he was intensely worried. Of course, he denied the charge most emphatically, but at the same time he wished me to proceed with the investigation and asked me to be kind enough to assist him in clearing his name of such a villainous and infamous charge. He then suggested that I send to the Rocky Mountain Detective Association in Denver, which was under the management of Dave Cook, whom I personally knew. I told Mr. Catron the territory had no funds for such an expenditure. His answer was, "Governor, I am asking that this be done and am willing to pay all expenses, for I know that you do not have any fund covering such an expenditure." I requested him to deposit a certain sum of money in the First National Bank to be used by me for this purpose, and he did this. I then had my secretary buy a book and open an account for all expenditures made, and sent a telegram to Dave Cook to send me his best man for the job. I received an answer

My Nine Years as Governor 97

saying that John W. Cook was coming to arrange all details. On the arrival of Mr. Cook at my office, I sent for Mr. Catron and he came over at once and I introduced him to Mr. Cook. I turned over to the latter the cipher notes and translations, also the chicken bones containing the strychnine, as well as all my memoranda regarding my interview with the convict and the names of all the men given me. Cook took them all. At this meeting I turned Mr. Cook over to Mr. Catron, and at the same time turned back to Mr. Catron the money he had deposited in the bank in my name, less some money spent for telegrams. I preferred that the transaction should be between Mr. Catron and Mr. Cook, and they were both satisfied with this arrangement. Mr. Catron expressed a desire that I take a personal interest in all the plans suggested by Mr. Cook, and I agreed to do so. One of the first things done by Mr. Cook was to experiment with the contents of one of the chicken bones, said to contain strychnine. He secured a couple of cats and gave them each a piece of raw meet with some of the crystals taken from the bone. They both became sick and died in a few minutes. The plans agreed upon between Mr. Catron and Mr. Cook were that Mr. Cook and an assistant from Denver should take the train to Joplin, Missouri, and at that point they were to purchase a farm wagon with bows and cover, together with a good pair of horses, harness, and all necessary equipment, such as a tent, camping outfit, bedding, and provisions. They were to disguise themselves as farmers and drive south to Neosho and contact the men mentioned by the convict. Mr. Cook carried out all his plans and remained in that country for several weeks. Finally, after being thoroughly convinced that the convict had been lying, he sold his outfit and returned to Santa Fe to make his report to Mr. Catron, who in turn reported to me.

When the convict in Colonel Bergmann's office had mentioned Neosho, Missouri, I had asked him who was the congressman from that district. He knew all right, for I later looked it up in the *Congressional Directory*. When I mentioned the name, Mr. Catron said that he knew the gentleman, and suggested that I see him on my next trip east. I was in Washington shortly after this and called on the congressman from Neosho. He said that he knew all the men whose names had been given me by the convict and that they were a pretty hard lot. However, he did not credit the story of the convict, nor did he believe that Mr. Catron could have visited Neosho without his hearing about it.

Of course, I could have given Mr. Catron considerable worry and trouble over this charge of conspiracy, had I been mean enough to do so, since a great majority of the Republican Party of the territory and the people as a whole were fully prepared to believe anything despicable and outrageous, whether true or untrue, if it was against Tom Catron. On the contrary, I put myself out to help him when he needed help. He, however, never appreciated what I did for him, as evidently his selfish nature predominated after his skirts were cleared of the conspiracy charge.

Of course, it is a well known fact by all familiar with criminology, that in every penitentiary or prison, there are groups planning escapes and conspiracies for what they believe to be for their interest. They never seem to care or consider what the consequences of their rash acts may lead to. Their only thought is for themselves and how to get out. These men are usually desperate and willing to take all chances.

Meanwhile, I had appointed Holm O. Bursum as superintendent of the penitentiary and he had assumed his duties. An investigation of the premises took place, assisted by Mr. John W. Cook. When this had been completed, Mr. Cook, Superintendent Bursum, and I went over to Las Vegas to interrogate some men who had been in the penitentiary as prisoners at the time W. H. Garner, alias C. H. Schultz, was there. From them we learned considerable about the conspiracy. They told us that the plot was well known among the prisoners, and that Henry Bergmann, the colonel's son, and O. L. Merrill, assistant superintendent and son-in-law to the colonel, were at the bottom of the whole affair. As soon as we returned to Santa Fe I had District Attorney Gortner file complaints against all three. However, they had left the territory. Mr. Catron and I discussed the matter as to whether it would be worth while to bring them back, and we finally decided to let things drop, as Mr. Catron knew that I was convinced from the evidence that he was innocent of the charge concocted by the penitentiary authorities for political purposes only.

One of the most infamous crimes committed during my administration was the brutal murder of Colonel J. Francisco Chaves. This occurred at Progresso in Torrence County, on November 26, 1904.

Colonel Chaves had been an outstanding political leader in New Mexico for forty years, and had a long record of public service. Born in Bernalillo County when it was under the Mexican flag, he had attended school in St. Louis and studied medicine at the New York College of Physicians and Surgeons. During the Civil War he had served as major of the First New Mexico Infantry, and had been promoted to the rank of lieutenant-colonel. During the next six years he was delegate to Congress for New Mexico. Having been given a seat in the territorial council at fourteen consecutive elections, he served as president of that body for eight sessions. He was also president of the constitutional convention of 1889. At the time of his death, he was superintendent of public instruction. He had just been elected to the thirty-sixth legislative assembly, but was killed before he could take his seat.

In addition to his political activities, Colonel Chaves was engaged in farming and stock raising in Valencia County. He was said to own about ten thousand acres of land, and many thousand head of sheep and cattle. A man of strong convictions, he was absolutely fearless. He had many friends, as well as bitter enemies. He waged unremitting war against a notorious band of stock thieves in his section of the territory, and was the cause of sending two of its members to the penitentiary.

Shortly before his death the colonel had received a note calling him down to Progresso. He showed me that note, and I advised him strongly not to go, as it was unsigned. He replied, "I am not afraid to meet those damn cowards." "I know you are not," said I, "but those are the very kind who will shoot you from ambush or in the back." My remonstrance did no good, and the brave old warrior went to his death. The assassination took place while he was eating supper with several friends. He sat at the head of the table and directly behind him was a window which looked out to the rear of the house. As the meal progressed, Colonel Chaves stood up to pass a plate of chili to a friend at the left. Just then a shot was fired through the window at his back, and in a second or two he pitched forward on the table, face downward, dead. He had been shot through the heart.

The murder occurred in a wild country—the most thinly settled in New Mexico. Whoever perpetrated this brutal act escaped on horseback, as a hurried investigation revealed footprints leading from the window to a corral nearby, where the assassin had tethered his animal. Progresso was sixteen miles distant from the nearest station on the Santa Fe Railroad, so the news was slow in reaching the authorities and the murderer had a good start. It was thirty-six hours before bloodhounds from the penitentiary took the trail, and they followed it for only a short distance. Every endeavor was made to find the murderer, but without success. One suspect was arrested on circumstantial evidence and brought to Santa Fe. However, the sheriff authorities later came to the conclusion that he had had nothing to do with the crime—an opinion at which most of the Progresso section had arrived some time before.

At the time, some were inclined to attribute the murder

to a dissatisfied element in the Republican Party in Torrence County which was supposed to have it in for Colonel Chaves. However, District Attorney Clancy, who was closely connected with and pretty familiar with the situation in the Progresso country, publicly declared that he was convinced that Colonel Chaves had met his death at the hands of one of the desperate band of stock thieves who had infested that region for many years. I took the same view of the case, and so did public opinion, generally.

The death of this distinguished citizen was a great loss to the territory, and to me personally, since he was my friend. The funeral of the murdered leader took place from the capitol four days after his body was brought to Santa Fe. The thirty-sixth legislative assembly appropriated $2,500 to be used in tracking down the assassin, but nothing was ever accomplished. Another had been added to the list of unsolved murders in the annals of New Mexico.

On August 17th, 1905, Judge Henry L. Waldo called at my home and told me he had just arrived from Glorieta and had learned from a lady there that a party of bandits, headed by an ex-convict, was on horseback riding up the Pecos for the purpose of kidnapping my son, Miguel, Junior. The night was stormy and pouring down rain, but I soon had reached several of the mounted police and appointing Charles Closson in command, I sent them immediately on horseback to find Miguel and bring him home. They started, heavily armed, and reached Miguel at the Red House before the bandits arrived, and conducted him back safely to Santa Fe. The group of bandits must have heard the posse pass the house in which they were sleeping or protecting themselves from the rain, for they disappeared from sight.

I gave considerable thought to the territorial penitentiary from time to time, but never again for such personal reasons as in the spring of 1899. There was so little restraint in frontier society, it naturally followed that it was one of the most important institutions of the territory during my administration, and hence claimed the governor's attention frequently. Its location in Santa Fe made it easier for me to keep an eye upon it than upon some of the other institutions of the territory. Mr. Bursum proved an able administrator, as well as a shrewd politician. He was ably assisted by Mr. James and William E. Martin. Mr. Bursum, Mr. James, and Mr. Martin came from Socorro County. Their management, plus the supervision of the board of penitentiary commissioners, which, of course, was appointed by me, kept the institution going pretty well.

One of the many charges which my enemies made against me was that I opened the door of the penitentiary, and turned a horde of desperate criminals loose upon society. I doubt if there ever was a governor who was not accused of abusing the pardoning power. As a matter of fact, my exercise of this power was never arbitrary. I had been governor for less than two months, when I issued an order that no pardons or commutations of sentence would be considered by me, unless the letters or petitions requesting the same were approved by the trial judge, the district attorney, and some of the jurors. These rules were printed in English and Spanish and were intended to do away with a good many annoyances which arose from the fact that the public had only a vague idea of the procedure governing the granting of pardons. It is, of course, true that during nine years in office I issued a good many pardons, and changed a good many sentences from death to life imprisonment. However, my records show that in each case there was a full investigation and my action was based on the recommendation of those who were in a position to know the merits of the case. Early in my administration I established the custom of holiday pardons. Each New Year's Day, Fourth of July, Thanksgiving, and Christmas I issued a pardon or commutation of sentence to "the most deserving convict" in the penitentiary, as recommended by the board of commissioners and the superintendent. I did this to encourage the convicts, that they might look forward to relief, provided they obeyed the rules of the institution and acted their part. These holiday pardons planted hopes in many breasts, and were very effective in maintaining good discipline and helped to protect the guards and other penitentiary officials.

In addition to these holiday pardons, I also issued a number of others where the circumstances seemed to call for such action. A few concrete examples will make this clear. On one of my first visits to the penitentiary, the superintendent called my attention to the case of Carlos E. Rievera. This prisoner was in the last stages of consumption. From his appearance I did not think that he could live a week. Besides, he was endangering the lives of other inmates. I sent for the penitentiary physician and had him make a report on the man's condition. On hearing this report, I immediately issued a pardon as an act of mercy. The released man was taken home and died a short time afterwards.

On Thanksgiving day, 1899, I issued a pardon to Francisco Villegos, of San Miguel County. He had been sentenced by Judge S. B. Axtell for a term of sixty years and had served twenty-eight years. I was reliably informed that when the judge was about to pass sentence he asked the usual question, if the accused had anything to say why sentence should not be passed. Villegos declined to answer and the judge sentenced him to forty years. Villegos then arose and said, "I now wish to say this sentence is unjust, and that I am not guilty of the charge." Judge Axtell then said, "You are adding a falsehood to the charge, and I now change the sentence just imposed to read sixty years instead of forty."

I took particular pains to get at the truth of the crime charged against Villegos, as he was from my county, and I had heard considerable about the case before becoming governor. From all the facts I could gather, I became convinced it was nothing more than political rivalry between two families. During the twenty-eight years Villegos had already served, he had never violated any rule of the penitentiary. His record was perfect.

I had been invited to attend the services in the penitentiary chapel, and was seated in the gallery back of the convicts. The scene was one of the most touching I have ever witnessed. Strong men and bad men were moved to tears, and everyone stood up to testify in eloquent words to God's mercies, as was spoken by one of the convicts. The pardon was read by William E. Martin, at that time the penitentiary secretary, in both English and Spanish, and was greeted with overwhelming applause. The convicts rushed to where old man Villegos sat and hugged and kissed him, or shook hands with him to congratulate him. The old man, who bore marks of suffering on his face, and had bright and intelligent features, was overcome and seemed as happy as a child with a new toy. He stammered a few words of praise to God, to me, and to the officials and friends who had assisted in securing his release. After leaving the penitentiary, he came to the executive mansion to thank me in person. In his enthusiasm he said, "Governor, this is the best act you ever performed."

As a matter of fact, this pardon proved to be one of the most popular ever granted by a New Mexican executive. The *New Mexican* had this to say:

Francisco Villegos, who was released on Thanksgiving Day from the penitentiary, where he was serving a sentence of sixty years, and who had served twenty-eight years of that sentence, having conducted himself all that time in a most exemplary manner, never transgressing a single rule of the prison, called at the *New Mexican* office yesterday and desired that his sincere thanks be publicly extended to Governor Otero for the great kindness in granting him a pardon as a Thanksgiving present. He also desired to thank his friends and the officials of the territorial penitentiary who brought his case to the attention of the governor. Although sixty years of age, the man looks quite young, not over forty-five. Says he expects to live some more years yet, and will from now on by his behavior show the governor and his friends that clemency in his case was properly bestowed. He learned a good trade in the penitentiary. Villegos returns to his family at Las Vegas tomorrow. He has had quite a history, having been a prisoner of the Apache Indians when quite a boy, when the dreaded Cochise was the chieftain of that tribe. As such prisoner he went through a good many hardships, was on many raids, and was finally liberated when Cochise and his band were taken prisoners by a squadron of the First California Cavalry during the early sixties.

The New Year's day pardon for 1900 was issued the day preceding to Eleuterio Padilla, Desederio Gallegos, and Emeterio Garcia, all of Santa Fe County. These three young men had been sentenced for murdering Marcelino Vigil. They were convicted entirely upon circumstantial evidence, and Judge N. B. Laughlin sentenced them to a term of fifteen years. Later, many mitigating circumstances came to light and there was great doubt as to who really killed Vigil. Judge N. B. Laughlin, J. H. Crist, who prosecuted the case as district attorney, and the then solicitor general, J. P. Victory, united with Judge John R. McFie, District Attorney R. C. Gortner, and Solicitor General E. L. Bartlett, together with a majority of the jurors who convicted the three young men and many prominent residents of Santa Fe County, in recommending the men for executive clemency; consequently, after a most thorough investigation of the case, I issued the New Year's pardon to all three.

On August 11th, 1900, I pardoned William M. Hightower, of Lincoln County. His case was a very meritorious one and clearly showed a miscarriage of justice. The district attorney, both grand and petit juries, and a petition signed by almost every citizen in the county, irrespective of politics, urged me to pardon him. Accordingly I had Colonel George W. Prichard investigate the case thoroughly. He advised me that the conviction was an outrage and that he unhesitatingly recommended that I pardon him, which I did.

The *New Mexican* for January 4, 1905, commented on my pardon of Walter Wade as follows:

Governor Miguel A. Otero gives a broken-hearted mother her chastened son. Governor Otero believed in her, and her sorrowful story and it appealed to him. Here is what she told the reporter: "Before we knew what was happening he had telephoned the warden that I was coming for my boy. Then Mrs. West and I cried, and I believe the governor did also." The governor pardoned her son, Walter Wade, so the mother might take him home to Raton. Wade's sentence was for ten years and he had served two and a half years.

I was just as careful in commuting a death sentence to life imprisonment as I was in exercising the pardoning power. I had scarcely entered upon my duties as governor when the case of Henry Daniels, of Grant County, was brought up. This man had been found guilty of murder and was sentenced to be hanged on September 17, 1897. The law at that time required the governor to issue the death warrant to the sheriff of a county where a death sentence had been given by the trial judge. I issued a death warrant in accordance with the sentence of the court, although I must confess I did not like the idea of the governor having to sign a death warrant without knowing anything about the case. Later a petition was filed in the case and I was visited by a large delegation of women from Silver City and Deming. I listened to all that they had to say, and finally promised them to grant a reprieve for thirty days. Naturally, with a human life in the balance, I felt a great responsibility, and determined to give the case a careful and full hearing. After doing this, I decided to commute the death sentence into life imprisonment.

A very similar case was that of Jose Chavez y Chavez, for whom I was asked to send a death warrant to San Miguel County. At his first trial this man had been convicted and sentenced to be hanged, but an appeal was taken to the supreme court on fifty-odd errors. The supreme court sent the case back for a new trial, but on the second trial there were sixty-nine errors. To save expense, the court affirmed the judgment of the lower court, but Judges Bantz, Hamilton, and Collier called on me and joined in a request that I commute the sentence of Chavez to life imprisonment. Accordingly after a hearing, I took the action recommended to me. The Democrats in Las Vegas called an indignation meeting, headed by Mr. A. A. Jones, who delivered a scathing speech against my action in commuting the sentence and charged me openly with being a "particeps criminis." Of course, this designation did not please me and Jones and I became bitter enemies. However, some years later he openly apologized and stated that my action in commuting the sentence of Jose Chavez y Chavez was one of the best acts I ever performed during my term of office. We became very close friends. In 1916, when he ran for the United States Senate against Frank Hubbell, I took the stump in his behalf and spoke in nearly every county in the state. Jones was elected and held his seat until his death, in 1927.

After the hearings on these two cases, in 1897, I became convinced that the law requiring the governor to sign a death sentence was not right. Accordingly, I had the law changed, so that these two death warrants were the last ones ever issued from the governor's office. Henceforth all executions were ordered by the court trying the case.

Naturally I was "cussed out" for taking action in some cases and for refusing to act in others. However, the territorial press, at times, was willing to testify that I refused to act because the circumstances did not warrant it. Thus the *Albuquerque Citizen* for June 2, 1900, said.

> Governor Otero deserves great credit for not interfering in the Ruiz murder case. Heavy pressure was brought to bear upon the governor to commute the sentence to imprisonment for life, and he examined the records very carefully, but could find nothing to justify executive clemency.

The case referred to was that of Jose P. Ruiz, who was hung in Old Albuquerque on June 1, 1900, for the murder of a five-year-old girl two years before. Everyone present at the execution expected to see Ruiz weaken at the last moment, but he proved to be one of the gamest men who ever suffered the death penalty in the Southwest. Before the sheriff placed the hood over his eyes, the murderer spoke a few words in Spanish, declaring that drink was the cause of his terrible crime.

The Fourth of July award, in 1905, went to William H. McGinnis, whose life sentence was commuted to ten years on account of valuable services rendered the penitentiary. He was a member of Black Jack Ketchum's gang of train robbers, so I shall give his history in the next chapter. However, I shall refer to his case here to illustrate the penitentiary regulations regarding good time allowance. An inquisitive friend, who knew little of prison regulations, wrote to ask how it was that McGinnis, whose sentence was commuted to ten years from October 10th, 1899, was actually released on January 10th, 1906. I, of course, wrote him that under our rules a prisoner was allowed one month for good time the first year. Then for the next five years his good time allowance would be one month more for each year. This meant that after five years, each year would be cut to six months. Consequently, the actual time for a ten year sentence would be seventy-five months, or six years and three months. Thus, when McGinnis, who was a model prisoner, was released, he had served his full sentence according to our rules.

When I first became governor, I originated the custom of rewarding a trusty in the penitentiary who performed any work for the territory, such as working on roads or buildings belonging to the government. I tried this out on the scenic road being built between Santa Fe and Las Vegas and also on the rebuilding of the capitol in Santa Fe. I had all the convicts assemble in the chapel and told them that I intended to remove the guards and place them on their honor not to try to escape. And that, if they conducted themselves according to my suggestions, I would reward each of them according to his merit. In October, 1897, a dozen prisoners were assigned to the capitol rebuilding board to work on the new capitol building. All of these men were either life or long time sentence prisoners, but they became model prisoners. Most of them were lifers, but they seemed to take as much interest in their work as though the building belonged to them. They had absolute confidence in what I promised them and really did not need watching, so gradually I ordered the guard reduced until not a man remained. Not once did they neglect their work, and I do not believe they ever had the slightest thought of attempting to escape. In fact, they acted as though they were proud of the fact that they were considered worthy of trust. It was a great pleasure to me to be able to help these poor fellows. I enjoyed it very much, and I never had a man or woman, who had been pardoned by me, returned to the penitentiary, which, I believe, speaks well for my judgment.

Two of the trusties who worked on the capitol building were Vicente and Elesio Sena, who were both in for life. They were stone masons, and did all the work on the pillars in front of the captiol, the design work above the doors, and they carved the motto. They were constantly on the job, and the architect, Mr. I. H. Rapp, told me that he had never had better workmen. The board of commissioners also praised their excellent work, and asked that they be rewarded for the same. They had had many opportunities to escape, but remained true to their promise to me. After the capitol had been completed, I pardoned them and they both became good citizens.

Many of the convicts worked on the Las Vegas road without guards. They realized that I would reward them as I did those working on the capitol building. Superintendent Bursum kept a record on each man, and when the time came, he recommended those who were most deserving for pardons. He and I occasionally made a tour of inspection of the road, which promised to be a beautiful one when finished.

Of course, not all of the inmates of the penitentiary were model prisoners, and there were several escapes, or attempts to escape, while I was governor. One attempt which I recall especially was made by three convicts on April 17, 1901. It happened that Mrs. Bursum, the wife of the superintendent, was expecting an arrival in the family that evening, and Dr. Knapp was in attendance. Mr. Bursum was pacing the hall when he suddenly heard a commotion below. Going to the top of the stairs, he saw George Stephenson, a life prisoner, peeping out of the front door with a pistol in his hand. The superintendent was clad in a night shirt only, but he ran to his room and secured a rifle. Seeing Stephenson in the act of firing, Bursum shot from the stair case and killed the convict instantly. He was too late, however, to save a guard, Felipe Armijo, who came in the front door just in time to be shot by Stephenson just before Bursum killed the latter. Armijo was painfully injured in the mouth, but the wound was not serious. Stepping to the window of the office, Armijo saw another convict, Simmons, in the act of holding up Dr. Knapp. He immediately fired a charge of buckshot into Simmon's back. Thinking that a trusty who entered just at that moment was in the plot too, Armijo fired the other barrel of the shot gun at him. The shell, however, contained small bird shot and the injury was slight. No one knew how that shell had gotten mixed with the buckshot, but it was there and certainly saved the life of the trusty. Simmons died later in the penitentiary hospital and the other convict, Frank Carper, surrendered. I drove out to the penitentiary after breakfast the next day and spoke to Simmons before his death. Stephenson's body had been carried to the carpenter shop where he was being fitted for a pine box coffin. He was soon on his way to the grave dug at the penitentiary burying ground for his worthless body. Frank Carper was, of course, sorry, but he lost all his good time.

Chapter VIII

THE FOLSOM TRAIN ROBBERIES

As I NOW remember, it was sometime late in the summer of 1897 that I learned that the Black Jack Ketchum gang had established their rendezvous in a thickly wooded canyon in northern New Mexico on the east side of the Taos mountains in Colfax County not far from Elizabethtown and within sight of Old Baldy. Learning this about two months after I became governor, I at once notified the sheriffs of Colfax and Taos counties to keep a close watch on the gang and to notify me promptly should they make any attempt to move. I learned that besides Tom and Sam Ketchum, the gang consisted of Will Carver, alias G. W. Franks, whose real name I believed to be Harvey Logan; William Walter, alias Broncho Bill; and Ezra Lay, alias William H. McGinnis. All five of these men were at their headquarters. Will Franks was a wonderful shot with either rifle or pistol, and was regarded as the most desperate man in the bunch. He was a plausible sort of fellow, a good mixer and a good talker, so he usually did the scouting for the party, and located the "easy money." Clayton, the county seat of Union County, was a comparatively new town and the headquarters for cattle, horse, and sheep men. In those early days it was overrun with gambling houses, saloons, dance halls, houses of prostitution, and rustlers. Much ready cash was in evidence, and the Colorado and Southern Railroad brought it in to Clayton from Colorado points almost daily. Franks soon learned all the facts and located the best point on the railroad right-of-way for a holdup, which was five miles south of Folsom near Twin Mountain. After acquainting himself with all the details, he mounted his horse and struck the trail for headquarters. He soon made known his plans to the gang and Tom Ketchum said, "We will try it. Let's waste no time, but get ready at once."

As soon as arrangements were made, Broncho Bill was left in charge of the "Robbers' Roost" and the others left on good horses in the direction of Folsom.

On the night of September 3, 1897, the south-bound passenger train of the Colorado and Southern Railroad entered New Mexico through Emory Gap without mishap. The engineer was Crowfoot, the fireman Cackley, and the conductor Frank Harrington.

The train stopped for a few minutes in Folsom. As it started south, a man jumped on the front end of the express car to the engine, and quickly climbed over on the tender. At Twin Mountain, where there is a slight grade, the man dropped from the tender into the engine's cab, where he covered the engineer and fireman with his rifle. "Stop the train," he yelled to Crowfoot. Finding himself looking into the barrel of a rifle, the engineer quickly complied with the order. When the train came to a stop, the engineer and fireman were ordered to jump off and line up. The strange visitor was none other than Black Jack and the three men walked back to the door of the express car where Cackley called out to the express messenger to open the door, which he did. At this point, Black Jack was joined by Sam, his brother, and Will Franks. The other member of the gang, McGinnis, was left to guard the four horses. Crowfoot, Cackley, and the two Ketchum boys climbed into the express car, while Franks stood guard at the door. "Open the safe," commanded Black Jack. "I can't," said Drew. "It is a through safe, and I don't have the combination." "You lie," said Sam Ketchum, striking Drew over the head with his rifle. The latter fell to the floor, stunned by the blow. "Hand up those sticks," said Black Jack to Franks. Several sticks of dynamite were passed to him and five of them were placed on the top of the safe. Throwing a quarter of fresh beef on top of the sticks, he lighted the fuse and the men stepped back. The explosion broke open the safe door and damaged the roof of the car. While the Ketchums were in the express

My Nine Years as Governor

car, Conductor Harrington came up from the forward passenger coach toward the disconnected express car, swinging his lantern. Franks called out, "Go back where you came from and put out that light before I shoot it out." A sack holding silver dollars had been torn open by the explosion and the contents were scattered over the car floor. Sam Ketchum, however, picked the silver up and made the sack secure. "Now get back to your engine," said Black Jack to the engineer and fireman, "and continue your journey south." On their arrival in Clayton, Harrington reported the robbery. Immediately after the robbery, which took about thirty minutes, the bandits mounted their horses and rode off towards their rendezvous in the Taos mountains.

Dixon, the rear brakeman, jumped off the rear Pullman and hurried back to Folsom to report the robbery. Posses were organized in Trinidad, Clayton, and Folsom. The next morning they visited the scene of the holdup, but the bandits had disappeared. The booty secured on this first holdup was reported to have been $3,500. "I made a careful investigation of the robbery," said W. H. Reno, "and secured information which convinced me the crime was committed by the Black Jack gang, but I was unable to locate their whereabouts."

Shortly after this first holdup of the Colorado and Southern, the Ketchum gang left their Taos Mountain rendezvous and took up their abode in the southwestern part of the territory. For nearly two years, Colfax and Union counties were at peace, so far as the Black Jack gang was concerned; but they made things interesting along the eastern line of Arizona and Grant County, New Mexico, until well-organized posses began a systematic round-up of all bandits. Then the gang found things too warm to remain in that locality. At this time, late in the spring of 1899, the gang had a falling-out with their old leader, Black Jack. Sam Ketchum was delegated to inform his brother of their determination to quit him. Sam had decided to go with the gang, and early one morning Franks and Broncho Bill gathered up their belongings, mounted their horses, and rode north. This time they located their headquarters on Turkey Creek, in a canyon ten miles above the town of Cimarron, where they had several horses and a good supply of grub and ammunition. Franks scouted around for awhile and finally decided it was about time to attempt a second holdup at Twin Mountain. Since the other bandits readily assented to the suggestion, preparations were in order. At this point, Broncho Bill decided to leave the bunch, so he told Sam Ketchum that he was disgusted with camp life and declined to stay in the camp during their absence. They cached their camp outfit, and the remaining three mounted their horses and soon reached their destination between Folsom and Twin Mountain.

On July 11, 1899, the gang again held up the southbound passenger train at the same spot where the first holdup had taken place. Frank Harrington was again the conductor, Engineer Tubbs was in the cab, and Homel Scott was in charge of the express car, which carried considerable money. As the train rounded the curve at Twin Mountain, Tubbs noticed a fire on the prairie ahead of his train. "Some sheep-herder's camp," he told his fireman. When the engine reached the fire, an uninvited guest with a pistol in each hand entered the cab from the tender. "Stop her," he ordered. The engineer promptly shut off steam, and the train stopped within three hundred yards of the scene of the first holdup. The stranger, who was Franks, forced the engineer and fireman to walk to the express car where he was joined by Ketchum and McGinnis. They fired a few shots to frighten the passengers and prevent their interference. The noise of these shots, however, informed the alert express messenger, Scott, that something unusual was happening. Accordingly, he hurriedly seized several valuable packages of currency from one of the safes and threw them among a pile of merchandise and fruit boxes, where the robbers failed to find them. A second safe was blown open with dynamite, and the bandits jumped out of the car with loot, which I was told, amounted to $70,000. The three bandits then crossed the track and made for their horses.

Meanwhile, Conductor Harrington had realized that another holdup was under way. Having secured a gun from a closet in the smoking car, he enlisted the assistance of two deputy sheriffs who happened to be on the train. The three men went through the train to the rear Pullman, and dropped to the ground. Seeing a bunch of horses by the light of the fire, they crawled toward them in the hope of preventing the escape of the robbers. Their share in the adventure being unknown to the engineer, the latter blew his whistle, and started the train without them. However, he soon realized that they had been left behind, and stopped the train and waited for them. As it turned out, the conductor and the two deputy sheriffs were too late. The bandits secured the horses and rode off in the direction of Turkey Canyon.

A posse was soon organized at Trinidad. This consisted of eight men: W. H. Reno; Sheriff Edward Farr, of Huerfano County, Colorado; F. H. Smith, of New York; H. N. Love, a cowboy from Springer, New Mexico; Perfecto Cordova; Miguel Lopez; James H. Morgan; and Captain Thacker. The two last named were employees of the Wells Fargo Express Company. A heavy rain fell in the vicinity of Folsom the night after the holdup and greatly interfered with the work of the posse. However, they were able to locate the camp where the robbers had slept the night before the robbery. Here they found the first real clue to the location of the gang's rendezvous. This was an envelope postmarked "Springer, New Mexico." It bore the address, "G. W. Franks, Cimarron, New Mexico."

Acting on this information, the posse then proceeded to Cimarron, where they were joined by United States Marshall Foraker with several deputies. On July 15, some of the posse drove into Cimarron and reported having seen three men leading several pack horses entering Turkey Canyon that morning. It was, at once, suspected that the trio were Franks, McGinnis, and Sam Ketchum. Quickly mustering their posse, Reno and Farr headed for some smoke which they took to be the Ketchum camp. On the following day, at five o'clock in the afternoon, they came upon the camp. According to one version of the fight which followed, McGinnis, who was on his way to a creek about fifty yards distant, was immediately put out of action by a bullet in his shoulder. Bullets flew so fast for awhile that no two accounts agree as to exactly what did happen. The robbers, unaccustomed to resistance on the part of the law, were cornered but fought desperately. Sam Ketchum was struck in the left arm by a bullet which shattered the bone and left him unable to continue the fight. Franks, the remaining desperado, was able, single-handed, to deal considerable misery to the posse. An expert shot, he fought like a bunch of wildcats against the eight men and got away without a scratch. As for the posse, Sheriff Farr fought with a wounded wrist until he was killed. Smith was wounded in the leg, and Love was killed with a shot through the breast. The battle lasted nearly an hour, Franks keeping up a fusilade of bullets the whole time. Finally he managed to get McGinnis on a horse, and carried him to a hideout in the mountains. Ketchum, painfully wounded, also escaped on horseback, but was captured not long afterwards, about twenty miles from the camp. He was taken to Santa Fe on July 20, 1899, and entered the territorial penitentiary as "No. 129." He refused to have his shattered arm amputated and died four days later of blood poisoning.

On leaving the battlefield, the posse headed for Raton. Realizing that the authorities had located their rendezvous, Franks decided to leave Turkey Canyon at the earliest moment. That same night he washed and dressed the wounds on McGinnis' shoulder. He then saddled two of their best horses and helped his wounded companion to

My Nine Years as Governor 117

mount. The two then left together for the southern country, keeping close to the mountains. After traveling all night and part of the following day, they succeeded in reaching a ranch belonging to a native family which was very friendly to the bandits, having received many favors from them. Franks gave them considerable money and the man and his wife agreed to care for McGinnis and not allow anyone to enter his room. Franks then went in the direction of Roswell and Carlsbad to a ranch in Eddy County that belonged to a Frenchman named Lusk who was taking care of some horses for the bandits. It was agreed that McGinnis would meet him at the ranch as soon as he was able to travel.

McGinnis remained with this family for about four weeks and received the best attention possible. Either the man or his wife was with him day and night and his wounds were kept clean and dressed every day. So far as McGinnis knew, no one suspected his being there. By the middle of August he had entirely recovered, so he decided to leave for the Lusk ranch. His Mexican friends cried on the day of McGinnis' departure, for they had tended him like one of the family. The robber showed the greatest appreciation and affection for both man and wife and presented each with a goodly sum of money with his thanks and a promise to come back and see them at some future day. His horse was in fine condition, and he left his benefactors at night, well equipped with rifle, pistols, and sufficient food to last until he reached his rendezvous with Franks.

Soon after the arrival of McGinnis at his ranch, Lusk became suspicious and notified M. Cicero Stewart, sheriff of Eddy County, of the two suspicious strangers at his place. Accordingly, on August 22, 1899, Sheriff Stewart, together with two deputies, J. D. Cantrell and Rufus Thomas, went with Lusk to arrest the two men. When they arrived, McGinnis was in the house, eating breakfast, while Franks was outside hunting their horses. A slight noise made by the posse while tying their horses to a wire fence alarmed

McGinnis, who dashed out of the door to get his rifle from his saddle. Seeing Thomas approaching the house, he fired at the latter with his 45 Colt revolver, striking him in the shoulder. Observing the ranchman, Lusk, in the group, and being satisfied that he had turned informer, he aimed at him, wounding him in the wrist. By this time Lusk had gotten his rifle into action and fired a shot which struck the outlaw on the side of the head. As McGinnis was stunned, he was quickly disarmed, handcuffed, and tied on a horse. Meanwhile, Franks, who had watched these proceedings from a hill about a mile away, disappeared. He was never captured, but his partner was taken safely back to town. The Colfax County officials having been notified of the arrest, the sheriff and two deputies went to Carlsbad and escorted McGinnis to Raton.

On August 16, 1899, just six days before the arrest of McGinnis in Eddy County, Black Jack Ketchum staged the third holdup of the Colorado and Southern at Twin Mountain. However, the affair turned out rather disastrously for the lone bandit. Having picketed his horse near Twin Mountain, he had walked leisurely to Folsom, where he prepared for his audacious attempt to hold up a passenger train all by himself. No one knows what prompted him to such a foolhardy undertaking. There was only one chance in a thousand that he would succeed. Very likely his pride was pricked because the other members of the gang had discarded him and he wanted to show them that he could accomplish single-handed what it had taken three of them to do. He certainly did not lack nerve, even if his plans were foolhardy. As a matter of fact, he came very near succeeding. He was defeated by one factor which he had not foreseen. He stopped the train on a curve and this made it impossible for the trainmen to uncouple the express car quickly. The resulting loss of time was the direct cause of his downfall.

The same routine was followed as in the two previous

holdups. Black Jack boarded the engine's tender at Folsom, and rode to Twin Mountain where he disappeared in the cab and compelled the engineer, Kirchgraber, to stop the train. The engineer and fireman were then marched back to the rear of the express car, and Scotty Drew, the express messenger, was forced to join them. Fred Bartlett, the mail clerk, stuck his head out of the door of the mail car to see what was going on. His curiosity, however, was quickly satisfied. Ketchum promptly sent a bullet through his jaw. The bandit accompanied his shot by yelling, "Get your damn head in there!" and Bartlett complied without delay. On reaching the rear of the express car, the three trainmen were ordered to uncouple it from the rest of the train. In vain they tugged and pulled at the couplings, which would not yield, owing to the train's being on a curve. "Hurry up or I'll kill every damn one of you," roared Black Jack.

Meanwhile, Conductor Harrington was preparing to take a hand in the affair. When the train had come to a stop, he walked to the platform of the car and got off. There was shooting up near the engine and he knew what that meant. His train was being held up again. It was the third time in two years and a second time within five weeks. He was getting tired of this holdup business, fearing the company might think he was in the play, as his train was always selected. Hurriedly, he got back into the car. He knew what the bandits were doing but he did not know how many there were in the party. Securing his double-barreled shotgun, he crawled through a small opening at the bottom of the partition between the smoking room and mail compartment, and pulled his shotgun after him. Harrington made his way to the front door and opened it slightly. The four men were only about ten feet away, all bunched together, so he was afraid to shoot for fear of hitting one of the crew. "Hurry, damn you," said the bandit, while the three men were making poor headway with the couplings. Drew stepped out of the line thus exposing Black Jack who was facing Harrington. "I wanted to hit the robber in the heart," said Harrington, "but in the dim light I misjudged. I had to be quick for I knew that when I opened the door I would attract the attention of the robber who was facing me, so I aimed as well as I could under the circumstances. I raised my shotgun, opened the door, and fired." Immediately another shot was heard. Eleven buckshot entered Ketchum's right arm just above the elbow, as a bullet from his gun went through the left coat sleeve of Harrington's coat. "His buckshot jiggled my aim," said Black Jack later. "I'd have killed him if he'd waited a fraction of a second; I had a bead on his heart, but he jiggled my aim."

Struck by buckshot from Harrington's gun, Black Jack fell. He got up and crawled under the express car and disappeared in the darkness, trying to reach his horse. His right arm was terribly lacerated and he bled terribly.

Kirchgraber and his fireman returned to the engine, while Drew went to his car. The holdup was over. Sheriff Saturnino Pinard and a posse from Clayton found the outlaw three hundred yards from the track astride his rifle, dazed, his right arm riddled with buckshot, his body drained of blood. He made repeated attempts to mount his horse, but was too weak to do so. As the posse came up, he waved them down with his huge black hat. He was then taken to Trinidad, where his wounded arm was dressed. However, his identity was not known at first. When asked his name he replied, "Stevens." After some correspondence he was taken to Santa Fe and entered at the penitentiary, on August 24, 1899.

As no one could properly identify the prisoner, Sheriff Shields, of San Angelo, Texas, was asked to come to Santa Fe. On his arrival he was taken to Ketchum's cell. "Halloo, Tom," was the sheriff's greeting. "I haven't seen you for some time. Where have you been keeping yourself?" The name of Stevens was no longer used. While Shields was in Santa Fe, Black Jack talked freely with him and told him of many things in which he had been engaged. As soon as it became generally known that Black Jack had been captured, the entire West breathed more freely. The press of the country applauded Conductor Harrington for his courage and two rewards of $1,000 each were paid to Harrington, one by the United States government and one by Wells Fargo Express Company. Several other rewards, aggregating $3,000, were never paid. One important matter had been finally settled, and Black Jack's career of crime was ended.

Shortly after Tom Ketchum's arrival at the penitentiary, his wounded arm began to bother him considerably. Dr. Miguel F. Desmarais, of the penitentiary staff, called me on the telephone, saying that gangrene had set in, and requesting that I would speak to Ketchum about the necessity of having it amputated. I drove out and had a talk with Tom, who agreed very readily to do as I advised. The arm was taken off at the shoulder. He recovered rapidly and began putting on flesh. He was an amiable prisoner, usually in a good humor. When Sheriff Stewart visited him in October, 1899, Tom said: "I am getting so fat that when they hang me they can eat me." The warden found in his cell a steel saw and a wooden pistol covered with tin foil. He was evidently preparing to attempt an escape from the penitentiary. The newspapers some times worried him. Thus when he read in the *New Mexican* that the Boers had held up a train and taken two million five hundred thousand dollars in English gold, he wept.

I took my son out to see Ketchum and they became great pals. Tom was very fond of peanuts and Miguel would bring him a sack whenever he visited him, which was quite often. One day Miguel told Tom he was going to beg his father to pardon him and he kept after me every day, saying, "Papa, Tom is an awfully good friend of mine, and I wish you would pardon him, as he promised me that he would be good and settle down."

One day Tom's oldest brother, Berry Ketchum, came to visit him but Tom declined to see him. He said, "Berry is my good brother. He is a Christian and belongs to the church. I will tell you how it all happened. He showed both Sam and me how to hold up a train. The three of us held up a train in Texas and secured about $100,000 in cash. Berry was the oldest, so he took the money and became a real Christian gentleman, and Sam and I had to rustle for a living. Once in a while, he would give us a horse and a few dollars but, believe me, the dollars were very few. He had taught us just how to hold up trains and get the money, so we kept it up. He worried every time we visited him, fearing we might give him away, but we never did. No, I do not wish to see him." Berry came over to see me and seemed to be a quiet and pleasant gentleman. He said Sam and Tom were always wild and would not follow his advice to settle down and go to farming. He said he had promised to give each of them a good farm if they would work it, but they declined. Berry went back to the penitentiary and left some money with the warden to buy Tom what he wanted, such as peanuts, candy, cakes, and pies, as he was very fond of sweets. At the same time, he asked the warden not to tell Tom what he had done. Berry returned to San Angelo without seeing his brother, but he visited Sam's grave and placed some flowers and a wreath on it. I felt sorry for Berry, as he appeared to be quite disappointed.

One day Doctor Sloan called at my office and asked if he might see Tom Ketchum and have a talk with him. Accordingly, I telephoned the necessary permission to Mr. James, the assistant warden. It seems that the doctor had been told of a buried treasure near San Angelo, Texas, where Sam and Tom had cached a considerable sum of money. Tom told the doctor a great story, drawing a map and locating the exact spot. Sloan did not tell any one, not even me, but he took a friend with him and, together, they drove to San Angelo and remained there several days looking for the place, but without success. On his return the doctor told me of his trip and his failure to find a fortune. Tom appeared to be disappointed over the doctor's failure and told him, "If I could go with you, I could show you the place in a minute." The doctor believed Tom and got up a great plan for me to allow him to take a large guard with him, with a promise to return Tom to the penitentiary, but I knocked all his plans into a cocked-hat and told him no, not even if the cache contained millions.

Sheriff Saturnino Pinard brought Black Jack's rifle to Santa Fe and presented it to me. I presented it to Colonel Theodore Roosevelt who was greatly pleased, especially when I told him that Ketchum wanted him to have it.

While the notorious train robber was waiting trial, public opinion all over the Southwest was greatly aroused as to the disposition of him. Arizona wanted to try him for the murder of Rogers and Wingate at Camp Verde, and made a requisition on New Mexico for him. They said, "Hand him over to us and we will see that he will trouble the frontier no longer." However, I refused to honor the requisition, telling the Arizona officers, "We'll attend to Black Jack ourselves."

He was tried at the regular September term of the district court sitting in Union County, in 1899. The indictment was for holding up a railway train with intent to rob it, which offense, according to territorial law, was punishable with death. Chief Justice Mills presided at the trial, while Jeremiah Leahy, of Raton, was the district attorney in charge of the prosecution. The latter was a splendid lawyer. He was absolutely fearless and was very successful in securing convictions. The court appointed William B. Bunker, a well-known attorney of Las Vegas, to conduct the defense.

Tom Ketchum made a very striking appearance at his trial. He was a tall, handsome man and stood as straight as an Indian warrior. His black hair was brushed back from his forehead and his face was clean-shaven except for a heavy, well-trimmed mustache. His eyes, which resembled black coals of fire, were piercing and radiant. He was neatly dressed, the end of his empty coat sleeve being tucked into a side pocket. His confinement had bleached and softened his usually rough and sunburned features. He stood calmly in the crowded court room, his eyes resting now on the judge, then wandering over the faces of the strange audience gathered to see the leader of the worst gang of outlaws the Southwest had ever known. It was the first time in his life that he had ever been hailed before a high court of justice. Unaccustomed as he was to such surroundings, he showed no signs of nervousness and seemed quite indifferent to what was taking place.

The imperturbable district attorney read the indictment and asked for the death penalty. The defendant's plea of "not guilty" was almost inaudible. Leahy put Kirchgraber, Harrington, and Drew in the witness box, and they testified that the man before them was the one who had held up their train at Twin Mountain on the night of August 16. Drew, the express messenger, was relating what happened when his train came to a stop on the fateful night.

"You say the prisoner pounded on the door of your car and commanded you to open it?" asked Leahy.

"Yes, sir."

"Well, what did he say to you?"

"He said, pointing his gun at me, 'Fall out of there damn quick!'"

"And what did you do?"

"I fell out damn quick. What would you have done, Mr. Leahy?"

"Is that true, Tom?" asked Bunker.

"You bet your goddamn life it's true and he didn't lose any time either."

The court suppressed the ripples of laughter that followed these remarks by Ketchum.

Bunker used his talents well but the testimony of the wit-

My Nine Years as Governor 125

nesses was very convincing and the summary by the district attorney was very damaging. The jury deliberated only a few minutes. When their verdict of guilty, which carried a death sentence, was read, the crowded court room was so quiet that a pin dropped on the floor could have been heard. However, Black Jack showed no emotion. He merely crossed his legs and gazed out of the open window. When Judge Mills asked him if he had anything to say, he promptly replied, "I'd like to shave the district attorney." The sentence of the court was that he be hanged in Clayton on October 4, 1900. Closely guarded, he was returned to the penitentiary in Santa Fe for safe keeping. For more than a year the attorneys wrangled on appeal. I ordered a stay of execution and set the day for the execution April 26, 1901.

On the morning of April 23, the gates of the territorial penitentiary opened to permit Tom Ketchum to pass them for the last time. He was taken to Clayton for execution. The usual legal routine had been accorded the prisoner to appeal to the supreme court of the territory for a new trial. This was denied. Only executive clemency could halt proceedings against Black Jack, and I decided not to interfere.

For several weeks rumors had been going the rounds that on the day set for the execution, his old companions in crime would be on hand in force to snatch the bandit from the clutches of the law. Conductor Harrington was to be waylaid and shot and similar treatment was to be meted out to those who had been responsible for Ketchum's downfall. I kept in close touch with conditions in Clayton and, as I expected, nothing unusual happened. To calm the people, I sent Captain L. C. Fort, of Las Vegas, to represent me and take charge of Ketchum's execution. The execution would have taken place at 8 o'clock, a. m., but for a spurious telegram received by the sheriff, purporting to be signed by me, granting a stay of execution. Captain Fort wired me at once, as he could not understand my changed attitude. The telegram was forwarded to me at Las Vegas, and I immediately went to the telegraph office and had the operator arrange with Denver to give me a clear line to Clayton. This was done and, through the operator, I carried on a conversation with Captain Fort, assuring him that no such message had been sent by me. Evidently the wire had been tapped near Clayton, as no telegraph office had sent the message. I told Captain Fort to proceed with the execution, and that my office would not interfere.

At twelve minutes past one, Ketchum, escorted by Sheriff Garcia and several guards, emerged from the jail, walked to the gallows, and ascended the thirteen steps. His left hand was chained to his side. His head was uncovered. He contemptuously refused the administrations of a Catholic priest. "Get a fiddle," he growled, "let's dance." He would not repent. A. W. Thompson, then of Clayton, now of Fort Collins, Colorado, visited Black Jack in his cell a short time before he was to mount the scaffold, and asked, "Are you nervous, Tom?" "Feel my pulse," the outlaw sneered, as he shoved his left arm through the bars. It was steady and strong. "Why don't they hurry?" the badman grumbled, cursing loudly. "I'd like to get to hell in time for dinner." Deliberately he took his place on the trap and cast his eyes downward to see that he was standing in the proper place. The guards bound his legs. A hangman's noose dangled above his head, and this was drawn down and placed about his neck. Black Jack moved his head from side to side to assist in the proper adjustment. The black cap was pulled over his head and tied.

Sheriff Garcia, hatchet in hand, stepped before the hooded figure.

"Are you ready?" asked the sheriff.

"Ready. Let her go," came the cheerful and audible response.

The sheriff raised his hatchet and it fell upon the rope that held up the trapdoor. The figure of the bandit shot downward. Descending a few feet it paused for a second and then dropped to the ground beneath the gallows. The noose, instead of breaking Ketchum's neck, had decapitated him. This was the terrible ending of Black Jack Ketchum.

The notorious train robber was buried in the old cemetery north of Clayton. In 1933, the owner of the cemetery, by permission, moved the body to the new cemetery. The disinterment was made on the afternoon of Sunday, September 10. It was a beautiful day and fully fifteen hundred curious citizens and strangers from every direction gathered for the occasion. It took two hours of careful work before workmen, under the supervision of Undertaker F. P. Kilburn, struck the outside box. Meanwhile, Mr. H. H. Errett, of Clayton, mounted on a truck nearby, told the story of Black Jack's history. When the top of the coffin was removed, the remains of the outlaw were found in a remarkable state of preservation after over thirty-two years. His black hair and long thick mustache had turned a maroon red. His black suit still covered his body, but it had turned to a red gray color. After having been viewed by the public, the remains were transferred to a new grave in the Clayton cemetery, where it, today, attracts thousands of visitors.

After his capture in Eddy County, William H. McGinnis was first taken to Raton but later transferred to the penitentiary in Santa Fe for safe keeping. His trial took place at the October term of the fourth judicial district court of Colfax County for 1899. It was held in Raton with Chief Justice Mills presiding and Jeremiah Leahy as district attorney. William B. Bunker was the lawyer for the defense.

McGinnis was indicted for killing Sheriff Edward Farr and H. N. Love, two of the posse at the fight in Turkey Canyon. As the case proceeded, the prosecution found that it had a difficult task upon its hands. The defendant insisted that he had not fired at the sheriff or any other member of the posse. He stated that, at the time of the attack by the officers, he was on his way to the creek for water and that he carried a canteen, not a rifle. He admitted that he had a pistol in his belt, but said that he was rendered unconscious at the very beginning of the fight and did not have time to draw it. The testimony of James H. Morgan, a member of the posse, was favorable to the accused. He stated that when the first shots were fired, McGinnis "had neither a gun nor a rifle," and that he fell immediately upon the first fire from the posse. Miguel Lopez, another member of the posse, testified that Perfecto Cordova, a third member of the posse, told him, after the fight, that McGinnis did not have a rifle when first seen by the posse. At the trial, however, Cordova swore that McGinnis did have a rifle in his hand when first seen and that, upon being ordered to surrender, he raised his rifle to his shoulder and fired at Sheriff Farr at the very moment the sheriff fired at him.

Other witnesses gave evidence to prove that McGinnis was in the vicinity of Cimarron shortly before the train robbery, in company with Franks and Ketchum, and that, on the day of the holdup, these three men were seen within a half mile of the very spot where it occurred. All of this testimony was more or less circumstantial.

The defense counsel objected to the introduction of this evidence, but Judge Mills overruled the objection. On cross-examination McGinnis refused to answer many questions put to him. He absolutely refused to answer all questions regarding his former life and his connection with the Black Jack gang. He answered only those relating to the fight in which Sheriff Farr was killed. When the district attorney insisted upon his answering questions regarding the train robbery at Twin Mountain, he addressed the court as follows:

> If the court please, I am here on trial for murder. I understand there are other charges against me for train robbery, other murder charges, and for interfering with the United States mail. I have been put on trial without being given a chance to procure many of my witnesses. I have no way to protect myself, and I positively refuse to answer any questions except

those asked by the district attorney concerning this fight, and I will not, under any circumstances whatever, answer any other questions attempting to incriminate myself.

McGinnis proved an exceptionally good witness, both as to intelligence and courage. His answers were prompt, without the slightest hesitation or show of fear and I believe that he told the absolute truth. It was very unfortunate for him that his trial took place just about a month after the conviction of Black Jack at Clayton. Public opinion was aroused to a high pitch against all persons connected with train robberies, and the courts were determined to stop this crime which gave New Mexico such a bad name for lawlessness, even though all points of law were not adhered to literally. Personally, I believe that all courts should be impartial and just at all times. Sometimes, however, popular clamor and political ambitions combine to banish the calm and careful consideration due to justice.

Being greatly interested in the case, I went to Raton and on the invitation of Chief Justice Mills sat beside him during the proceedings. I listened very attentively to all the witnesses. I do not pretend to know what changed Perfecto Cordova, but any person who heard his testimony could tell that he was following instructions. In fact, after the trial, he admitted to several that he had been mistaken about McGinnis firing his gun. I was particularly impressed with Morgan's testimony and believed that he and McGinnis both told the truth. I noticed that every ruling in the case was against the defendant. I have never believed that McGinnis had a fair trial; it seemed to me that he was convicted before he was tried. From all of the evidence given at the trial, I came to the conclusion that Franks killed both Sheriff Farr and H. N. Love, as both McGinnis and Ketchum were down and out after the first volley of bullets fired by the posse.

When the arguments had all been finished, the jury deliberated for three hours, finally bringing in a verdict of guilty of murder in the second degree. The court thus sentenced McGinnis to the penitentiary for life. Perhaps it was fortunate for him that he was not tried for train robbery, because he might have received the same sentence given Black Jack.

The court room was packed throughout the trial, many people having been turned away. One session lasted until 11 o'clock in the evening. The money used by the defense was donated by the cowboys of the Mogollon district of Socorro and Grant counties, where McGinnis was well known and quite popular.

McGinnis proved a model prisoner, never violating a rule of the penitentiary. He was a trusty for some time and on two occasions assisted the authorities in suppressing outbreaks by the convicts.

The first mutiny occurred at four o'clock in the morning, when two prisoners, who were being conducted from the cell house to the bakery, attacked the deputy warden and locked him up in the key room. They were equipped with pistols and ammunition, which had been smuggled in by a discharged convict, and could help themselves to any keys they wanted. They tried to capture the armory but met determined resistance from the prison guards who knew that, if they succeeded, it would mean many deaths and very serious trouble. A large number of shots were exchanged in the fight and the night captain of the guards was seriously wounded, as well as a trusty, Pedro Sandoval. The mutiny was finally suppressed and the two convicts were shot. One died during the night and the other died a few days later in the penitentiary hospital. The captain of the guard and the trusty recovered.

During this affair, McGinnis was night engineer at the power plant. He remained loyal to the authorities and helped to suppress the mutiny. Without his timely assistance many others would have been killed.

The other insurrection occurred some years later. On

this occasion they used a young boy, the brother-in-law of Superintendent Bursum, as a shield to keep the guards from firing on them. Armed with knives, the prisoners surrounded the cell house keepers and demanded the keys to the armory. Mrs. Bursum; Mrs. James, wife of the deputy warden; and Mrs. Martin, wife of the penitentiary clerk; ran to the top story of the administration building, where they could see the mutinous convicts below. They called out to McGinnis, who was a trusty, to get help. Jumping on a gray racer belonging to Mr. Martin, the latter rode a mile to town. In a short time he returned with a squad of territorial militia and the mutiny was soon over.

Accordingly, on the eve of the next regular holiday, July 1, 1905, upon recommendation of penitentiary authorities, I issued an order commuting McGinnis' sentence to a term of ten years. As a matter of fact, McGinnis was released on January 10, 1906, as his actual time was shortened by good behavior to six years and three months. After he became free, McGinnis, whose real name was W. E. Lay, was in the saloon business at Shoshoni, Wyoming, for a short time. Later he became interested in oil lands and moved to Los Angeles. He married a very fine woman and they had two children. Mrs. Lay told a friend that I was the only person about whom her husband spoke except in the very highest terms.

Chapter IX

I TAKE A HAND IN TERRITORIAL POLITICS

As T. B. CATRON had been the boss of the Republican party in New Mexico for many years before I became governor, it was natural that he should attempt to play the same role after my appointment. He could not boss me, and time was to show that he failed in his efforts to have me removed. One thing he could do—that was to fight me for the political control of the territory. Catron passed as an astute politician, though I scarcely think his reputation was altogether deserved. He was, however, very greedy for office and power, and was quite willing to scheme and spend money on every election, no matter how minor the office or offices involved.

His determination to beat me in politics, no matter what the cost to the party, may be illustrated by something that happened in the spring of 1900. At that time Catron realized that, although he was chairman of the Republican committee for Santa Fe County, "the Otero faction," as he called my supporters, would probably win the city election unless he resorted to desperate measures. Accordingly, through several conferences with members of the Democratic committee he arranged a fusion ticket, made up of Democrats and "Catron Republicans," which carried the election. That the defeat of the regular Republican ticket was due to his animosity against me was proven nine months later by affidavits made by Honorable Charles F. Easley, Arthur Seligman, and A. B. Renehan, the Democratic leaders with whom he had bargained. These gentlemen stated under oath that Catron had said that "he did not care if not a single Republican was elected to a city office," that "he wanted to get even with 'the gang' to down Governor Otero," and that he "was willing to bust up the Republican Party of Santa Fe County to do so."

My Nine Years as Governor

The perseverance with which the Republican boss of Santa Fe County pressed charges against me in Washington was only matched by the determination and lack of scruple with which he fought me in election after election. Every Republican territorial convention was the scene of a fight between us. Usually it ended in a defeat for him and a victory for me. Thus, while I did not attend the convention held in Socorro in the spring of 1900 and boss the Republican delegates, as the Democratic pop sheets of the territory prophesied, I was elected a delegate at large from New Mexico to attend the Republican national convention at Philadelphia.

The patience of my readers would be exhausted, were I to refer to all of the minor elections in which Catron hoped, by hook or crook, to wrest some advantage from me. I shall, therefore, confine myself during the remainder of this chapter to speaking of the elections for delegate to Congress. This official was the most important one chosen by the voters of the territory. He had to be elected every two years. While he had no vote in Congress, he was the official spokesman of the territory at the national capital. He was in a good position to suggest needed legislation and to gain the friendship and support of congressmen and senators who could vote. If a delegate worked harmoniously with the governor, the two might do much good for the territory. If the two were unable to work together, little would be accomplished for the territory by Congress. Furthermore, if the delegate were opposed to the governor, the delegate became the spokesman, not for the territory as a whole, but for the disgruntled element in the party. This, of course, would be a source of great embarrassment to the governor, and might lead to his removal. Consequently, I usually took an active interest in the question as to who would represent the territory in Washington.

Having defeated Catron in 1896, Honorable Harvey B. Fergusson was the delegate to Congress when I became governor. He was an Albuquerque attorney, a Democrat, and an ardent free silver man. An election for this office took place again in the fall of 1898, soon after the soldiers had all been sent to the front. The Republican convention, which was held in Albuquerque, was favorable toward me, and adopted the following resolution:

> We congratulate Governor Otero upon the success of his administration and commend him for his efforts in behalf of good government and the advancement of the material and financial interests of New Mexico, both at home and abroad, and we tender to the President of the United States our thanks for the appointment of a governor from the ranks of the people, a man who by reason of his lifetime residence in New Mexico, and his intimate acquaintance with the needs of our people, is best able to perform the duties of an executive in this territory.

While the convention was in session, Mrs. Otero, Miguel, and I were in Albuquerque as the guests of Honorable and Mrs. William B. Childers. However, for several good and sufficient reasons, I did not attend the convention. I was of the opinion that Captain Maximiliano Luna should have been nominated for delegate. However, the convention could not agree on Max because his uncle, Solomon Luna, opposed his nomination. Many of my friends who were favorable to the nomination of the dashing young soldier got themselves appointed by the chair as a committee to invite me to a seat on the platform. They started out to find me. While I was strongly in favor of Captain Luna, I declined to interfere with the action of the convention, so my friends had to report that I could not be found. The result was that Pedro Perea, who had been supported by Catron for the governorship the year before, was nominated. This mild-mannered gentleman succeeded in defeating Mr. Fergusson, and held the office for two years.

While the man of my choice was not named for delegate, my party did elect its candidates for Congress and the legislative assembly by a strong majority. This result occasioned the following comment in the territorial press:

My Nine Years as Governor 135

The sweeping Republican victory in New Mexico is a living reminder to the enemies of Governor Otero, that while he may not have pleased those who are interested in the territory of New Mexico "for revenue only" his administration has been entirely satisfactory to the great majority of the people, and to prove it they endorsed him at the polls on election day. His firm adherence to the principles of right and justice has endeared him to the people of the territory in a manner that will not be soon forgotten. So much for the "boy governor" as the *Optic* has been pleased to call him. If New Mexico could have a few more officials as efficient as the "boy governor" for a few years she would realize an increase in immigration that would open her eyes to the necessity of having an honest administration of public affairs all over the territory.

Another newspaper declared that I should feel proud of the results at the polls—that it was "Glory enough for the governor for one election." A third paper commented as follows:

By their votes cast at the recent election the people of New Mexico paid a well deserved compliment to Governor Otero, by endorsing his official acts for the past seventeen months and upholding him in his efforts to give the territory a good, clean and just administration. Ever since Governor Otero took his office the Democratic press of the territory has never failed to misconstrue his acts as an officer, pervert facts and to accuse him of exercising the prerogative of his office for partisan reasons, even though he was only obeying the mandates of the law, and could not have acted otherwise had he desired. The election of a great majority of the candidates on the Republican tickets in the various counties clearly indicates that the voters believe in the honesty of purpose and sincerity of desire which have actuated the governor in everything he has done as an officer and the executive of the great territory of New Mexico. Governor Otero has conscientiously endeavored to do his duty in every act imposed upon him by his office and it must be gratifying to him to know that the voters of the territory believe in him and so express themselves at the polls, despite the efforts made by the Democrats to discredit him by misrepresentations and malevolent attacks. As matters now stand, the governor has every evidence that his efforts to advance the interests of the territory are appreciated by the great majority of the people of New Mexico, and strength will be given him to continue his course of action without regard for the desires of the extreme partisans among his opponents, and in utter contempt for enemies and their newspapers and supporters.

Mr. Perea accomplished very little in Congress and, consequently, was not regarded as a strong candidate to succeed himself when the election of 1900 came around. In that year, I took a very prominent part in the nominating convention and in the campaign. The convention was held in the chamber of the house of representatives in the new capitol building in Santa Fe on October 3. The description, as told in the *New Mexican,* is quoted in full in the Appendix (p. 369).

During my speech I was frequently interrupted by great applause. An editorial in the *New Mexican* characterized my address as "a concise and clean summing up of the issues" which had created very favorable comment.

For some reason the nomination for delegate to Congress nearly went begging. Soloman Luna was one of those who declined it. While he possessed character, wealth, and influence, Sol did not have much formal education and was rather bashful when it came to speaking before a crowd. In fact, Sol never made a speech in his life. After some thought on the subject, I gave my support to Bernard S. Rodey, who accepted the nomination offered him. Mr. Rodey, an Albuquerque attorney, was a native of Ireland and a very fluent speaker.

Ten days after the convention Rodey came to Santa Fe to see me. He was very blue, because he had no money for his campaign expenses. He had been "cussing out" the railroad for years, so they naturally regarded him as a radical and would not give him any passes. He told me that he was really up against it, and would have to resign from the ticket. I encouraged him as best I could, and promised that I would write for passes and let him have some cash. I gave him my check for fifty dollars, which he accepted with a grateful smile, saying: "Governor, you have saved my life." I wrote the president of the Denver and Rio Grande and also Judge Waldo, counselor for the Santa Fe, for passes for the candidate. These were sent at my personal request, and Mr. Rodey remained as my guest until they arrived.

When the transportation had been arranged, I invited Messrs. A. M. Bergere and William E. Martin to join me, in company with our candidate for Congress, in some campaigning. We first started out on a week's trip through Rio Arriba, Taos, Mora, and portions of San Miguel and Colfax counties in the northern part of the territory. Our first destination was Tierra Amarilla, where we planned to attend the county Republican convention. I had an axe of my own to grind in that neck of the woods. L. Bradford Prince, former governor of the territory, was an avowed candidate for the territorial council from Rio Arriba County. I was determined to defeat Prince, and to see that Honorable Thomas D. Burns received the nomination. The latter did not want the place but finally consented to accept the nomination. Prince's name was placed before the convention, but the nomination was not seconded. When Burns' name had been brought up, he was unanimously nominated by a standing vote. I, of course, was greatly pleased. I then made a short talk and ended up by introducing Mr. Rodey as the Republican candidate for delegate to Congress. Rodey made a splendid speech, Mr. Martin acting as his interpreter.

The next morning I arranged by telegraph for wagon transportation from Tres Piedras to Taos. We drove to Chama and took the train for Tres Piedras. We found the wagon hitched and waiting, so without delay, Rodey, Bergere, Martin, and I jumped in and away we started for Taos. After crossing the Rio Grande, we climbed the south side of Arroyo Seco and on top of the hill was a large number of people out from Taos to welcome us. They had a string band and played all the way to Taos. The plaza was crowded and a brass band started up with "There will be a hot time in the old town tonight," and the cheering was loud and happy. After dinner we were escorted to the court house. As usual I made a short address and introduced the candidate. The next morning we started for Mora over the United States Hill. The road was a fright, the mud being over a foot deep. We were in an open wagon drawn by four sprightly horses, our driver being an American who knew his business. However, the load was heavy and it began to rain. As we were going down hill at a lively trot, the wagon upset, sending us flying, but fortunately, no one was hurt. After getting things straightened out we all got back in the wagon. When we reached Agua Negra the whole valley was under water about two feet deep. We hired a native and had him walk in front of the team to show us the road. We proceeded in a walk until we reached Cleveland and drove up in front of Dan Cassidy's store, where he drew the whiskey from a barrel in a tin cup. It was fine liquor and as the tin cup was passed around, I suppose we took more than an ordinary drink, so when we started for Mora we were all feeling very happy. The rain kept up and we did not reach our destination until about 1:30 a. m. Chief Justice Mills was holding court there and the town was crowded with people. Bergere and Martin got out the brass band and paraded around to lively music. Everybody got up and soon the court house was filled to overflowing. We had a great meeting which lasted until morning. As usual I spoke first and introduced the candidate, who made a great hit with the people.

About noon the next day, we started for Las Vegas. On arriving there, I sent Rodey and Martin to Colfax County for a meeting, while Bergere and I stopped over in the town. The next day, our party being again united, we all started for Santa Fe, which we reached on the afternoon of October 20th. Our campaign through these northern counties had taken a week exactly. I personally paid all the expense, and it amounted to $400 in cold cash. However, we had cordial receptions wherever we went, and promises of big Republican majorities.

The *Chama Tribune* for October 22 made the following comment on our trip:

> Truly it cannot be said of Governor Miguel A. Otero, in his exalted position, that he distributes all his attention and favors to the rich and influential citizens; quite on the contrary, for from the exalted heads that wear the crown, down to the humble and lowly sons and daughters of toil, the governor is found mingling among them, always with a kind word of cheer and a

friendly handshaking for all. The presence of the governor at the Rio Arriba County Republican convention last Monday was the first time in the history of Tierra Amarilla that an executive of the territory was known to visit that town. The governor's presence added untold brilliancy to the convention.

While in Las Vegas, I saw my old friend, James S. Duncan, who was a member of the territorial council for several terms. "Jim" and I endorsed Rodey's note at the bank for five hundred dollars and gave it to him with instructions to use it carefully. Rodey gave us a mortgage on some lots in Albuquerque as security, and after a long time he finally paid the note, but it was an uphill job. Frank A. Hubbell, the chairman of the Republican central committee, was hot because Mr. Rodey refused to turn over to him one hundred dollars which Justo Armijo had given him for his campaign. Hubbell even attached Rodey's library, but I succeeded in quelling the trouble and having the attachment dismissed. Later, after we had twice elected Rodey to Congress, he double-crossed me with Frank Hubbell, and this brought about his defeat for the third nomination.

Three days later, Rodey and I took the early morning train from Santa Fe to Las Vegas to attend the San Miguel County Republican convention, which convened that day, October 23rd. On the arrival of the train we were met at the depot by a reception committee and were driven to the court house in the old town where the convention was being held. In the carriage with me were Chief Justice Mills, Hon. Eugenio Romero, and Mr. Rodey. When we entered the convention hall, the delegates and onlookers stood up and cheered. The enthusiasm was immense, and the cheering continued for several minutes. Finally, when order had been restored, I was taken to the rostrum and introduced to the chairman, who in turn introduced me to the convention. I made a speech which appeared to be well received, from the frequent interruptions and cheers from the delegates. When I finished a recess was taken, and a regular reception took place for I had to shake hands with everybody present. The chair announced that the noon hour had arrived, and the recess would continue for lunch and until 1:30 o'clock. On the reconvening of the convention Mr. Rodey made a splendid speech which was well received. After he had finished, we retired so the convention might proceed with its business. We promised to return for the evening session to ratify the nominations to be made by the convention. Rodey and I arrived about 9:00 p. m. The convention had finished its work, and the hall and galleries were crowded with people, many ladies being in the large assembly to hear speeches from us. I was introduced first and spoke for about an hour to a very appreciative audience. Mr. Rodey followed me and, as usual, made a good impression. Every person seemed happy and they promised large Republican majorities for San Miguel County.

The *Las Vegas Republican* for October 29 commented upon my address as follows:

> Governor Otero's speech in this city last Monday evening did a lot of good. The people here are now talking of territorial affairs more than of the national issues. That is right. There is plenty to do right here at home in the way of self government, and when we learn to attend to our own business right well, as we have in the past three years, perhaps the people of the states will consider the claim of New Mexico to statehood.

The following day Mr. Rodey and I started out on a campaign trip through San Miguel and Guadalupe counties. Leaving Las Vegas at six o'clock the morning of the 24th, we visited nearly all the principle precincts. Everywhere we were received with great enthusiasm and promises.

November 7th was a happy day for me. Election returns throughout the states showed that McKinley and Roosevelt had been elected, and the returns in New Mexico showed that Rodey had been elected as delegate to Congress. In Santa Fe County the Republicans carried their ticket with one exception. Charles F. Easley was elected to the territorial council instead of Thomas B. Catron. This was expected, as Catron was fighting the Republican administration of the territory. Some people get what they deserve. Of course, Catron contested the seat before an overwhelming Republican majority in the council, but that was as far as he got. Mr. Easley retained his seat throughout the session.

Republican papers throughout the territory interpreted the Republican victory at the polls as a strong endorsement of my administration. Practically all of them printed my picture at the head of the editorial column. Below was the inscription: "For the governor of New Mexico from June 7th, 1901, to June 7th, 1905. Miguel A. Otero." The *New Mexican* for November 14th said:

> The Republicans of New Mexico elected Mr. Rodey and no mistake about it. It was the party as a whole that did it, aided and supported strongly by Governor Otero and the territorial administration. It will do well to remember this fact in the future.

The *Carlsbad Argus* for November 23rd said:

> New Mexico, during the past two years, under the honest, conservative and business-like administration of Governor Otero, has prospered in an exceptional degree, and it is most pleasing commentary upon the wisdom and appreciation of the people of the territory that by their vote on the 6th instant, they made entry on the official record. "Well done, thou good and faithful servant."

The *Albuquerque Citizen* for November 22nd said:

> It is our belief that Governor Otero will join in favoring every measure of legislation beneficial to the territory. He has made the best governor New Mexico has ever had, and deserves reappointment by President McKinley.

Chapter X
I AM REAPPOINTED IN SPITE OF MY POLITICAL ENEMIES

THE *Albuquerque Citizen* for April 8, 1901, said: "The opposition to Governor Otero is concentrated in Santa Fe, and consists of a half-dozen disappointed office-seekers." Though few in number, these men were loud-mouthed and very active. Consequently, before discussing my reappointment by President McKinley, it is necessary to pay my compliments to the little group which fought bitterly and absolutely without scruple to blacken my character and belittle my achievements. How desperately they hoped to oust me from my position, or at least to prevent my reappointment when my first term expired on June 7, 1901!

The leader of this gang was Thomas Benton Catron. He was, without doubt, one of the ablest lawyers in the territory, but he devoted his brains and energy to crushing opposition to himself, with no thought of public welfare. Having taken up the practive of law in New Mexico a year or two after the Civil War, he had, in one way or another, acquired an interest in large land grants in the territory. Many of the descriptions of the old Spanish and Mexican land grants had been very loosely worded, and Catron had shown great ingenuity in interpreting them to the advantage of his clients and himself. In fact, he came to be the largest landholder in New Mexico. At the same time, he became very influential in the Republican Party in the territory. Referring to Catron in *The Leading Facts of New Mexico History* (Volume II, p. 520) Twitchell says:

> Until the year 1896 he was recognized as the leader of the Republican Party, framed its policies, wrote its platforms, controlled its conventions, represented the party in national conventions, and was a member of the Republican national committee. With the administration of Governor Miguel A. Otero, aided by the executive, a powerful party machine was erected and

Mr. Catron was compelled to divide the leadership with younger men ambitious for political preferment and recognition in the party councils.

While he aspired to the role of party boss in the territory, Catron lacked the leadership which made Tom Platt and Matt Quay supreme in New York and Pennsylvania for so many years. A blunt and determined man, he could not inspire loyalty in others, but sought to bully them instead. Catron was always ready to spend money on elections, and this fact helped to make him available as a candidate. In 1894, I had been responsible for his nomination as the Republican candidate for the office of delegate to Congress. I never knew how much money he spent in that election, but he spent so much that he had to borrow $2,000 from me, and he succeeded in defeating Antonio Joseph of Ojo Caliente, a wealthy Democrat who had been delegate to Congress for ten years. Once elected, Catron had been forced to spend much of his time and thought in defending some of his friends who were finally hung for the murder of Frank Chaves. The excessive zeal which he showed in this case, the so-called Borrego case, nearly led to his being disbarred from law practice in the territory. However, one judge was prevailed upon to change his mind—he moved to St. Louis shortly afterwards—and thus Catron and Charles Spiess, his partner, were saved. Not satisfied with this outcome, Catron's friends called a meeting of the bar association and elected him president. All of this whitewash, however, did not prevent the delegate from New Mexico from being known in his true character in Washington. Denied any real influence in the national capital, Catron schemed to get some fradulent bonds validated, and to have one of his sons appointed to West Point and another to Annapolis. He also cultivated the acquaintance of Tom Reed, speaker of the house. In 1896, Catron favored Reed for president, although as a "goldbug" the man from Maine was opposed to the admission of any more territories to the Union. Later, when McKinley had been nominated and elected, Catron had the brass to pose as a McKinley supporter and to assume that the men he recommended would be appointed to office in New Mexico. For governor of the territory, Catron supported Pedro Perea of Bernalillo. Naturally, he was grieviously disappointed when I was made governor instead.

It was inevitable that we should come to conflict. He was dictatorial and absolutely ruthless in his methods, whereas I did not propose to be dictated to or bullied. The President had made me governor, and I intended to control things myself. Furthermore, Catron was a corporation lawyer, while I was a tribune of the people.

At first, however, Catron hoped to work with me. Always greedy for office, he was determined to have himself appointed United States district attorney. Never a very good judge of character, he was blind and egotistical enough to think that he could get my support. However, I knew him of old. Realizing that he had owed his nomination as delegate to Congress to me, he had written me on November 9, 1894, that "if it may be in my power to be of any service to you in any manner whatever, from now on, I wish you to command me freely." Later, when I was a candidate for the position of United States marshal in the spring of 1897, he had promised me in the presence of Mrs. Otero and many others that he would support me for that office. Yet he had no sooner arrived in Washington than he did everything in his power to have Solomon Luna appointed and ignored my candidacy entirely. Just as he promised Richard Hudson to support him for the position of United States collector of internal revenue, and then, when he got to Washington, did his best to have A. Staab, of Santa Fe, appointed instead. It happened that I was in the lobby of the National Hotel when Dick told Catron to his face that he was "a damn liar and an ingrate," and that he would not believe him on oath, and Catron took it.

As I had very definite convictions regarding the value

of Mr. Catron's promises, and had become governor without any assistance from him, I had no reason to support him for the position he coveted. I did tell him that between himself and Eugene Fiske, I would much prefer him. As a matter of fact, I knew that Catron had no chance, as both President McKinley and Senator Mark Hanna were dead against him. Hanna knew that Catron had opposed the nomination of McKinley, and had done all he could for the nomination of Reed, and even if I had supported Catron, it would have done him no good, and would have hurt my own influence in Washington. Furthermore, the President chose not to replace the man whom President Cleveland had made United States district attorney for New Mexico, in 1896. This was William B. Childers, a native of Tennessee who had settled in Albuquerque a month before the railroad had reached that place. One of the best lawyers in New Mexico, he always performed his duties fearlessly and impartially. An outstanding Democrat, he had been chairman of the Democratic central committee of the territory for several years. In 1896, however, he supported the "gold" wing of the party. Naturally, McKinley felt that he should recognize the Gold Democrats in some way, so Mr. Childers was left undisturbed in office for nine years. He was about the only Democrat who held an important federal office in New Mexico while I was governor. Childers was a courteous southern cavalier, and we were very warm friends. He had a lovely family, and we visited back and forth frequently, as I shall describe in a later chapter.

Mr. Catron never remained friendly toward anyone whom he could not boss. He had a row with me less than a week after my first inauguration as governor, and I plainly told him where he might head in. However, during my first year, even though I knew he was bitterly against me, I did everything within my power to harmonize all differences between us for the sake of the Republican Party. His only thought, however, was for himself.

Catron's chief ally in New Mexico in the fight against me was Eugene A. Fiske, of Santa Fe, who was also a candidate for the position of United States district attorney in 1897. As long as they were rivals for the same office, each said some pretty mean things about the other. Later, when they realized that neither had a chance of getting the appointment, they combined forces and concentrated all of their venom on me.

A third member of the conspiracy was Frederick Muller, of Santa Fe. Prior to the war with Spain, "Fritz," as he was usually called, had been the captain of a cavalry troop at Santa Fe, whose principle occupation on Sundays was to congregate at Fischer's brewery and drink beer. They had a rule that no Mexicans were allowed to join the troop. Fritz was foxy and knew his onions, and was popular with a certain group. He was a good drillmaster and a thorough soldier. When the first call was made for volunteers, his troop was the first to volunteer. When the troop was accepted by the government, I appointed Muller as captain —as he had been in the original troop. As a Catron Republican, he had been elected collector for Santa Fe County, and was holding this position when he went off to the war. During his absence from the county, Catron attempted to have his office declared vacant, so that he could put another Catron man in his place. I took the position that there was no vacancy—that a citizen who was fighting for his country should not be considered absent from his civilian office. The case was tried before the district court, and my views were sustained. However, Fritz did not appreciate the favor which I had done him. Colonel Theodore Roosevelt liked him, and this went to his head. Most of the Rough Riders supported me, but Fritz was too much under the influence of my enemies. They played constantly upon his vanity, and made him believe that, if Roosevelt as president removed me, he would be appointed as my successor. Stupidly, Fritz swallowed all the lies they told him, and signed several letters addressed to Roosevelt against me. The latter once handed me a letter written by Muller, and asked: "Who do you think writes these letters for Fritz? Of course, I know that he never wrote them; he couldn't, for he has a very limited education." I replied that I knew who wrote them and that it was Eugene A. Fiske. I afterwards verified this by both Fritz and a notary public who worked in Fiske's office.

Catron, Fiske, and Muller were my most active enemies, but there were others who were associated with them from time to time. Fiske was lined up with the Raton gang, mostly Ohio men under the leadership of a newspaper publisher named T. W. Collier, who had himself been a candidate for the governorship. Abe C. Voorhees was looked upon as a scout for the Collier-Fiske combination. He was always on the job, moving about noiselessly in a secretive and pussy-footing manner. At intervals he reported imaginary tales of political intrigue to the wiseacres gathered at the round-table, hatching plots and schemes which never developed into anything but foul air. On one visit to Washington, Fiske was jubilant: he had discovered a "real find." He had made the acquaintance of the Reverend Mr. Madden, a Methodist preacher from McKinley's home town, Canton, Ohio. It was generally believed by the gang that their new friend was the pastor of the church where the McKinleys worshipped, and was a frequent visitor in their home. It was even reported that Madden would, doubtless, occupy the guest room in the executive mansion as soon as the President and Mrs. McKinley learned of his arrival in Washington. Fiske introduced his "find" to the gang as a "sure-shot" who could be counted upon to "bring home the bacon." I frankly admit that I was greatly impressed, and had little doubt as to the final success of Fiske and his Raton bunch. Fiske smilingly admitted that he had everything his own way, and we all regarded him as a true "captain of political industry." But, alas, the much overrated Madden failed to get past the outer doorkeeper at the executive mansion, and wandered around Washington like a "lost spirit in Hades." However, he remained with the gang as long as they paid his expenses, which was not long.

L. Bradford Prince was also a member of the gang that opposed me. President Harrison had appointed him governor of New Mexico, and he had hoped for a reappointment when the Republicans were again in power in Washington. He took himself very seriously, but was not too dignified to hit below the belt when he had a chance.

Catron's "man Friday" in the fight against me was William M. Berger, a New Yorker who had soldiered a while during the war between the states. Coming to Santa Fe in 1880, he had set up a law office and dabbled in real estate, insurance, and newspaper work. Berger was ready to do the dirty work for the bosses, and to follow orders implicitly. For five years, from 1897 to 1902, he ran the *Santa Fe Capital*, a yellow sheet which weekly denounced "the little governor" and the "ring" which was said to surround him. This paper was one of the very few in the territory which failed to support my administration. Catron and his crowd backed it, of course, but it had very little circulation and no influence, though some of my friends at times derived great amusement from its attacks. A fly-by-night concern, the *Capital* shortly went on the rocks, and the editor moved to Belen, where he consoled himself by launching another paper. Berger was a tool for the gang.

Quinby Vance also ran with "the gang." His brother-in-law, R. W. Tayler, was a congressman who represented the Ohio district which McKinley had formerly represented. While he was surveyor-general of New Mexico, he did not amount to much, and was not even reappointed himself. However, Fiske and Wallace made him believe that the President might appoint him governor.

While Catron and I were working together to clear him of any connection with the alleged conspiracy to poison me,

I thought that we had become friends again, and that the hatchet had been buried again for all time. I was confirmed in this belief by the fact that when the Republican convention was held for the city of Santa Fe about this time, it was Mr. Catron who introduced the following resolutions which was adopted unanimously:

> We also fully and unequivocally endorse the territorial administration of Governor Otero, and pledge him the hearty support of the Republican Party in the interest of economy, law, and order, believing that his administration is far superior to any that has preceded it.

However, strange to say, after the conspiracy case had been settled, he resumed his unreasonable tactics in fighting my administration and more particularly myself, leaving no stone unturned to injure me, both personally and politically, if within his power. Mr. Catron's ambitions, his extreme jealousy, and his desire to dictate knew no bounds. He was so bitter against me that he would have resorted to anything to have gotten rid of me. He was very resourceful when it came to removing anyone who opposed him, but he was afraid to go the limit with me, as he knew that I had many friends. However, he fought me in the territory and in Washington, in small matters and in those of more importance.

As the Republican boss of Santa Fe County, Catron fought me in election after election—all of which I have described in other chapters. The determination with which he fought me at the polls was only matched by the perseverance with which he filed charges against me in Washington. President McKinley and I had wisely kept our intention to make me governor to ourselves until my name was sent in to the Senate so that I could at least be confirmed before the usual barrage of charges began. I say "usual," because it is well known in the national capital that the favorite pastime of disgruntled politicians in the territories is to prefer charges against the governor and other territorial officials. One wonders how they can think up so many tall tales, but their discontent stays with them night and day and is bound to give birth to malicious lies of infinite variety and pattern. Their charges cannot be proven, nor can they be easily disproved. The result is vexation of spirit and expensive and time-consuming trips to Washington to refute these idle tales. And there is always the chance that the higher-ups in Washington will be worn out by such persistence, and will remove those against whom so many charges are being made—in the hope of getting a little rest. However, if I was cursed by being set upon by a whole gang of bitter enemies, I was fortunate in having friends in power who showed the greatest of patience and good judgment in weighing the papers submitted against me. It was not simply that McKinley had confidence in me; he also knew Catron and sized him up at his true worth.

I had not been governor of the territory long before charges began to pile up against me. I cannot take time to specify all of them. As early as the war with Spain, when I was so busy I had to work in my office until late at night, I was advised by the secretary of the interior that Catron and Fiske and some of their miserable satellites had preferred additional charges against me. I had appointed Mr. Charles A. Spiess district attorney for the counties of Santa Fe, Rio Arriba, and Taos. Charlie was a former law partner of Catron, but the two men had had a falling out. My every move was a signal for a counter move on their part, so they immediately attacked this appointment. Spiess later served with ability in the assembly, where he helped to pass some good laws and even presided over the council. However, Catron and Fiske alleged that he was a notoriously bad man who had only recently served a term in the penitentiary. They declared that he was corrupt, dishonest, and untruthful—an all-around scoundrel, unworthy of trust, and a grafter who would stoop to the lowest methods. Spiess had been sent up for contempt of court, but had been guilty of no other offense. I told Charlie that I would go to Washington at once and refute the charges and place those two character assassins where they belonged, since neither of them was worthy of belief and their affidavit was not worth the paper it was written on.

On my arrival in the capital, the first thing I did was to go and see the secretary of the interior regarding these charges. The secretary was very nice, and listened attentively to all I had to say. My opinion of both Catron and Fiske seemed to amuse him very much. He laughed heartily and said: "Do not worry, governor. I merely advised you, as we do in all such cases. However, these men are well known here, and we give little or no attention to their complaints, as we supposed the charges were made just as you have stated. The charges will be dismissed." Having settled the matter satisfactorily, I immediately telegraphed Charlie the facts. This was the beginning of one of the most infamous batches of affidavits ever concocted and filed in Washington. The purpose was to injure, or destroy, if possible, the reputation of those who refused to be governed by this group of high-binders. However, they were unable to accomplish their designs, for the authorities in the national capital knew them like a book, as I pointed out above.

Not satisfied with filing charges against me with the President and secretary of the interior, Catron and Fiske also worked on Vice-President Roosevelt. They hoped to turn him against me by writing malicious letters and getting Fritz Muller to sign them. While in Chicago in August, 1901, I met Mr. Roosevelt on Jackson Boulevard, and we stopped for a little talk. That evening I received a note from him asking me to come to his room at the Annex, as he wanted to see me. He was dressing for a dinner at the Chicago Club when I arrived, and I stayed with him until he left. During the conversation, he told me that he had been receiving some letters from Captain Muller that were very much against me. Mr. Roosevelt promised to give me the letters when he returned to Washington.

The following is a sample of the Fiske-Muller concoction:

Santa Fe, N. M., April 25th, 1901.

To the Honorable Theodore Roosevelt,

My Dear Colonel:

Late yesterday afternoon I learned that Ex-Governor Prince, of Santa Fe, and Flushing, L. I., expected to go to Oyster Bay and assist when you took your new degree, which, I understand, was to be conferred last evening, so I telegraphed you to see him and I knew he would tell you truthfully of the *bondage, politically speaking, that we are under here in New Mexico*. Governor Prince will leave for home in a day or two, and it seemed too good an opportunity to have him meet you, to stand on any formality about the matter.

Many charges against Governor Otero have been sent to Washington. *I have sent a copy of one set to you.*

Some of the laws of the last legislature, which convened in January last, are the worst signed by any governor. They were all *his* laws in the beginning. Some men came here to attend the session, who were clean and honest, but before very long the promise of a position made them Governor Otero's *tools*.

The organic act governing this territory is wrong. It should prohibit any member of either house from receiving any appointment during that session; instead of that being the case, the entire legislature is *debauched* by promises of "snaps" of some sort.

The taxation has been doubled. There is no *surplus* as Governor Otero asserts. *Any money in the treasury is already appropriated* to pay insurance and interest.

Governor Otero, not content with the salary which the U. S. gave to other governors, has had the territory allow him "Contingent Expenses" of $4,800, and when vouchers were spoken of, he said it would be against his dignity to give an account of the money.

He has had the laws changed giving him power to remove any county official at his own will, if they do not do his absolute bidding. So, *the voice of the people* is to be nothing. He has surrounded himself with "a ring," composed of *some of the most corrupt and unscrupulous men in the territory*. His plan is to have an enabling act passed by Congress next December, and he is to go to the U. S. Senate. Any man of independence who will not bow the knee to him is to be prosecuted.

The courts have never been so venal. The judge of this district and the *chief justice, a Democrat from the state of Connecticut, do just as he wishes them to do.* He has given it out plainly that the *President says he may have anything he wants,* so they are afraid of his threats.

I was working for Secretary Wallace to be the new governor, but he died about ten days ago. *We* want a change out here, and almost any one will be welcomed if *we* get Otero out.

The people want *Ex-Governor Prince,* irrespective of party, and he is *my* choice *above all other men.* He was a very prominent candidate four years ago, and had the finest recommendations any man has ever had. Every member of the New York legislature, both houses, recommended him. Mayor Strong and hundreds of others, but on account of *some bonds the Coler's beat him,* he would have protected *the people.* The present governor has played into their hands, and has had his "expenses" paid by them in New York and Washington.

Governor Prince is not a candidate, and knows nothing of this letter, but if the President will appoint him as the *dark horse,* he will do more for New Mexico than he can by appointing any other man.

I am not writing you in any selfish interest, but because *I* know that *Prince* was the *best governor New Mexico ever had.* He served under President Harrison. *Everything was peaceable, honest and for the public good.*

Will you write to the President and ask him not to make the appointment for governor of New Mexico until his return to Washington in June? Governor Otero's time does not expire until June 7th. *I* will go on, *if necessary, and explain matters to him.*

We pray for relief from the present administration, which is run solely in the interest of self. *We* in New Mexico are not living under a republican form of government, but under an *absolute monarchy. Help us, Colonel,* to be *free.* Llewellyn knows all about it, but he says he is a *pie-eater,* at Otero's lunch counter, so can say nothing.

I shall write on other matters later, but this is a *call for relief.*

Very respectfully,

(Signed) Fred Muller.

Governor Otero's Most Recent Humiliation, the Crowning Disgrace. Republicans Made Ashamed

The Republican Party is proud of its name and its history; and properly so, for its success has been synonymous with the greatness and prosperity of the country.

New Mexico is asking for statehood and, of course, should show her ability to govern her own affairs.

Both have been disgraced and humiliated by the action of Otero and his "gang" *in Washington during the last few weeks.*

He has disgraced *the party* by bringing *Democrats* before the President and the Senate, as better representatives than Republicans. Before his nomination, *Judge Albert B. Fall, the most rabid and intense Democrat in the whole Southwest,* was appointed the *leader of the Otero party,* and made the argument for Otero before the President, and drew his answers to the charges on file. *The rest of the gang, like a lot of curs,* followed the lead of Albert

B. Fall, the man who, through his whole life, has been the bitterest enemy of the *Republican Party*.

Before the Senate committee last week, *Democrats* were much more conspicuous than *Republicans*. Even the dispatch sent by the governor's press agent to the *New Mexican* confessed that five of the *Otero* supporters were *Democrats*. *William H. Pope,* who is an intense Georgia *Democrat,* was specially conspicuous, then came Charles H. Gildersleeve, once chairman of the Democratic territorial committee in New Mexico, and Judge Thomas Smith, the *Democratic ex-judge.* For Otero to send them as his representatives, showed that *he had no hold on the Republican Party,* but that only affected himself. The real *danger* was in making it appear to Senators *that the Republicans here have to depend on Democratic leadership.*

Worse than this, especially as to statehood, *was the disgrace to the territory.* Before the President, Otero had to *send to Texas for Albert B. Fall,* his chief spokesman, *and the brains of his party.* And before the Senate he was represented by U. S. Attorney Matt G. Reynolds, from Missouri; Judge Thomas Smith, from Virginia; Mr. Charles H. Gildersleeve, from New York; Judge Edward P. Seeds, from Iowa, and a lot of other outsiders. *This was virtually admitting* that *New Mexicans have not the ability to govern themselves,* but have to rely on outside aid.

The course of the *"Otero crowd"* has all the time been dangerous to statehood. By insisting on pushing his reappointment *they* brought before the world the wretched condition of the administration here. *But now they have done far worse.* They have shown to the Republican Senators that their faction, *while calling itself Republican, yet has to submit to Democratic leadership,* has to go to distant states to get its spokesmen before a committee.

The Republican Party ought to rise and repudiate this false position, and the people of the territory should indignantly declare their capacity for *self-government* without the aid of *demagogues from Georgia, Missouri, Texas, New York, Iowa, Virginia, and California.*

At the time President Roosevelt gave me the Catron letter,* he expressed himself as being very disgusted with Fritz Muller for giving him such a letter, and said: "The crazy Dutchman does not give me credit for seeing through such a vile and worthless piece of manufactured lies written by selfish candidates." I, too, was disgusted.

When Captain Muller had returned from the war, at first he had been very bitter against Catron for his attempt to oust him from his political job in the county, and had been grateful to me for holding it for him. However, he soon joined Catron and Fiske in their fight against me, as they assured him, he would be appointed to my place, as

*For copy of letter and Muller-Fiske affidavits see Appendix, pp. 371-385.

My Nine Years as Governor 155

governor of New Mexico, and, naturally, this went to his head, and he did his very best to turn Colonel Roosevelt against me. Fortunately, however, Major Llewellyn and other former Rough Riders, who were friends of mine, also had the colonel's ear, and did not hesitate to write him about me.

The letters, concocted by Fiske and signed by Muller, were interesting reading, and both the President and myself had a hearty laugh over them, for they amused us greatly. However, it is time that I allowed some of those who supported my administration to have a word. I always felt considerable gratitude at the attitude which the territorial press took toward me. There were only two or three yellow journals that wanted to oust me. The situation was summed up by the *New Mexican* for April 20, 1901, as follows:

> The Republican newspapers of the territory, with but an unimportant exception or two, are supporting Governor Otero for reappointment. The decent Democratic papers would also like to see him reappointed, a few Populist sheets are opposed to him, this must be expected; Governor Otero must have enemies, and they are very bitter and vindictive; they have good cause to be, for he has spoiled many of their nefarious, rotten and dishonest schemes.

The *Chama Tribune* for June 3 paid its respect to my enemies as follows:

> Governor Otero's enemies cannot prevent his reappointment. As the time draws near for the appointment of a man to succeed Honorable Miguel A. Otero as territorial governor of New Mexico his opponents and enemies are redoubling their efforts to encompass the defeat of the present executive as his own successor. Their rantings and ravings have indeed reached the rabid stage and in the frenzied ambition to shelve Governor Otero they are making use of means which will only act as a boomerang, and instead of accomplishing the desired result, will rebound and do far more injury to the slanderers than to the man at whom they are directed.
>
> Governor Otero has made some strong enemies during his administration, but of the whole bunch, individually and collectively, he may justly feel proud, for their bitter enmity has been engendered wholly and simply because the governor would not be dictated to by these men, ...
>
> Governor Otero has turned a deaf ear to the counsels of those men who would have the territorial government conducted in a manner that would enable them to be benefited in a pecuniary sense at the expense of the public and to the depletion of the territorial treasury; for this he has been condemned by his enemies ...
>
> Governor Otero has insisted upon the exercise of his right to surround

himself with officials whose ideas correspond with his own regarding the conduct of territorial affairs. He has not allowed the "gang" to dictate his appointments nor in any way to influence his decisions upon matters of state. . . .

Governor Otero has insisted that the revenues of the territory be promptly collected and that they should only be expended in a businesslike manner and for purposes calculated to benefit the territory at large and not a favored few who, with itching palms, stood ready to plunge their greedy hands deep into the public exchequer. . . .

Governor Otero has labored unceasingly to maintain and enhance the credit of the territory and to reduce her indebtedness with the result that today New Mexico stands upon a higher financial plane than she ever did before. For this the clique condemns him.

In every official act of his administration Governor Otero has had an eye single to the public good and to the upbuilding of the territory so that she might ask for *statehood* with a reasonable degree of assurance that her demands would not be turned down. . . .

The motive behind this virulent opposition to the governor is too apparent to deceive anybody. Actuated by malice, born of defeated ambition and blasted political hopes, these men now seek the defeat of a man under whose banner they would have most gladly enlisted as subservient tools and henchmen, ready to do the bidding of their master in everything which would redound to his and their personal benefit. But Governor Otero soon gave them distinctly to understand that their aid in the conduct of his office was not sought, would not be solicited, and if tendered would be spurned, and from that time on they became his implacable foes, who now are leaving no stone unturned to bring about the governor's defeat as his own successor. Will they succeed? The *Tribune* predicts not.

The *Albuquerque Citizen* spoke well of my achievements as governor. It said:

The territory is in better shape than it ever was before. Governor Otero's term of office expires in June, and he deserves reappointment from President McKinley. Four years ago, when Mr. Otero was appointed governor, the public affairs of the territory were in bad shape. The last year of Governor Thornton's Democratic administration showed a deficiency of over $100,000. The territory appeared to be on the eve of bankruptcy and the new governor faced a heavy responsibility, which he nobly met. During his term of office a new capitol has been erected in Santa Fe, the public credit has been restored, enabling the territory to refund its bonded indebtedness at the low rate of 4 per cent interest. No scandals of any sort can be truthfully brought against Governor Otero. He has served the people faithfully and has neglected no duty. He has made the name of New Mexico creditable at Washington, and secured for the territory recognition in all departments of the government.

As my term neared its close, the *Citizen* said, on June 4:

The term of office of Governor Miguel A. Otero expires June 7th. He will undoubtedly be reappointed. He has the entire Republican Party of the territory urging his return to the office. The late legislative assembly endorsed him in a body. The national Republican committeeman for New Mexico, the

My Nine Years as Governor 157

delegate to Congress, the chairman of the territorial Republican committee, nearly all the county committees and officials, and the entire Republican press of the territory endorse his candidacy. Nearly everybody in New Mexico, with a half a dozen sore-head exceptions, favors his reappointment. He has made the best governor New Mexico has ever had and the people earnestly desire his retention in office.

The editor of the *Lordsburg Liberal* did not profess to be "in the know" as to who would be the next governor of the territory, but he was hopeful. An editorial for June 3 said:

Next week marks the end of the four years of Governor Otero's term of office. The *Liberal* is not sufficiently in the confidence of President McKinley to say whether he will be reappointed or not. There are papers whose editors claim to be so intimate with the President that they know for a certainty that another man will be appointed governor next week. There are papers which claim, with equal certainty, that the governor will be reappointed. As said before, the *Liberal* does not know, but judging from the good record made by the governor, and President McKinley's known inclination to keep a good man in the right place, he will reappoint the governor. He has made a record as governor that will meet the approbation of the great mass of the people of the territory. He has labored under difficulties in doing this, but he has overcome these difficulties, and the people are satisfied with what he has done. Even the leading Democrats of the territory say that if we must have a Republican governor, and there is no way of getting around this, that the present incumbent is the man for the place. Like all positive men, he has made enemies, but their enmity comes from personal reasons, not from any mistakes he had made in his official capacity. Because of this personal enmity, they are doing everything in their power to prevent his reappointment, but it is doubtful if they succeed, and it is to be hoped that they will not.

I have in my files, as I write, a number of other editorials from newspapers all over the territory. In one way or another, they all reëchoed the sentiment expressed by the slogan of the *Las Vegas Record,* which called for "Four years more of Miguel A. Otero and a clean administration."

In spite of all the charges filed against me in Washington, I was naturally buoyed up by the support which the territorial press gave me and by my faith in the justice of President McKinley. On June 1, I left for the national capital to meet the charges filed by the "gang." The "busy bees" certainly had been at work, and I was greatly surprised to find that several "pussy-footers"—men who, like the kaw bird, looked one way and flew the other—had joined the little bunch of marplots. These were such men as J. M. Cunningham, E. D. Bullard, Daniel T. Hoskins, Frank Springer, E. L. Hewett, and others unknown to me. Of course, I expected Otto L. Rice, S. O. Fletcher, J. A. Carruth, and C. T. Jordan to work with Catron and Fiske, as they had all been busy for four years and belonged to the die-hard crowd.

My friends were very loyal and the newspapers continued to work in my behalf. The only fear I had was that they might tire out my Washington supporters, but I always felt very sure of President McKinley. He was my friend and, fortunately for me, knew the men who were fighting me.

Having arrived in Washington on June 4, I called at the executive mansion the following afternoon, and had a very agreeable talk with the President. He told me that he had instructed the secretary of the interior to give me all the original letters and petitions filed against me. He suggested that I answer each of them separately, attaching my answer to the document in question. I promised to do this, took a carriage and drove to the Department of the Interior, where I saw Secretary Hitchcock. He was very pleasant, and said the President had just called him on the phone and told him that I was on the way to see him, and that he should turn over the documents to me. With my hands full of papers, I then drove to the Cochran building, where I engaged three stenographers whom I instructed to be at my apartment in the Shoreham Hotel at 8 o'clock the following morning.

Just as I was leaving my room, the next day, the stenographers arrived and, of course, I gave up my breakfast and started to dictate. I did not leave that room until eleven o'clock that night. The girls worked in relays. During the day, Mr. Jefferson Raynolds and Mr. H. O. Bursum came in and offered their assistance. However, I felt equal to the task and told them I was a pretty good dictator myself. Bursum laughingly remarked: "That is exactly what they are accusing you of being." Later I met them again when I went for breakfast, about midnight. The next day, the stenographers were busy typing their notes, so I was left alone until noon. Then two girls arrived and I finished the rest of the answers. They promised to have all the work completed on the following day.

Bursum and Raynolds seemed as interested in the outcome as I was, and, when the papers were delivered, we three checked over all of my answers. I then delivered the original papers and my answers to Secretary Hitchcock and he took them home with him. The next day he told me they were the best and most complete answers he had ever read and complimented me most highly, saying: "I know the President will be pleased."

On June 15th, the President sent for me and I was ushered into the cabinet room, where I found him with Judge Nathan Goff, of West Virginia. Both men were smiling as I entered the room. The President was in the act of signing my commission, which he blotted and handed to me, saying to Judge Goff: "Nathan, the 'gang' of corrupt politicians in New Mexico thought they had my governor, but they never touched side nor bottom." Turning towards me, he said: "Now, governor, accept this commission, go back to New Mexico and administer the affairs of your big territory as you have been doing for the past four years, and it will meet with my hearty approval." We talked for a few minutes and I said goodbye, as I had decided to leave that same evening for Santa Fe. I was not long in finding Mr. Raynolds and Mr. Bursum and we were all happy, and began sending telegrams to New Mexico. The Associated Press had the news, and already I was receiving telegrams from the territory and my family.

I had no sooner departed from the executive mansion, when Quinby Vance and his brother-in-law, the Ohio congressman, called on the President to tell him what they thought of the governor of New Mexico. After listening to their "little tale of woe," President McKinley told them he had just settled the governorship of New Mexico by signing and delivering a new commission to Governor Otero, and he did not wish to hear anything further on that subject.

William M. Berger, who styled himself the representative of the taxpayers of New Mexico, was not admitted to the executive mansion as the President had left instructions through his secretary that he did not wish to see Berger or any of that Santa Fe outfit who was opposing my appointment.

This same order was issued by the secretary of the interior, so the "gang" having no place to go, took the train for New Mexico at once. I believe L. Bradford Prince and Mrs. Prince also left Washington that same evening. They had remained in their quarters on "G" street all day, fearing that they might run into me on the street. I think Quinby Vance was with them.

It was a great victory for me and my administration and the "gang" hid their faces and went into retirement for a short time.

Both the President and Secretary Hitchcock assured me that I would be confirmed by the Senate as soon as Congress convened in December.

I shall close this chapter with the following summary of the circumstances of my reappointment taken from the *Washington Post* and reprinted in the *New Mexican* of June 15, 1901:

> Miguel A. Otero was appointed governor of New Mexico today. The term of the governor expired on June 7th, but the appointment was held up at the request of parties in the territory. Communications were received at the interior department several weeks ago protesting against the reappointment of Mr. Otero. Various allegations were made relative to his management of territorial affairs. The secretary of the interior, Mr. Hitchcock, took up these communications and had each one carefully investigated. Mr. Otero answered each, and the special agents of the department made reports on them. The result was the complete vindication of the present governor and, as he had the backing of the territorial organization of the party, Mr. Hitchcock recommended his reappointment.
>
> Both the President and secretary of the interior pronounced the answers filed by Governor Otero to be the most complete and perfect set of answers they had ever read.
>
> Tonight Mr. Otero received upwards of one hundred telegrams of con-

gratulations at his appointment. He left today for New Mexico and expects to reach Santa Fe on Wednesday, June 19th.

The President today sent for Governor Otero and signed his commission as governor of New Mexico to succeed himself in the presence of Governor Otero and Judge Nathan Goff, of West Virginia. .... All in all there were 15,000 pages of typewritten evidence in the case, but by far the greater part of it was commendatory of the administration of Governor Otero and came from Democrats and Republicans alike. When he came to examine the papers, Secretary Hitchcock found that the protests against Otero's reappointment all dealt in generalities, no special charges of any consequence being filed. ... As far as his administration was concerned the secretary and the President were firmly convinced that Governor Otero had made an excellent record, above reproach, and his reappointment was speedily determined upon when the case was once summed up.

I went home with the comfortable feeling that, with William McKinley as President, I was secure in my position as governor for another four years—unless New Mexico became a state before my term of office was up. I had no anticipations of the terrible tragedy which was to occur within fifteen months, and which was to inspire my enemies to renew their attacks upon me.

Chapter XI

MY SECOND INAUGURATION

THE NEWS of my appointment spread rapidly through the territory. Dispatches expressing approval of the President's action were received by the *New Mexican* from every county seat with telegraphic communication. My reappointment was certainly popular with the people. The *New Mexican* for June 15, 1901, said:

> The news of Governor Otero's reappointment spread like wild fire in the city this afternoon and on every hand were heard expressions of satisfaction at the wise course of President McKinley in heeding the wishes of the people of the territory and reappointing the governor who has given New Mexico a thorough business administration. The event will be celebrated this evening with bonfires and serenades.

The following dispatches are representative:

Albuquerque, Bernalillo County:
> The reappointment of Governor Otero caused great satisfaction to all classes of our people, specially the business interests that have prospered during the past four years beyond expectation. The Republican Party is stronger than ever in this county owing to the reappointment of Governor Otero.

Carlsbad, Eddy County:
> Satisfaction with the reappointment of Governor Otero is great throughout Eddy County and this town, and is joined in by nearly all our citizens, although many of them are strong Democrats. They, however, realize that Governor Otero deserved reappointment.

Gallup, McKinley County:
> The news of Governor Otero's reappointment was hailed with delight by the citizens here who have found him a staunch friend and who knew him to be a first class executive. Had we the shaping of affairs we would keep him in for governor for the next forty years.

A week after the event the *New Mexican* announced that it was "still receiving advices from all over the territory to the effect that the reappointment of Governor Otero is eminently satisfactory to the people. The people of New Mexico are level-headed and there is no mistake about it."

As was to be expected, editorials appeared in newspapers from one end of the territory to the other touching on my past achievements and congratulating the people upon the fact that I would administer the territory for the next four years. The following from the *McKinley County Republican* may be taken as representative of the attitude of the weekly press:

> The Republican County of McKinley rejoices with the territory at large in the reappointment of Governor Miguel A. Otero to be his own successor, an honor never before accorded to a governor of New Mexico. The action of President McKinley in this matter is appreciated by the Republican Party which has stood squarely by Governor Otero in all his actions since he received his appointment as governor on the 7th of June, 1897. It is but natural that in the great amount of business which has passed through the governor's office in the past four years that he should have made some personal enemies. In view of this it is remarkable how few in number they are, and the small amount of influence they brought to bear on the administration. The territory was never so prosperous as today. The finances are in good condition; the 4 per cent bonds of the territory are now at a premium, where in former years 6 per cent bonds sold at a discount; there is a large surplus in the treasury and all obligations are paid in cash. The increasing demands of our admirable school system are complied with as soon as made, and the percentage of illiteracy is less today in New Mexico than in several of the states. New business enterprises are springing up everywhere, several railroads are under construction, new towns have been founded, and prosperity has come to stay and will remain with us so long as business enterprises are given the protection and fostering care of the honest administration of public affairs which they have received during the past four years. Governor Otero is a typical New Mexican and ably represents the people, and right now we present him as the proper man for governor of New Mexico from June 7th, 1905, to June 7th, 1909. It is a little early, but we want to get the start of the next dozen or so of kickers that will probably show up by that time.

A number of these editorials were reprinted in the *New Mexican*. There were so many of them, however, that the paper was forced to take refuge in such announcements as the following:

> The *San Marical Bee, Alamogordo News, Taos Cresset, Raton Range, Otero County Advertiser, Chama Tribune, Pecos Valley Stockgrower, Red River Prospector, Albuquerque American, Farmington Hustler*, all printed lengthy articles in favor of Governor Otero.
> The press of New Mexico reëchoes the joy of the people at the reappointment of Governor Otero. Even Democratic papers admit that Governor Otero has given the territory a clean, economical, and efficient administration the past four years and that during his administration New Mexico has prospered as never before and has gained an enviable reputation among the other commonwealths of the Union as a progressive and growing territory that ought to be admitted to statehood upon the ground of merit alone, not to speak of its theoretical right to that boon.

Naturally, I was pleased, not so much by the amount of printer's ink which was spread out in my honor, but rather by the tone of the editorials. Of all of these comments, perhaps the one which I appreciated the most was one which appeared in the *New Mexican* itself and which came from the hand of that able newspaper man and firm friend of mine—Max Frost. Here it is:

> To Governor Otero belongs the distinction of being the first governor of this commonwealth or of any other territory to be reappointed after serving a term of four years. The reasons which induced the President to break this precedent must have been weighty and are found in the fact that Governor Otero has given the territory a clean, economical, and remarkably efficient administration, an administration so honest and so manifestly for the best interests of the territory that the most skillful lying and the most cunning insinuations against his character and his acts failed to make even a temporary impression at Washington.
>
> . . . .
>
> To sum up: Governor Otero was re-appointed because he was able not only to disprove specifically and fully by official records and affidavits every charge against him, but also because the people demanded his reappointment and because President McKinley, after thorough investigation, was convinced that Governor Otero has given the territory one of the best administrations it ever had, that under it every interest has prospered and that it would be the height of inexpediency to place another man in the gubernatorial chair at this time.
> Governor Otero will not disappoint the President nor the people of New Mexico and will to the fullest extent of his ability continue to give the Sunshine territory an administration which will compare favorably with that of any other state or territory in the Union and which will push New Mexico on to statehood and prosperity.
> And now for a rousing reception to Governor Otero. The people of New Mexico have secured the governor they desired. President McKinley has put the people of New Mexico under lasting obligations by reappointing Governor Otero. Every man, woman, and child in New Mexico is invited to be at the territorial capital on Saturday to attend the inauguration of Governor Otero. It was the people of New Mexico against a small ring and the people have won. President McKinley recognized the voice of the people of New Mexico in reappointing Governor Otero and the people of New Mexico are correspondingly grateful to him. There must be a few men in New Mexico or now on their way to New Mexico, who not only feel small, but are deemed so insignificant, that the territory wouldn't mind if they were to pack their trunks and emigrate to Mexico or return to the states from whence they came.
> President McKinley was too experienced and sagacious a statesman and knows human nature too well to be induced to do an injustice. He saw through the web of lies and falsehoods, misrepresentations, and false affidavits made by a few marplots and turned them down accordingly by reappointing Governor Otero.

My Nine Years as Governor

Western newspapers outside of New Mexico did not allow my reappointment to pass without comment. The following editorials are representative:

The Denver Republican: The reappointment of Governor Otero, to be governor of New Mexico will be received with favor by a majority of the people of that territory. He has made a good executive, in some respects the best the territory has ever had, and nothing would have been gained by his removal.

Governor Otero is a representative of the Spanish-American class of the population, which is a large element in New Mexico. This in itself was a recommendation in his favor, nearly all the governors of the territory having been appointed from states east of the Missouri river. He is a man of intelligence and sound judgment, and he belongs to one of the old and well-known families of the Southwest.

He is one of the earnest advocates of *statehood* for New Mexico, and it is probable that his influence in behalf of that cause will be increased by the approval the administration has placed upon him by his reappointment to the office of territorial governor. . . .

In Governor Otero the members of Congress may see an example of the ability of the natives of the territory to administer their political affairs with credit to themselves and safety to public interest. . . .

The *Los Angeles Times:* In the reappointment of Miguel A. Otero to the governorship of New Mexico for the next four years the President has again displayed an admirably keen knowledge of western men and measures. When Governor Otero assumed control of New Mexico four years ago this month he courageously gave it out that he would tolerate no sort of political dictation. He wished to be untrammeled in his efforts to build up and improve the territory. Affairs financially, educationally and otherwise were in bad shape, and popular regard for law and order was at a minimum. Now all this is changed. . . .

It is a fact generally known, but borne out by government statistics, that New Mexico now leads all other states and territories in the number of her sheep, having nearly 7,000,000 head. The territory has many natural resources, among which are its vast coal and iron deposits. Under the new order of things, capital from the outside is readily obtainable for development.

Governor Otero has been bitterly opposed from the start by some influential members of his party at home, but under his administration the territory has been solidly Republican, returning largely increased majorities at the last two general elections, so that it may now be said that New Mexico can be counted as safely within the Republican column. Governor Otero cherishes the hope that the territory may be admitted as a state before the expiration of his second term. He is certainly working along the right lines to attain that object.

My return to Santa Fe was like a triumphal procession from the time my train crossed the Colorado-New Mexico line. From the very hour that the news of my reappointment had been received in the territory, committees were named and elaborate plans launched to give me a rousing reception.

Democrats joined with Republicans in these preparations. The reception committee met me at Lynn, the first station we came to in New Mexico. Judge John McFie made a fine welcome address, and I responded appropriately, I hope. The citizens of Raton had made preparations to keep me and my party for a day in order to have quite an elaborate reception. I declined to allow time for this, but did stop over and take a later train the same day. The crowd there was large and enthusiastic, and I was in the best of spirits. I was accompanied by Solomon Luna, H. O. Bursum, and Miss Mary La Rue.

The ovation I received at Springer is best described by the *Springer Sentinel*. The issue for June 25 said:

> Long before the train bearing Governor Otero and the several committees on hand who had gone to Raton to meet him, had arrived in *Springer*, a large number of citizens, including the band, assembled at the depot. Strains of music greeted them as the train steamed into the depot, and as the party alighted from the train the governor was welcomed by an enthusiastic throng anxious to express their congratulations on his reappointment. Miss Hannah Jacobs presented him with a beautiful bouquet which he highly appreciated. The few minutes the train remained at the depot was far too short to give the governor an adequate idea of the high esteem in which he is held by the people of Springer.

An immense throng cheering hoarsely awaited me at Las Vegas. Extensive preparations had been made for giving me a royal welcome, including a ball. However, I declined to stay over night, so that part of the program, arranged by the citizens of my home town, was postponed until after the inauguration.

However, in accordance with my promise, I went to Las Vegas a few days later to give the citizens of my home town the opportunity of celebrating my reappointment. I was accompanied by Mrs. Otero, my son, my sister, Mrs. Harry J. O'Bryan, and her two children, Aileen and DuRoss, as well as several friends. Upon our return to Santa Fe, the following brief account of the celebration appeared in the *New Mexican:*

> Mr. and Mrs. A. B. Renehan, Judge Frank W. Parker, Hon. William E. Martin, and Judge John R. McFie returned last evening from Las Vegas

My Nine Years as Governor 167

where they attended the functions given in honor of Governor and Mrs. Otero. The procession, banquet, reception at the court house, and reception and ball at the Duncan Opera House Thursday were the finest affairs of the kind ever had in Las Vegas. They state that everything went off according to program and most amiably and smoothly. The welcome to Governor and Mrs. Otero was very enthusiastic, many strangers were in town, the streets were crowded and east and west Las Vegas were gaily decorated and every one seemed to be happy and joyful.

My arrival at the territorial capital was described by the *New Mexican* for June 20 as follows:

Governor Otero arrived this evening at 11:40 o'clock, the regimental band was at the depot and despite the lateness of the hour there was present a large crowd of people cheering Governor Otero loudly. His trip from the New Mexico-Colorado line to Santa Fe was a continuous ovation by crowds of enthusiastic people. And still they come. From every part of New Mexico come expressions of joy to the *Santa Fe New Mexican* on account of the reappointment of Governor Otero.

Naturally the continual ovations given me by an enthusiastic people were climaxed by the inauguration. Saturday, June 22, was the date selected by the citizens committee for this event, which brought visitors from every part of the territory and beyond.

The plans for the day were outlined by the *New Mexican* as follows:

Judge John R. McFie is to administer oath of office on the west front of the capitol, on the steps. Colonel J. Francisco Chaves to deliver an address of welcome in English, and Hon. W. E. Martin an address of welcome in Spanish. The parade is to pass in review of the governor. In the evening, a public reception will be held on the second story lobby of the capitol building, at which the governor and Mrs. Otero will receive.

The events of that day stand out in my memory as though it were yesterday. However, it would be impossible for me to improve upon the beautiful and complete write-up given by the *New Mexican,* which said:

No more perfect day ever dawned upon Santa Fe than this, the second inauguration day of Governor Miguel A. Otero. By early morning light loyal and willing hands flung to the breeze the Stars and Stripes from almost every house along the route which the inaugural parade took this afternoon. The city had a holiday air. There were visitors from all parts of the territory at the hotels, upon the streets, and in the plaza. It was a festal day which not only Santa Fe but New Mexico will remember for many years to come and to which those who participated in the events of the day will always refer with pride.

At noon the roll of drums and sound of bugle gave the first sign of the coming inaugural parade. The different military companies gathered at their barracks. Later, Carleton Post G. A. R. assembled at its headquarters and then marched to the executive mansion to act as a guard of honor to Governor Otero. By half past one, the grand marshal, George W. Knaebel, had the inaugural procession pretty well in hand, and promptly at two o'clock it moved from Washington Avenue up Palace Avenue to Cathedral Street, to and down San Francisco Street to Galisteo Street and on Galisteo street to the capitol, where Governor Otero and those with him in carriages alighted and walked up the wide capitol stairs to the first platform where they took position, while the remainder of the procession entered the southern gate on the west side of the capitol grounds.

The procession was an imposing one and included the military as well as civic organizations, and many carriages occupied by officials and private citizens.

There was a hush as Judge McFie administered the oath of office which Governor Otero repeated with clear, strong voice, though with visible emotion, as follows:

> I, Miguel A. Otero, do solemnly swear that I will support and defend the Constitution of the United States against all enemies foreign and domestic; that I will bear true faith and allegiance to the same, that I take this obligation freely, without any mental reservation or purpose of evasion; and that I will well and faithfully discharge the duties of the office on which I am about to enter; so help me God.

The manner of Judge McFie in administering the oath was impressive and deep silence reigned while the solemn words were spoken. After the obligation had been taken, Judge McFie presented the new Bible, on which the governor had taken the oath, to Governor Otero.

The inaugural address, which followed, was greeted with cheers.

Governor Otero spoke as follows, his address being interpreted into Spanish by Hon. Jose D. Sena: [For address see Appendix, p. 385.]

At the conclusion of Governor Otero's inaugural address, the governor's salute of seventeen guns rang out while the multitude cheered.

A cavalry band struck up a selection, after which *Hon. William E. Martin,* who is undoubtedly one of the most brilliant orators in Spanish in the Southwest, made an address in Spanish which brought forth cheer after cheer from the people. The address was translated for the *New Mexican* by Colonel J. Francisco Chaves, and is as follows: [See Appendix, p. 387.]

Following the beautiful speech delivered by Hon. William E. Martin, the band played a couple of selections after which Colonel J. Francisco Chaves, president of the late legislative council, delivered the address of welcome, as follows: [Appendix, p. 388.]

The inauguration ceremonies were brief and inspiring. The address in Spanish by Hon. William E. Martin was a masterpiece of eloquence that stirred the audience to outbursts of enthusiasm. Colonel J. Francisco Chaves always reaches the hearts of his hearers and the address he made this afternoon in welcoming Governor Otero was a splendid oratorical effort. Governor Otero's inaugural address was delivered in a dignified tone and its logic convinced his audience of the sincerity of his utterances. The carriage in which Governor Otero rode was a mass of asparagus vines, blossoms, and

My Nine Years as Governor

patriotic colors. The four white horses that drew Governor Otero's carriage wore garlands of roses.

To this account from the *New Mexican* may be added one striking detail from the *Albuquerque Citizen* for July 1, as follows:

> Eastern people have the idea that New Mexico is a desert and that flowers do not bloom in this arid soil. If they could have seen the *parade in Santa Fe* last Saturday they would have changed their mind. The carriage containing Governor Otero was decorated with four thousand roses.

Chapter XII
MY RELATIONS WITH PRESIDENT McKINLEY

I HAVE ALREADY pointed out that my original appointment as governor of New Mexico was due solely to my acquaintance with William McKinley and to the confidence which he felt in me. He was an experienced judge of men and, at a time when a score of politicians were clamoring for the post, felt instinctively that he could depend upon me—only a young man—to do the job to the best of my ability. It was a difficult position, far from the national capital, but I always felt that he kept me in mind and expected me to make good. He always referred to me as "my governor" or "my man in New Mexico" and made me feel that he was risking his personal judgment against that of the politicians and the charges of my enemies that I would succeed. Naturally, I could not afford to let him down.

Officially, President McKinley always gave me his strong support. He showed this when he allowed me to pick the majority of the judges for the territorial bench—in spite of all the political pressure which was being brought upon him by Eastern politicians to appoint other men. Again, almost four years later, he again demonstrated the strong support he was giving me by patiently sifting through all the charges which malice and political animosity had trumped up against me and then giving me a commission for another four years.

But McKinley never thought of stopping at official support. He was not only the President, but also a man, and one who had a genius for friendship. He seemed to like me from our first meeting in Minneapolis. This chance acquaintance developed into a strong friendship which lasted until his death at the hands of a cruel assassin. McKinley was always kindly and considerate. He was never cross, and there was not a single unpleasant incident to mar the pleasant relations between us. He was a great President and a great man.

I remember once McKinley complimented me in a very delicate manner. It was a month after my first inauguration. I was in Washington to confer with him regarding territorial appointments, as I have described in my first chapter. Before I left the White House, he said that he had agreed to hear the Folsom case on the following morning and asked me to be present at the hearing. S. M. Folsom was president of the Albuquerque National Bank and had been convicted by the federal court of banking irregularities and sentenced to a term in the federal penitentiary. He was formerly from Vermont and had many warm friends in New Mexico. When I arrived the next day and was ushered into the cabinet room, I found Mr. McKinley alone. He asked me to take the chair beside him on his right, and explained that he wished me to listen carefully to what the attorneys said. In a short time, Senator Redfield Proctor, of Vermont, came in. I soon learned that he was a great friend of the Folsom family in Vermont, and was there in the interest of a pardon for Folsom. With the senator were Frank W. Clancy and Neill B. Field, both of Albuquerque. Senator Proctor introduced them to the President, after which they both shook hands with me, telling the President how pleased they were that I was present. I greeted Senator Proctor, for I had had the pleasure of meeting him before. When the hearing began, I listened very carefully to the arguments. At the close—much to my surprise—the President turned to me and asked what I would do if the case were before me as governor. I quickly answered: "I would pardon Mr. Folsom." The President then turned to Senator Proctor and said: "Well, you heard what Governor Otero said. He has decided the case, and the pardon will be granted." We all shook hands and thanked President McKinley. He merely smiled and told the others: "You better thank Governor Otero," which they did.

Whenever I was in Washington on official business, I was always warmly greeted by President McKinley at social functions. However, I shall describe these occasions in a later chapter.

President McKinley visited New Mexico once while he was in office. It was in the spring of 1901. He was on his way to San Francisco to attend the launching of the battleship Ohio. As soon as I heard of his plans to come west, I sent him a telegram, inviting him, in behalf of the people of New Mexico, to visit Santa Fe. However, George B. Cortelyou, the President's private secretary, wired me that it would be impossible for the President to accept my invitation, as the itinerary had already been arranged over the Southern Pacific Railroad. This, of course, was a great disappointment to the people, as well as to myself. However, the presidential train was to make a stop at Deming, so I arranged a special train to go to Deming to meet the President and his party. Already many rumors were floating around that the "gang" which was fighting me was arranging an opposition party to meet the President in El Paso with petitions and affidavits against me. Catron, Fiske, Fritz Muller, and five or six others engineered the plot. They carried letters and petitions, and were thus loaded for bear, and felt very sure of their ground. John Roberts, formerly of Canton, Ohio, and a brother of Mrs. Joshua S. Raynolds, and Quinby Vance, were being groomed for my job—a case of "any port in a storm." They intended to tell President McKinley just where to head in, and things were supposed to work perfectly for their cause. However,

> "The best laid schemes o'mice and men
> Gang aft a-gley;
> And leave us naught but grief and pain
> For promised joy."

My good friend, Mr. Jefferson Raynolds, went to El Paso and kept me advised of all that was happening.

Meanwhile, every preparation was being made to give the President a warm welcome in Deming. On May 4, I left for Deming, together with Mrs. Otero and Miguel, Junior, as I wished to get there a few days before the presidential train arrived. Quite naturally, I was annoyed over what was to happen in El Paso, as the "gang" had circulated all kinds of stories. On May 6, I received a very cheerful telegram from Jefferson Raynolds advising me to keep a stiff upper lip and not allow the wild rumors manufactured by Fiske et al., to bother me. The next day the President and his party arrived. Meanwhile, a special train from the northern part of the territory had arrived with about two hundred citizens and a brass band. Deming was decorated with flags and banners. One large banner facing the train windows displayed in large black letters the words "McKinley and Otero." I was ushered by Mr. Cortelyou to the rear platform. As President McKinley walked out to greet me, I turned and presented the President to the large crowd, in the following words:

> Mr. President, in behalf of the citizens of New Mexico, I extend to you a most cordial and hearty welcome to our territory, and can assure you that there is not a state or territory in the Union that has a greater admiration and love for President McKinley than has New Mexico. Our greatest regret is that your previous engagements have prevented your making a longer stay in our territory so that you might have visited some of our larger cities in the north. As your time here is so limited, I will not detain you longer, but will now take great pleasure in introducing to you our citizens here assembled.

The President made a few happy remarks and shook hands with all those who could reach the rear end of the car. Loud cheers for Governor Otero came from every direction and as the President stepped back in the car, he said to Secretary Hitchcock: "My governor is all right, the people are with him."

Seeing Mr. Swartz, of Mimbres, on the platform, with a basket filled with his delicious apples, I called him to the car and he presented the President and Mrs. McKinley with the fruit. They were so pleased that they asked him to send a barrel of the apples to the White House. Later, I received a letter from the President asking me to have Mr. Swartz send him a barrel every year, for they were the best apples he and Mrs. McKinley had ever eaten.

I told the President and the secretary of the interior that there had been no defalcations by county collectors during my administration, and the President laughingly remarked to the secretary: "Here seems to be a strong basis for another charge against Governor Otero."

Mrs. Otero and I were the recipients of many courtesies by prominent citizens of Deming during our few days' visit with them.

A few days after President and Mrs. McKinley made their hurried visit to New Mexico, the Associated Press gave out that the latter was very sick in San Francisco. Later, it was announced that she was very low, and that the President had cancelled all side trips and would return to Washington at once. Mrs. McKinley recovered very nicely, while her husband was soon stricken by the hand of an assassin.

Four months after the President had stopped at Deming —less one day—the tragedy occurred. I was enroute to Denver with my wife and son. The conductor of the train knocked at the door of our drawing room and told us that McKinley had been shot by an anarchist at the Pan-American Exposition, at Buffalo, New York. The great shock I received is reflected in the following interview which appeared in a Denver paper the next day:

> A reporter, learning of the arrival of Governor Otero of New Mexico in Denver, found him at the residence of his brother-in-law, Mr. Harry J. O'Bryan. He had just arrived from Chicago with Mrs. Otero and son, Miguel Junior. He was deeply affected by the news of the attempted *assassination of President McKinley,* and said: "I heard the news as I was entering the railroad yards in your city. It is a great shock to me, as it must have been to all persons. I hardly know what to say or think. It comes so swift and sudden it seems as though it must be a dream or something unreal. One of the greatest Presidents the country ever had, and to think he should be marked for the assassin's bullet. It is awful, awful. In all my relations with President McKinley, I have learned to love him as I would a member of my own family. His is the kindest, most lovable disposition I have ever seen in a man. His loss will be a national calamity."

I immediately sent the following telegram:

Denver, Colorado, September 6th, 1901.
Hon. George B. Cortelyou, Secretary to the President,
Buffalo, New York.

I cannot sufficiently express the profound sorrow of Mrs. Otero and myself on hearing of the attempt upon the life of the President. Our hopes and prayers are for his recovery.

Miguel A. Otero.

For several days the press reported that the President was recovering. Every issue stated that he was better and still better. However, on September 13, a telegram said "President McKinley is reported to be dying." Another message on the following day announced, "President McKinley died at 2:15 o'clock this morning."

On the same day the *New Mexican* said:

The appalling and sorrowful news of the death of the President, at Buffalo, early this morning, was received by the many warm friends and admirers of that great and wise statesman and pure man, and by the people of this city and territory with great sadness and sorrow. Expressions of sincerest sympathy with Mrs. McKinley and of universal regret of the President's death were heard everywhere and from everybody throughout this great territory. In Santa Fe, especially, was this the case, and amongst the many who are mourning the demise of William McKinley, now with the silent majority, are many of the leading and most prominent citizens of the territory; as the dead President had endeared himself officially and personally in many ways, to them and specially to Governor Otero.

A representative of this paper called upon the governor and found him in the executive office looking and feeling as if the death of his father had again occurred. In answer to an inquiry, the governor handed the *New Mexican* a copy of a dispatch which he had just sent to Mrs. McKinley, which is published herewith, and said: "I cannot express my feelings in this matter any better than to say, it seems to me that the father who was kind loving, and helpful to me from the moment of my birth to his death has again left me, never to return. I have known President McKinley for fifteen years or more, and in that time have learned to love, respect, and admire him as much as such feelings can agitate a human heart and mind. His uniform kindness, courtesy, and sincere friendship to me naturally would have won my gratitude, love, and admiration, but those in addition to his grand character, officially and private, his wisdom, his statesmanship, and his great knowledge of men, their motives and affairs, grew upon me from time to time, that for years past I set him before myself for emulation and as an example of what a citizen of this country should and ought to be. Words are inadequate to express my great sorrow and grief at his death and time alone can assuage this grief and sorrow. Mrs. Otero, who had also been honored with the friendship of the President and Mrs. McKinley, feels as strongly as I do."

The governor was preparing then and there to issue a proclamation, setting apart the day of the funeral, of the late President, as a day of memorial and sorrow on the part of the people of New Mexico. Governor Otero had sent another dispatch to Mrs. McKinley, as follows:

Santa Fe, New Mexico, September 14th, 1901.
Mrs. William McKinley,
Milburn House, Buffalo, New York.

Accept profound sympathy of Mrs. Otero and myself in your great bereavement. New Mexico mourns with the whole people, not selfishly for their own irreparable loss, but for you who are left alone.

Miguel A. Otero.

PROCLAMATION FOR A DAY OF FASTING

Governor Otero recommends that on the day of the funeral of President McKinley memorial services be held—a loss to the world and to humanity. Governor Otero today issued the following suitable and fitting proclamation:

PROCLAMATION FOR A DAY OF FASTING AND PRAYER

Executive Office, Santa Fe, N. M.
September 14th, 1901.

WHEREAS, our beloved chief magistrate of the nation, William McKinley, President of the United States, has succumbed to the assassin's bullet, after a week of hopeful lingering, and now lies dead at the festival to which he had gone and honored with his presence; and whereas, his untimely death is mourned not only by the people of the United States, but by the whole world as a loss to humanity and the best and truest principles of statesmanship and administration; and

WHEREAS, for the third time in the history of our Republic, the nation has had to mourn for its head, foully stricken down by a murderous hand,

Now, THEREFORE, I, Miguel A. Otero, governor of the territory of New Mexico, by virtue of the power vested in me by law and usage, hereby ordain and proclaim the day upon which the funeral of the late President is held, to be a day of fasting and prayer in New Mexico; that all public business be suspended on that day, and that private affairs be transacted only so far as may be actually necessary; that all public schools and institutions be closed, except as memorial services for the honored dead may be held therein; that the flags on all public and private buildings and school houses be half-masted from the date of this proclamation until after the funeral ceremonies.

And it is earnestly recommended that every church and house of worship on that day hold a memorial to commemorate the life and services to his country of one of the most distinguished and exemplary Americans since the birth of the Republic; and that all our citizens laying aside their usual avocations and employments on that day, assemble at their respective places of worship, there to unite in the solemn service for the dead we mourn, and to offer their prayers for the stricken widow and family in their sore bereavement, and to pledge themselves as American citizens to earnestly support and uphold any and all measures to prevent the recurrence of such a dastardly outrage as causes our mourning today.

In witness whereof, I have hereunto subscribed my hand and caused to be affixed the great seal of the territory of New Mexico.

Done at the Executive Office this the 14th day of September, A. D. 1901.

Witness my hand and the great seal of the territory of New Mexico,

(SEAL)   Miguel A. Otero, Governor of New Mexico.

By the governor:
J. W. Raynolds, Secretary of New Mexico.

President Roosevelt also issued a proclamation directing that the day of the funeral should be observed as a day of fasting and prayer.

On the day after McKinley's death, I left Santa Fe for Canton to attend the funeral. I was joined at Lamy by Major Llewellyn and, together, we journeyed to Chicago. During the rest of the way we traveled in a special Pullman, which had been chartered for our party which consisted of Senator Thomas H. Carter, of Montana; Senator Charles W. Fairbanks, of Indiana; Senator Henry C. Hansborough, of North Dakota; and Hon. Perry Heath, the postmaster general. There were also several others who have escaped my memory. My immediate party was made up of Major Llewellyn, who acted as my adjutant-general; Messrs. Foley and Pierce, of Chicago, two friends of mine; and myself.

When we arrived at Canton, we found the little city crowded with visitors. However, all of our party had been assigned to rooms in the Barnett House. When the train arrived with the remains of the late President, we all stood on the second story porch and with bared heads watched the funeral procession pass by. It went on up the street to the McKinley home, where the body was placed on a stand in the living room facing the street, while a military guard surrounded the house.

The next day the body was removed to the court house and thousands upon thousands passed it in review. In fact, the crowd was still moving slowly by when the hour was reached in the late afternoon to take the body back to the house. The funeral was the next day. On this occasion four seats were reserved for me and my party on the left side of the church in the front row. It was a beautiful day. My open carriage was just ahead of the one occupied by the governor of Illinois and his party. Major Llewellyn, as my adjutant sat beside me, while Messrs. Foley and Pierce rode opposite us. All the way to the cemetery the streets were lined up with military and other organizations, and I was kept busy saluting flags as we drove past.

I shall conclude this chapter by giving an eulogy on President McKinley, which I wrote at the request of the Continental Assembly for a book gotten up by General Grosvenor, of Ohio:

EULOGY

The death of President McKinley is too recent and too shocking for any one who has the ability and feeling to properly eulogize him in whom

> Unbounded courage and compassion joined,
> Tempering each other in the victor's mind,
> Alternately proclaim him good and great,
> And make the hero and the man complete.

For nearly forty years he has lived and moved in the fierce light that beats upon our public men and reveals the slightest flaw in motive or in character, and like the perfect gem this light brought out in him the latent beauties of his nature, which were his chiefest hold upon the people whom he knew and loved so well.

It was not his mastery of political science, his statecraft, or his wisdom that brought him closer to the people than any one before him and made his untimely death felt as a personal grief to every home in our country, which stayed the wheels of commerce between the Atlantic and Pacific and caused the telegraph to pause and the heart of this great nation to stand still for five solemn moments, while his sacred remains were sorrowfully entombed by loving hands on the green hillside near the little city which was his home.

It was the clear, honest, kindly Christian character of the *man* which the nation mourned, and it is this which will place the name of William McKinley highest among those great of whom it can be said: "He loved his fellow men."

He has passed from us in the prime and pride of life, just after he had uttered words of peace and goodwill to all the world, at a festival in honor of the brotherhood of men and to exemplify the peaceful arts which have made the Americas great and one in purpose.

To us who mourn, it seems that his life work was scarce begun, there is so much to do, and he who is gone appeared to us the best equipped for its doing. But to Him who doeth all things well, it was otherwise. His time had come and found him fully ready. His first thought was for the loved wife whom he had shielded and protected so long, his next was forgiveness to the unhappy man who had slain him and his last, complete resignation to the will of God. His, a model life, a Christian death. The whole world mourns.

> He was a man, take him for all in all,
> I shall not look upon his like again.

Chapter XIII

I TRIUMPH OVER MY ENEMIES AGAIN

ON THE EVENING of the funeral, we left for Chicago. Here I remained for a couple of days in the hope of ascertaining just what would happen after the President had become settled. I found out soon enough. I had been reappointed in June, but since the Senate was not in session at the time, the appointment figured as a vacation appointment. This meant that it would have to be sent in again as a permanent appointment and confirmed by the Senate. While McKinley was in office, the bitter attacks of my enemies "had never touched side nor bottom," as the President put it. However, with the inauguration of Theodore Roosevelt, I was up against a different proposition altogether.

The gang started in right away on my new chief, and were re-inforced by several Rough Rider statesmen (?) who succeeded in getting his ear. Roosevelt made me go over everything again, without paying the slightest attention to the findings of President McKinley and Secretary Hitchcock. The conspirators were so desperate that L. Bradford Prince, in spite of his ambition to be governor of New Mexico, was willing to step aside so that they might recommend a Rough Rider captain for the appointment. Roosevelt was quite partial to the members of his regiment, and it was thought that he would fall for this suggestion. I was rather surprised that he didn't.

A "New Mexico Republican Reform League" was organized and blank petitions were sent out, asking for my removal and the appointment of Captain Frederick Muller as governor. These papers were circulated in Santa Fe, Bernalillo, San Miguel, Eddy, Chaves, and other counties. Quinby Vance was mentioned in some of the petitions as an alternate.

The gang established headquarters in Washington in the little brick house on Twelfth and G street where Mr. and Mrs. Prince resided. They secured two stenographers and worked them day and night, getting up charges against me. The newspaper men were all good friends of mine and would bring me the Prince stuff almost as soon as it reached their hands, so that I was kept fully advised as to what my enemies were doing. Their efforts were rather crude and childish; the gist of the charges they put out being that I was an uneducated Mexican who favored Spain—a rather unusual statement in view of the assistance I had given in raising troops for the war!

However, they succeeded in lining up some formidable allies. By working through the Beardsley family—Mrs. Prince was a daughter of Colonel Sam Beardsley of the Iron Brigade—the Princes persuaded Senator John T. Morgan to promise assistance. The senator, who had been a Confederate brigadier, represented Alabama in the Senate for thirty years. A man of seventy-seven years of age at this time, he was known for the independence of his views and the length of his speeches. Another ally in the enemy camp was General Lew Wallace, who had been governor of New Mexico in the seventies, when Billy the Kid was winning his reputation as a killer. One of my enemies, whom I shall call Mr. X, had lined up the Indiana man on their side, as they were old friends. I began to fear that my goose was cooked, sure enough! In addition to the old gang, I now had several Rough Riders fighting me, as well as two former governors of the territory. And one of the latter was a celebrated author, like President Roosevelt. The gang felt very confident of success. One of them laughingly remarked, "You know, these literary fellows all stand together, so we will surely oust Otero now!" I was becoming so disgusted with the attitude of my new chief that I felt very much like resigning. However, I knew that was exactly what they were working for, so I declined to fall into their trap.

At first, I knew nothing of these re-inforcements of the enemy but I soon heard of one of them. President Roosevelt called me to the White House and said, "Governor Otero, my old friend, General Lew Wallace, was here with Mr. X and he vouches for the truth of all that this gentleman says against you. Now, I am inclined to follow General Wallace, but I want to be fair with you and tell you just where I stand in the matter. I care nothing for what Tom Catron, Ex-Governor Prince, and those other fellows have told me, as I know them well and know their motives. But, when a distinguished literary man, a friend of mine, brings Mr. X here and vouches for him, it becomes a very different proposition. Now, what have you to say for yourself?"

Of course, I did not say what I wanted to say. I was "hot under the collar," as mad as could be. Controlling my temper as well as I could, I told the President that I had the highest respect for General Wallace, but that he was being imposed upon by a gang that would do anything to oust me from my position. Furthermore, I told him some things about the members of this gang that made him open his eyes with amazement. I told him that the man who had come to the White House with General Wallace was a man who could not be believed. I said that Captain A. B. Fall, one of the officers I had appointed during the war, was in Washington at my request and that he had told me of a case in which a man of some wealth and prominence had been indicted for adultery, and Mr. X forced him to pay $2,500 before he would dismiss the indictment. After this sum had been paid, Mr. X told his victim, "I forgot to tell you that there was another count in that indictment—fornication—and, unless you pay me an additional sum of $2,500, I shall be compelled to prosecute you on that charge." The outraged man had then taken his case to Mr. Fall, who secured an immediate dismissal by threatening to report the matter in Washington. I cited a similar case in another county, in which the defendant, who happened to have been a classmate of Roosevelt's at Harvard, had been forced to secure the services of Mr. Fall to free him from blackmail, after he had already paid Mr. X his first demand of $800.

"Now, Mr. President, I know my word is absolutely good, and I make these accusations against this man X to show you just how General Wallace and yourself are being imposed upon."

"Did you say that Captain Fall was here in the city?" the President asked.

"Yes, sir."

"Well, find him at once, tell him that I want him to come to the White House, and see that he does it promptly."

Finding the captain down town, I took him to the White House and introduced him to President Roosevelt. After the introduction, the latter did what I thought was a very ungentlemanly act. Telling me to stay where I was, he took the captain to the other end of the room, where I would be unable to hear the conversation. Before Mr. Roosevelt had a chance to speak, Fall said, "Mr. President, I understand from Governor Otero why you wish to see me. Before going into this matter, I wish to say that Mr. X is at present at the Ebbitt House in this city. I would like for you to send for him and I will tell you all I have to say in his presence."

"No," Mr. Roosevelt replied, "if what Governor Otero has told me is true, I don't want that fellow X to ever darken the door of the White House so long as I am President."

Captain Fall then proceeded to tell the President all that I had told him and much more that I did not know. At the close of the conversation, the latter thanked the captain and said that he would see that the door-keeper was instructed to forbid "that scoundrel" from entering the White House, should he ever present himself. Furthermore, he said he would write General Lew Wallace fully. As the President was standing near the door of the cabinet room, he left the room that way without saying good-bye to either of us.

On leaving the White House, Captain Fall and I went

directly to the Ebbitt House where we found Mr. X sitting in the lobby of the hotel. We walked up to him and the captain told him all that he had said to the President. The gentleman (?) turned deathly pale and beads of perspiration rolled down his face, mingling with two streams of tobacco juice from his mouth. All he could say was, "Fall, you ought not to have done it."

My counter attack put the whole bunch of conspirators to confusion and most of them scattered like a covey of quail. Mr. X and his followers left the city that night, but a few of the gang remained around the Prince headquarters, hoping to defeat my confirmation by the Senate. Realizing that this would be their next move, my friends and I decided that I had better remain in Washington until the matter had been definitely settled. Mr. Jefferson Raynolds and Mr. Bursum felt that they must get back home, but Colonel G. W. Prichard and William B. Childers agreed to stay with me.

The President sent in my reappointment to the Senate on December 18, and the matter was referred to the committee on territories. By January 7, 1902, Catron, Fiske, and Berger returned to Washington ready to lead the fight against my confirmation by the Senate. They were invited to appear before the committee and to present proof of their charges. However, while visiting on the floor of the Senate, I was assured by Senators Mark Hanna and J. B. Foraker and many others that they would support me. Senators daily received telegrams by the score requesting my confirmation, and a number advised me that there was not the slightest chance of my being turned down.

On January 13, I appeared before the committee and it took me just three minutes to convince the members present that the charges against me were absolute fabrications and rested on nothing but envy, malice, and disappointed ambition. Two days later, Eugene A. Fiske presented the committee with another batch of charges and some protests against my confirmation, signed by members of his gang. While he was reading the charges, the chairman, Senator Beveridge, stopped him several times and rebuked him severely. Mr. Fiske wished to present an affidavit signed by Frederick Muller but the committee declined to accept this until the bearer had made a second affidavit, swearing that the first one was genuine.

At the last hearing, held by the committee, on January 16, my friends were there in force. Those present were:

Bernard S. Rodey, delegate to Congress from New Mexico; William B. Childers, United States district attorney for New Mexico; George W. Pritchard, district attorney for the fifth district of New Mexico; Matthew G. Reynolds, United States attorney for the court of private land claims; Judge Thomas Smith, former chief justice of New Mexico; N. B. Field, Albuquerque attorney; William H. H. Llewellyn, district attorney for the third judicial district of New Mexico; Charles Springer, of Colfax County, New Mexico; Dr. Nathan Boyd, of the Elephant Butte construction in New Mexico; William H. Pope, who was later chief justice of New Mexico; Charles H. Gildersleeve, former chairman of the Democratic central committee for New Mexico; Edmund Burke, a friend from Iowa; Brigadier-General H. B. Freeman, U. S. A.; Judge Edward Seeds, former associate justice of New Mexico.

Messrs. Catron and Fiske were in Washington at the time, but they lacked the guts to make their appearance for the final battle. It was given out at their hotels that the former had been "unavoidably detained" in New Mexico and that the latter had been called home, but the truth was that both had gotten cold feet. The sole representative of the gang which had been fighting me so actively for almost four years, who was present for the final showdown, was William M. Berger. The editor of the *Santa Fe Capital* appeared with documents enough to perfect a treaty with Great Britain. He was allowed to read everything he had brought against me and to make a statement regarding each paper. At one time he made some nasty statements regarding several of the men whom I had appointed to office in the territory. Senator Beveridge stopped him and asked me three questions, all of which I cleared up in two minutes. Having resumed his testimony, Berger, at one time, so grossly misrepresented the facts that in the presence of the whole committee I called him a "contemptible liar" and "whelp unworthy of notice." I jumped from my seat, grabbed an inkwell, and started to throw it at him. However, Senator Dillingham, of Vermont, caught my arm and the chairman ordered me to take my seat. While I apologized, my action served to disconcert the nervous man in the witness chair and he soon stopped talking. The committee did not ask him a single question. Senator Beveridge merely asked if that was all and Berger answered "Yes." He then gathered up his papers and left the room. Our side was not put on the stand. I was preparing to give some testimony myself, but the chairman said, "It is not necessary. We have heard all we want to know," and Senator Carter, of Montana, moved that the committee go into executive session. Accordingly, my friends and I all retired and waited results in the hall. In much less than two minutes the door opened and the senators came out smiling. Each one stopped to shake hands with me, and I was told, "You were unanimously recommended by the committee for confirmation." Messrs. Childers, Prichard, and Judge Smith then joined me and we all drove to the Shoreham.

On the following day the report of the committee was taken up in the Senate. Senator John Tyler Morgan, of Alabama, and Senator Hernando de Soto Money, of Mississippi, bitterly opposed my confirmation, doing everything in their power to defeat me. During the debate, Senator Morgan read some letters from Rev. O. J. Moore and Rev. E. L. Eustis, both of Santa Fe. These sanctified gentlemen were handling the truth rather carelessly in order to describe what a terrible man I was. At this point, Senator Thomas J. Patterson, of Colorado, always a friend of New Mexico, arose and asked if the gentleman from Alabama would yield the floor, as he wished to read some letters from clergymen in Santa Fe who knew Governor Otero. Thinking that the letters would be in line with those he was reading, the unsuspecting southerner consented. Senator Patterson then read letters from the Right Reverend Peter Bourgade, Archbishop of Santa Fe, from Rev. W. A. Cooper, of the Methodist Church, and many others—all of whom praised me very highly. As he had the floor, my Colorado friend then moved for my confirmation. I was duly confirmed, with only two negative votes, which were cast by the two senators who had spoken against me.

Senator Morgan told me later that the only reason he opposed my confirmation was because of a promise he had made to Mrs. Prince and her husband, who were very bitter against me and whose statements seemed very plausible. I told him that Prince was a candidate for my position and that he and his wife would resort to any method to oust me. The senator laughed and said, "Oh! That explains their attitude, then."

I received my new commission on January 24, 1902. After calling at the White House to thank the President and say goodbye, I left at once for Santa Fe. A dispatch sent out from Washington by the Associated Press said:

Governor Otero has been receiving telegrams by the hundreds every day congratulating him upon his victory and his vindication. He expressed his gratitude to all those who stood by him. Yesterday, Mrs. Otero and Mrs. Anson Mills were receiving and some of the best known ladies in the United States called. Governor Otero and his family will leave for Santa Fe tonight. They will stop one day in Chicago where they will be guests at the Annex.

The conclusion of the long, bitter fight called forth the following comment in the *New Mexican* for January 24:

The old man who paid the freight on the anti-Otero trains between New Mexico and Washington is out several thousands of dollars, but then he has gained some experience.

Senator Morgan, of Alabama, may know a great deal about the construction of a canal across the Isthmus of Panama, but he knows blamed little about conditions and affairs in New Mexico. This is a private opinion of many of New Mexico's citizens publicly expressed.

The bitterly unjust, unfair, and untruthful fight made on Governor Otero and other leading citizens of the territory did nothing but harm and injury to New Mexico. If the "gang" behind this fight aimed at injuring the territory and defaming the people of New Mexico, they have certainly succeeded well.

Before leaving Washington I decided that my inauguration should be simply the taking of my oath of office in the supreme court room before Chief Justice Mills and the other judges of the supreme court, with only my family and a few special friends in attendance. This I communicated by wire to Acting Governor James W. Raynolds.

I remained in Chicago longer than I had intended and did not reach Santa Fe until January 31. The inauguration, which took place the next day, was followed by a reception and ball arranged by Santa Fe citizens of both parties. The whole affair was described by the *New Mexican* for February 1 as follows:

> Governor Otero and Mrs. Otero, and son, Miguel, upon reaching the Colorado state line yesterday were met by General Manager J. E. Hurley, of the Santa Fe Railroad, and Mrs. Hurley and were brought to Santa Fe in Colonel Hurley's private car. At Las Vegas Miss LaRue joined the party and came over to Santa Fe as a guest of Governor and Mrs. Otero. At Raton, Springer, Wagon Mound, Watrous, and Las Vegas there were large crowds at the stations who welcomed Governor and Mrs. Otero back home in a most hearty fashion. The train arrived at 9:00 o'clock last evening in Santa Fe and the party was met by the general committee on arrangements, by the band of the First Regiment of the National Guard of the territory, and a large concourse of enthusiastic citizens. Amidst loud cheering and band playing the gubernatorial party was escorted to the executive mansion, where for an hour or two an informal reception was held, the justices of the supreme court, territorial officials, and many citizens paying their respects and extending their hearty greetings and congratulations to Governor and Mrs. Otero.
>
> During the forenoon, many citizens called at the executive mansion and expressed their gratification and congratulations at the governor's reappointment and confirmation. At 3 o'clock this afternoon, Governor Otero had the oath of office administered.
>
> The entire affair from the arrival of Governor Otero on yesterday evening until the ending of the dance tonight was unostentatious and of a quiet character, as it was considered that the governor having been sworn in and inaugurated in June last after reappointment to be executive of the territory of New Mexico, such would be the proper course.
>
> The people infer from the attitude of Governor Otero that he has no fear of being catronized.

Chapter XIV
ANSWERS TO THE CHARGES AGAINST ME

DOUBTLESS, BY THIS time, my readers are curious as to the charges that were so persistently urged against me. They may also be inclined to jump at the conclusion that "where there is smoke, there must be some fire." Over against this bit of proverbial wisdom, however, is the fact that I served as governor of New Mexico for four years after a supreme effort had been made by the "gang" to oust me. My enemies, undoubtedly, obtained the ear of Honorable Ethan Allen Hitchcock, secretary of the interior, and a very conscientious public servant, and also that of President Roosevelt himself. Furthermore, they had several hearings before the Senate committee on territories, and used the influence of a leading eastern family to make sure of a spokesman on the floor of the Senate. Yet, after all they could say or write, *or swear to,* had been thoroughly investigated, the President sent my name to the Senate and the committee unanimously endorsed the nomination, and the Senate—with only two dissenting votes—confirmed my appointment.

Six weeks before this, my friends had had little doubt as to the final outcome. This is shown by the following dispatch which the Associated Press sent out from Washington, on December 1, 1901:

> The name of Governor Miguel A. Otero will be sent to the Senate for confirmation as governor of New Mexico. This statement can be made without reservation. Charges made against the governor have not been substantiated to the satisfaction of the government officials.
> The charges were general in their nature, alleging incompetency and the appointment of corrupt minor officials in the territory. Later more charges of the same general tenor were added, but investigation failed to substantiate them, hence the determination to send the name to the Senate.

Newspaper men are usually "in the know" and their confidence that I would survive the campaign of lying propaganda directed against me, was completely justified. For the benefit of my readers, I have incorporated these infamous charges against me in this book, Appendix, pp. 371-385; 393-394. Unfortunately, however, these documents are so lengthy and detailed and repetitious that they would exhaust both the patience of the reader and the resources of the publisher, hence I left out considerable of the trash. T. B. Catron's letter of October 28, 1901, and the Fritz Muller and Eugene A. Fiske affidavits of January 10, 1902, are included in the Appendix.* I have carefully preserved my papers and these will be available to students who wish to get behind the statements made in this book.

I will say this for my enemies: they were very thorough and exhaustive. They concocted every imaginable charge against me, and at the same time, exhausted their energies and the patience of the Washington authorities needlessly. They charged that I was personally unfit to govern the territory, that my appointments to office were bad, that I was largely controlled by Max Frost, and that I debauched the legislature by appointing its leading men or their relatives to office. Furthermore, they declared that I was breaking up the Republican Party in the territory by my attempt to boss it, and that my support for reappointment came altogether from office-holders, people who expected favors from me, or Democrats who hoped to create dissension in the Republican ranks.

In concluding his letter to the President, Fritz Muller stated that my friends claimed that the President was under obligation to me, since I had helped him get up the Rough Riders Regiment. Fritz added to this statement, gratuitously, "when hell would not have kept them from you." He also offered to go to Washington, where he said he would say much worse things about me and my "gang," than he cared to put on paper. President Roosevelt had quite a good laugh over this letter, and evidently had but little faith in Fritz's judgment, as he did not invite him to come. Apparently, his own "gang" also distrusted him. Probably they

*See pages 152-153 for the April 25, 1901, letter of Fritz Muller to Theodore Roosevelt.

were afraid that a cross-examination would reveal the fact that the stupid German had merely signed letters which a Santa Fe lawyer had written, and had the willing tool sign.

All of these charges and misrepresentations made me angry, but I resolved to control my temper and to keep at the task which my friend, President McKinley, had given me. The memory of his faith in me gave me strength; for his sake I had to "carry on."

I scarcely need to refute these charges. If they had been true, I would have been removed from office. Furthermore, I would not now be giving them publicity by summarizing them in this book. However, I shall not let them pass without saying a few words in defense of myself and those who were associated with me in my administration.

When Chief Justice O'Brien appointed me clerk of the fourth judicial district, I wished to resign the county clerkship. My friends, however, declared that if I did so an incompetent politician, recommended by Tom Catron, would succeed me. The county commissioners did not want me to give up the job either, since Eugenio Romero and Lorenzo Lopez, the two most powerful Republican leaders in the county, were ready to precipitate a scrap to see whose candidate would get the place. Accordingly, I put Byron T. Mills in as deputy and turned both duties and fees of the office over to him. So, for all purposes I was out. The White Caps were committing many crimes in the county at the time, such as cutting down fences and burning houses and haystacks, and the county commissioners were appealed to for protection. Two members of the board agreed to hire detectives under fictitious names and to pay them in cash, so that their identity would not be known and there would be less danger of the men being killed out of revenge. Apparently the money, supposed to be paid out in this way, was simply stolen by the two commissioners, but I had no part in it and knew nothing of it, at the time. On becoming governor, I removed one of these men from a territorial office and he became very bitter against me. Evidently, he went to Catron and admitted that he had been a thief, in the hope of connecting me with the crime, as county clerk. However, I knew nothing of it until I saw Catron's letter. All county warrants are issued by the board of county commissioners and are signed by the chairman.

Catron says I was discharged from the San Miguel National Bank. This is untrue. On my return from Europe I resigned for good and sufficient reasons, as set forth in the second volume of *My Life on the Frontier* and on my *demand* for so doing, receiving full salary for a year thereafter, together with the advance price I placed on my stock.

The other charges against my character and fitness for office obviously need no answer from me as no one would believe such idle gossip and false statements.

In regard to my appointments to office, I did appoint my father-in-law, Judge Lafayette Emmett, as territorial librarian on a petition signed by every member of the bar. Judge Emmett had formerly been chief justice of Minnesota for nine years and was in every way competent and an honor to the office.

My brother Page wanted to fight the Spaniards and I made him a first lieutenant. I also made Mr. Catron's son, John Catron, a first lieutenant in the same regiment, but no objections were raised on the latter appointment. A vacancy occurring in the regiment, I advanced my brother to the rank of major. After the war he was appointed a clerk in the legislature by the members. He was qualified for the work and never asked my support, for he knew that I was opposed to nepotism. He was appointed clerk of the United States land board through the efforts of Solomon Luna and other politicians, who were his personal friends, and the appointment was made by the secretary of the interior, *and not by me. I* had absolutely nothing to do with either of these two appointments. Page was a great fisherman and hunter and no one in New Mexico was better acquainted with the wild life of the territory. It was Page who succeeded in having the legislature pass the game law, and while the law was in process, the members of the legislature petitioned me to appoint Page as the first game warden in the territory and stated in the petition, if I refused to appoint Page, they would kill the bill. I was anxious to have the bill passed, so made the promise. Accordingly, I later appointed him territorial game and fish warden. I never heard of a single objection to either the Judge Emmett or Page Otero appointments except from Tom Catron, and even he did not object to the appointments, his venom was directly aimed at me. Personally, I was opposed to both of these appointments on principle of nepotism. However, we Oteros were connected by marriage with the Lunas and Chaves' as well as other prominent families in New Mexico. Accordingly, if I had refused to appoint to office everybody who was related to me, I would have deprived the territory of a good deal of talent; besides, I was not considering Catron, Fiske, and Muller.

I knew absolutely nothing of the crimes which Catron charged to have been committed by men whom I appointed to office. Of course, I did know that "Billy" Martin had served a term in the territorial penitentiary for killing a man and had been pardoned by Governor Ross. I had also investigated the exact circumstances, which I have related in *My Life on the Frontier*. Furthermore, Billy was a warm personal friend, could speak well in English and in Spanish, and was the best interpreter and translator in the territory. Accordingly, I felt that his services were indispensable. The fact that he had been quicker on the trigger than a tough character who was about to shoot him could not be allowed to deprive New Mexico of his services. Catron's statement that I had detected Billy Martin in the embezzlement of school funds was absolutely untrue. I never knew of Martin doing anything of a dishonest nature.

Another appointee of mine was alleged to have killed a

My Nine Years as Governor 193

man back in the state of Tennessee, some years ago, and was said to have destroyed the court record. However, I was assured by a judge from that state, who was acquainted with all the facts, that the act was completely justifiable. Catron got all worked up over this case and even sent Gus O'Brien, one of his office men, to Tennessee to secure a requisition from the governor to have the alleged fugitive returned to stand trial. However, I told him that he was wasting his time as I would not honor such a requisition, if it were presented to me, so he dropped the matter. Some years later, this friend, whom I had saved from the inconvenience of a trial for murder in a distant state, showed his gratitude to me by deserting me and going over to the Catron camp. Catron and myself were both candidates for the United States Senate, and my old friend worked and voted to send my old enemy to Washington, as against me. He was a member of the first state senate and, of course, his vote counted for Catron. Such is life in the far west.

The charge of forgery was made against another man who held office under me. This charge is certainly amusing, for this fellow was almost always controlled by Catron. I remember that, at the time, he was favoring my friends during an election, Catron called him a "low down son of a bitch." Later, the fellow went with Catron and one of my friends remarked to him: "He is with you now; quite recently you were calling him a son of a bitch." "Yes," replied Catron, "at that time he was your son of a bitch, now he is my son of a bitch."

Catron charged one of my appointees with embezzlement. I did not learn of this charge until long after this appointment. The gentleman who had held this position had gone off to the war and I had to fill the vacancy at once. I was not well acquainted with the man whom I appointed to take the place but he was strongly recommended, especially by many of the G. A. R. Later, I removed him for cause.

The bribe, said to have been given another of my territorial officials, and the article in the Silver City paper in which Catron says this charge originally appeared, were unknown to me. I doubt very much whether this statement of Catron's or the article he mentioned would have had any effect on me. Furthermore, I appointed this gentleman to office, not because of any deal with him, but because he was well qualified for the office. I realize now that I made some mistakes in my appointments, but others were praised as good appointments by the territorial press, the people generally, even the school men, in fact, by almost everybody, except a few disappointed politicians who were anxious to make trouble for me in Washington.

Catron is wrong in saying that Max Frost controlled me. If ever a governor was his own boss, it certainly was I. No man on earth could control me and that was the very reason Catron and Fiske hated me. It is true that Frost was indicted for some irregularities in the United States land office, but that was years ago. Frost was a saint compared to Tom Catron. Possibly half a dozen New Mexicans were involved in the famous Star Route frauds,* but Max Frost was not one of them. As for the "corrupt ring" which was supposed to control me, I might point out that it included such men as the following list of some of the principal gentlemen, citizens of New Mexico, who supported my administration during those days:

Jefferson Raynolds, Joshua S. Raynolds, James W. Raynolds, Henry L. Waldo, James F. Hinkle, Holm O. Bursum, Solomon Luna, William J. Mills, John R. McFie, Frank W. Parker, John S. Clark, Charles Springer, Thomas D. Burns, James S. Duncan, W. A. Hawkins, William H. H. Lllewellyn.

H. B. Holt, David J. Leahy, Charles A. Spiess, Albert B. Fall, Joe E. Sheridan, W. H. Newcomb, W. D. Murray, Secundino Romero, B. C. Hernandez, Amado Chaves, O. N. Marron, C. M. Foraker, Bernard S. Rodey, Elfego Baca, William C. Reid, A. W. Pollard.

N. B. Field, Byron T. Mills, Max Frost, A. L. Morrison, W. E. Gortner, Charles Ilfeld, A. B. Smith, J. A. LaRue, Jan Van Houton, J. A. Mahoney, W. B. Bunker, E. W. Fox, W. H. Andrews, W. C. Porterfield, H. J. Hagerman,

---

*Investigations in the early 1880's revealed that a ring of grafters, headed by the Second Assistant Postmaster General, Thomas J. Brady, and Senator S. W. Dorsey, had been drawing 38 per cent of the total cost of the postal service for carrying mail over certain routes in the west.

W. S. Hopewell, Edward A. Cahoon, Jeremiah Leahy, William G. Hayden.

Malaquias Martinez, Numa Reymond, Ramon A. Sanchez, Jesus M. Sandoval, Edward L. Bartlett, Venceslao Jaramillo, William G. Sargent, Rufus J. Palen, William T. Thornton, Nathan Jaffa, George W. Prichard, Alfred Grunsfeld, Levi A. Hughes, William H. Pope, James M. Hervey.

Stephen B. Davis, Jr., Frank W. Clancy, E. C. Abbott, Jose D. Sena, J. H. Vaughn, Charles V. Safford, C. T. Brown, A. A. Keen, H. D. Bowman, W. B. Childers, George Curry, Jesus Romero, R. P. Barnes, Frank Springer, N. B. Laughlin, J. E. Hurley, H. W. Kelly, Fred H. Pierce, Juan Navarro, M. Brunswick, M. W. Browne, M. R. Otero, M. W. Mills, E. G. Austen.

G. A. Richardson, A. W. Thompson, W. R. Tipton, E. S. Stover, W. B. Walton, S. G. Cartwright, and many other prominent Republicans and Democrats in every county of the territory.

When one considers the fact that the thirty-fourth legislative assembly was composed of as fine a body of men as ever assembled in any legislature in New Mexico, it is preposterous to think that they were debauched by me or anyone else. Certainly none of the "gang" would have dared to make such a statement in their presence. My enemies criticized the legislature for appropriating additional money for the governor's office, although the expenses of the office were increasing every day, and the charges filed by them kept me busy going to Washington to answer them. As for the appropriation for those extra employees, Catron knew that they were vetoed by me but were passed over my veto. He also knows that the best legal authorities in New Mexico and Washington said that revenue for schools could not be raised in connection with the inspection of coal oil. Three successive inspectors have won their suits to retain all of their fees. Another thing I wish to contradict and emphatically deny, is the statement made by Tom Catron when he said that I had told the committee in the legislature that it was "beneath the dignity of the governor to return vouchers or take receipts for his disbursements."

I agree that the assessed valuation of the territory was far too low. However, I was not responsible for this condition. The assessors were elected by the people and men like Catron failed to make true returns of their property. Catron claimed that he was the biggest land owner in New Mexico. He probably was the chief tax-dodger in the territory and did more to contribute to this bad state of affairs than anyone else. However, financial matters were in better condition throughout the territory than ever before. Catron knew this but he hoped to injure me by misrepresenting the facts.

When Catron says that I broke up the harmony of the Republican Party, what he really means was that I destroyed *his* power as boss of the territory. It was natural that he should fight me, as I was the only governor of New Mexico to oppose him. He could not dominate me as he had former governors. I never outraged the best interests of the real Republicans of this territory, though I did fight the faction which followed Catron. I encouraged D. M. White to run on an Independent ticket. This split the Republican vote as I had foreseen, and resulted in the election to the council of Charles F. Easley, a Democrat, but an honest man who could be trusted to do what he believed was right. I advised some of the members of the council to defeat any contest Catron might file and I succeeded in keeping him out. I wanted to show him that he was no longer running things in the high handed mannner to which he was accustomed. Catron, compelled to admit defeat, gave many reasons why he was not in the council, but one was sufficient—he did not have enough votes. His statement about the use of armed deputies at the Santa Fe convention of 1900 is simply ridiculous. I did not attend the territorial convention at Socorro and boss the convention as the opposition prophesied. Yet the convention endorsed my administration and I was elected to head the delegation to the national convention at Philadelphia.

My enemies willfully charged that my administration was likely to make New Mexico a Democratic state. I can truthfully say that the bitter fight which they made on me in Washington did more than any other one factor to injure the cause of statehood and to keep New Mexico out of the Union for another ten years.

Regarding my relations with the territorial courts, every intelligent citizen in New Mexico knew that I never attempted to interfere in any way with the judges, nor to interfere with the drawing of jurors. Every judge I recommended for appointment to President McKinley, William J. Mills, John R. McFie, and Frank W. Parker, made good and were continued in office by President Roosevelt and President Taft. It is ridiculous to say that their decisions were rendered at my orders. All this talk about a "ring" surrounding me is a pure invention. Catron was the head of the old "Santa Fe Ring" which was responsible for a good deal of sorry political work throughout the territory. Consequently, it suited his fancy to say that I was the head of another. "People who live in glass houses should not throw stones."

I do not deny that on my recommendation the law was changed so that I could oust dishonest county officials. Someone was needed to crack down on them and force them to quit stealing public money. It was my business to do it and I did it. I appointed honest men in their places, too.

Naturally officials whom I appointed were actively interested in politics and strongly supported me for reappointment. Many Democrats also signed petitions endorsing my administration. Some of them took the trouble to go to Washington and tell the Senate committee on territories that the opposition to me was because I had the courage and nerve to fight Catron, and that the latter was ruination to good government and a dangerous man when given power. However, it is a gross misrepresentation on the part of my enemies to say that my support for reappointment came solely from office-holders, Democrats, and those expecting political favors. The great majority of the Republicans of the territory and all but about two or three of the newspapers backed me, as I have shown in previous chapters of this book.

I have given more space to these infamous charges than

they deserve. Catron and Fiske would not have dared to file such rot with President McKinley, but with the assistance of "Rough Rider Fritz," they succeeded in getting the ear of President Roosevelt. They took a chance and failed. After being fully investigated, their charges were dismissed as groundless by President Roosevelt, and were filed away in the department of the interior, where they were left to gather dust, while I continued to administer the territory of New Mexico for four additional years.

Chapter XV

MY PART IN THE MOVEMENT FOR STATEHOOD

EACH YEAR while I was governor, I drew up a report which gave a detailed description of the resources, institutions, and prospects of the territory. This was submitted to the secretary of the interior and was printed by the government printing office. Thousands of copies were distributed by the government and by the bureau of immigration of the territory. My reports were much more complete than those of my predecessors, and the chief of the government printing office wrote me in January, 1900, that the report which I had recently sent in was the best report ever made by a governor of any territory. All of the territorial papers and a number of papers in the East and West commented very favorably on my reports.

The *Doña Ana County Republican* for February 5th, 1900, said:

> We acknowledge receipt of a copy of Governor Otero's excellent report to the secretary of the interior. It deserves and is receiving much praise and will undoubtedly be the means of correcting many erroneous ideas current in the East relative to New Mexico. The document is said to be the most complete report ever submitted by a governor of a territory.

Referring to the same report, the *Clayton Enterprise* said:

> This office wishes to acknowledge receipt of the report of Governor Otero to the secretary of the interior. The report is far reaching in its scope, over 400 pages..... The maps and pictures incorporated therein are magnificent and the pleas made for statehood are simply unanswerable.

Frequently the press notices quoted from my reports. Thus, the first one I submitted received the following notice in a Washington paper:

> The secretary of the interior has received the annual report of Governor Otero of New Mexico. The governor says that the population of the territory has increased by 100,000 since the last census of 1890, and that it is capable of supporting 5,000,000 people. He dwells upon the mineral and agricultural resources of the territory. He says: "Information which is reliable from

the gold camps throughout the territory strengthens the hope that New Mexico will soon reap the benefit of a genuine mining boom." He makes strong grounds in favor of statehood, claiming that the people are entirely capable of self-government. He argues that admission into the Union would be beneficial alike to the proposed state and the United States.

Each of my reports contained a plea for the admission of New Mexico to the Union. I was heartily in favor of statehood. I had been opposed, in 1888 and 1889, feeling, with Numa Reymond, that the territory was too poor to pay the expenses of a state government. However, New Mexico had developed a great deal in ten years. The hard times of the nineties were over, and the territory and the nation were starting in on a period of prosperity. The *New Mexican* and other papers of the territory kept up the agitation for statehood, and I gave the movement my full support. It is true that I did not refer to it in my first inaugural. The fact was that I was lucky to be able to say anything at all. A comparatively young man, I unexpectedly found myself the governor of a great territory. Naturally, my friends and I were jubilant over my sudden elevation, and more in a mood to celebrate than to think out the policies to be pursued during my administration.

The circumstances were very different four years later. In spite of the bitter fight which my enemies made on me, I was confident that I would be reappointed. Of course, my friends and I consumed a considerable quantity of choice liquor after the commission had actually been handed to me. But there had been more time to think about the future. Immediately on my return to the territory, I took a strong stand in favor of statehood. In concluding my inaugural address, I predicted that I would not be able to complete my term of office, since New Mexico would be a state in less than four years. I believed this strongly and, in time, began to have my ambitions for the day that a star would be added to the flag for the state of New Mexico. Whenever there seemed any likelihood of an enabling act being passed by Congress, the territorial politicians would plan to array

My Nine Years as Governor 201

themselves in senatorial togas. Catron and Fall, Rodey and Andrews, looked forward to seats in the United States Senate for years. I was charged with having the same bee in my bonnet. This, however, was inaccurate. I liked my job as governor so well that I wished to be the first governor of New Mexico to be elected by the people.

In January, 1903, my attention was called to a statement made before the legislature of California regarding New Mexico. Accordingly, I sent the following telegram to Senator W. H. Savage, Legislative Assembly, Sacramento, California:

> I understand that Senator Hahn of Pasadena, states that our people as well as myself are opposed to statehood for New Mexico. Such a statement, if made, is absolutely untrue. Delegate Rodey's majority last fall of nearly 10,000 on a statehood plank certainly expressed the wishes of the people on that question, and my attitude in favor of statehood of New Mexico is too well known to need any explanation on my part. My annual report to the interior department, messages to the legislature, and frequent calls for statehood conventions will thoroughly answer any such statement.
>
> (Signed) Miguel A. Otero, Governor of New Mexico.

In addition to boosting statehood in my annual reports, I also helped to give the movement publicity through press interviews and by appearances before congressional committees, as well as through personal work with congressmen and other officials. During my frequent visits to the national capital, I always called at the House and Senate, if Congress were in session. Frequently, I made my plea before the committee on territories of one body or the other. At other times, I simply talked statehood with the members, many of whom I came to know quite well. At times, I found the outlook very encouraging; at other times, it was the reverse.

Naturally, the work which I was able to do in Washington was sandwiched in between attentions to many other matters. This may be illustrated by quoting the announcement made in the press regarding a trip to Washington which I made in December, 1898. I had left Santa Fe on December 12th, being accompanied by my wife and son. Before taking my departure, I informed the people through the territorial press that my principal object in making the trip was to:

> take up the act passed by the last session of Congress, granting lands to the territory for the use of the public schools and territorial educational institutions, with the Department of the Interior and the members of Congress for the purpose of having it amended in a manner to enable New Mexico to avail itself of lands granted. As the law now stands almost $20,000 will be required to pay the entrance fees in the land offices of the territory, and the condition of our treasury will not permit this expenditure. I am in hopes to be able to secure a recommendation from the department and a concurrence by Congress in my recommendation whereby the lands granted may be selected and entered without cost to the people of the territory. If this can be done the committee composed of the governor, solicitor-general, and the surveyor-general can organize and proceed with the work. I look upon this matter as one of the greatest and most important necessities needed for New Mexico, and am very anxious to secure this legislation and secure some changes in the present law which will remove the obstacle now confronting us. In regard to statehood, I shall do what I can to secure the introduction and favorable action by Congress on an enabling act. It seems to me that New Mexico is entitled to statehood by reason of its constantly and rapidly growing population, its wealth in natural resources, and its possibilities in the way of development.
> .... I feel that I will be of benefit to the many interests of New Mexico by going to Washington at this time.

To the above statement, the *New Mexican* added:

> Governor Otero has many friends among the members of Congress and in the departments, is well liked by all who know him in the East, and his presence in Washington during the time Congress is in session can only result in helping along the cause of statehood, the amending of the land grant law, and other matters which are of benefit to the territory at large.

While en route to Washington we stopped over in Chicago for a few days and I was interviewed by the different papers on the subject of statehood, the Republican victory in New Mexico, and New Mexico's attitude on sound money. The *Inter Ocean* said:

> New Mexico is in perfect harmony with the Washington administration on all matters pertaining to the welfare of the territory. Governor Otero is a young man, being under forty years of age, and was appointed by President McKinley in June, 1897, without his being a candidate for the office and without the usual political endorsements.

A few days later, on December 19th, the *Washington Star* said:

> Governor Otero arrived in Washington today. He will ask Congress for $20,000 to pay fees of the register and receiver in the United States land

offices in New Mexico, or, an amendment to the present land grant act whereby the lands granted to the territory may be selected and entered without cost to the people of New Mexico. He will also visit congressional committees on territories in the interest of statehood for New Mexico. The governor is much liked, and is certainly a live wire.

The people back home naturally appreciated the fact that I was not traveling for my health or for a good time, as the following notice from the *Clayton Enterprize* shows:

> Governor Otero's trip to Washington is proving anything but a vacation for him. Ever since arriving in the nation's capital he has been hard at work advancing the interests of New Mexico, and his efforts in that line will not be without beneficial results. This great territory is fortunate in having a man for its governor who is indefatigable in his endeavor to secure legislation which will advance the welfare of every citizen, and to bring about the admission of one of the richest sections of the Union as a state.

By the time I had been in office for two years or more, many of the eastern papers were taking up my plea for statehood. Arizona, of course, was also clamoring for admission to the Union. Governor N. O. Murphy and I were warm personal friends, and we always worked together. We consulted frequently in Washington. When passing through New Mexico, Murphy would often send me a wire to meet him at Lamy Junction. We were both in Washington in December, 1899, and felt greatly encouraged over the work we were doing. As the Christmas holidays approached, we decided to leave for the Southwest in a private car and take some guests along. The party consisted of Senator George L. Shoup, of Idaho, chairman of the Senate committee on territories; Senator C. D. Clark, of Wyoming, chairman of the Senate committee on foreign relations; Honorable Binger Herman, commissioner of the general land office; General F. C. Ainsworth, U. S. A., of the war department; Governor Murphy; Honorable Solomon Luna, member of the Republican national committee for New Mexico; Colonel R. E. Twitchell, of New Mexico; and myself. At Baltimore we were joined by Honorable George R. Peck, general attorney for the Santa Fe Railroad; and Senator A. G. Foster, of Washington. Stops were made at

Raton and Las Vegas, at which places I introduced the party and speeches were made from the rear platform of the private car. On our arrival at Santa Fe, carriages were at the depot platform and the party was driven around the city. We visited the territorial penitentiary, the old San Miguel Church, and all other points of interest. Luncheon was served at the executive mansion, after which the party was driven to the depot to meet a special train from Albuquerque containing a reception committee consisting of O. N. Marron, mayor of Albuquerque; United States District Attorney William B. Childers; Honorable Frank W. Clancy; Honorable Mariano S. Otero; Honorable E. V. Chavez; W. L. Hathaway; C. W. Ward, of the *Journal-Democrat;* Thomas N. Wilkinson; Colonel E. W. Dobson; Judge J. W. Crumpacker; A. A. Keen; E. P. McGinness, tax commissioner of the Santa Fe-Pacific Railway; and other citizens. The Albuquerque committee had expected to meet our party at Lamy, and seemed somewhat disappointed that it had consented to visit the capital and remain there until the afternoon. Judge McFie, Honorable H. O. Bursum, Honorable R. L. Baca, and I accompanied the party to Albuquerque where the visitors were driven around the city in carriages handsomely decorated with flowers. After a splendid dinner at the Armijo House the visitors were escorted by the committee, headed with a brass band, to the Commercial Club where a grand reception took place.

The *Albuquerque Journal-Democrat* said:

> The party was received by an immense crowd at the depot. All the members of the Washington party made short addresses, as did also Governor Otero who was enthusiastically cheered. At the Commercial Club a most successful reception was tendered the visitors. They all made addresses. Governor Otero spoke most eloquently and was roundly cheered and applauded.

The *Albuquerque Citizen* added:

> Governor Otero seemed to be a great favorite with the visiting senators and the Washington officials. They consulted him frequently and exhibited their regard and friendship for him upon every possible occasion, and if statehood is secured for New Mexico at this term of Congress, and the prospects

of that being accomplished are very bright, the greatest honor is due to Governor Otero, for it was through his effort that a committee for the first time in the history of the territory visited New Mexico with the express purpose of conferring with its people about statehood. Should there be a delay of another year or two, credit will nevertheless be due to Governor Otero, for he has made the way smoother for succeeding efforts to have the territory admitted as a state.

After the day in Albuquerque, the party left on a special car for Ash Forks, Arizona, where they found another committee awaiting them and had a grand reception. The private car was then switched to a special train for Prescott and Phoenix, where more receptions had been arranged.

Meanwhile, I had returned home on December 27th, after a strenuous and exciting week. My family physician, Dr. J. H. Sloan, immediately ordered me to bed, where I remained for several days. I developed a severe cold and no visitors were allowed, but my private secretary came every day with the mail, and I was able to keep up with those important duties which accumulate at the close of the year.

In January, 1901, I met Governor Murphy in Chicago. After my conference with him, I gave out an interview, the gist of which was: Both Governor Murphy and I have come to the conclusion to postpone pressing our petitions for admission of the two territories to statehood until the next session of Congress.

One of the schemes which Governor Murphy and I planned together was to hold a convention in each of the two territories to promote the statehood movement. We agreed to have them about the same time, and that each of us would attend both conventions and speak on both occasions. The one in New Mexico was planned in connection with the territorial fair in Albuquerque, while the Arizona affair was to be held in Phoenix a week later. On September 13th, 1901, I issued a call for the convention in my territory to be held on the fifteenth of the following month.

Two days before the fair opened I visited Albuquerque for another occasion. This was described by the *Albuquerque American* for October 11th as follows:

> Governor Otero arrived in Albuquerque today as a guest at the banquet to be given by the Retail Merchants Association. He was given a most hearty and enthusiastic reception. At the banquet he was introduced by Mayor O. N. Marron. The governor yielded gracefully and even pretended he liked it. The mayor had just delivered a ringing speech on the future of Albuquerque. The governor responded heartily and most effectively to the call of the toastmaster, Mr. Ruppe, the entire gathering was standing and calling loudly for Governor Otero. Mayor Marron in introducing the governor declared that he was as much the governor of Albuquerque as he was of New Mexico, and the speaker drew great applause when he said at the outset that he looked forward to making his home in Albuquerque ere long.

I returned to Santa Fe on the midnight train, as I was quite busy completing preparations for the statehood convention. I had also accepted the invitation of the fair association to open the fair. On the afternoon of October 13th, I returned to Albuquerque, accompanied by my family and my very efficient private secretary, Miss Clara H. Olsen. On our arrival, we were met by a large committee of citizens headed by Mayor Marron and Sheriff Hubbell. The street and the platform of the depot were a perfect jam. It took the committee several minutes before they were able to open a lane to the carriages for our party. Finally, we were ushered to an elegant barouche covered with flowers and drawn by four horses. The Albuquerque Guards under Captain Borrodaile then escorted our carriage to the Commercial Club. On the following morning, I headed a lengthy parade to the fair grounds where a large gathering of people from all over the territory had assembled. As I entered the grand stand, the band started playing "Hail to the Chief," and the cheering from the many thousands who were present was great and very inspiring. Having been introduced by Mr. Marron, I made a brief speech, declaring the fair now formally open. I was then escorted around the buildings and grounds, where I met many of the visitors. Finally, my family joined me, and together with Miss Olsen, we returned to the Commercial Club, where a committee was waiting to take us to lunch. All of the Albuquerque papers made favorable comments on my visit to their city, even going so far as to say that my address was "timely and eloquent."

The statehood convention met at 10 a. m. on October 15, in the spacious ballroom of the Commercial Club, delegates from every part of the territory being in attendance. I called the meeting to order and Colonel J. Francisco Chaves was elected chairman. The address of welcome was made by Mayor Marron, the response by Colonel Chaves. Mr. Edwin Munger then made the principle address of the day. As the president of the Hamilton Club of Chicago, he pledged the support of that strong and popular organization for statehood for both New Mexico and Arizona. His remarks were well received. Governor Murphy, who was in Albuquerque as my guest, then made a powerful appeal for the admission of both territories. He was quite a wit and many times during his remarks he had the convention in an uproar of laughter. However, his general remarks were solid and impressive. His many reasons why we should be admitted were strong and to the point. He made a splendid speech, and when he took his seat every delegate stood up and cheered him.

Colonel Chaves, the chairman, then called upon me. My speech is given in full in the Appendix (p. 389.)

The *Santa Fe New Mexican* reported:

When Governor Otero finished his speech he was greeted with prolonged cheers. His impressive and eloquent address hit the nail on the head. He fearlessly told the delegates from every county in New Mexico where the trouble was located and called on them to do their duty.

On October 18th, the same paper said:

Governor Otero, Mrs. Otero, and Miguel, junior, returned this noon from Albuquerque. The governor was enthusiastic over the great success of the fair and the statehood convention. "We crowded sixty days into two," said the governor, in speaking of the results achieved by the statehood gathering.

Less than a week after my return to Santa Fe, I took the train for Arizona to help Governor Murphy with his convention. The latter met me and my party at Ash Forks with a special train. Here I also met Honorable Thomas Ryan, first assistant secretary of the interior, who had been on a visit to Phoenix with his wife. We tried hard to persuade him to return with our party. Mrs. Ryan was anxious for the secretary to accept, but because of limited time he was unable to do so. Governor Murphy had his surgeon-general with him. I had mine with me, and the two doctors amused the entire party by filling prescriptions at stated intervals. We reached Prescott early in the afternoon and were met by a large delegation of citizens with carriages, who drove us around the town and to some of the mines. We were given an elegant banquet at the Burke Hotel. About two hundred citizens were in attendance and everything was served from cocktails to cafe-noir with a pony of brandy. In my party were Colonel J. Francisco Chaves; Dr. William R. Tipton, my surgeon-general; Thomas S. Hubbell; Adjutant-General William H. Whiteman; and C. J. Gavin, of Raton. Colonel Chaves had commanded the expedition in 1863, when the territory of Arizona was organized, and his speech at the statehood convention was listened to very attentively and with great appreciation by all present. The colonel related a story about their arrival on the banks of Salt River. He said: "We were dirty from our long march across the desert and the river looked so good, we all stripped off our clothing and went in for a good swim." Observing the ladies in the private boxes, he gracefully waved his arms in their direction and added: "But there were no beautiful ladies present at that time." This remark brought down the house and it was several minutes before the colonel could resume his speech. Everybody was standing up, cheering, and laughing and the ladies threw roses at the colonel.

While I was in Prescott, the *Prescott Journal Miner* had this to say:

> Governor Otero is a young man, not yet forty years of age, and is so prominently identified with New Mexico and so enthusiastic over its advancement and government as to recently receive a recess appointment from our late President as governor for four years more. He is a pleasant gentleman, easy and graceful in his manners and has that western characteristic and demeanor that makes his fellowship agreeable from start to finish.

After a very pleasant visit in Prescott, we boarded the train for Phoenix and arrived about 8:00 p. m. The depot platform was crowded with citizens, and a brass band. The Phoenix paper said:

> Governor Otero was given an ovation as is seldom given a visitor to another commonwealth. The governor of New Mexico is popular wherever he goes and his popularity adds to the renown of New Mexico. He knows how to say and do the things at the right time and the world appreciates men who are heartily sincere and honestly enthusiastic.

Rooms had been reserved for myself and party at the Adams Hotel and we were driven there, headed by the band and many carriages. On our arrival, we found the lobby and adjoining rooms crowded, and the governor introduced me to many of his friends. We then hurried up to the parlor where Mrs. Murphy and some of her lady friends greeted us.

The following day was the convention at the opera house. The building was beautifully decorated and the interior was magnificently emblazoned with flags, bunting, and flowers. Back of the stage was an immense American flag and across it a wide silk ribbon, white, with the word "Statehood" in gold letters.

Our party was seated on the stage together with Governor Murphy and all the territorial officials and prominent citizens of Arizona, while the private boxes were filled with beautiful women, and believe me they were beautiful in their handsome gowns of different colors seated in the midst of American beauty roses of the long-stem variety. It was a picture long to be remembered.

After the convention had been organized, the chairman called on Governor Murphy who delivered a splendid oration on statehood and ended with an address of welcome to the visitors from New Mexico, coupled with a very flattering introduction of me. When I took the floor, the cheering and hand-clapping were continued for some minutes, while the ladies threw American beauty roses at me. I was so overcome at this sudden demonstration that tears came to my eyes. I had a touch of "buck fever" and was completely unnerved, and found myself wishing for about three fingers of good brandy.

As soon as the cheering had subsided, I walked to the center of the stage, and gave my address. (P. 391, appendix.)

That same night, after the convention had adjourned, Governor and Mrs. Murphy tendered me a grand reception at the Adams Hotel. I had the pleasure of sending Mrs. Murphy six dozen long-stemmed American beauty roses. The reception was a huge success, and I believe nearly every resident of Phoenix was there. We were all in the best of spirits for we had just attended a magnificent banquet in the hotel dining room. The reception lasted for hours, but the guests and particular friends of Governor and Mrs. Murphy remained long afterwards, and it was daylight before the main body left the hotel. It certainly was a whole night.

We succeeded in getting a few hours sleep and, after a good breakfast, took the special train back to Ash Forks. We stopped for a few hours at Prescott and had a most enjoyable time. I visited the newspapers with Mr. Dennis Burke, and here is what the *Prescott Mining Courier* had to say later:

> Governor Otero, of New Mexico, accompanied by Honorable Dennis Burke, of Prescott, called on the *Courier* yesterday. Governor Otero has been in attendance on the statehood convention at Phoenix. He is sanguine in his expectations as to statehood for the territories. In our short talk with the governor we discovered him to be one of those few public men whom one feels perfectly at ease with at first sight. What a pity he is not a Democrat, but that he cannot be and hold his job.

After a very pleasant time in Prescott, we took our train for Ash Forks. On our arrival, we found we had plenty of time to walk around the little town and see the sights. Governor Murphy took us to a small restaurant where we had a few bottles of champagne and some cake. When the train arrived we boarded the Pullman cars and were soon sound asleep for we were all rather short on sleep and were very tired.

The next day, October 29th, we arrived in Santa Fe, and

none of our party could speak too highly of the splendid treatment we all enjoyed in Arizona.

Naturally the territorial newspapers had much to say of my visit to Arizona. *The New Mexican* for November 4th said:

> Arizona exchanges point to the fact that Governor Otero made a very pleasant impression on his recent visit to that territory. The Arizona newspapers seem to be a pretty good lot.

Two days later the *Dona Aña County Republican* summed both conventions up as follows:

> Notwithstanding the war that some of the territorial newspapers have waged against Governor Otero, he still remains one of the most popular men in New Mexico. This fact was strikingly shown at the territorial fair and the statehood convention. Wherever he appeared he was welcomed with unmistakable evidence of the esteem in which he is held by the people. No speaker at the statehood convention was more enthusiastically applauded at the close of his address, with the possible exception of Colonel J. Francisco Chaves, whose speech touched the hearts of his hearers in a peculiar manner on account of its reminiscent nature. Governor Otero has been in Arizona recently to attend the statehood convention at Phoenix.
>
> A reception was tendered him at the Adams Hotel, and it was one of the social events of the season in that beautiful city. The *Arizona Gazette* says the governor has a winning air about him which captivates those he comes in contact with. His address at the convention called forth complimentary notices from the press. It is pleasant to know that our governor made an equally favorable impression in Prescott, where he spent a few hours. Referring to his personal characteristics the *Prescott Journal Miner* among other things said: "He is a pleasant gentleman and has that western characteristic and demeanor that makes his fellowship agreeable from start to finish."

The statehood convention held in Albuquerque requested that I appoint a delegation of an equal number of Republicans and Democrats to visit Washington in the interest of the cause. After the Fifty-seventh Congress had convened, I accordingly appointed the following:

> Republicans: Frank A. Hubbell, Solomon Luna, J. H. Elliott, Charles A. Spiess, George W. Prichard, J. Francisco Chaves, William H. Andrews, A. W. Harris. Democrats: O. N. Marron, A. B. Fall, G. A. Richardson, William H. Pope, H. B. Fergusson, F. A. Manzanares, Anthony Joseph, Willard S. Hopewell.

These gentlemen, at least a good number of them, went to Washington and materially assisted Delegate Rodey in his work in Congress. Finally, on May 9th, 1902, I received a telegram announcing that the omnibus statehood bill had passed the House of Representatives that day. This bill provided for the admission of New Mexico, Arizona, and Oklahoma. This victory, of course, simply transferred the fight to the Senate. The territorial press thought that I should appoint another delegation to go to Washington and help our delegate get the bill through that body. However, Mr. Rodey wired me that he was coming to New Mexico soon, and that the Senate intended to appoint a committee to visit New Mexico, and that it would be useless for us to send a committee to visit the national capital at that time.

The Senate committee arrived in Las Vegas on November 12th, for the alleged purpose of making an investigation to see if New Mexico and Arizona were really fit for statehood. Albert J. Beveridge, of Indiana, was the chairman. Other members were Henry E. Burnham, of New Hampshire; William P. Dillingham, of Vermont; and Henry Heitfield, of Idaho. Thomas R. Shipp, private secretary to Senator Beveridge, acted as the secretary of the committee. L. G. Rothschild, of Indianapolis, who was known as "the Baron," acted as "the outside man." He would sneak around in the slum districts and meet impossible people in order to make an adverse report of conditions as found by him. Absolutely, not the slightest attention was paid to the favorable side of the territory, and no inquiry was made covering education, industry, manufacturing, banking, stock raising, mining, or farming. The sole intention seemed to be to gather the unfavorable side. Mr. Rothschild visited the saloons and dance hall districts, especially the low down class of humanity. He would photograph a lewd, dirty prostitute or a drunken scoundrel stretched out in some alley, lying in his own filth. These exhibits were to be used to convince eastern people that such were the general conditions of society in New Mexico. I must admit I was disgusted with Senator Beveridge as he seemed to be the whole thing and managed the plans, through the "Baron," to perfection. The other senators, Burnham, Dillingham, and Heitfield were gentlemen, and had little to say. The Indiana senator was playing his part to perfection. "He certainly knew his onions," and undoubtedly was a good representative of the interests opposing statehood for New Mexico and Arizona. The official reporter was State Senator Ogborne, of Indiana, and the committee messenger was S. A. Henshaw, presumably from Indiana, and R. C. Simon, Washington, official interpreter. The humorist of the burlesque show was the "Baron," who laughingly said: "I am serving as porter, baggage-master, footman, and maid." The party traveled in a private Pullman. The committee was met at Raton by a delegation from Albuquerque, headed by Delegate Bernard S. Rodey, Judge B. S. Baker, Dr. G. W. Harrison, Honorable William B. Childers, and Honorable O. N. Marron. This committee did not stop in Las Vegas, but continued on to their home city. The senators' car was sidetracked at Las Vegas, the place selected for the first hearing.

I had secured the necessary consulting rooms and the parlor in the Castañeda Hotel for the ordeal. I, of course, met the committee and the retinue of helpers, and took them to lunch. They were very secretive, Beveridge particularly so. After lunch the committee asked to be left alone in the parlor, where, evidently, the final instructions were to be meted out to the "Baron" who carried a small satchel and a kodak for his invasion into the slums of "Fair New Mexico." The first victim examined was Jesús María Tafoya, county school superintendent of San Miguel County. He was duly examined in philosophy, rhetoric, algebra, biology, etymology, and syntax. Jesús was frightened and somewhat nervous, still he held his own and, no doubt, did as well as the average school teacher in the wilds of Indiana. However, he was not a real educator and the "Baron" knew it. Jesús was simply a good politician and knew how to secure votes for the Democratic Party, but he made an excellent witness for the committee. Two or three justices of the peace were found who could not speak English, and they made good witnesses, too. This went on until supper time, when Senator Beveridge telephoned to Superintendent Hurley for an engine to take his car to Santa Fe, and this was refused. At this point Senator Beveridge got what was coming to him. He found that his authority did not extend to railroad officials, as the superintendent advised him that he would have to wait for the next passenger train which would pass through Las Vegas the following day. Beveridge, for the first time, appealed to me and I asked why he had not spoken to me before, as I thought I might be able to secure an engine. He seemed in great distress. I telephoned Mr. Hurley and he at once said: "Of course, Governor, you may have an engine if you want it, but that committee, never." I asked him to kindly attach an engine to the private car and I would accompany them to Santa Fe, and this was done. The next morning, in Santa Fe, the committee carried on the same tactics. I had invited them to take dinner with Mrs. Otero and me at the executive mansion and afterwards to drive around the city, and this was accepted. So their examination in Santa Fe was very light. Late that same evening they went to Albuquerque where they put on the final touches, and where a rather amusing story gained credence and was soon in the city of Washington. The county superintendent of Bernalillo County, Mr. Esclavio Vigil, was called before the committee. The story, as related by the "Baron," was that the witness was nervous and timid. Suddenly, Senator Beveridge pointed his finger at him and asked: "Who discovered America?" Esclavio was clearly embarrassed and answered, "I no know him." "Well," said Beveridge, "don't you know that Christopher Columbus discovered America?" "No, I no know him," promptly answered Esclavio. "Don't you know that Christopher Columbus is dead?" asked Beveridge, and Esclavio answered: "No, him dead, too bad." Esclavio was excused and the examination soon closed. The whole affair was a joke, but it served its purpose. Beveridge's report was made to the United States Senate and "Joint Statehood" was brought forth.

At the dinner, given to the senators by Mrs. Otero and myself at the executive mansion, were Secretary Raynolds, Judge John R. McFie, Mrs. A. M. Bergere, and Miss Nina Otero.

Considering the nature of the investigation made by the Beveridge committee, I was not surprised when, on December 3rd, I received word from Washington that President Roosevelt and the Republican Party were opposed to statehood for either New Mexico or Arizona. During the remainder of my term of office I worked consistently for separate statehood for New Mexico, and opposed joint statehood for New Mexico and Arizona. The movement to join the two southwestern territories and admit them to the Union as one state started early in 1903. The new state was to be called New Mexico. I knew, of course, that the people of Arizona would never stand for that. I was personally against such a move and determined to join with Arizona in opposing it, if New Mexico was foolish enough to fall for it. Nor was my attitude affected in the least when I heard that Delegate Rodey and Solomon Luna and Holm O. Bursum were all willing to approve such a bill.

Secretary Raynolds returned from an eastern trip on Christmas day, 1902. Leaving him in charge in the territory, I took the train for New York and Washington the same day. Mrs. Otero and Miguel accompanied me, and we planned to be gone for five or six weeks. When Congress resumed after the holiday recess, I went to Washington, while my family remained in New York.

Beveridge's infamous report on his visit to the territories was followed by a filabuster which lasted for weeks. The omnibus statehood bill was finally killed, without any vote having been taken. I heard a part of the debate. I remember especially sitting on the floor of the Senate with Senator

Knute Nelson, of Minnesota, and Senator Mark Hanna, of Ohio, both of whom were opposed to the admission of New Mexico. I listened to the former senator until the Senate adjourned for the day. The senator resumed his tirade the following day and spoke against the bill for a solid week. I continued to listen, no matter how badly I felt over his unjust speech.

On January 8th, 1903, I called on President Roosevelt and he told me that he was against statehood for both New Mexico and Arizona, as he believed it to be for the best interest of both territories, and added: "If I were in your place I would remain a territory as long as the United States government will pay your running expenses." He then spoke of dishonest judges, saying: "With statehood you will be burdened with dishonest judges and will be forced to keep them, while as a territory they can be removed and their places filled by the President." Mr. Roosevelt became very much excited when I did not agree with him, and in most eloquent words tried to impress me that all judges in the West were corrupt. He wound up his spleen by saying: "Governor Otero, I think a corrupt judge ought to be taken out to the corral, tied to a cow's tail and sh— to death." I smilingly agreed to his statement, but insisted that we had many honest and capable judges in New Mexico, much better than those sent out to us by politicians in the East.

I had several meetings with the New Mexico statehood committee while I was in Washington. Besides myself, Solomon Luna, Frank A. Hubbell, W. A. Hawkins, A. B. Fall, W. H. Andrews, and William H. H. Llewellyn were there. I was thoroughly disgusted with the attitude of Bernard S. Rodey, Solomon Luna, and Holm O. Bursum on the statehood question. I felt that jointure might carry in New Mexico, with these gentlemen behind it, but was quite certain from a talk I had with Governor Murphy, that it would never carry in Arizona.

On January 14th, my family and I arrived in Santa Fe

after an absence of a little more than three weeks. The regimental band and a large number of citizens greeted us at the depot on our arrival and escorted us to the executive mansion, where, as usual we held an informal reception. The following morning I was at my office quite early as I had a great amount of mail to handle and I was anxious to get to work. I gave out the following statement to the press:

> The people here know as much about the statehood question as do those in Washington. There is no more information to be had there than there is here. While East and in Washington I lost no opportunity to say and do all I could for statehood. I am opposed to the union of New Mexico and Arizona as one state and opposed the suggestion while in Washington. I am in favor of the passage of the omnibus bill as it passed the House and on that basis I did all I could. No one can say what the outcome will be today.

In November, 1903, Alexander O. Brodie, who had succeeded Murphy as governor of Arizona, made a statement opposing jointure of New Mexico and Arizona. He said: "The people of Arizona will rather forego admission as a state, than to be admitted as one state with New Mexico." I agreed with him in all he said and made a statement that "The people of New Mexico will rather forego admission as a state, than to be admitted as one state with Arizona."

On December 8, President Roosevelt sent his message to Congress, and he failed to mention statehood for the territories. I was not surprised, neither was I disappointed, for I well knew that he never favored statehood, even though he had promised it. His personal statement to me was enough to satisfy me that we could not count on his support, and I believed he would have vetoed any bill passed by Congress for the territories, whether for single or joint statehood.

Two days after the President had sent his message to Congress, my family and I left Santa Fe for New York, Washington, and other cities, expecting to be gone for a month or six weeks, depending largely on what Congress did in the matter of statehood. We stopped in Chicago for a couple of days and reached Washington, December the fifteenth, making our headquarters at the New Williard Hotel. I found Mr. Solomon Luna in town, and he and I went, in company with Delegate Wilson, of Arizona, to the White House to call on President Roosevelt and discuss the statehood proposition. Mr. Wilson told the President that the people of Arizona were opposed to joining New Mexico and Arizona into one state, and would fight such a proposition to the bitter end. Mr. Luna and I expressed the same views as to the sentiment in New Mexico, telling the President that joint statehood would be unfair to both territories. Our talk did not seem to impress the President in the slightest degree, and we could plainly see that he was against us.

Throughout the year 1904 I continued to fight joint statehood. On February 12, a reporter called at my office to get my views on the subject. I told him that I was strongly against joint statehood, that I thought it unwise and believed that the people of the territory were almost solidly against it. Delegate Rodey's one aim was statehood. He was so persistent in fighting for it that the people dubbed him "Bernard Statehood Rodey," his middle initial being S. He made a good fight, but was finally forced to accept jointure. Consequently, when the joint statehood bill was passed by the House on April 19, he announced that he was strongly for the bill. I read this announcement with regret, for I was strongly against the bill and hoped to assist in its defeat. Time was to show that I would be the only one of the so-called leaders in the Republican Party in New Mexico who would stand out to the last against joint statehood. Rodey was one of the first to desert, but even Luna and Bursum failed to stand out to the bitter end. On May 25, I received a letter from Stephen B. Elkins, the West Virginia senator who as delegate to Congress from New Mexico back in 1876, would have gotten the territory into the Union but for

My Nine Years as Governor

the unfortunate handshake incident.* Elkins wrote that he thought I was right in my stand on statehood, that he was strongly opposed to joint statehood himself, and hoped that the territory would wait for a few years. He thought that New Mexico could be admitted separately in four or five years, and asked her to wait. Of course, I felt that this was good advise. I agreed with him entirely, and time was to show that we were right.

Many citizens, however, came to think that joint statehood was our only hope, and the efforts of those who worked to defeat it were not appreciated. Thus, about June 20, just after my return from the Republican national convention in Chicago, the *Albuquerque Citizen* said editorially: "The fossils in Santa Fe did good work." It added: "Having knocked out statehood, the fossils at Santa Fe will doze another three hundred years." I was not having as lonely a fight at this time as I was to have later, and the *New Mexican* replied as follows:

> The fossils of Santa Fe didn't want any of your joint statehood humbug and, therefore, went to work to knock it out. They are in favor of single statehood within present territorial limits and upon that line they will make their fight for the rights of the people of New Mexico, regardless of a few interested newspapers and politicians. "The fossils in Santa Fe" in this fight were aided by Governor Otero, who hails from San Miguel County; by National Committeemen Solomon Luna, who comes from Valencia County; by Chairman of the Republican Territorial Central Committee, Frank A. Hubbell, whom the esteemed *Albuquerque Journal* is pleased to call "the Boss of Bernalillo County"; by Delegate H. O. Bursum, who is one of the leading citizens of Socorro County; by Delegate David J. Leahy, who registers from Raton, Colfax County; by Delegate William G. Sargent, who is proud to write El Rito, Rio Arriba County, after his name. In addition, "The fossils in Santa Fe" were helped and abetted in this fight for the best interests of the patriotic people of the territory by a great majority in the Republican territorial convention held last March, as well as by a greater portion of the county conventions held this spring, and by many prominent citizens of the territory, Republicans and Democrats as well. This time surely "the fossils of Santa Fe" were in very good company. Naturally the *Citizen* is hot in the collar. This is easily explained, hence the *New Mexican* cannot bear its esteemed contemporary and its genial editor the least bit of ill will, quite the reverse. If "beefing" helps to clear the atmosphere why go ahead. Governor Otero is strong for single statehood and very much against jointure.....

On December 13, I left for Washington, accompanied

---

*Hammond and Donnelly, *The Story of New Mexico*, The University of New Mexico Press, Albuquerque, pp. 131-132.

by my family. William H. Andrews, who had just been elected delegate to Congress from New Mexico, met me there and we put in about two weeks working to defeat the joint statehood bill then pending in the Senate. My family and I then spent the Christmas holidays in New York, leaving for Santa Fe on the 26th. My efforts were evidently appreciated by many of my fellow townsmen. When we arrived in Santa Fe, we were met at the depot by a large crowd of citizens with the military band, and they all escorted us to our home.

The year 1905—my last as governor of New Mexico—found me still standing out against joint statehood, which Senator Beveridge and other congressmen were trying to force upon us, whether we wanted it or not. In May, I received an invitation from Governor Joseph H. Kibbey, of Arizona, asking me to attend an anti-joint statehood convention at Phoenix. I decided that I could not accept this kind invitation, although my sympathies were one hundred per cent with the movement. My belief was that this was purely an Arizona affair, and New Mexico had better attend to her own affairs and not mix with the Arizona people in this matter.

A few days later I received a telegram from Mr. W. Scott Smith, who was in Arizona, visiting his friend, Honorable W. S. Sturgis. Mr. Smith stated that he would be in El Paso on the 25th, en route to Washington, and asked that I meet him there, if possible. This I did, going with him as far as Pastura, New Mexico. From this point I drove out to my ranch for a day, then returned to Santa Fe by way of Pastura and Torrance. Four days later the *Arizona Republican* announced the result of my conference with Mr. Smith. It said:

> National Committeeman W. S. Sturgis, of Arizona, read the following telegram from Governor Otero of New Mexico to the anti-joint statehood convention in Phoenix, which was received with thunderous applause and had Governor Otero been present he would have received the ovation of his life:

My Nine Years as Governor 221

"I appreciate fully your very kind invitation and would be with you at Phoenix on Saturday, but official duties prevent. Can say, however, that I am heartily with you in spirit, thoroughly sympathizing in your movement. While New Mexico has a most friendly feeling for Arizona, we will oppose jointure. I have never halted nor hesitated in my declarations for single statehood for both territories. This, I believe, is the sentiment of a very large majority of our people. Solomon Luna, our member of the national committee, and H. O. Bursum, chairman of the Republican central committee, are of the same opinion. We will join with you in opposition at the proper time. Arizona is large enough, prosperous enough, and rich enough to maintain and support a separate state government without being annexed to any territory. We know the good people of Arizona believe the same conditions to exist as to New Mexico. May great success attend your convention is my earnest wish.

"(Signed) Miguel A. Otero, Governor of New Mexico."

On December 20, about two weeks before I was to step out of the governor's chair, I was interviewed by a newspaper reporter from Denver as to my future attitude to joint statehood. I told him exactly what I had told every man, woman, and child who asked me that question: "I am not for joint statehood with Arizona." He asked: "In the event of the bill carrying, where do you think the capital will be located?" I answered: "I do not know, but I think it should be located in New Mexico. Whether it will remain in Santa Fe or not I am not prepared to say, as I have not made myself sufficiently acquainted with that phase of the question, for I am so bitterly opposed to any thought of jointure that I decline to believe that there is the remotest chance of the bill passing, so why bother about the location of the capital?"

The threat of jointure with Arizona was hanging heavy over our heads when I went out of office. There were too many "yes, yes" men in the territory who could be persuaded to fall in with administration policies adopted in Washington. Fortunately for us, Senator Joseph B. Foraker, of Ohio, who had fought ably for single statehood in 1902, had the forethought to introduce an idea which defeated joint statehood. Congress passed the bill, but with the Foraker amendment, which meant that if a majority of the voters of either territory refused their consent, the whole thing was off. In the election on November 6, 1906, New Mexico carried for joint statehood by a majority of 11,460. Arizona, however, voted against the proposal by a majority of 13,124. Thus the matter was ended, much to my satisfaction. Glory enough for one day.

Chapter XVI
BULL ANDREWS GOES TO CONGRESS

IN SPEAKING of my reappointment by President McKinley, the *Pecos Valley Stockman* for July 8th, 1901, said: "Otero's victory over the Catron-Fiske-Berger-Vance faction places him permanently as the leader of the Republican Party in this territory, a position whose honors the governor will doubtless wear gracefully and easily as becomes a courteous gentleman and capable official." This was to prove an accurate prophecy for the future; at the time, it was a little premature. I have already described how the accession of Roosevelt to the presidency led my enemies in my own party to renew their assaults on me. And even after I had been reappointed the second time, they continued to fight me for the control of the party.

This fight waxed especially warm in the summer and fall of 1902, when there was an election for the members of the territorial assembly and the delegate to Congress. Catron, who was sometime "the Republican boss of Santa Fe County" and at all times a local politician, "started the ball a-rolling" through his position in the county. His methods were described by the *New Mexican* as follows:

> The faction known as the "Tom Catron faction" in Santa Fe County, who are against the territorial administration, are making strenuous efforts to control the Santa Fe County primaries and the county convention for the election of ten delegates to the Republican territorial convention at Raton and later for the county Republican convention for the nomination of legislative and county ticket, that will be hostile to the administration.
>
> The Catron methods of running primaries and conventions in Santa Fe County are disagreeable to the respectable Republicans and these methods will no longer be tolerated. Stick a pin right there, this means business. It is Catronism vs. the Administration in this county, and more or less so in the entire territory. The result is not doubtful. The friends of the administration in the Republican Party in Santa Fe County and in the territory at large will win hands down.

On October 6th, the administration delegates to the Santa Fe County convention badly beat the "Tom Catron faction" and elected the following delegation: E. C. Abbott, A. M. Bergere, M. A. Ortiz, J. V. Conway, James D. Hughes, M. R. Otero, Gus R. Johnson, D. M. White, Jose D. Sena, and Amado Chaves. The "Tom Catron faction" bolted and named a contesting delegation, but were badly beaten in the territorial convention.

Catron was a member of the territorial Republican central committee, and he cast the only negative vote at the meeting.

The Republican conventions in every county in the territory endorsed my administration in the strongest language possible, which was very gratifying to me, owing to the fact that the Catron faction and all his "button gangs" were fighting me personally as well as my administration.

Catron's defeat is indicated by the fact that the Republican territorial convention, which met in Raton, strongly endorsed my administration and renominated Bernard S. Rodey for delegate to Congress. The resolution passed by the convention was as follows:

> We most heartily endorse the administration of Governor Miguel A. Otero in the territory, which has resulted in improving our financial standing and moral credit at home and abroad. It has induced new capital to come into the territory, and protected what was already here. And especially we endorse his personal and official efforts to improve the method of assessments and taxation which have resulted in adding one and one-half million dollars to our tax rolls for the present year. His official and personal conduct has been subject to the most searching scrutiny by two Presidents, and two Senates with the result that it has been approved by them, and in that result we sincerely congratulate him.

Rodey had been nominated and elected, in 1900, largely through my influence and assistance during his campaign so that he was generally regarded as the administration candidate. The passage of the omnibus statehood bill by the House in the spring of 1902 was regarded as quite a feather in his cap. On his return from Washington, toward the last of July, his friends in Albuquerque gave him a grand reception at the Alvarado Hotel. I was present, and stood with the delegate. I gave him further assistance in the campaign that fall, accompanying him and William E. Martin to Otero County toward the last of October. I also made speeches in several precincts in and around Santa Fe.

Being very much interested in the election returns, I remained up practically all night with a messenger running between my office and the Western Union Telegraph Company. From the early returns I felt we had won, but I never anticipated such overwhelming majorities as were given the Republican ticket in New Mexico. Let me quote what the *Santa Fe New Mexican* had to say:

> The people of New Mexico on Tuesday last gave the lie direct to the snide reformers who have been assailing and slandering Governor Otero and the officials of the territorial administration. They spoke mighty emphatically and the verdict is right and just.
>
> The territorial administration of Governor Otero received a splendid testimonial and endorsement by the citizens of New Mexico at the polls on Tuesday last. The greatest majority ever given in the territory for delegate to Congress and for legislative candidates was cast on that day.
>
> Mr. H. B. Fergusson realizes by this time that the people of New Mexico are not in a humor to countenance unjust attacks and slanders upon the territorial government.....
>
> The greatest victory of all is the splendid endorsement that the administration of Governor Otero has received in New Mexico. The Democrats and snide reformers made their principal fight on the line of attacks upon Governor Otero and his friends. The people properly resented these attacks by rolling up a majority of over 9,000 votes for Delegate B. S. Rodey, by electing a legislature that is almost solidly Republican and by electing two-thirds of the Republican candidates for county office throughout the territory.....
>
> It is not necessary to seek far for the reasons of the splendid majority which New Mexico gave on Tuesday for the Republican ticket. It means an unqualified approval of the acts of the territorial administration and the personality of Governor Otero and his official advisers. The opposition thought it played its strongest card when it accused Governor Otero and the territorial administration of corruption, dishonesty, and inefficiency. But the people supported the territorial Republican platform which endorsed completely and enthusiastically the administration of Governor Otero, and the other territorial officials..... It is as plain as if it were written in characters of fire against a cloudy midnight sky: "We the people of New Mexico with overwhelming majority, endorsed the administration of our popular and capable governor and we demand statehood from Congress and the President of the United States, approving most heartily the brilliant statehood campaign of our indefatigable delegate to Congress." The people with almost one voice say: "Well done, Governor Miguel A. Otero and members of his territorial administration. Continue in the paths in which you have been so successful for the glory of the commonwealth and the good of its people."

On November 11th, the *Las Vegas Record* said:

New Mexico returned an emphatic answer to the slanderers of Governor Otero and his administration..... This is a glorious endorsement and vindication of which Governor Otero has good cause to feel proud.

Administration candidates for the legislative assembly and for Congress were elected in 1902 and again in 1904. In an early forecast of the political situation in the last named year, the *Albuquerque Citizen* said on February 5th:

Through the conservative and safe administration of Governor Otero the Republican Party of New Mexico is assured of victory next fall. The party is harmonious and united in nearly every county and the factional dissatisfaction is very small. In fact there is almost no opposition to Governor Otero. There is the best of feeling in all sections toward him, and he has reason to be proud of his excellent management of public affairs.

However, this appearance of harmony was to prove deceptive, and the campaign of that year was to split the party, temporarily at least.

Ralph Emerson Twitchell, who was something of a politician as well as a historian, has testified to the effectiveness of my political methods. Speaking of me in *The Leading Facts of New Mexican History*, volume II, page 524, he says:

During his incumbency, under his leadership, and with the patronage of his office, the Republican Party organized a political machine so powerful that even the appointment of notary public was considered in some localities a great favor and mark of political recognition. Induced to ally themselves with a political party so well organized, through the favor of the executive in the matter of political appointments, many prominent men, formerly occupying exalted positions in the councils of the Democratic Party, flocked to the standard of Republicanism set up by a leader who acknowledged no equal and brooked no rivalry in his leadership. Under his domination and at his instance the Republican territorial convention of 1904, a majority of whose delegates had been instructed to cast their votes for the renomination of Bernard S. Rodey, who has been chosen delegate to Congress in 1900 and 1902, the last time by a majority of nearly ten thousand votes, repudiated their instructions and voted for the nomination of William H. Andrews, one of the delegates to the convention and himself instructed to cast his vote for Mr. Rodey. So potent was his leadership while executive, that he was enabled to remove from office and utterly destroy politically the leaders in some counties offering any opposition, among them the chairman of the Republican territorial central committee.

The throwing over of Rodey, the nomination of Andrews, and the ouster of the Hubbells were all closely connected. The action took place mostly at the Republican territorial convention of 1904, which convened in Albuquerque on September 12th. This convention was the most important one held in New Mexico during my administration, so I shall discuss it in full.

The Hubbells practically controlled Bernalillo County. Frank A. Hubbell was county superintendent of education, while his brother, Thomas S. Hubbell, was sheriff. The action of the former in connection with the Springer school bill showed that he was more interested in graft than in public service. Frank W. Clancy, whom I had appointed district attorney in Bernalillo County, reported that grave irregularities were practiced by both of the brothers. Clancy charged that Frank Hubbell, under the Springer school act, had collected three annual salaries from the county in one year and that many of his accounts had been padded. In the case of Thomas Hubbell, it was charged that he was in league with a justice of the peace in Albuquerque who was one of the Hubbell "gang." At that time, the sheriff received large amounts for the feeding of prisoners. In one instance, cited by the district attorney, the sheriff was said to have arrested eight or ten tramps going through Albuquerque en route to California. They were brought before the justice of the peace and found guilty on three different counts. Having been sentenced to six months in the county jail on the first count, they were committed to the custody of the sheriff. According to the charge, the latter then took the tramps to the outskirts of Albuquerque and asked, "If I turn you loose, will you hike for California and never come back here?" Of course they answered "yes." "Then go to it!" said the sheriff. Yet it was reported that these men were carried on the books for six months and that Tom collected for feeding them. Furthermore, it was charged that at the end of six months he made his return to the justice of the peace, and that that obliging official issued another commitment for six months on the second count, and that Tom collected from the county for an additional six months' board for these men.

At the end of this period Clancy claimed that Hubbell rendered another return and, in exchange, received the third committment for six months. The county was said to have paid the sheriff for eighteen months' board for these vagrants, although it was said that they had never eaten one meal in the county jail. It was said that Tom could get away with things like this, because his father-in-law was chairman of the board of county commissioners, and no questions were asked. Thousands and thousands of dollars were said to have been taken from the county in this manner. Still another graft was charged in connection with the law which permitted growers of grapes to sell wine which was made by them from their own grapes without the payment of a license to the territory or the county. It was said that Tom allowed his friends to start saloons in many precincts and that they purchased liquors and sold the same without payment of a license, but that each saloon paid Tom a retainer for the privilege of carrying on this illicit business.

While Clancy had the reputation of being an honest official, the Hubbells declared that he had brought these charges against them for political purposes. The Bernalillo County Republican convention passed a resolution which denounced him as "a submissive and pliant tool" of their political enemies and as a "traitor to his party...."

Besides being strongly entrenched in control of Bernalillo County, Frank Hubbell, for four years, has been chairman of the Republican central committee for the territory. In this position he presumptuously assumed that he represented the whole Republican Party in New Mexico, and took upon himself the place of a dictator. He had insulted Rodey in his first race for Congress, by demanding every dollar subscribed. Rodey did not have a cent to pay railroad fare, meals, or lodging. If it had not been for Jim Duncan and myself, he would have had to drop out of the race. It would have served Hubbell right if Rodey had thrown him over when he ran again, in 1902, since as the nominee of the party for Congress he had the power to appoint the chairman of the central committee. However, Rodey reappointed Hubbell. When the former was reëlected by a very large majority, the latter claimed it as *his* victory, which Mr. Rodey allowed, as he gave in to Hubbell on all occasions.

On September 12th, 1904, the day of the convention, the *New Mexican* said:

> Governor Otero took a determined stand last week and insisted that there must be a change in the chairmanship of the Republican territorial central committee, having become convinced that Frank A. Hubbell was an improper man for the position. In this view the governor is strongly supported by all good and decent Republicans and by the people regardless of party. He took his stand at the right time and in the right place. The party and the people are certainly grateful to him for his timely, steadfast and strenuous attention to the good of the commonwealth.

I had taken my stand a few days before the convention. Rodey had called at my home, accompanied by the Hubbells, Solomon Luna, and William H. Andrews. During the conversation I told Rodey that I could not support him for renomination at the convention, unless he would promise me not to appoint Frank Hubbell as chairman of the central committee. The Irishman was evidently "feeling his oats." The county delegations seemed to favor him strongly, so he showed considerable independence and a large amount of temper. He replied: "Governor, I already have 85 per cent of the delegates named for the convention, and I can tell you, I intend to appoint Mr. Hubbell as my chairman. I can tell you further, I will receive the nomination, the governor to the contrary notwithstanding." "Well," said I, "then you do not want my assistance, and you may let it go at that." All of them left my home in a body, except Mr. Andrews, who remained as the others went to the depot to take the train for Albuquerque. I asked him if he had heard what Rodey had said, and he answered "yes." I then said: "Mr. Andrews, will you accept the nomination for the delegateship?" His answer was: "No, Governor, I cannot, for I am on the Bernalillo delegation and am instructed to vote for Rodey." I said: "I do not ask you to change that vote, but you can give your proxy to Mr. Childers and instruct him to cast your vote for Rodey, that is the honorable thing for you to do. I believe I can secure your nomination at the convention, if you will give your consent to run, otherwise I shall go in myself and accept the nomination. I will give you until 4:00 p. m. to give me your answer."

About 3:00 Mr. Andrews came to my home and said he would accept if nominated. We were to leave the next day for Albuquerque. I telephoned my adjutant-general to have my band ready to go with me on the following day, and to have them wear their artillery suits with helmet and red plume. I telegraphed the Alvarado Hotel for rooms. The next day I started for Albuquerque with my candidate, William H. Andrews; my adjutant-general, W. H. Whiteman; and my private secretary, Miss Olsen. All the details had been made. We reached Albuquerque late Thursday evening, but not too late for the band to commence playing in the front yard of the hotel. Considerable feeling had been aroused by Rodey and Hubbell and their followers in Albuquerque and large crowds began to gather around the band. Just before leaving Santa Fe, I received a telegram from Mr. Rodey, saying: "I understand you are fighting my nomination, I warn you not to do this, for I will be nominated." I answered him by saying: "I suppose you mean your telegram as a threat. If so, it has not the slightest effect on my system." On Friday, I met several Republican politicians, who came to the hotel to offer their assistance. I told them to get busy as I needed their help and would appreciate their efforts. On Friday night, the delegations began to arrive. Luna, Rodey, and the Hubbells were in the hotel lobby meeting each delegation and reminding them that they had been instructed for Rodey, but they were met with a statement from each county: "We want to see the governor first," and they would come to my room and register for Andrews. I was so busy I did not touch my head to a pillow, day or night, neither did I leave my rooms. People called at all hours to see me. The convention was to meet on Monday morning and I personally "stood guard." I never relaxed my vigilance for a moment from Saturday morning until the following Monday night, after the nomination had been made. There was so much wrangling going on that the convention did not come to order until 3:30 p. m., when Mr. Hubbell rapped the convention to order and proceeded to deliver an oratorical classic which would put to shame a Billingsgate fishmonger. Referring to my candidate and myself during the course of his rambling remarks, he said: "We have here at the Alvarado Hotel today a couple of gentlemen. One has got a barrel of money under the bedstead, and the other the offices of the territory."

The convention was then organized by the election of Colonel J. Francisco Chaves, as chairman. Following a report from the committee on rules, Hubbell made another speech vilifying my candidate. Andrews was not as good a public speaker as Rodey; consequently, Hubbell objected to the rule: "And no addresses be made except by members of the convention until after nominations are made." Hubbell shouted, "If Mr. Andrews gets the nomination, it will be through corruption. No decent or self-respecting man will vote for Mr. Andrews. He is not fit to represent the party and not fit to be brought before the convention. He is ashamed to appear and his friends are ashamed to bring him on the platform. They do not dare to show such a man in public." These slanders were interrupted by hissses, but Hubbell continued, nevertheless. He was warmly seconded by his brother, the sheriff, who yelled at individual delegates: "How much did you get for your vote?" At David M. White, of Santa Fe County, he hollered: "You sold your vote for a railroad ticket to Albuquerque." Standing in his seat he waived a handful of greenbacks above his head and shrieked: "One hundred dollars to one that you are all afraid to bring your candidate into this convention."

R. E. Twitchell supported Hubbell, and moved to strike out the objectionable rule. Charles A. Spiess also spoke in favor of the amendment, saying that if it were adopted "the gentlemen who are in favor of W. H. Andrews as delegate will have the privilege of presenting him before the people of the territory of New Mexico and let them judge whether or not he is as able to represent the people of New Mexico as Bernard S. Rodey has been. I do not think he is. I passed sixty days in the legislative council of New Mexico with W. H. Andrews representing Socorro County, and I do not hesitate to say that he was not able to represent that county."

The amendment having been lost, nominations were then in order. Mr. George S. Klock, of Albuquerque, placed Bernard S. Rodey in nomination. Major Llewellyn, of Doña Ana County, placed in nomination William H. Andrews, also of Albuquerque. The roll of delegates was called with the result that Andrews was nominated with 101½ votes, Rodey having received only 65½. The nomination was then made unanimous, and Thomas S. Hubbell pledged Bernalillo County to roll up a majority of 2,500 votes for the candidate.

After the convention the new central committee met and H. O. Bursum was elected chairman. The headquarters, which had previously been in Albuquerque, were moved to Santa Fe.

This is the first time the inside history of the nomination of Andrews has been told. I had given Rodey strong support in his earlier campaigns, helping to elect him in 1900 and again two years later. Doubtless my action in throwing him over in 1904 was not anticipated by most people, and seemed quite sudden, and arbitrary. However, I had good reasons for the part I played in the affair—first of all, my devotion to single statehood. Rodey's willingness to accept joint statehood was selfish. With him it was "any port in a storm." He was anxious to pass a statehood bill. He was shrewd enough to see that Congress would not allow single statehood just then, and he was afraid that his failure to get some action out of that body would stand in the way of his securing a renomination. On the other hand, if New Mexico and Arizona were admitted as one state, he reasoned that the former territory had a much larger vote than the latter and her leaders could, therefore, secure all the offices. Hence he would stand an excellent chance to land a senatorship. However, I believe that he was wrong in his calculations. The people as a whole did not want jointure with Arizona and would have resented such a move.

My other reason for throwing over Mr. Rodey was his determination to stand by the Hubbels. Frank and Thomas Hubbell were able politicians, and Frank had served as chairman of the central committee for four years. However, the cause of good government demanded that he and his brother be ousted from the place which they held in the politics of Bernalillo County and the territory. Of course, it meant a real fight. But even my enemies cannot say that I was ever afraid of a fight.

Rodey, of course, did not know when he was beaten. Two weeks after the convention it was reported on the streets of Albuquerque that he had accepted a nomination for Congress tendered him by the Independent Republicans, or Hubbell faction. The report also had it that the Democratic Party had offered to give him four thousand dollars for campaign expenses, if he would make the race. At first undecided, a month after the convention Rodey made up his mind to run. Of course, the Hubbell-Rodey ticket was doomed to defeat before it really started. The sole object was to defeat the regular Republican ticket and throw the election to the Democrats.

On October 12th, Holm O. Bursum, the new chairman of the central committee, decided to inaugurate the Republican campaign at once. Accordingly, the next day, the campaigners left over the Denver and Rio Grande Railroad for

Tres Piedras, and from there went by carriages to Taos. Our party included William H. Andrews, the candidate; Jose D. Sena, interpreter; A. S. Adams, reporter; Chairman Bursum, and myself. However, Mr. Bursum was called back from Embudo.

Two days later the *New Mexican* gave the following report of our success:

> The popularity of Governor Otero is a great factor in the campaign. The *Albuquerque Journal* does not take too optimistic a view of the political situation in northern New Mexico, when it remarks editorially as follows:
>
> "William H. Andrews, Republican nominee for delegate to Congress and Governor Otero, have been making a vigorous campaign through the northern counties of the territory, and all accounts from that section agree that the progress of the gentlemen from point to point has more resembled a triumphal demonstration than an ordinary electioneering tour."
>
> Governor Miguel A. Otero is especially popular in the northern counties, and his friends, who number pretty nearly all the people of the country, turned out to welcome him, for many miles around, and all assured him of their earnest and enthusiastic support of the Republican nominee.
>
> Wherever Governor Otero and Senator Andrews have gone, so far, they have made a very favorable impression and votes for the Republican territorial, legislative, and county tickets.....

On October 15th, 1904, our reporter, A. S. Adams, wired the *Santa Fe New Mexican* as follows:

> A rousing ratification was given Governor Otero and Senator Andrews by Taos Republicans on Thursday night. The campaign party led by Governor Otero and Senator Andrews met with a reception in this town (Taos) last night, the like of which has never been equaled. Owing to rain and bad roads Taos was not reached until nearly ten o'clock. For miles in the distance sky rockets could be seen as they were set off to apprise the travelers of the welcome in store for them. No sooner had the carriages entered the town limits than a huge bonfire was lighted and the plaza covered with burning red lights. As the carriage raced into the Plaza a cannon was fired giving the governor's salute of seventeen shots.
>
> After an elegant supper, during which time the band played, and no sooner had the last person laid down his fork than the great crowd broke into the hall. Dr. T. P. Martin called the meeting to order, a committee being at once selected to wait on the guests and escort them to the hall. The entrance was spectacular. It was different in many ways to anything seen in Taos before. It was very difficult for any one outside to gain admittance to the hall, because of the great number who were crowded about the doors. Never before have the people of any county in the territory entered so heartily into the spirit of a meeting. Every time the name of Otero was mentioned cheers rang out true and strong. The band constantly played between the speeches and the speakers were repeatedly interrupted by loud cries of approval. Governor Otero made the speech of his life. He thanked the citizens of Taos County for their cordial welcome and it was clearly evident

that the words were not those formal superfluous expressions common in many campaigns. Just as soon as the meeting adjourned we had to take our carriages back to Tres Piedras in order to catch the early morning train for Santa Fe, so as to connect with the evening train for Las Cruces, as we were due there on day after tomorrow at the Doña Ana County Republican convention.

We reached Santa Fe early in the afternoon of October 16th, in plenty of time to catch the evening train for Las Cruces. We arrived in Las Cruces the next morning and were met by Colonel Llewellyn and a delegation of Republican voters and escorted to the hotel for breakfast after which we went to the Llewellyn home for a much needed rest. The Republican county convention was in session. Among the resolutions passed was the following:

> We heartily endorse the national, territorial, and county administrations of public affairs, and point with pride to the splendid financial record of the territory under the able management of our worthy chief executive, Honorable Miguel A. Otero, who has so largely reduced the burden of our public debt, during the seven years in incumbency of his office.

Our party remained in Las Cruces over night and traveled to Santa Fe the following day, arriving early in the evening. On my arrival, I sent for the adjutant-general, and directed him to furnish tents and blankets pertaining to the National Guard of New Mexico, to the San Marcial flood sufferers. I also sent them my personal check for two hundred dollars as a donation to help towards their immediate needs in the way of provisions and food. Senator Andrews also sent the same amount as soon as he was informed of the situation. This prompt and timely action by Mr. Andrews and myself was greatly appreciated by the people living at San Marcial.

On October 19, our campaign party left Santa Fe at 1 p. m. over the Santa Fe Railroad in the private car, "Rocket." In addition to the original members, there were also Judge A. J. Abbott, A. M. Bergere, and David J. Leahy. Quite an extensive tour was planned, including meetings at Mora, Las Vegas, Springer, Raton, Folsom, Clayton, Alamogordo, El Paso, Carlsbad, Roswell, Deming, Silver

City, Lake Valley, Hillsboro, Socorro, Los Lunas, Gallup, Albuquerque, Estancia, and Santa Fe.

While in Las Vegas, just as I was leaving for the court house in the old town, I was handed a telegram from Santa Fe announcing the death of my dear friend, Solicitor General E. L. Bartlett. The train going south was in and I took it for Santa Fe. I remained there until after the funeral, and then took the Mexican Central Railway to Torrance where I caught the campaign party. The campaigners were in splendid humor saying they had had very large and enthusiastic meetings everywhere. We reached Carlsbad on November 1st, and here is what Adams telegraphed his paper:

> At Carlsbad Governor Otero spoke, not devoting his time to politics but to a business discussion of the needs of the valley, which he had not visited for over twenty years. Governor Otero talked as a governor to his constituents and not as a supporter of any candidate. He brought the subject of irrigation to his hearers as a plain business proposition, asking them if Mr. Money, in the event that he was elected, could expect to receive consideration in a Republican House. After the meeting we were driven to the elegant home of Mr. George H. Webster where we enjoyed a splendid lunch and other refreshments. We were then driven to the depot where our private train was in waiting. Besides the "Rocket" we had a parlor car for the band, a baggage car, and an engine and a full crew of trainmen, so we were never delayed. Our private car had a conductor, a chef, and a porter, and the larder was filled with choice meats, chicken, ducks, fruits, vegetables of all kinds as well as the choicest liquors, cigars and cigarettes, in fact everything necessary for a complete outfit "fit for a king." Senator Andrews did not overlook anything. When we arrived at any place where there was to be a meeting, the band would form in front and the party would follow in regular order to the court house or the hall.

After leaving Carlsbad we went to Roswell where a platform had been built in the square for the speakers and hundreds of seats arranged for the large crowd present. We visited the military institute, the club house, and the Hagerman orchard. Mr. Hagerman sent two barrels of fine apples and a half dozen fat turkeys to our car. We had an elegant meeting at Roswell, notwithstanding the fact that Chaves County was the banner Democratic county of the territory and was frequently called "Little Texas."

We next went to Deming, Silver City, Lake Valley, and

Hillsboro. In all of these places we had large crowds. We then went to Socorro, where practically the whole town turned out. The court room, where the meeting was held, had been decorated with beautiful flowers and I was presented with a handsome bouquet of roses by a committee of ladies. The meeting was a great success and the local speakers promised to give Senator Andrews a large majority, which they did. Our next stop was at Los Lunas, county seat of Valencia County, the strongest Republican county in New Mexico. Here Mr. Money only received six votes while Andrews received 1,811 and Rodey 31.

We then went west to Gallup and back to Albuquerque, the home of both Andrews and Rodey. The Hubbels had boasted that Bernalillo County would give Andrews a majority of 2,500. The result, however, was very different. Rodey received a plurality of 760 in the county, while Andrews received only 717 votes. However, we had expected treachery on the part of the Hubbels, so were not disappointed in the result. From Albuquerque we went to Estancia, Torrance County, where we held a big meeting. Andrews carried this county by a plurality of 496. Our next stop was at Santa Fe where we closed our campaign with a tremendous meeting. Thomas B. Catron, R. L. Baca, Marcos Castillo, and Celso Lopez all ran on the Democratic ticket and worked hard against Andrews. While they carried the county ticket by about five hundred majority, Andrews only lost by 41. It was perfectly correct for Catron and his following to fuse with the Democrats but for the administration forces to do so was treason, according to Catron's ideas. On election day, I went over to Las Vegas to cast my vote, and returned to Santa Fe that same night.

A few days before the election I predicted that Andrews would have a plurality of 5,200. I missed it for his plurality was only 5,180. When the territorial board had canvassed the vote, it made the following report:

William H. Andrews, Republican 22,305
G. P. Money, Democrat 17,125
B. S. Rodey, Independent-Republican 3,419

However, I did not have to wait for the official figures. The night of the election, the Western Union people kept a messenger running from their office to my home, bringing the reports from the different counties; long before midnight I became convinced that my candidate had been elected by a good plurality.

On November 12, the citizens of Santa Fe arranged a delightful reception and banquet in honor of the delegate-elect and myself for the great victory at the polls which had thoroughly vindicated the territorial administration and given Mr. Andrews such a large majority. It was a regular jollification and everyone seemed happy. Many appropriate toasts were drunk to both Andrews and myself.

A few days after the territorial board had made the official canvass of the vote. Senator Andrews asked that I appoint him a colonel on my staff, which I did. He immediately wired for uniforms. He was a fine looking officer and took an interest in his duties as an aide-de-camp. He was present on all occasions when called for duty.

Naturally my action in throwing over Rodey and causing Andrews to be nominated and elected was misrepresented in Washington. The following telegram, which tells its own story, was sent from Washington to my office in Santa Fe, from where it was forwarded to me in New York:

> Governor Otero has an anonymous enemy in Washington who takes every opportunity that presents itself to attack him. During the past week every senator and representative in Congress has received a printed circular, entitled *The Deep Damnation of Rodey's Taking-Off,* without signature or anything to indicate the author. This cowardly and anonymous attack is doing statehood a great deal of harm, and is making friends for Governor Otero. Senators and congressmen do not like cowards and are too often troubled by similar annoyances and anonymous attacks upon themselves to pay any attention to such dirty truck. All these charges were fully examined by the Senate committee on territories some time ago and found to be absolutely untrue and false. Upon a thorough and reliable investigation, it was found to be the work of Mr. and Mrs. L. Bradford Prince, Thomas B. Catron, Eugene A. Fiske, Fritz Muller, William Berger, A. C. Voorhees, J. F. Man-

ning, Quinby Vance, George H. Wallace, T. W. Collier, Preacher Madden, Preacher Moore, and Preacher Eustes, all sworn enemies of the governor, and whose influence is absolutely worthless.

Fortunately for me, I had foreseen that official Washington might be interested in what happened at our territorial convention. Accordingly, at my request, the secretary of the interior had sent his private secretary to New Mexico to attend the convention. This gentleman, Mr. W. Scott Smith, and his daughter, Miss Edna, were our guests at the executive mansion and accompanied me to Albuquerque. They attended the convention regularly and returned to Santa Fe with me. They were disgusted with the Hubbell-Rodey combination and congratulated me on the manner in which I had defeated them. Smith made his report to his chief strongly in my favor.

William H. Andrews was the last delegate to represent New Mexico in Congress. He was reëlected three times and was still serving in that capacity when President Taft signed the proclamation which made the territory a state. My selection of him for the post was wholly justified by his achievements in Congress, and particularly by the service which he rendered in getting an enabling act passed. Even the historians have vindicated me. As a friend of Rodey and a member of the convention of 1904, Ralph Emerson Twitchell was anything but an impartial on-looker at the time. He was very bitter against Andrews and heaped abuse on all who did not agree with him. He left the hall without voting, and his account of this convention in *The Leading Facts of New Mexican History* is unjust, unfair, and absolutely false. Yet, he admitted that my candidate proved an excellent man for the place. He says in the book just referred to, volume II, page 545: "Laboring day and night for his constituents, Mr. Andrews, in his capacity as delegate, has no superior in the Congress of the United States."

As for the Hubbells, I shall conclude the story of their "ouster" in the next chapter.

Chapter XVII

I REMOVE THE HUBBELLS

MANY PEOPLE FELT that I took a much needed step at the territorial Republican convention in Albuquerque, in September, 1904, when I forced Frank Hubbell out of the position which he had held for four years as chairman of the Republican central committee. However, Hubbell was still treasurer of Bernalillo County, his brother, Thomas, was sheriff, and their henchman, Eslavio Vigil, was county superintendent of public schools. Between the three, they had a strong grip on one of the most important counties in the territory, and it was predicted that graft and corruption would flourish as long as they held these offices.

Frank W. Clancy, the district attorney for the second judicial district, was a fearless official who had fought the Hubbells for years. Public opinion was becoming aroused, and this strengthened him in the determination to redeem Bernalillo County from the pernicious influences which dominated it. He filed charges in my office against the three men, on April 15, 1905. On reading them over, I decided to give the accused officials a fair hearing. I had no personal feelings in the matter, but felt that such charges called for a thorough investigation.

The accused, at first, did not regard their predicament as serious. They knew that there were no funds in the territorial treasury which could be used to bring witnesses to Santa Fe for an investigation of their conduct. I was well acquainted with this point myself, but quickly got over the difficulty by ordering that the hearings be held in Albuquerque at the Alvarado Hotel.

It took a good deal of time before the cases against the three men were finally settled. More specific charges were filed on June 26 and August 16, and briefs for the defense were filed by the attorneys for the accused. I made several trips to Albuquerque and spent some days there, presiding over the hearings in person. The proceedings were judicial in character, and a full record was kept by my private secretary. The territory was represented by Attorney General George W. Prichard and District Attorney Clancy.

The charges came under the heading of malfeasance and misfeance in office, non-performance of duty, and violation of certain sections of the compiled laws and of the session laws of the territory. The general charge was that they had appropriated public funds of the county to which they were not lawfully entitled, and various other violations of the statutes. The specific charges in each case may be summarized as follows:

Frank A. Hubbell, treasurer and ex-officio collector for Bernalillo County, was charged with having used $12,000, collected to pay the current expenses for the year 1904, to pay such expenses for 1903, in violation of the law; that he paid out $354.79 on warrants drawn by the county superintendent of schools for expenses that could be incurred only by the directors of the school district; that he paid out $215 for expenses of the county institute of 1903, although there was only $100 in the county institute fund. That he retained and refused to distribute to the proper funds $3,192.08 received for license moneys; that, while he was superintendent of public schools of Bernalillo County, he drew $2,025 for visiting the public schools, charging for 415 days of visits when only 225 days of visits were possible. In other words, he was charged with having collected for three full years in one.

There were thirteen charges against Thomas S. Hubbell, sheriff of Bernalillo County. The first ten charges were that he made the county pay for eighteen months of board at the rate of 75c per day for the keep of ten prisoners after they had been discharged from the jail. He was also charged with permitting three specified individuals to retail liquor without a license.

The charges against Eslavio Vigil, county superintendent of public schools for Bernalillo County, were similar in character. He was charged with having collected for more days of school visits than he could possibly have made, with having retained fees received from teachers attending the county institute, and with having drawn upon the county treasurer for the expenses of the county institute for more than the fund allowed. It was also charged that he falsely certified to the territorial superintendent of public instruction that a certain school had been held for seven months and $400 paid to the teachers, while actually the school had been held for only three months and $150 paid the teachers, and that he made similar false statements in regard to two other schools.

As some of the ten tramps for which he was said to have collected board from the county had departed for California or parts unknown, a few of the first ten charges against Thomas Hubbell could not be proven. With this exception, all of the charges against the three officials were established. Accordingly, on August 31, I issued three executive orders, removing them from office. At the same time I made the following appointments to fill the vacancies which had been created: Justo R. Armijo, to be treasurer of Bernalillo County; Perfecto Armijo, to be sheriff; and Andrew B. Stroup, to be superintendent of public schools.

The character of the men I chose to supplant the ousted officials is shown by the following press comment:

> The new appointees are well known throughout central New Mexico. Justo R. Armijo is a native of Bernalillo County, a man of strict business integrity and of high business attainments and of much experience in public affairs; he has been probate judge and has held several other offices of honor and trust in the county government. He also served one term as postmaster of the city of Albuquerque. Wherever placed he has performed the duties of the office satisfactorily and well. Perfecto Armijo is a native of Bernalillo County and there is no better known man in the county. He has served several terms by election to the office of sheriff. He is fearless and in every way qualified to fill the office with great credit. Andrew B. Stroup has been a citizen of Albuquerque for several years, is a teacher by profession, and has served as superintendent of the public schools of Albuquerque, giving satisfaction in the position.

My Nine Years as Governor 243

The *New Mexican,* for September 1, gave a thorough review of the case, in which it said:

Governor Otero saw his duty and did it. "The mills of the gods grind slowly but they grind exceedingly small." The official and political history of Bernalillo County for some years past is an open book to the citizens of New Mexico who care to look. It is not necessary to iterate and reiterate the many charges of official misconduct which from time to time have been made against certain officials of Bernalillo County who held office for many years and who upon the face of the returns have been elected by very heavy majorities to the offices which they have held for years.

After summarizing the charges against the three officials and the outcome of the cases, the *New Mexican* continued as follows:

That Governor Otero acted within the powers of his office and strictly in accordance with the letter and spirit of the law .... is fully conceded by all who understand the situation, lawyer and layman. The governor acted as he should have done and his action will meet the approval of all law abiding and patriotic citizens as soon as it is known throughout the Sunshine Territory.

Governor Otero acted under the law, within the law, and for the best interests of the people; his action will be conducive to bringing about better and more efficient government in counties and a more honest and capable financial administration to them. It will teach county officials no matter how many votes they have behind them, and no matter how strong they think themselves politically, that they are not beyond the law and that they should be the first citizens scrupulously to obey the statutes and perform the duties of their offices within the spirit and the letter of the law.

The governor's action means that a new day has dawned upon county administrations and that officials must and shall do their duty properly and honestly hereafter or they will be removed from office, if proper complaint is proven. This is the dictum, and it had better be recognized throughout the Sunshine Territory by every official, high or low.

The governor did his duty and for that the people will applaud and commend him. That this performance of the duty of the executive will be of the greatest benefit to the cause of good government and to the well being of the people will be acknowledged by all those who understand New Mexico conditions and will also improve New Mexico's good reputation and fair name throughout the land.

Judgment has been pronounced and it is universally believed that it is a just judgment. Much and great pressure was brought to bear upon the governor to be lenient in the cases, and not to carry out the provisions of the law and to let the accused officials down easily.

Upon becoming satisfied that the charges were proven and that the accused were guilty as charged, the governor brushed all other considerations aside and pronounced the verdict as announced yesterday. He did his full duty. *"He seen a duty, a dead sure thing, and went for it there and then!"*

Governor Otero is in receipt of numerous telegrams of congratulations from all parts of the territory upon his action in removing Frank A. Hubbell, Thomas S. Hubbell, and Eslavio Vigil from their offices in Bernalillo County.

One prominent financier of the Southwest concludes his telegram with the quotation, "Righteousness exalteth the nation."

Naturally, my action caused considerable excitement in Albuquerque. It was rumored that the three ousted officials would barricade themselves in their offices and attempt to retain possession of them by force, that the national guard would be called out, and that bloodshed would result. However, the court recognized the new commissions which I had issued, and the new officials were duly installed in office.

This, of course, was not accomplished without some unpleasant incidents. Thomas S. Hubbell proved a hard man to deal with. However, on September 29, the district court committed him to jail, and Sheriff Perfecto Armijo executed the order. He found the ex-sheriff in his former office behind the counter with the gate locked. Armijo jumped over the counter and served the court order. Taking Hubbell by the arm, he then marched him to the gate and kicked it open. He then marched through the hallway and over to the county jail, pushing his prisoner in front of him. Finding the jail locked, he broke down the door and took possession, locking Hubbell up in one of the cells.

On October 19, Judge Ira A. Abbott denied the petition of counsel for Frank Hubbell, asking for an injunction against Justo R. Armijo to restrain him from taking possession of the office of the county treasurer in the court house. The petition asked further that Frank Hubbell be allowed to remove certain records from the office as personal property. By the court order, Armijo was given full possession of the office, and made free to enter the vault. Later, Armijo went to the office of the *Bandera Americana,* a weekly paper published in Albuquerque and belonging to Frank Hubbell. He met the latter there and asked him for the keys to the vault. Hot words were exchanged, after which the two men went for each other in pugilistic style. However, they were separated by Nestor Montoya, the editor of the paper. Shortly afterwards, J. J. Sheridan, Hubbell's former deputy, appeared at the court house and delivered the keys to Armijo.

On September 30, Frank Hubbell and Eslavio Vigil were both indicted by the grand jury and each gave bond for $1,000. None of the three men, however, was given any further punishment after having been ousted from his position. In December, Thomas Hubbell filed charges against Frank Clancy, but after reading them I promptly dismissed them.

The Hubbells were probably the most powerful officials I fired during my administration, but they were, by no means, the only ones. I have already described how I disposed of several territorial officials whom I had inherited from the preceding administration. Charges against this or that man were continuously being filed in my office. I disposed of them on their merits, firing some and retaining others. During my first year in office, I found that in many of the counties the officials were not giving proper attention to their duties. Hence, I decided to take severe measures to compel the county commissioners and the collectors to do their duty in the matter of tax collections. I realized that this would not be popular, but felt that something had to be done. Naturally, in some cases, my actions were misinterpreted by the press. Thus, in the spring of 1898, the press in northeastern New Mexico asserted that I had asked for the resignation of all the county commissioners in Union County. I had taken no such action, but I was resolved to take prompt action if they failed to do their duty. Later, charges were filed against one of these commissioners, Dolores Romero. After a hearing in my office, on September 6, I decided, without hesitation, in favor of the defendant, as none of the charges were proven. The case was dismissed. In commenting on this case, the territorial press said:

Governor Otero can be relied upon to act without fear or favor and with deliberation, justice, and backbone in any cases of charges against county officials of malfeasance, misfeasance, or corruption in office. Such charges have been made in one or two counties, and they will receive proper attention.

Three months before this, a delegation from Raton, Colfax County, came to my office and stated that J. F. Ruffner, who had been elected as county commissioner for their county in 1896, had failed to furnish a bond, as required by law. When I was satisfied that this was a fact, and that his failure to qualify left the vacancy to be filled by me, I appointed Mr. Joseph B. Schroeder, of Raton. Some of the rabid Democrats of Raton resented my action in declaring that a vacancy existed, and sent the following telegram to the Denver *Rocky Mountain News:*

> Raton, New Mexico, June 6th, 1898. It is believed here that the governor has taken this action for no other reason than that Ruffner is a Democrat. In several cases, Governor Otero has done this same thing, and the people are getting tired of having their elective officials removed by the President's appointee.
>
> The people will resist this assumption of authority to the bitter end and will give the governor to understand that he is not yet czar of New Mexico.

Of course, well informed citizens realized that there was utter disregard for legal requirements in the counties, and that the territory needed a chief executive who would remedy this situation, and enforce the law without fear or favor. While Mr. Ruffner had been duly elected, he had not furnished bond, even after the matter had been called to his attention. Consequently, when the matter had been presented to me by the district attorney, my plain duty impelled me to take the course I did.

Besides, I found that my Democratic predecessor, Governor William T. Thornton, had done exactly the same things three years before. He had removed two Republican county commissioners in Doña Ana County on the charge that they had not furnished the bond required by law, and, therefore, were not legally qualified. And he filled the vacancies by appointing two Democrats. Both elective and appointive officials were removed during the Democratic administration preceding my own, not because the law authorized such removals, but simply because *might* was

My Nine Years as Governor

right. I, however, was very careful to keep within the law in making any removals.

Occasionally, I was forced to take action, although very reluctant to do so. As an illustration of this, I shall give the case of Mr. Thomas J. Bull, of Mesilla, a member of the board of regents of the Agricultural College. On account of charges filed against him, I was forced, in February, 1898, to cite him to appear before me to answer the same. This was very disagreeable to me, as he was a warm personal friend of my father, and I had known him since childhood. In order to put him to as little inconvenience as possible, I went down to Las Cruces with Mr. Joshua S. Raynolds, a close friend of another member of the board of regents. Here I gave Mr. Bull an opportunity to tell me all the facts. However, instead of appreciating what I was trying to do in his behalf, he became very arrogant and declined to answer even a simple question. After calling several witnesses, some of whom were friends of his, and after a thorough hearing, I suggested to my father's friend that he resign. At this he became white with rage, saying: "I'll be damned if I do! Now you have my answer, go to it!" The meeting was adjourned at once. I promised to render my decision when I reached Santa Fe, as I still hoped that the old gentleman would change his mind, after thinking the matter over quietly. However, I had no such luck. Accordingly, on March 8, I removed him and appointed another old friend, Don Jacinto Armijo, to fill the vacancy. The *New Mexican* commented upon the case as follows:

> Governor Otero will do his duty under the law, and in a direction calculated to benefit the best interests of the territory. Howls and insinuations from Democratic papers and politicians who desire to keep corrupt or dishonest officials in office will affect him not. Governor Otero is not a very large man physically, but corrupt officials will find out in due course of time that he has a good sound, straight, big backbone. This is not a Democratic administration; not by a good deal.

Occasionally, I was forced to make a removal on account of the idiosyncrasies of individuals. Thus, when the county seat for Colfax County was removed from Springer to Raton, the county clerk, Mr. Manuel M. Salazar, refused to allow the records of his office to be moved. As much as I disliked to do it, I was compelled to remove him. I appointed Mr. A. L. Hobbs, of Raton, to fill the vacancy.

When I removed an official or a member of a board, he stayed removed. Thus, on February 3, 1902, I removed L. Bradford Prince from the board of the College of Agriculture and Mechanics Arts and appointed Rev. W. A. Cooper, of Santa Fe, in his place. Mr. Prince filed an application with Solicitor-General E. L. Bartlett, asking that he be granted a writ of *quo warranto* to test the legality of Mr. Cooper's appointment. The solicitor-general promptly denied the request, which, of course, was what I wanted him to do.

Chapter XVIII

SOCIAL LIFE IN OLD SANTA FE

NINE YEARS of official life naturally included a good many social functions, some of which I shall attempt to recall in this chapter. I shall include formal dinners and receptions, as well as more exclusive affairs. Some of these I shall describe rather fully, while giving only a passing mention to others, and omitting some entirely. However, I hope that the reader will get some idea of the gay social life of the "ancient city" in the nineties and the early nineteen hundreds.

One of the first social affairs, after we had moved from Las Vegas to make our home in Santa Fe, was a dance which Mrs. Otero gave, on October 20, 1897, at the Palace Hotel. This was in honor of Miss Mary LaRue, of Las Vegas, who was visiting us for a few days. Miss LaRue will be mentioned often in this chapter, since she was almost like one of the family. We had known her since her birth, and she had been a bridesmaid at our wedding. She was beautiful and one of the kindest and most lovable girls I have ever met.

On October 30, Mrs. Otero gave the most brilliant receptions of the season to her lady friends in Santa Fe, many ladies coming from Albuquerque, Las Vegas, and other points in the territory. The beautiful floral decorations were a perfect dream, and the refreshments from Denver could not have been more elegant and choice. The ladies attending the reception pronounced it as being the best ever seen in Santa Fe.

On February 18, 1898, Mrs. Otero and I gave a reception to Chief Justice William J. Mills and his wife. Judge Mills and his family arrived in Santa Fe only a few days before this, and were our guests at the executive mansion. The judge qualified as chief justice on the 16th. The *New*

Mexican pronounced the reception "One of the most elegant social funtions ever given in the territory and at its capital."

In April, we had as our house guests for some weeks, Misses Mary LaRue, Beatrice Atkins, Ruth and Kate Raynolds, all of whom were from Las Vegas. On the last night of the month the young men of Santa Fe gave a grand ball at the Palace Hotel in honor of our guests. The event was one of the most enjoyable social functions of the season.

In June, Honorable and Mrs. William B. Childers, of Albuquerque, were house guests at the executive mansion for a week. During their stay Mrs. Otero gave a luncheon in honor of Mrs. Childers. The decorations were in yellow, and the affair was pronounced one of the most exquisite ever given in Santa Fe.

On June 17, Mrs. Otero and I entertained the judges of the United States land court at dinner. The decorations were lavendar and cerise. The guests present were Chief Justice Joseph R. Reed, Associate Justice Wilbur F. Stone, Associate Justice Thomas C. Fuller, Associate Justice W. M. Murray, Associate Justice and Mrs. Henry C. Sluss, and Honorable and Mrs. William B. Childers.

On January 27, 1899, Mrs. Otero and I gave a reception at the executive mansion to the members of the legislative assembly. This brilliant social affair lasted from 8 to 11 p. m. More than two hundred guests were present. The members of my staff were all there, wearing their full-dress uniforms for the first time. The adjutant general stood at the head of the line and introduced the guests as they arrived. Later he told a reporter: "The stream of visitors seemed incessant and from the heartiness of the congratulations offered it was plain to be seen that the present executive is justly considered one of the best governors the territory of New Mexico ever had."

After the line had broken, many of our close friends remained until the "wee small hours." The brass band on my staff was in attendance and the well selected program was greatly enjoyed by all.

The very day that the invitations were issued to this affair, Mrs. Otero was presented with one of the handsomest and most valuable vases ever brought to this country. The presentation was made by Mr. J. J. Leeson, of Socorro County, the representative for New Mexico at the Omaha exposition. The vase was quite large and was made of Bohemian glass inlaid with solid gold and silver. Naturally this gift was on display at the reception and greatly admired.

Just about this time, Mr. and Mrs. Alfred M. Bergere gave a delightful dinner party in honor of Mrs. Otero and myself. The other guests were former Governor L. Bradford Prince and Mrs. Prince, Captain and Mrs. Maximiliano Luna, Hon. Thomas B. Catron, and Mrs. Charles A. Spiess.

In August, the very day after our return to Santa Fe from a fishing trip on the Pecos, our dear friends, Mr. and Mrs. Jacob Gross, of St. Louis, Missouri, arrived for a visit. They remained with us for ten days, during which time we had something very much like a real family reunion. "Jake" Gross, as we called him, had been a close associate of the Otero family since we lived in Leavenworth, Kansas, in 1864. "Sister Carrie," his wife, was the daughter of dear old Doctor Moses Linton, who had been our physician when my brother, Page, and I attended St. Louis University, in 1869. We tried hard to keep them for at least another week, but the large family of growing children were calling loudly for them to return home, and they felt they must obey the summons. Mrs. Otero, Miguel, Junior, and I went with them as far as Las Vegas. The Grosses went on their way home, while we stopped in Las Vegas for a little visit with friends. After a couple of very pleasant days we returned to Santa Fe.

Two days after our return home, Mrs. Otero gave the principal and most elaborate social function of the year at the executive mansion, to the ladies of Santa Fe. It was an afternoon reception and tea. The flowers were beautiful and contrasted with the lovely gowns worn by the ladies, and the refreshments from Denver were greatly enjoyed. Music by an Italian quartette, harp, two violins, and a mandolin, was beautiful and added much to the occasion.

On August 30, the executive mansion was the scene of much merriment among the younger set, occasioned by a birthday party for my son, Miguel. Games were played and delicious refreshments were served.

On the day after Miguel's party, Mrs. Otero and I entertained Judges Murray, Fuller, and Sluss of the United States court of private land claims, Judge Emmett, Doctor and Mrs. Cones, Hon. William B. Childers, Land Commissioner A. A. Keen, Mrs. R. J. Palen, and Mrs. Hite.

One of the most interesting and pleasing incidents which happened while I was governor of the territory occurred on October 4th, 1899, when the investiture of the sacred Pallium was conferred on Archbishop Peter Bourgade at St. Francis Cathedral in Santa Fe.

The investiture of the sacred Pallium upon Archbishop Peter Bourgade took place at the Cathedral, and at the banquet served by the Christian Brothers at St. Michael's college to a great number of invited guests; Father Phillips of Denver, Colorado, was toastmaster. When the festal occasion had reached the stage for toasts, I, as representative of the territory of New Mexico, was called upon and spoke as follows:

> Your Grace, and gentlemen: I desire to congratulate you upon this most auspicious occasion, when, for the fourth time in the history of this ancient city, the solemn and impressive ceremony of investiture of the sacred Pallium has been witnessed.
> As chief executive of this territory, charged by law and my oath of office with the execution of its laws and the acts of the Congress of the United States applicable to it, I am glad to greet the head of that great church which for so many years has been the support and stay of the law throughout the largest diocese in the United States, without whose aid and assistance the administration and execution of the laws in the vast domain included in New Mexico and Arizona would have been most difficult, if not impossible.
> While under our constitution and system of government church and

state must always be distinct and separate, yet in the practical administration of affairs we find that each relies upon the other.

It was your church, most reverend Sir, that first brought Christianity to the people of this land, and dotted the western side of the continent with missions, convents, schools, and churches from the bay of San Francisco to the highest part of the Rocky Mountains. To it and its servants the people owed not only their religious knowledge and instruction, but were indebted for most of their material progress and comforts in earlier years. The priests of your church introduced sheep and the vine, pears, apples and other fruits which were unknown here before, and which have become so great a factor in the material advancement of this western country, until the fame of California, Arizona, and New Mexico fruits and grapes has become almost world wide, and the "Mission" grape of the early fathers is acknowledged as the best of all its kindred; while sheep and their products in New Mexico bring us more revenue than all our other resources combined.

For all of this, and much more, our people are indebted to your church; and it is most appropriate that the ceremony of today should have occurred upon the very spot where, two hundred years ago, De Vargas reconquered the City of the Holy Faith, from the savage Indians, and caused the solemn services of your church to be executed in thanksgiving and praise to God for his victory, and where he made the vow in its commemoration which is faithfully observed until this day in the procession to San Rosario.

I congratulate your Grace upon assuming the Pallium. I congratulate our people upon having a prelate who has lived among them so long, and knows so well their needs and wishes. And I congratulate myself and the government I represent in having, in the exalted position which you occupy, so able, distinguished, and patriotic an American citizen as yourself.

The speech was greeted with loud applause.

That evening Mrs. Otero and I entertained Archbishop Bourgade and Bishop Matz at a dinner at the executive mansion. The decorations were crimson and pink and were greatly admired by the guests. In addition to Archbishop Bourgade and Bishop Matz, Ex-Governor Prince, Solicitor-General Bartlett, Judge McFie, Judge Emmett, Vicar-General Fourchegu, Father Gerard, Father Phillips and Mrs. A. M. Bergere were guests. After the dinner we all went to my offices in the Old Palace as Bishop Matz and Father Phillips were anxious to see the Ben Hur room and my offices.

During the first week in January, 1900, Chief Justice Mills was a guest at the executive mansion. On the sixth we attended the annual meeting and banquet of the territorial bar association, which was a brilliant affair. Honorable H. D. Estabrook, of Chicago, was the orator of the day. The banquet was held in the dining room of the Palace Hotel, which had been superbly decorated under the artistic management of District Clerk A. M. Bergere. Colonel R. E. Twitchell, president of the bar association, was the toastmaster. The following toasts were given: The Judiciary, Chief Justice William J. Mills; The Territory, Governor Miguel A. Otero; The Bar, Honorable Thomas B. Catron; The Bar and the People, Honorable Frank Springer; The Last of the Circuits, Honorable L. Bradford Prince; The Trial Court, Honorable R. P. Barnes.

The meeting was a great success and lasted until very late. Many good stories were told and enjoyed by every one present.

On January 13, I received a telegram from Governor Murphy, of Arizona, saying that he would be on a southbound train passing Lamy Junction that afternoon. Accordingly, Chief Justice Mills, Associate Justices Frank W. Parker, and J. W. Crumpacker, and I met him at Lamy, and accompanied him on his journey as far as Albuquerque. At Lamy, Murphy introduced us all to two members of the staff of the *Chicago Journal* who were on their way to Santa Fe. On the following day I saw these young women at the Palace Hotel, and Mrs. Otero entertained them at lunch. In the afternoon we drove them around the capitol building, the penitentiary, and the United States Indian School. They seemed delighted with their visit and the courtesies shown them. On the following evening, Honorable L. Bradford Prince and Mrs. Prince entertained them at a buffet dinner and card party. After breakfast the next morning I saw Prince "hot hoofing" it to the Palace Hotel with the evident intent of being the first Romeo on the scene. He was a past master in this particular art and was never known to side track an opportunity. He was "Johnny on the spot." His well-trained nostrils had scented something the evening before, and he was just following it up, but alas, he was too late. Both women were quite pretty, and had attracted the attention of two young mining men from New Jersey who were also stopping at the same hotel. These young men were never known to overlook a bet. They were interested in the Fraser copper mine near Taos, and were heading for the mine that very morning. Accordingly, the two women gave up their plans to go on to Arizona, and accepted the invitation of the young men to accompany them to Taos instead. We all called to say good-bye just as the ladies were taking the hack for the depot. However, as it turned out, they went to the Denver and Rio Grande railroad station, and together with the two jolly miners left for Tres Piedras where they were all driven to the mine in a light spring wagon.

About ten days later, I was both surprised and shocked on seeing the four miners (?) enter Conway's restaurant for breakfast. That same afternoon they all left for Albuquerque and registered at the Highland Hotel. Unfortunately for him, a prominent gentleman happened to be stopping there just then. He was invited to a cocktail party in their rooms one evening and the hilarious drunks made the night hideous. The next morning they were all ordered to leave the hotel, including the said gentleman. This was the beginning of the trouble which finally brought about his removal from office. I always believed that he was guiltless of any wrong doing, but his enemies based their charges on immorality and he was doomed, although Elihu Root and I did all in our power to help him.

Some weeks later I received a letter from Chicago from the husband of one of the young women. He made certain inquiries regarding his wife, which, however, I declined to answer. Nevertheless, I learned later, through the press, that two divorces had been granted in Chicago. I wrote Governor Murphy fully about the whole exciting affair, and told him never to do it again.

On February 2, Mrs. Otero gave an elaborate luncheon at the executive mansion in honor of Mrs. Max Frost, a recent bride.[1] The green and white decorations were very artistic and a bouquet of white carnations graced the center of the beautifully appointed table. At each place a corsage bouquet of bride's roses was placed. The viands served were delicious. The guests remained after luncheon in agreeable social intercourse for several hours. The following were the guests: Mrs. Frost, Mrs. Prince, Mrs. Palen, Mrs. Bergere, Mrs. Day, Mrs. Newberry, Mrs. Turner, Mrs. Arthur Seligman, Mrs. Gulliford, and Miss Baker.

In September, Miss Jeanette LaRue, of Las Vegas, arrived for a visit at the executive mansion to remain for a month or six weeks. The LaRue family, while not related to the Oteros, is very close indeed. Miss Jeanette was a very charming young woman, and enjoyed her visit so much that she returned again the following April.

Mr. James Wallace Raynolds became territorial secretary of New Mexico in the spring of 1901. Mr. Raynolds was a personal friend of mine. After his promotion, he and his charming wife began to play a more prominent part in the social life of Santa Fe. The *New Mexican* for February 12, 1902, describes an affair in their honor:

> The reception of last Tuesday evening of this week by Governor and Mrs. Otero in honor of Territorial Secretary and Mrs. Raynolds was, without a doubt, the most brilliant of the many functions they have given in their five years' residence in this ancient capital. The executive mansion on Washington Street was ablaze in glory of electric lights and from 9 o'clock in the evening until after midnight, a steady and large stream of guests entered, representing the beauty, the grace, the wit, and the gallantry of Santa Fe society.
>
> The interior of the mansion was a vision of beauty. The guests entered by way of the hall reception room, rich and quaint with its Indian effects and decorations. The drawing room to the left, where the receiving party stood, was an artist's dream in green and white. Festoons and swaying portieres of smilax formed a vivid background for the masses of white carnations used. In an adjoining room there was dancing all evening to the enlivening strains of the First Regiment cavalry band, which was stationed at the top of the stairway in the hall of the second floor.

---

[1] After the death of her first husband, Mrs. Frost became the second wife of Governor Otero. They were married October 1, 1913. She is still living.

Delicious punch was served in the library by the young ladies, the room being a profusion of smilax and pink carnations. Portieres of smilax were on every side, a dainty and unique fancy. The dining-room, where an inviting collation was served, was also profusely decorated with the delicate smilax, in conjunction with subdued lights, from many pink shaded candles, but here the flowers used were bride's maid roses. In the center of the beautifully appointed table was an immense cluster of these lovely blossoms, while the color scheme was further carried out by four pink tapers which were surrounded by broad shades of pink silk, each made to represent a rose.

Mrs. Otero was a vivacious and charming hostess, who looked lovely in an all-white costume of silk and chiffon veiled in Cluny lace and carrying American beauty roses. Her gown was a master creation of a skilled modiste. Mrs. Raynolds looked handsome and queenly in an exquisite gown of pink chiffon over pink silk trimmed with roses of the same tint and carrying a bouquet of violets. Those who assisted in receiving were Mrs. McMillan in white lace, Mrs. Frost in blue, Mrs. Palen in gray crepe, Mrs. Hughes in black, Mrs. Keen in rose-colored crepe de chine, Miss LaRue in white organdie, Miss Palen in white net over satin, Miss Nina Otero in cream-colored crepe de chine, Miss Hurt in white chiffon and Miss Massie in gray, all beautifully gowned and as handsome and bright a receiving party as ever gathered at a social function in Santa Fe.

The reception marks a bright page in the social history of Santa Fe, rich in its memories of gala events. It will be long remembered as the gayest, the most enjoyable, the most brilliant society affair of the season which was closed by Lent the day following.

> The lights, the beauty and blossoms
> And from eyes in fair faces the gleam,
> The music, the laughter and radiance,
> They came and went like a dream.
> A dream of the fragrance of roses,
> A dream of a sweet low refrain,
> A dream of love's softest whisperings,
> But a dream that will not come again.

In 1902, Mrs. Otero and I had quite a few house guests from time to time, and there were numerous luncheons, dinners, and card parties in their honor. My sister, Mrs. Harry J. O'Bryan, of Denver, came in May, accompanied by her husband and their two children, Aileen and DuRoss. Miss Julia Freeman, of Ohio, visited us for a couple of months in the summer. She was greatly missed after her departure, as every one was in love with Julia. Mr. and Mrs. William B. Childers were with us for a week in September. Our dear friend, Miss Mary LaRue, also visited us about the same time.

Early in January, 1903, Miss LaRue came back for

another visit and remained with us during the session of the legislative assembly. During the following June she was married to Mr. Stephen B. Davis, Jr. Mrs. Otero and I went to Las Vegas for the happy event, regretting however, that it would render her visits to us less frequent.

On January 31, Mrs. Otero and I gave a dinner at the executive mansion in honor of the members of the council. The guests were Territorial Secretary Raynolds, Hon. Solomon Luna, Land Commissioner A. A. Keen, Colonel J. Francisco Chaves, James S. Duncan, Venceslao Jaramillo, Amado Chaves, George F. Albright, Thomas Hughes, Malaquias Martinez, W. A. Hawkins, and Albert B. Fall.

On February 6, we gave a public reception in honor of the members of the thirty-fifth legislative assembly. The event was indeed a superb social function and one of the most delightful that was ever held at the executive mansion. Those in the receiving line or assisting were: Secretary and Mrs. J. W. Raynolds, Judge and Mrs. J. R. McFie, Mrs. Jefferson Raynolds, Mrs. J. A. LaRue, Mrs. Fred H. Pierce, Mrs. E. D Raynolds, Miss LaRue, Miss Jane LaRue, Miss Blanche Rothberg, Miss Palen, Miss Nina Otero, and Miss Clara H. Olsen.

During the summer, Mrs. Otero and I had the honor of entertaining some distinguished military men. On July 27, we gave a dinner for Brigadier-General Frank D. Baldwin, U. S. A., his wife, and members of his staff. A little later General John C. Black arrived with his wife and daughter. General Black was the commander-in-chief of the Grand Army of the Republic. A vast crowd of people assembled in the plaza to hear him speak after I had introduced him. After his address, we drove to the executive mansion where Mrs. Otero gave a luncheon for the visitors.

On January 19, 1904, Hon. Abraham Staab, the leading merchant of Santa Fe, gave an elegant dinner and smoker in honor of "Governor Otero and the Supreme Court of New Mexico." We all had such a delightful time, that we

My Nine Years as Governor

remained with our genial host until early morning. Indeed, we wanted to stay for breakfast, and Mr. Staab said: "Stay and I will promise sausage and buckwheat cakes." I believe another bottle of champagne might have settled the question in favor of staying, but we decided we had enough of a good thing, and said "good-morning" and "adios."

In February, Mrs. Otero and I gave an elegantly appointed dinner in honor of the judges of the territorial supreme court. The decorations were in red and green. Covers were laid for twelve. The following were the guests: Chief Justice William J. Mills, Associate Justice Frank W. Parker, Associate Justice W. H. Pope, Solicitor-General E. L. Bartlett, Major R. J. Palen, Mr. A. M. Bergere, Associate Justice John R. McFie, Associate Justice B. S. Baker, Secretary James W. Raynolds, Judge N. B. Laughlin, Hon. W. S. Hopewell.

On April 15, we gave a dinner which was described by the *New Mexican* as follows:

> Governor and Mrs. Otero entertained at dinner last evening in honor of Mr. and Mrs. J. C. Osgood and party of Denver, Colorado, who were vistiors to the capital yesterday. The table and dining room decorations were in pink and consisted of carnations of that color, most attractively arranged. The table presented a beautiful appearance and covers were laid for twelve. There were present besides the host and hostess, Mr. and Mrs. J. C. Osgood, Mr. and Mrs. Delos A. Chapell, Mr. and Mrs. G. W. T. Traen, George W. Bowen, Secretary and Mrs. J. W. Raynolds, and W. S. Hopewell. The Osgood party came to Santa Fe at the direct invitation of Governor and Mrs Otero and spent a most pleasant afternoon and evening here. They had just visited the Grand Canyon of the Colorado in Arizona and were returning to Denver, for which city they left last night in their special car.

On June 15, Solicitor-General E. L. Bartlett gave a smoker at his residence on Hillside Avenue. This was in honor of the seventh anniversary of my inauguration as governor of New Mexico. One participant described the affair as:

> Great indeed, and I never heard more witty and interesting talks, nor better speeches anywhere, although I have been much in Washington, New York, and other great cities, have met many prominent men of the nation and have attended many social functions.

Genuine enjoyment reigned and there was a sincere flow of soul and high order of rhetoric indulged in. The goodly company consisted of friends and well wishers including, in addition to the guest of honor and the host, the following: Secretary Raynolds, Associate Justice McFie, Associate Justice Parker, Associate Justice Pope, Major R. J. Palen, Territorial Treasurer J. H. Vaughn, Hon. John H. Knaebel of Denver, Hon. W. S. Hopewell, Superintendent H. O. Bursum, Traveling Auditor Charles V. Safford, Hon. Arthur Seligman, Territorial Auditor William G. Sargent, Hon. A. Staab, Land Commissioner A. A. Keen, Hon. H. B. Holt of Las Cruces, Hon. Levi A. Hughes, Surveyor-General M. O. Llewellyn, Hon. James L. Seligman, District Attorney E. C. Abbott, Supreme Court Clerk Jose D. Sena, District Court Clerk A. M. Bergere, and Game Warden Page B. Otero.

In September, Miss Edna Scott Smith, of Washington, D. C., was our guest for a week. Miss Smith was the daughter of my friend, Mr. W. Scott Smith, private secretary to Secretary Hitchcock of the department of the interior. Both Mrs. Otero and Mrs. James W. Raynolds entertained in her honor.

On New Year's Day, 1905, open house was observed at the executive mansion during the entire day and we received numerous callers, who greeted both Mrs. Otero and myself most heartily.

Our reception in February for the members of the legislative assembly was described by the *New Mexican* as follows:

> Grand reception at the executive mansion to members of the 36th legislative assembly. In line, besides Governor and Mrs. Otero, were President John S. Clark, of the council; and Speaker Carl A. Dalies, of the house; Hon. Solomon Luna, and Mrs. Luna. Assisting Mrs. Otero and the receiving party were Mrs. James W. Raynolds, Mrs. Max Frost, Mrs. A. M. Bergere, Mrs. Arthur Seligman, Mrs. Stephen B. Davis, Jr., of Las Vegas; Mrs. N. B. Field, of Albuquerque; and Miss Nina Otero.
>
> For Mrs. Otero the reception was another triumph added to a brilliant social career as the first lady of the territory. Those who were present pronounced the society event superb and elegant in every arrangement and de-

tail, and one of the finest that has ever occurred in the interesting social history of New Mexico's capital.

June 14, my eighth anniversary as governor of New Mexico, was celebrated by a smoker. Invitations had been sent out by a committee four days in advance. Among those present were a number of friends from out of town, as follows: Frank W. Clancy, E. L. Medler, F. J. Otero, Chief Justice William J. Mills, Jacob Gross, Harry W. Kelly, James G. McNary, Solomon Luna, E. D. Raynolds, Jefferson Raynolds, and John S. Clark. Major R. J. Palen, Levi A. Hughes, James W. Raynolds, H. O. Bursum, A. M. Bergere, and others from Santa Fe were also there. At this smoker a beautiful ebony gold-headed cane was presented to me by my numerous friends. Every one present had some pleasant remarks to make, especially Mr. Jacob Gross, who recited many interesting stories of the frontier days when we both enjoyed hunting buffalo and other game, so plentiful then. Mr. Levi A. Hughes spoke mostly on the lines of my administration and expressed the hope that I might continue as governor of New Mexico for at least eight years more. Altogether, the smoker was a great success.

However, my official duties were nearly over. On December 23, Mrs. Otero and I gave a dinner in honor of Hon. Herbert J. Hagerman, who was to succeed me in a few days. The future governor's brother, Mr. Percy J. Hagerman, a prominent attorney of Colorado Springs, was also present. The *New Mexican* described the affair as follows:

The color scheme was pink, and pink chrysanthemums were the principal flowers. These filled a large cutglass vase in the center of the dining table, as well as smaller cutglass vases on the mantle of the old-fashioned fireplace in the dining room. Pink cutglass candlesticks with lighted pink tapers and electric lights in pink bulbs added to the brilliancy and artistic effect of the cutglass and the old silver in front of each guest. The dinner was elegant and in many courses. Interesting conversation took place during the serving. In addition to the guests of honor and the host and hostess there were present: Secretary and Mrs. James W. Raynolds, Mrs. John R. McFie, Major and Mrs. Rufus J. Palen, Colonel and Mrs. Max Frost, Attorney-General and Mrs. George W. Prichard, and Surveyor-General and Mrs. Morgan O. Llewellyn. It was a social function as elegant as ever took place in the executive residence, which is a very historic building. It was built in

1870 and for twenty-five years was occupied as the residence of the commanding officer of the district of New Mexico, and thereafter became the official residence of Governor Otero. Many are the social functions that have been held there, but none was more charming or more enjoyed by the participants than Wednesday evening's dinner.

The final social affair of my administration was described by the *New Mexican* for January 20, 1906, as follows:

Attorney-General and Mrs. George W. Prichard, last evening at their residence on East Palace Avenue, entertained in honor of Governor Otero at dinner. The affair was one of the most delightful and exquisitely appointed that has ever taken place in the capital city. The decorations were American beauty roses and the color scheme was pink and green. The dining table, at which covers for sixteen were laid, presented a beautiful appearance. The viands were as palatable as the best culinary efforts could make them. During the dinner the following dispatch from Delegate Andrews was read: "Your kind invitation to attend dinner in honor of Governor Otero received. Yes, I will be there in spirit if not in person. Toast Governor Otero for me." A letter was also read from Hon. Herbert J. Hagerman, in which Mr. Hagerman regretted that he was unable to accept the invitation extended to him as he would not arrive in Santa Fe until Saturday evening, one evening later than the day of the dinner. After the dinner a very handsome and large solid silver loving cup artistically chased and engraved was presented to the guest of honor by Chief Justice William J. Mills in a very appropriate and neat speech on behalf of the six member of the supreme court of the territory, as a token of the respect and esteem in which Governor Otero and his character both official and private were held by them. Governor Otero, who was quite overcome at the unexpected and handsome gift, replied in a very heartfelt and sincere manner. The following is the engraving on this fine specimen of the jeweler's art: "Presented to Governor Miguel A. Otero by the Members of the Supreme Court of New Mexico, William J. Mills, John R. McFie, Frank W. Parker, William H. Pope, Edward A. Mann, Ira A. Abbott, January 19th, 1906." On the reverse side is engraved the monogram composed of the initials of Governor Otero's name, M.A.O.

Then came after-dinner speeches by every member of the party present in the happiest vein, all of them eloquent and interesting, and some of them very witty. Some of the speakers made very happy hits and all remarks, besides being very appropriate and in the best of spirits, bore the stamp of cordial friendship, great esteem, and high respect for Governor Otero. The speeches took up about four hours, but all were thoroughly enjoyed, and as it was indeed "a feast of reason and a flow of soul," no guest noted the speed with which time passed and all were astonished when it was discovered that after the singing of "Auld Lang Syne" the "wee small hours" of the morning had arrived.

It was an occasion which will be ever remembered by the guests that were fortunate enough to attend as one of the charming and best incidents in their lives, and will certainly be treasured by Governor Otero as a gratifying memory and memento for all time to come.

Those present, besides the host and guest of honor, were: Chief Justice William J. Mills, Associate Justice John R. McFie, Associate Justice Frank

W. Parker, Associate Justice William H. Pope, Associate Justice Ira A. Abbott, Associate Justice Edward A. Mann, Territorial Secretary James W. Raynolds, Superintendent H. O. Bursum, Colonel Max Frost, Major R. J. Palen, Hon. Amado Chaves, Surveyor-General Morgan O. Llewellyn, Clerk of the U. S. District Court A. M. Bergere, and A. B. Renehan.

Chapter XIX

HERE AND THERE IN THE TERRITORY

WHILE official duties kept me in Santa Fe most of the time during my governorship, I paid many short visits to other parts of the territory. I have already dealt with some of these trips, especially with those taken during various political campaigns. In this chapter, I shall try to bring together other trips which may or may not be worth recording, but which, at any rate, will contribute toward an accurate picture of the activities of a territorial governor. Official duties, private business, social obligations, or the need for recreation furnished the occasion for most of these trips.

Frequently official duties prevented my accepting invitations which were showered on me. Thus, shortly after I became governor, Mrs. Otero and I received an invitation to the wedding of our good friends, Mr. Jose A. Baca, Jr., and Miss Marguerite Pendaries. The bride was the youngest daughter of Mr. and Mrs. John Pendaries, of Rociada. She was considered the most beautiful young lady in northern New Mexico. Both of her parents were born in France and the daughter showed the sprightly vivaciousness and other chacateristics of the French people. The groom was the son of Don and Doña Jose Albino Baca, of Upper Las Vegas, one of the most distinguished families in New Mexico. Both Mrs. Otero and I greatly regretted our inability to attend the wedding, which took place on June 23, 1897.

I had to go to Washington several times during my first year as governor, and these trips and the necessity of getting acquainted with my new job kept me from doing much traveling around the territory. However, I did spend almost a week in Albuquerque during the territorial fair in September. A delegation headed by Mr. C. C. Hall, invited me to open the fair. I accepted, promising to have my staff and as many members of the territorial militia as possible there on the occasion. Accordingly, I arranged to have a meeting of the militia while I was in Albuquerque. Adjutant-General H. B. Hersey and a dozen other officers of the militia accompanied me when I left Santa Fe. My escort on the opening day of the fair consisted of more than one thousand men on horseback. The largest single delegation was from Pajarito, home of Hon. Frank A. Hubbell, who won the silver loving-cup. The reception tendered me, on this occasion, was the largest ever given in New Mexico to anyone. There was also a grand parade on Governor's Day. The militia held the called meeting on September 13. The organization was perfected by the election of the following officers: Governor Miguel A. Otero, president; Col. H. B. Hersey, first vice-president; Col. John Borrodaile, second vice-president; Major O. Parker, third vice-president; Lieut. H. J. Emerson, secretary; Col. Venceslao Jaramillo, treasurer.

After the fair had closed, I received a copy of the *Albuquerque Citizen* which said:

> Governor Otero returned to his official home this morning feeling that it had been good for him to be here. His six days' visit in Albuquerque was a continuous ovation, and what should be especially gratifying is the fact that the demonstrations were no less tokens of the esteem in which our people hold him personally, than of respect to the high office which he holds. We have the highest respect for Governor Otero, but when it comes to real, warm friendship, with heart in it, that's for Gillie.

During the following month, I paid a much shorter visit to Las Cruces. On my arrival, I was met by a committee of citizens and escorted to the court house, where a grand reception was given me. A parade headed by a band followed and covered all the principal streets which were lined with cheering men, women, and children. When we reached the newly erected stand, I was introduced by Major Llewellyn to the crowd, which was very large. I made them a short talk, thanking them for their kind welcome and regretting that official business prevented me from extending my visit at that time. I returned to Santa Fe on the evening train.

In the spring of 1898, on the eve of the war with Spain, I made a visit to Silver City. I went down to gather information and material for my forthcoming report on the resources and conditions of New Mexico. Adjutant-General Hersey and Captain James, U. S. A., accompanied me. At Lamy, we were joined by Chief Justice Mills and Marcus Brunswick, of Las Vegas. The chief justice had mining interests in Grant County that needed attention, while Mr. Brunswick went along for the trip, and certainly had the time of his life. He was one of those old timers who thought money was only intended to spend, and with him it flowed like water over a dam. He was one of the most liberal men I ever knew, and was always looking out for the comfort and enjoyment of his friends.

When we arrived in Silver City, we were met by a large and distinguished body of citizens. It was my first visit there since becoming governor, and the people wished to make it a memorable event, so that every little detail had been worked out to perfection. Rooms for our party had been provided at the Timmer House. One of these rooms had been turned into an improvised clubroom, where we found a sideboard, large bowls of cracked ice, cigars, cigarettes, and every known kind of liquid refreshment, together with an expert mixer of drinks. That night there was a large banquet in the dining room and about two hundred and fifty of the leading citizens attended. Many fine speeches of welcome were made, some of which were very amusing. Sometime during the early morning hours I was handed a telegram, announcing that war had been declared against Spain. I immediately wired to Colonel James E. Hurley, at Las Vegas, asking for a special engine to take me back to Santa Fe. However, we soon figured out that we could make better time by taking the regular train. In the meantime, I kept in close touch with my office, and went ahead with the program arranged by the committee in Silver City. It was quite late, or I should say, quite early in the morning before we got to bed.

After a little sleep and a very light breakfast, we drove out, the next morning, to Fort Bayard to visit Colonel Ed Moule, as had been previously arranged. On reaching the fort, I was honored by the usual salute of seventeen guns, and escorted to the headquarters of the commanding officer. Here an elegant lunch was served by Mrs. Moule and other ladies. The colonel's wife, who was a native of France and spoke with a very strong accent, was a dear little woman and very anxious to please. Her husband was a small man and as profane as a "drunken sailor." Since the fort was about to be abandoned, the soldiers were all busy packing and there was much confusion. While we were there the colonel drove to the guard house and called out the guard. As they were a little slow in turning out, he gave them a cursing such as I had never heard before. He called them everything under the sun, and the poor fellows showed their embarrassment very plainly.

Since we expected to drive from the fort to Hanover, we invited the colonel to join our party. He did so, taking a government ambulance and four army mules along. We went by way of Central City, where we stopped for a few minutes to see some friends who had gathered at the Murray brothers' store. One of the principal Republicans I met there was a justice of the peace, named J. Crockett Givens, who seemed to be quite a leader in the community. He was a mulatto, a rather clean-cut fellow with heavy sideburns, and very gentlemanly and respectful. The people at Central City offered us some refreshments, of which, however, we partook very sparingly. We then drove directly to Hanover, where I accepted an invitation to go down to the bottom of the mine in an ore bucket. The miners were very careful that no accident should occur, and I enjoyed the experience very much. Before starting back for Fort Bayard, we ate the excellent lunch which Mrs. Moule had provided. On arriving at the fort, we left our escort and Colonel Moule, and went on to Silver City, which we reached in good time to take the train for Santa Fe. During the trip I secured an option on the Hanover mine, which I afterwards sold to some New York people for ten thousand dollars cash. However, I had to give Judge Mills half of the profits, as he and I had a gentleman's agreement as partners in such matters. This arrangement turned out very unfortunately for me, as the judge never produced anything to divide. On reaching Santa Fe, we found great excitement over the war. Men from every section of the territory were pouring in, anxious to enlist.

After the New Mexico squadron for Roosevelt's Rough Riders had gotten off to Cuba, I paid a couple of visits to Las Vegas, taking Mrs. Otero and Miguel with me. Here in my home town we naturally received many courtesies and attentions. We were handsomely entertained by many friends who showered so many dinners, luncheons, and receptions on us that we were on the go constantly. These kind friends were Chief Justice and Mrs. William J. Mills, Mr. and Mrs. John W. Zollars, Dr. and Mrs. Atkins, Mr. and Mrs. Joshua S. Raynolds, Mr. and Mrs. Jefferson Raynolds, and Miss Sadie Holzman. When we returned to Santa Fe, Misses Mary LaRue and Beatrice Atkins accompanied us to be our guests for a few weeks.

Toward the end of July, these young ladies, together with Colonel and Mrs. Austin and Colonel and Mrs. W. R. Tipton, went with us to Taos to attend the marriage of Cololen Venceslao Jaramillo to Miss Cleofas Martinez. We traveled by the Denver and Rio Grande Railroad to Tres Piedras, and from there by carriage to Taos. Our train was in a wreck just north of Española. Several cars, including ours, jumped the track, and our party was badly tossed about. Rev. Father John Roux was jammed between two cars and killed, while Mr. John Conway and Mrs. Gross, of

Denver, were slightly injured. Our entire party escaped injury.

On reaching Taos, I held an informal reception at the court house in accordance with the wishes of the people assembled there from all over the county for the wedding. I was called upon for a speech, but confined myself to a few personal remarks which seemed to be well received by all, as they cheered me with much vigor. Every man, woman, and child crowded around to shake my hand and extend good wishes. It was very gratifying to me for everyone expressed himself as being pleased with my appointment and pledged their earnest support to my administration.

The wedding was a grand affair and every person present seemed happy and pleased. The ceremony took place in the old Catholic Church which was filled with relatives and friends. The decorations and flowers were beautiful. The gowns worn by the ladies were handsome and charming to look at, but, of course, the women themselves were much like a picture, for there were many beautiful young women in attendance. Most of the gentlemen wore the regulation fulldress suits, while the officers wore fulldress uniforms in honor of Colonel Jaramillo. After the church ceremony, we went to a handsomely decorated hall and enjoyed a splendid dance. The orchestra came from Santa Fe. At midnight refreshments were served and much champagne was in evidence, and toasts to the happy couple were many. It was a grand affair from beginning to end. The next morning our party returned safely to Santa Fe.

The most memorable trip within the territory that I made, in 1899, was one taken in February to Alamogordo, the county seat of the newly created county of Otero. The act which had created this county and named it in my honor provided that all the county officials were to be appointed by me. Accordingly, I arranged to leave Santa Fe on February 17. Mr. C. B. Eddy had sent his private car, "El Paso del Norte" to Santa Fe for my use in making the trip from that point to Alamogordo, via El Paso. He was very careful to supply the car with almost everything for which one might wish. The ice chest and larder were filled with the choicest foods and drinks and the chef and porter were experts in their line.

Many of my friends wished to accompany me on the trip, so Mr. Eddy provided an extra Pullman to accommodate the party which consisted of the following: Mrs. L. Bradford Prince, Mrs. Rufus J. Palen, Mrs. William Guilliford, Hon. Solomon Luna and wife, Major Max Luna and wife, Chief Justice William J. Mills, Associate Justices Frank W. Parker and John R. McFie, Adjutant-General William H. Whiteman, Colonel R. E. Twitchell, Colonel E. G. Austen, Colonel E. W. Dobson, Colonel V. Jaramillo, Captain George Curry, Senator James S. Duncan and wife, Hon. Marcial Valdez, Mr. John S. Clark, and Major Eugene Van Patten.

The main object of the trip was to look over the field and consult the citizen's committee regarding the appointments for county officials, which, of course, was up to me, and secondly, it had been arranged for Mrs. Otero to formally christen the new county in the usual way by smashing a quart bottle of champagne on the rear end of the private car as it crossed the county line.

From the time we left Santa Fe we received ovations at every railroad station en route. At Albuquerque our party received an immense delegation of citizens, headed by a brass band. We visited with them for some time before taking our departure for El Paso, which we were due to reach early the next morning. On the arrival of our train at El Paso, we were welcomed by a large reception committee and the McGinty brass band and orchestra. I was requested to come out on the depot platform, and as I did so, the band struck up "El Capitan," and the crowd commenced cheering. It was an inspiring scene, and one long to be remembered. A line was soon formed, and Colonel J. A.

Eddy, who stood next to me, introduced all the people. I shook hands with each and exchanged a few words with some of my old friends.

After the introductions and hand shakings, Mr. Eddy announced that some little delay would be necessary on account of adding some additional day coaches to the train, as the El Paso reception committee together with the brass band and all the citizens on the platform had decided to go. Every car on the train was crowded to its full capacity. When we reached the county line, the train slowed up so as to allow Mrs. Otero to break the bottle of champagne and pronounce these words: "I hereby christen you *Otero*." The train stopped for about ten minutes, while the band played "The Star Spangled Banner" and everyone stood at attention with bare heads. When the ceremony was over the band played "There'll Be a Hot Time in the Old Town Tonight" and started a march in which all the passengers joined, singing and cheering. Finally, the conductor called "all aboard" and we were soon on our way to Alamogordo.

Before leaving El Paso, Mr. Eddy had additional eatables and drinkables placed in one of the coaches together with several hundred pounds of ice. At the noon hour lunch was served to all our guests and was greatly enjoyed. Cool beer, hot coffee, and tea were served with the lunch, and everybody seemed happy. When the train pulled into Alamogordo, an immense concourse of people surrounded the private car, and a timely address was made by the president of the Alamogordo club who presented me with a beautiful floral key to the city. I replied in a very few words, as carriages were waiting to take us to the hotel. At 6 p. m., our party was royally entertained at a magnificent dinner by Colonel Eddy and his charming wife, and at 8 p. m., an immense procession passed our hotel headed by the brass band and followed by a large number of beautiful floats and hundreds of people on horseback and on foot. After marching through every street in the city amid red fire and bonfires, ringing of bells, blowing of whistles, firing of anvils, sky rockets, Roman candles and other fire works, the procession finally halted in front of the Alamogordo Hotel, where I was called upon for a speech. Considering the great applause, I felt that my remarks were duly appreciated, and, of course, that was very pleasing to me. After a few short talks, Mrs. Otero and I were escorted to the hotel parlors where a public reception had been arranged as the people were anxious to meet us both. At 10 p. m., an elaborate banquet was served by the Alamogordo Club. This ended the festivities for the day, and it was well past midnight when we retired to our rooms and beds. It certainly was a grand day and not a moment dragged from the time we left El Paso.

The following morning we were up bright and early. After breakfast, I met with the citizens committee to go over suggestions, made by each member, regarding the appointments to be made for county officials. I listened very attentively and took a list of all people named, promising to take immediate action on my return to Santa Fe. This meeting completed all my official obligations.

The railroad company had arranged for an excursion to take us all up to Cloudcroft over the corkscrew road, and believe me, I think it was well named. It surely was a great climb, and many times I feared the little narrow gauge engine would be unable to make the grade, but we finally reached Cloudcroft on the summit of the Sacramento Mountains. Near the depot, the people of Cloudcroft had erected a large evergreen arch, which we were to pass through in going to the hotel where rooms had been engaged for our party to spend the night. An elegant dinner was served at the Lodge, after which the McGinty orchestra played sweet music for a dance which lasted until early morning.

The next morning we took the train for Alamogordo, and as it was down hill, we were not long in reaching our destination. We remained here until after luncheon, spending our time discussing the proposed officials for the new county. I listened to all the citizens had to say, but made no promises. We soon boarded our train and began our homeward journey. Our El Paso friends insisted that we stay over in that city for the night and the next day, and we felt that we must accept their very kind invitation. We had the private car and the Pullman so only those who wished to go to a hotel did so. Carriages were waiting at the depot on the arrival of our train and we were driven at once to the club where a large crowd had assembled and a brass band was playing popular music. Cocktails were passed around and soon we were ushered into the dining room, where a regular banquet was served. Many prominent residents and business men of El Paso were present with their wives, and soon we were just a happy family. The brass band came to give us a serenade, a number of people called to say "How," and plans were arranged for the following day, which included a visit to Juarez, Mexico. No mention of the international dam project was permissible, and we New Mexicans could not ask for kinder treatment. It was late when we returned to our cars, but it was not long before we were all in bed enjoying a good rest. The chef had a late breakfast for those who remained. Many in the Pullman drove up to the city for breakfast, but we had arranged to meet at the club at a certain hour. We planned to take our luncheon in Juarez at a popular resort, visit places of interest, and return to El Paso in time to take our train for Santa Fe.

Our party was not allowed to spend a cent while in El Paso. We were treated as guests of the city, and the committee in charge did things in fine shape. The hospitality of the El Paso people was simply grand, and could not have been improved upon. We reached our train in ample time and the chef had dinner arranged for those who took the

Juarez trip, while those who preferred to remain in El Paso had their dinners in the city.

Honorable Marcial Valdez, one of our party and a member of the legislature from Doña Ana County, got in telegraphic communication with friends in Las Cruces and arranged to have our party stop there on our return trip. As Las Cruces is less than fifty miles north of El Paso we were soon there. A large delegation of citizens met us, headed by a brass band, carriages, and hundreds of people carrying torches. Our party entered the carriages and the procession started for the business center of the city. From the main street we proceeded to a nicely decorated hall where a short address of welcome was made to which I responded briefly, as our time was limited. A reception being in order, Mrs. Otero and I were introduced to everyone present. The music started and the dance began. An elegant lunch was served by the ladies, and it was long after midnight when we again started on our homeward journey.

The next morning we reached Socorro and were met by a large delegation with carriages and escorted to the plaza where people were still gathering, as it was early morning. A brass band was playing in the plaza. At my request, speeches were dispensed with. Chairs had been arranged for our party and Mrs. Otero and I stood on a slightly raised platform and met and shook hands with all the people present. So many beautiful flowers were given our party that everyone carried a bouquet. In a very few words I thanked the people for the kind welcome given our party and for all the flowers.

We made short stops at Belen and Los Lunas and, finally, reached Albuquerque where a large delegation awaited us with carriages. We were driven to the Armijo House where an elegant luncheon was served, with cocktails and wine. After lunch, we were driven to the old town plaza and met many people. It was rather late in the afternoon when we took our train for Santa Fe. We stopped for a few minutes in Bernalillo to shake hands with the people gathered at the depot. The chef served a nice farewell dinner for us which we greatly enjoyed. About 9 p. m. we reached Santa Fe and found carriages waiting to drive us home. A vote of thanks was given to the chef and porters, and everybody who made up our party said it was a great success from start to finish.

Early in August, Chief Justice Mills and I went to Silver City again on business. We remained there only a few hours, as we planned to go with friends on a rather extensive fishing trip to the headwaters of the Pecos River. In this party were Associate Justice Crumpacker, United States District Attorney William B. Childers, District Attorney Frank W. Clancy, District Court Clerk A. M. Bergere, Sheriff Thomas S. Hubbell, and Doctor J. H. Sloan. Mr. Childers turned his club house over to us. We secured a first class cook from Las Vegas, a colored man from the Hot Springs Hotel, and a helper to do the house work and wait on the table, besides two men to look after the horses. We had a large wooden refrigerator with shelves, and it was anchored in the river with the cold stream running through it. We kept all perishable meats, vegetables, fruits, watermelons, and bottled beer in this improvised refrigerator. Judge Crumpacker brought along several large beer glasses, each of which held a quart. Each glass bore the name of a member of the party in large gold letters. Under the name, also in gold letters, was an original motto, *"One more won't hurt."* We fished, played cards, rode horseback, climbed the highest peaks on the Pecos, rested in hammocks, pitched horseshoes, drank cold beer, and had an all-around good time. We left Santa Fe on the morning of Monday, August 7, and returned Wednesday evening. Fish were plentiful. Going out each morning at daylight, some would return for lunch, while others took lunch with them and spent the whole day fishing. Our catch ran into the hundreds each day.

In September, Mrs. Otero, Miguel, and I spent a very

pleasant week at the territorial fair in Albuquerque as guests of the city. We stayed at the Commercial Club. The first night we were serenaded by the ninth cavalry brass band of the United States Army. I opened the fair for the third time. Many social attentions and courtesies were showered upon us while in the city.

In October, I made the opening speech at the fair given by the New Mexico Horticultural Society. This, of course, was held in Santa Fe. My speech was followed by an address by Dr. Frederick W. Sanders, president of the Agricultural College. He pointed out the great encouragement I was giving to horticulture and to his institution.

During 1900-1901, there were trips to Las Vegas, Raton, and Albuquerque, and also several trips to my sheep ranch, in Guadalupe County, in the southern part of the territory, sometimes spending ten days or two weeks there. Secretary Raynolds, who was my partner in this business, frequently went with me. At times, we were met at the ranch by Eastern wool buyers. These trips were taken intermittently for several years during the spring or summer.

During the year 1901, my enemies kept me busy "hotfooting" it to Washington to answer charges they preferred against me, so my trips around the territory were few. The following year, however, gave me more opportunity to visit around among the people of the territory.

In February, 1902, I went to Albuquerque at the invitation of the mayor of that city to attend a reception to General Arthur McArthur, U. S. A., accompanied by Colonel Jaramillo and Adjutant-General Whiteman. Early in June, I went to Mesilla Park to preside over the intercollegiate meet. Mrs. Otero and Miguel went with me. Following this, I made several short trips to the ranch, to Las Vegas, and to Albuquerque.

My trip to Raton, in July, stands out in my memory because of my meeting with General Fred Funston. I had gone up to attend the celebration of the Fourth. Adjutant-

General Whiteman went with me, and Chief Justice Mills joined us at Lamy. We met the captor of Aguinaldo on his private car, with his wife and baby. He had come to Raton to deliver an address, but had been stopped by a telegram from Washington. He merely said: "My lips are padlocked from Washington, so I can only say I am pleased to meet you all." After the ceremonies we were all invited to go and see the starting of the drill on the new oil well near Raton.

Shortly after my return to Santa Fe, my private secretary, Miss Olsen, had planned to go to Colorado Springs for about three weeks on her annual vacation. Consequently, I decided that this was a good time to take a vacation myself, and planned a trip to El Paso and Cloudcroft. Mr. Eddy kindly tendered me the use of his private car, "Cloudcroft," for the journey, so that everything promised a splendid visit to Otero County. The private car arrived in Santa Fe on August 2. Miss Julia Freeman, Miss Nina Otero, Eduardo and Manuel Otero, accomanied my family and me. While we were in El Paso, Mr. Eddy arranged for a coach and four to drive our party to Juarez. I particularly cautioned Nina and Julia about their purchases and advised them not to buy any cigars or silk hose. Nevertheless, when they returned, Julia was sitting up on the front seat with the driver, her feet extending to the dashboard and a dozen silk stockings dangling beneath her dress. And Nina was found with two boxes of cigars. Everything was taken from them and sent to Pat Garrett, the slayer of Billy the Kid, whom Roosevelt had made collector for the port of El Paso. The girls asked me to see Mr. Garrett in their behalf, but I declined to do so. The cigars were retained by the collector, but Julia was allowed to keep her hosiery. We had a delightful trip to Cloudcroft. On our return we had another pleasant little visit in El Paso, and then started for home. We were gone nearly a week.

In October, my family and I again attended the territorial fair in Albuquerque. While there we were the guests of Hon. William B. Childers and Mrs. Childers. As we were there on my birthday, October 17, the Childers gave me a nice party and I received many congratulatory telegrams from friends all over the country. It was a very pleasant week, indeed. We spent the week of the fair in Albuquerque again in 1903, the following year. We had a most delightful time, as the people of that city are splendid entertainers and are always cordial and hospitable to their guests, and especially to the governor and his family.

On January 14, 1904, Mrs. Otero and I were again in Albuquerque. This time it was to attend a reception and ball at the Alvarado, given by Hon. and Mrs. Solomon Luna. It was an elegant affair and lasted until morning. The buffet dinner, topped off with champagne and anything else you might wish for in the drinking line, was simply fine. It was an occasion long to be remembered by those who were fortunate enough to be invited.

During the last week of May, Secretary Raynolds and I visited Judge Frank W. Parker at Hillsborough and went with him to the Animas to inspect a gold mine recently discovered by a Mr. De Bois and a few other miners. On our visit to the property we stopped at the Hot Springs and took a bath. A small lake had formed a short distance below the bathhouse, and was filled with wild ducks. Judge Parker walked over to the carriage and got an automatic pistol and was returning toward me with the pistol in his hand, when suddenly it went off, the ball passing through my coat, not two inches from my heart. It was a very close call and the judge was more frightened than I. We reached the mining camp about dark. After supper, we made our beds on the ground in a small corrall. I cannot forget that night, for a mare with a bell kept sticking her head over the low fence near my bed and the bell rang constantly. Next morning, we all went to the De Bois mine. The owner pointed out the rock he wanted us to take, which ran high in gold.

However, we were suspicious and took several pieces from the same lead above and below his selections and did not find a trace of gold. Consequently, we quickly decided that Mr. De Bois had salted the mine for our special benefit. Our horses were lost and we had a devil of a time finding them, but finally got started for Hillsboro, reaching that place late at night. The next day Judge Parker gave us a fine dinner at his home, after which we attended a ball at the court house. I think everybody in and around Hillsboro, men, women, and children, were at that dance, and it lasted until sunrise. That afternoon, we started for Nutt station en route home and slept all the way.

On the evening of July 16, I left Santa Fe for Las Cruces to examine, personally, the condition of the Mesilla Valley and the scarcity of water for irrigation in that part of the territory. While there, I appeared on a program with several other speakers: Martin Lohman, Marcial Valdez, and Albert J. Fountain.[1] While I was talking, a heavy rain began to pour down and the people cheered for me, saying that my visit was responsible for the first rain they had had for months. I promised to do all in my power to see that they secured a diverting dam in the bed of the Rio Grande at Peñasco Rock, eighteen miles from Las Cruces. That evening the people of Las Cruces gave me a grand reception at the court house, together with an elegant buffet supper, furnished by the ladies. I returned to Santa Fe the next morning. The people of Mesilla Valley were enthusiastic over my meeting and the three-hour rain which drenched the valley made every farmer living down there happy. I stopped with Colonel and Mrs. Llewellyn, and sat on the porch. Shortly after the speaking, some farmers passing Colonel Llewellyn's home noticed me sitting there. One of them waved his hat and said: "You are a very good man, Governor; you bring rain to our people."

On August 11, I went to Las Vegas to inspect the New

---

[1] A son of the man of the same name who was murdered in 1896.

Mexico National Guard. The inspection was held at Camp Otero on the 13th. On the 17th, Mrs. Otero, Miguel, and I left for the Pecos river, where we were the guests of Mr. and Mrs. Niell B. Field at their summer home. We enjoyed our visit immensely. There were plenty of fish and mushrooms and other good things. About a month before our visit, Mrs. Field had sent us a large speckled trout which she had caught in the Pecos River herself. She was very proud of her catch, which was supposed to be the largest fish ever caught in that locality. It measured twenty-five and one-half inches and weighed seven pounds before it was cleaned.

Unless I was very busy running the territory, I was usually ready to go fishing. So I shall conclude this chapter by describing two fishing trips in the spring and summer of 1905.

About the middle of May, I decided to make a trip to the Red House on the Pecos River, as I had promised my brother, Page B. Otero, territorial game and fish warden, to go there and watch him place several hundred young trout in the river. I arranged with Mr. Charles Closson to have a relay of horses sent out to the town of Pecos the day before, so when we reached that point we changed our team for the fresh horses and drove to the Red House, where we met my brother with his son, Page, Junior. In my party were Mrs. Max Frost and Miss Nina Otero. Mr. Closson did the driving and we had an elegant time. We watched the placing of the trout in the stream and then returned to the Red House for a lunch fit for a king, which the ladies had provided. After lunch we started back to Pecos and changed our horses. We altered our original plans by taking the road to Lamy, where we had a Harvey House dinner, after which we started for home, and arrived in Santa Fe before midnight. It certainly was a most enjoyable trip. Both ladies enjoyed the drive immensely and, of course, Mr. Closson and I had an equally good time.

This was before the automobiles appeared upon the scene in New Mexico. We started from Santa Fe at six o'clock in the morning and got home before midnight. The whole distance, including the trip to Lamy, was about eighty miles or a little more. A brilliant idea concocted by Mrs. Frost was to inspect my hand bag, which contained two pint flasks of fine whiskey, taken along in case of snake bites. She emptied the two flasks and refilled them with water. It happened, however, that the snakes were not bad that day, so the whiskey was not needed. I discovered the joke some days later in Santa Fe and we all had a good laugh. The only damage was the loss of one quart of very good whiskey.

The second trip, which was also to the Upper Pecos, was in the latter part of July. Judge Matt. G. Reynolds, of St. Louis; Levi Hughes; and I took the Santa Fe train to Glorietta. I had arranged to have a carriage meet us there to take us to the Red House. We stayed there two days as the guests of my brother Page. His son and mine were also there. We caught several nice speckled trout and Page cooked them and served them in beautiful fashion. We returned to Santa Fe on August 1. We had quite an experience on the return trip, since our carriage broke down and we had to walk several miles to Glorietta. On arriving there, I telegraphed to Superintendent Hurley, who arranged for an engine to take us over to Lamy Junction. Here we caught the regular train for Santa Fe. We arrived in the ancient city o. k. after a short but very enjoyable trip.

Chapter XX

MOODY MERRILL

A TERRITORIAL governor naturally came in touch with all kinds of people, and I shall devote this brief chapter to one of the smoothest rogues this side of Sing Sing.

Charles F. Grayson was a newcomer to New Mexico, but he seemed to be a very substantial business man. He became president of the Silver City National Bank, and seemed to be well connected with big financiers in New York and Boston. He, at once, took a great interest in New Mexico bonds and mining property. Judge McFie introduced him to me as a financier who wished to bring about a refunding of all the securities of the territory. Naturally, I was greatly interested. At Grayson's request, I introduced him to Chief Justice Mills. At that time the judge and I were negotiating with Thomas B. Catron for an option on the Hanover copper mine. I told Grayson of the matter, and he volunteered to arrange a deal to my entire satisfaction, which he did by securing the option from Mr. Catron and turning it over to me. I had some New York people who wanted this property, and Grayson helped me materially in putting over the deal. Naturally, I felt very kindly toward my new friend.

Soon after this, the Silver City banker spoke to me about his refunding proposition. He and Judge McFie called at my office and presented the matter fully. In spite of the fact that the judge strongly endorsed all Grayson said, somehow it did not appeal to me. Consequently, I said frankly that I did not like the proposition, and that I did not think it favorable to the territory. Grayson went away quite disappointed, but I did not realize that I had made an enemy who would be heard from in Washington.

However, on my next trip East, I found that Grayson

and a friend of his, Mr. L. H. Hole, of the firm of W. N. Coler and Company, New York brokers who were heavily interested in New Mexico securities, had called at the department of the interior and presented charges against me.

On learning this, I wished to know more about this man Grayson. On my return to Santa Fe, I asked R. P. Barnes, of Silver City, about him. Barnes seemed rather embarrassed, and I guessed that he wished to tell me something, but had promised his informant to keep whatever it was a secret. Just as he was leaving my office, he gave me a good look, and then dropped a piece of paper which I picked up after he had gone. The paper contained only two words, "Moody Merrill." I put two and two together, and concluded that this was a clue that would put me on the track of my man. I, at once, began an inquiry, and finally found that some years before this Moody Merrill had lived in Roxbury, a suburb of Boston, and that he had been president of the street railway in Boston, and of the school board of Roxbury. However, he had absconded from Boston with several hundred thousand dollars of the city's money, and his whereabouts were unknown. I got on his trail and found that he had gone to the interior of Mexico, where he went to work for a man named Charles F. Grayson, who owned a large gold mine. Merrill made himself very useful about the property. The workers in the mine were illiterate Mexicans, so that when the owner died, Merrill assumed the name of Grayson and carried on. In time he sold the property for a considerable sum, and went to El Paso. Here he got in touch with a woman whom he had known in his early days. After some correspondence, she went to that city and they were married; after which they took up their residence in Silver City as Mr. and Mrs. Charles F. Grayson. Having acquired sufficient stock in the Silver City National Bank, he had himself elected president of that institution. He had friends in Boston who kept track of him all this time, and kept him advised as to how things were going. However, he never ventured to go back to Boston, though he did go to New York, where he became associated with Mr. Hole, who, I believe, knew his history.

After I had gathered all the information I thought necessary, I had my friend, Mr. Jefferson Raynolds, go to Boston to see if Grayson's picture was in the rogue's gallery. It was, so he got a copy of it and gave it to me in Washington, where I had gone in answer to a letter from Hon. E. A. Hitchcock, secretary of the interior. The latter showed me a letter signed "Charles F. Grayson," which he had received and which even out-did Catron and Fiske, since he was backed by a Wall Street firm. The letter stated that I was hurting the credit of the territory and recommended that I be removed from office. Accordingly, I related my story. Mr. Hitchcock listened attentively to all I had to say and became perfectly furious. He said that Grayson had better never darken his door again, and that he would write Coler at once.

I left the secretary's office and started for my hotel, walking up Pennsylvania Avenue. When I reached Eleventh Street, I noticed Grayson walking toward me, evidently on his way to see the secretary. When he was about to pass me, the hypocrite stopped and offered his hand to me. Looking him straight in the eye, I said, "I will not take your hand, you low-lived thief. How dare you to address me? If it were not for your age, I would knock you down right here, you damn cur!" He backed away and called "Police." When an officer appeared, I was the one who spoke up. I told him that this man was Moody Merrill who was wanted by the police in Boston. The policeman proceeded to arrest the man. The next day the papers were full of the story of the absconding financier who had finally been caught. Officers came from Boston and took him back, where he was identified without difficulty. His bond was fixed at $15,000 and he had to go to jail until his friends got enough money together.

I got my revenge on Charles F. Grayson and received compliments from all directions, from the President down. Shortly after this, Grayson returned to Silver City, humble and sick. He soon died of pneumonia. I still have the little slip of paper which Mr. Barnes dropped in my office with the name "Moody Merrill" written across it. It was a physician's prescription blank, and I am afraid it let our Silver City bank president in for some rather bitter medicine. The opposition to me was always in bad luck. None of them ever succeeded in doing more than causing me some expense, running back and forth from Santa Fe to Washington to answer their lying charges. However, Catron, Fiske, and Muller were not as sensitive as Grayson and refused to die at the proper time.

Chapter XXI
I VISIT THE STATES

I HAVE HEARD that Grover Cleveland was never in Washington until he went there to be inaugurated as President of the United States. This is a surprising fact when one considers that he had already served a term as governor of one of the greatest states in the Union. I don't believe that he could have gotten by with that even for two years, had he been governor of a territory. The territories naturally faced toward Washington, just as in former days the American colonies had faced toward London or Madrid or Paris. The Republican platform had been declaring for "home rule for the territories" for some years before I became governor, but that did not save me from keeping the trail to the capital hot. It seemed to me that I was always going to Washington. There were various reasons for these trips: the President might wish to see me regarding territorial appointments—I might be needed to fight the international dam treaty, or to see the President regarding the permanent location of the territorial capital, or to lobby for statehood, or to settle some practical difficulties arising out of the Fergusson Act, or to answer charges preferred by the gang that was fighting me. Of course, life in Santa Fe was dull at times so that these excursions to the East were usually interesting and exciting. While I always had railroad passes, I paid my other expenses out of my own pocket; otherwise, I might possibly have wished to be on the go oftener. However, it worked to the advantage of the territory. This aspect of the matter was referred to by the *El Paso Times*, in June, 1899, just after I had returned from a trip to Chicago and Washington which saved New Mexico thousands of dollars. The *Times* said:

> Governor Otero is doing considerable travelling this year in the interest of New Mexico. It is well for the people to know, that the governor pays all

his own expenses. The territory had no funds for traveling or paying such expenses.

I have already referred to a number of these trips, but will try to complete the account in this chapter. Business was generally mixed with pleasure; social affairs were sandwiched in between interviews with officials. I shall not try to unravel them any more than I have done heretofore, but will, perhaps, dwell more on the lighter side of life in this chapter. I shall try to relate my story without any attempt at generalization, feeling confident that my readers will get a fair bird's eye view of official society from the standpoint of a territorial governor.

Of course, I was in Washington in June, 1897, when President McKinley gave me the surprise of my life by calling me in and telling me that he intended to appoint me governor of New Mexico. Later, I returned to the national capital to confer with the President and the secretary of the interior regarding territorial appointments. I was, by no means, the only one there from the territory at that time, as the following New Mexicans were registered at Washington hotels on July 17: Ex-Delegate Thomas B. Catron, Judge John R. McFie, Judge A. A. Freeman, Mr. Frank W. Parker, Mr. Quinby Vance, Mr. Karl A. Snyder, Mr. Frank W. Clancy, Mr. Ralph E. Twitchell, and Eugene A. Fiske. I reached Washington about this time and made my headquarters at the Normandie Hotel. Mr. Solomon Luna was also in Washington, with headquarters at the National Hotel.

A few days later, Mr. Luna was taken very sick, and I became greatly alarmed over his condition. I did not like his room in the National Hotel and wanted him to move to some hospital. Accordingly, I consulted Senator Elkins, who introduced me to Senator Chandler, of New Hampshire, who was a doctor. The latter recommended the Garfield Hospital, which was under the management of the Sisters of Charity. I drove out there and made all arrangements, securing a splendid private room. I drove back to the National Hotel and assisted Luna in dressing and gathering up his effects and helping him down to the carriage. I took one of the bellboys with me and soon had Solomon comfortably provided for in a fine room. I telegraphed his wife and she came to Washington. I remained with him until she arrived, visiting him every day, and seeing that he got the best doctor, as well as nurses, and that they showed him every attention. Solomon was a very sick man and had he been allowed to remain in the hotel under the house doctor, I believe he would have died. He remained in the hospital for several weeks before he was able to travel west.

An amusing incident happened the day I took Solomon to the hospital. The mother in charge and the sisters guessed from his name that he was a Jew. However, when the nurses undressed him for bed, they discovered that he was wearing scapulars. The mother superior told me how surprised they all were when they made this discovery. I then explained fully, and also told Solomon, who seemed to enjoy the joke.

In October, I went to Denver to attend the celebration of the "Knights of the Silver Serpent." Governor Alva Adams, of Colorado, had invited me to be present, and the Denver and Rio Grande Railroad tendered me, complimentary, a train consisting of two Pullmans, three day coaches, and two baggage cars. These ample accommodations were provided so that I could bring an infantry company and the band along, as well as my family, staff, and invited guests. The latter included Page B. Otero and wife, Col. John Borradaile, Captain T. J. Matthews, Captain James, U. S. A., Major N. L. King, Judge Wilbur F. Stone, of the court of private land claims, Hon. and Mrs. James H. Reeder, and many others.

While in Denver, Governor Adams remarked, in the presence of governors from Illinois, California, Utah, and Wyoming, that the troops from New Mexico made the best appearance and manifested the most perfect discipline of any troops in the city. We had gone up on the 3rd and returned to Santa Fe on the evening of the 9th.

The last of November found me again in Washington in response to a telegram from President McKinley, who wished to consult me regarding the appointment of judges for the territory. I was accompanied by Mrs. Otero and Miguel. As some friends were staying at the Hotel Wellington, I telegraphed for reservations at that place. After seeing the President, we went on to New York. Leaving my family there, I took the train for New Haven, where I had a pleasant visit with Honorable William J. Mills, who was shortly after this appointed chief justice of New Mexico. The judge took me to lunch at the Quinnipiack Club. In the afternoon I went by train to Farmington, to visit my niece, Miss Bonnie Ransom, at the young ladies college. From the depot I was driven in an old fashioned stagecoach to the school where I saw her and some of her girl friends. I cannot remember seeing so many pretty young ladies at any place I ever visited, as I did here. The only man I saw was the driver of the coach. I returned to New Haven and had a nice visit with Judge Mills at his mother's home and, after dinner, took the train back to New York.

By the year 1898, I had gotten most of the territorial appointments straightened out, and my enemies hadn't had time to file many charges against me, so I had less journeys to make than the previous year. However, I did go to Washington about the middle of August, as the *Washington Post* for the 17th announced:

> The governor of New Mexico is a guest at the Shoreham. He is one of the youngest chief executives in the country, but had had a wide experience in business and politics, and on account of his personal popularity the news of his appointment was hailed with great satisfaction.

From Washington, I went on to New York, as I frequently did on these eastern trips. I always stopped at the Waldorf-Astoria while in the big city. I was well known there and was popular with everyone from the manager down to the bellboys. Among the many people with whom I became acquainted at this famous hotel, my friend, F. Augustus Heinze, the Montana copper king, stands out in my memory. After he had acquired a little mining experience as a young man, his grandmother had died, leaving him fifty thousand dollars. He had gone immediately to Germany, where he took a thorough course in mining engineering. Returning to Butte, he made a fortune in the mining game. He also allied himself with William A. Clark, a millionaire mining man who represented Montana in the Senate for eight years. As Clark was a timid speaker, while Heinze was quite an orator, he gave his friend effective aid in his political campaigns. Heinze finally sold his interests in Butte to the Standard Oil Company for over ten million dollars. Later he lost the Clark support, and became reckless. He went into the banking business in New York City, but Standard Oil broke him finally, during the panic of 1907.

At the time I met Mr. Heinze, I found him a delightful acquaintance. He was always very cordial and agreeable. He was ten years younger than I, and while somewhat shy, was greatly admired by women. In appearance he was very good looking, even distinguished—and his conversation showed him to be a man of education and culture. He was never regarded as a braggadocio and I never heard of his boasting of any of his exploits in Butte. Of course, my meetings with him were merely of a social nature. I greatly admired him and liked to be in his company.

I saw Mr. Heinze many times on my trips east. However, the occasion which I especially love to recall was a trip to New York, in August, 1898. I was passing through the lobby of the Waldorf-Astoria one morning, when I heard my name called. I turned and saw my wealthy friend coming toward me. Having explained that he was giving a dinner that evening to some of his lady friends, he said: "Governor, I will feel highly honored if you will join us.

The dinner is to be here in a private dining room, and Oscar is attending to all arrangements." I told him I would be pleased to accept. Later I was informed there would be two other gentlemen in the party and sixteen delightful young women.

The table was beautifully decorated, a perfect gem: It was set for twenty. I sat across the table from my host, with four ladies to my right and four to my left. Mr. Heinze had the same number of beautiful women on each side of him. Two other gentlemen sat at the ends of the table. The place cards were very handsome and unique. At each lady's place was a beautiful corsage bouquet and an English walnut. These, however, were no ordinary nuts. The inside of each had been removed, and the shell equipped with a small gold hinge and a gold catch. On being opened, each favor revealed a crisp new one hundred dollar bill. Heinze played no favorite, all were treated alike. The ladies were all very handsomely gowned and wore exquisite hats; each was a picture, and a beautiful one at that. Heinze certainly had good taste.

The menu was faultless. I never enjoyed a better dinner in my life and we all voted that Oscar had out-done himself. Wine and the choicest of liquors went with each course. The conversation was witty and brilliant, without even a suggestion of being coarse or indelicate. Everything passed off most pleasantly and we all had a splendid time. I certainly enjoyed meeting these beautiful and intellectual women. It was a great treat and I can never forget Mr. Heinze's kindness in selecting me from his list of personal friends to join him that evening. Fortunately, such parties were of rare occurrence. It was sometimes hard to get back to earth the next day, and there was usually work to be done.

The Fergusson Act, which had been passed by Congress in June at the insistance of Delegate Harvey Fergusson, was supposed to give a large amount of land to the territory for schools and colleges. However, due to the way in which the act had been drawn, it was discovered that New Mexico would incur heavy expenses in securing possession of this "gift." Consequently, I had gone to Washington to see if I could get this adjusted in some way. In December, I returned and appeared before Honorable Binger Herman, United States land commissioner. I argued for an appropriation of twenty thousand dollars to carry the provisions of the act into effect. At first the commissioner was strongly against the proposal. However, I won him over. After hearing my argument, he said that he concurred in what I said, and would make the recommendation to Congress. This he did, and that body made the appropriation.

On returning to my hotel, I found awaiting me my brother, Major Page B. Otero, and Captains Albert B. Fall, W. C. Reid, and William Strover. I took them at once to the White House and introduced them to President McKinley and later to the secretary of war, Honorable Elihu Root. On a suggestion made by the officers we all proceeded to a photographer and had group pictures taken.

New Year's Day, 1899, found my family and myself still in town and very much in official society. On this day, Mrs. Otero, Miguel, and I were warmly greeted at the White House by both President and Mrs. McKinley, and were singularly honored by being invited to pass behind the receiving line, where we remained and mingled with the distinguished guests of the day. The flowers and decorations in the Blue Room were very beautiful and well arranged and everyone in the receiving line, and behind the line, was happy. It resembled a large family, for everyone seemed to be acquainted, and those who were not, introduced themselves, as formality was not noticeable on New Year's Day at the executive mansion. Very little official business was transacted during this holiday week, for it kept one busy attending dinners, luncheons, receptions, teas, and theater parties. The fact of our having been behind the line at the executive mansion, and being personal friends to President and Mrs.

McKinley, opened the door to us for several social distinctions and honors, and we were entertained so much that our time was almost entirely taken up with social duties. While it all was very pleasant, I felt that I had much business to dispose of before the different departments and before Congress. However, it was a week of pleasure, and heads of departments were not expected to attend to business, unless absolutely necessary and, at those times, it was impossible to see them. I would not have had any difficulty in extending my leave of absence, but I was anxious to return to the territory and had set Friday as the day for our departure.

In May, I went to Chicago to attend to matters relating to the building of the capitol. Mrs. Otero, Miguel, Junior, and Miss Mary LaRue accompanied me. When I had finished my business, I was called to Washington. I went alone, while the others remained in the breezy city and returned to Santa Fe some days later. My arrival in the national capital on May 22 was noted in the *Washington Post* the next day: "The governor of New Mexico, Hon. M. A. Otero, who is at the Shoreham, brings good accounts of the conditions in his territory. Governor Otero is, perhaps, the most popular man in New Mexico, and he has friends galore in the East as well."

Among my many trips to Washington, this one stands out in my memory very distinctly. In fact, it was a very special occasion. The Peace Jubilee, which lasted three days, brought the largest crowd to the city that it had ever seen since the Grand Army of the Republic had assembled there, fifty thousand strong. Everything was conducted on a grand scale, regardless of expense. Everywhere could be seen flags of different countries and bunting in great profusion. The court of honor which extended for three blocks in front of the White House, treasury, state, war, navy, and department of justice buildings, attracted the greatest attention, with flags, bunting, statues, and thousands of electric lights of red, white, and blue artistically arranged in a manner calculated to attract the eyes of the thousands of citizens and visitors in the city. On each of these memorable three days, I occupied a position of honor on the grandstand, close to the President and members of the cabinet and their ladies. The fireworks each evening, in some respects, surpassed those at the McKinley inauguration. As the President left his carriage at the foot of the Washington Monument hill, he happened to see me sitting with some friends in one of the boxes, so he sent one of his secretaries to invite me to join his party in his private box. I shall never forget that evening for this was an exceptional honor, not only to me, but also to the territory of New Mexico.

Decoration Day, this year, was celebrated by official Washington, at the Arlington Cemetery and at the Soldiers' Home, on a grander scale than usual. The military men started early to the respective grounds, accompanied by numerous brass bands. It was a perfect day. Upon a special invitation, I had the honor of acting as an escort to Mrs. John Addison Porter, wife of the private secretary to President McKinley. She and I rode in her open carriage, immediately after those of the President and members of the cabinet. Upon the arrival at the cemetery the carriages of the President, members of the cabinet, and Mrs. Porter, were the only ones admitted to the grounds.

Mrs. Porter had gone to town at 5 o'clock in the morning to secure flowers, and had passed most of the morning in arranging with her own hands, four beautiful wreaths and a five foot set piece to decorate the graves of the Roosevelt Rough Riders. The flowers almost hid Mrs. Porter and me in our carriage.

In the seating arrangement on the platform overlooking the cemetery, in the front row of honor were President McKinley, Secretary Alger, Mrs. Alger, Secretary Wilson, and I. As President McKinley stood to allow the other guests to pass to their seats, to his left, I quietly and politely

My Nine Years as Governor

expressed my regrets to Mrs. Porter, who was seated immediately behind the President, that I had to be separated from her, and my remarks caused the President to smile.

The Memorial Day oration was delivered by the assistant secretary of the interior, Honorable Webster Davis, and it was acclaimed one of the best ever delivered at Arlington. It certainly was a classic, and with his closing remarks every person stood, while the President shook his hand warmly.

Thousands of people began decorating the graves with flowers. I took the massive set piece and Mrs. Porter took the four wreaths, and with the solemnity due the occasion, placed them to the best possible advantage on the graves of the Rough Riders, who sleep the sleep that knows no waking, in the most historic cemetery in the United States.

This trip to Washington was very successful, as I succeeded in getting the millions of acres of land for public institutions in good and workable shape. While in Chicago, I was also able to save the territory more than two thousand dollars in freight on material to be used by the capitol rebuilding commission.

Less tangible results of this and other trips were referred to in the territorial press from time to time. Thus, regarding this particular trip, the *Elizabeth Town Miner* had this to say:

> New Mexico is getting a great deal of advertising throughout the East in the interviews Governor Otero had while on his recent trip to Chicago and Washington. They have been published in all the Eastern papers. The governor is loyal to the territory and has on each occasion given New Mexico a good send off as to her climate and resources.

In October, I went to Chicago to attend the laying of the corner stone of the federal building of that city. Mr. W. D. Washburn, a member of the committee, called at my office and invited me. Mrs. Otero, Miguel, and Adjutant-General Whiteman went with me. President McKinley delivered the address, and I had the pleasure of meeting him several times. I dined with him at the Union League Club, and attended a luncheon at the Hamilton Club at which he was present. After a week in the city, our party returned in the private car of J. E. Hurley, superintendent of the Santa Fe Railroad. As it happened, we arrived in Santa Fe on my birthday, October 17.

I always liked Chicago, and two months later, when I was in Washington on territorial business, the following dispatch appeared in the *Denver News* for December 18:

> Governor Otero of New Mexico tells a reporter, that if he had a vote in the Republican central committee, meeting in Washington today, he would cast that vote for Chicago to hold the next Republican convention, for the purpose of nominating a candidate for President and vice-president of the United States. He has been invited to attend the grand reception to the supreme lodge, Knights of Pythias, tonight, and will deliver an address at the banquet which follows the meeting.

In the spring of 1900, I visited Los Angeles twice. Mrs. Otero's health had not been good, so it was decided that she and Miguel, Junior, and Miss Mary LaRue should spend a month or more in California. I went out, in March, and secured permanent quarters for them at a beautiful little hotel known as the Bellevue Terrace. Mrs. Otero's health improved greatly, and they all enjoyed their stay very much. I returned to the coast again, in April, and spent two weeks with them; after which we came back to Santa Fe together, on the 21st.

Early in June, I took the train for Chicago, Washington, and Philadelphia. I planned to attend the Republican national convention, which was to be held in the last named city, as I had been elected delegate at large from New Mexico. I had not attended the territorial convention held in Socorro in March and, therefore, did not boss the delegates, as the Democratic pop sheets had prophesied I would. I headed the delegation from the territory to Philadelphia because the masses of the Republican voters of New Mexico desired this to be the case.

While our delegation was in Washington, the Associated Press sent out the following dispatch:

Governor Otero, Hon. Frank A. Hubbell, Hon. A. Abeyta, Hon. Secundino Romero, and Hon. Solomon Luna, held a conference of half an hour with President McKinley at the executive mansion. Hon. Solomon Luna is the national committeeman of the Republican national committee for New Mexico and the other gentlemen are members of the New Mexico delegation to the Republican national convention at Philadelphia. The delegation is instructed for William McKinley for the nomination of President of the United States.

At the National Convention, I helped to get a statehood plank into the platform. Regarding the methods used, I later told a Washington correspondent: "We went to Philadelphia early, engaged rooms at a leading hotel, and talked and entertained for New Mexico. The result was the strong recommendation for statehood in the party platform." We also refused to say what we would do in the fight over the vice-presidency, declaring that we would "Vote as a unit for what seems to promise most for New Mexico."

During the convention I enjoyed a splendid conference with Senators Quay and Penrose in the Wigwam. Later I had the pleasure of sitting with Mrs. Theodore Roosevelt. She confided to me that she was absolutely opposed to her husband accepting the nomination for vice-president. She said: "It is simply an attempt of Senator Platt, of New York, to sidetrack him, so he cannot accept the renomination for governor of New York."

However, through the insistence of Senator Quay, Colonel Roosevelt was forced to accept the nomination, although it was well known that both President McKinley and Senator Mark Hanna were strongly in favor of Secretary John D. Long, of Massachusetts.

I was elected on the notification committee to inform President McKinley of his nomination. As I was unable to attend, I telegraphed Hon. Solomon Luna, who was in Washington, to act for me, and he did so. I had some important official duties to attend to in Santa Fe and had to return home by the first train.

I was in Chicago and Washington several other times before the year 1900 closed, but nothing unusual happened.

However, the *Washington Post,* for September 18, had this to say:

> E. K. Somborn, of Chamberlain's, has received a large and excellent photograph of Governor Miguel A. Otero, of New Mexico, which will be hung in the gallery of portraits of distinguished men, which is one of the noted features of the famous hostelry. Mr. Somborn and Governor Otero are warm personal friends, and in the letter that accompanied the photograph, the governor expresses the hope that it would be worthy of "occupying a small place in the 'home I love so well'." Governor Otero is well known in Washington. His visits to the capital are about twice a year. He is greatly admired by President McKinley, and has many warm friends among men in public life.

Generally my trips to Chicago, during these years, were connected with the rebuilding of the capitol or other business of the territory. However, on August 28, 1901, I went to Chicago to bring Miguel, Junior, and his mother home. Two weeks before, my son had been badly bitten by a dog in the yard of Judge McFie. I had grabbed a Winchester rifle and rushed over and killed the animal. Mrs. Otero, who frequently went to Chicago on shopping trips, left for that city that evening, so that the boy could take the Pasteur treatment. After their arrival in Chicago, the *Chicago Tribune* said:

> Miguel Otero, the eight-year-old son of Governor Otero, of New Mexico, at the Annex yesterday afternoon said: "My mother and I both think I am all right. I am not certain that the dog that bit me was rabid. I think it was afraid for its puppies, and so leaped over the fence at me. Dr. Lagorio gives me an injection of virus through my stomach. He will give me thirty injections, which will take two weeks. I do not feel at all afraid myself. It is a very curious process, this Pasteur cure.

Meanwhile I was called to Las Vegas on important business. I made a quick trip of it and then left for Chicago to bring the boy home as soon as his two weeks were up at the Pasteur Institute. I found Miguel completely recovered, and anxious to get home. We returned by way of Denver, visiting my sister, Mrs. Harry J. O'Bryan, for a few days. From Denver, we were accompanied back to Santa Fe by Mrs. A. M. Bergere and Miss Nina Otero.

While in Chicago, Mrs. Otero and I were the dinner guests of Admiral and Mrs. Schley, who later invited us to join their box party at the Studebaker Opera House. We had a most enjoyable time.

It was just as we were getting into Denver on the trip just mentioned that I heard the tragic news of the assassination of President McKinley. I have already described my trip to Canton, Ohio, to attend the funeral.

On December 9, I left for the East, together with my family. During the month, we visited friends and relatives in New York, Boston, and other places. On the last day of the year we returned to Washington, where we planned to remain until after the Senate had passed on my nomination for governor. Accordingly, we celebrated New Year's Day, 1902, by attending the reception at the executive mansion. A Washington correspondent wired his paper:

> Mrs. Otero, wife of Governor Otero of New Mexico, received a most cordial invitation from President and Mrs. Roosevelt to assist in receiving at the White House on the New Year's reception in the Blue Room, while Governor Otero entered with the senators and members of the House of Representatives.

After a most cordial greeting from President and Mrs. Roosevelt and the cabinet ladies, I joined Mrs. Otero behind the line and we remained until the reception was over. At the time, I recalled that three years before Mrs. Otero and I had both been behind the line at the New Year's reception of President and Mrs. McKinley. I was happy to think that the same cordial relations seemed extended to the present administration from the last. Many congratulations and good wishes were extended to us on that New Year's Day. Every one seemed sure that I would be confirmed by the Senate the following week.

Senator Foraker's daughter was married while we were in Washington. Mrs. Otero and I attended the wedding and also the wedding breakfast at the Foraker home. During our long sojourn in Washington, both Mrs. Otero and I were the recipients of many invitations to receptions, dinners, theatre parties, and other entertainments, many of which we were unable to accept. Mrs. Otero was chaperon to Miss Julia Freeman, her cousin, and daughter of Brig.-General H. B. Freeman, U. S. A., at the Charity Ball at the New Willard Hotel.

Soon after Congress assembled in December, 1903, I returned to Washington to work for statehood and to attend to other territorial business. The very last day of the month, I attended a meeting in Delegate Rodey's room regarding the transfer of the military reservation in Santa Fe to the public schools. This was held at the request of the secretary of the interior. In addition to Mr. Rodey and me, Mayor Sparks, of Santa Fe, and Mr. George Curry were also there. As we all agreed on the transfer without difficulty, we went to Mr. Hitchcock's office and I presented our opinion to him. He approved our plan, and asked us to take up the matter with the President. This was done and the transfer was made in short order.

On New Year's Day, 1904, Mrs. Otero and I attended a reception at the White House. My wife was one of the receiving ladies, while I passed behind the line and mingled with the distinguished guests. We had a most delightful day and, later, were invited to dinner. The large dining room was nicely decorated with flowers on each table. There were many small tables for four, while the President's table seated eight. I had two reasons to remember this dinner. One because I had been invited by President and Mrs. Roosevelt, and the other because I was seated just across from the President at a table with Edward Everett Hale, author of *The Man Without a Country*. I enjoyed being with Mr. Hale, and loved to hear him talk. He was so interesting and pleasant I can never forget him.

A few days later, Mrs. Otero, Miguel, and I went to New York for the opera. One night, on our return to the Waldorf-Astoria, from the Metropolitan Opera House, I had a memorable experience. There was a deep snow, the wind was blowing, and the night was bitter cold. As we entered the hotel, I noticed Senator Mark A. Hanna seated in what was known as "Peacock Alley." I was heading toward the elevator with Mrs. Otero. The senator called me over where he was seated and asked me to visit with him, so, beckoning to Mrs. Otero to go on up to the room, I sat down beside the senator. He said that he had been to Cooper Hall to make a speech and had been in a draft and had taken cold. He added that he felt feverish so wanted to sit there and rest and wished some one to keep him company. We talked for about an hour, but I could see he was getting no better, so I suggested that he go to his room and said that I would escort him to his door. This I did, turning him over to his wife when we reached his suite.

It was the last time I ever saw the senator. He did not seem to improve and finally decided to go back to Washington. He ordered a private car and he and Mrs. Hanna left for Washington. Later, he developed a case of pneumonia which proved fatal, death occurring on February 15, 1904, at 6:45 p. m. I felt that I had lost my best friend in Washington.

We left New York and arrived in Santa Fe on January 11, after a splendid trip.

Mrs. Otero and her guest, Mrs. Bergere, spent a week or ten days in Chicago, in May, where they had a very enjoyable time. On their return, they were accompanied by Mrs. Bergere's daughter, Miss Anita, who had been in school at Cedar Grove, a boarding school of the Sisters of Charity of St. Joseph, near Cincinnati, Ohio.

Just a month after my wife's return, I left for Chicago to attend the Republican national convention there. There was nothing especially noteworthy about the convention, as it was a foregone conclusion that Roosevelt would get the nomination. However, Hon. Thomas F. Walsh, of Colorada, a millionaire mining man who was a member of the delegation from his state, gave quite an elaborate dinner in connection with the convention. I was invited and, of course, accepted. There were a great many present and Governor Peabody, of Colorado, made a splendid speech.

I have already spoken of my visit to Sagamore Hill in July, when I served on the notification committee. On our return to New York, I stopped at the Waldorf-Astoria for several days. While there, I met Lilburn G. McNair, Arthur Seligman, and former Chief Justice William A. Vincent. We had quite a reunion, which reminded me of the early days in Las Vegas, before I became governor. McNair was an old schoolmate of mine at St. Louis University, and had spent one summer in Las Vegas at the Hot Springs. Arthur Seligman and I left New York for Washington together as I had some business there. It did not take me long to finish this so we went on to Buffalo, New York, where we stopped for a day to visit Hon. Norman E. Mack and Mr. John A. Ellwood. These gentlemen showed us an elegant time. We called on Mayor Knight, and all had a splendid dinner together. Later we drove to the park. While there, Mr. Mack played one of his jokes on me. Two policemen rounded me up as I was sitting on the grass, and arrested me for trespassing, but the mayor and Mr. Mack appeared and got me out of the scrape. We then adjourned to a nearby club house and took a few bottles of good champagne. We had a splendid time and I shall never forget that day in Buffalo. Seligman and I then stopped off at Cleveland, Ohio, where we had a pleasant visit with his wife's family. I certainly enjoyed the drives around the city. We then left for Chicago where we stopped for a couple of days, reaching Santa Fe on August 8, after a most enjoyable trip.

The middle of December found me in Washington, working against joint-statehood, although I spent Christmas with my family in New York.

During my last year in office, I was somewhat run down in health and greatly in need of rest. Consequently, Mrs. Otero, Miguel, and I, with Miss Nina Otero as our guest, left for the Pacific coast, on March 27, 1905, where we visited San Francisco, San Jose, Santa Barbara, Monterey, Los Angeles, and San Diego. We met New Mexicans almost everywhere we went.

During the latter part of September, I made a trip to Denver, Chicago, Washington, and New York. At this time, especially while I was in the national capital, I renewed many acquaintances with men who were shaping the destiny of the nation, among them friends from New Mexico. Among these were Colonel Max Frost and Hon. C. T. Brown, of Socorro, who were in Washington, attending a convention of the thirty-third degree Scottish Rite Masons.

On the opening night at the National Theater, Maude Adams was to present Peter Pan for the first time, and I secured one of the large private boxes and had the pleasure of taking Mrs. Max Frost, Mrs. Brown, and the three daughters of my good friend, W. Scott Smith. We occupied the upper box on the left side facing the stage. Of course, we had an excellent view of the large crowd in attendance. Many senators bowed to us, and Senator Carter, of Montana, remarked to Senator Hansborough: "Look at that box! There is Governor Otero of New Mexico with five of the prettiest women in Washington." After the theater we had a fine meal of broiled lobsters and oyster stew washed down with cold champagne. It was a night long to be remembered.

On getting into Chicago on my trip home, I encountered my old friend, Mark Smith, who had served as delegate to Congress from Arizona for several terms. Mark was getting ready to go to French Lick Springs, Indiana, and I decided to join him. I remained there a few days, and then took the train back to Denver, where I visited my sister for a couple of days before going on to Santa Fe. Home again, I felt greatly improved in health and ready to settle down and dispose of the large amount of business which had accumulated during an absence of several weeks.

Chapter XXII

THE LOUISIANA PURCHASE EXPOSITION

NOTHING IS quite so good for a territory as advertising, and New Mexico needed both capital and immigration to develop its almost untouched resources. Realizing this, I was also aware of the splendid opportunity which the various expositions offered to advertise the products of New Mexico. The Pan-American Exposition at Buffalo, New York, in 1901, and the South Carolina and West Indian Exposition at Charleston, South Carolina, the following year, were so far away that little interest was manifested in them in our territory. However, the Hyde Exploring Company volunteered to send an exhibit to Charleston. This firm, which was located in Farmington, New Mexico, with trading posts in Albuquerque and New York, did quite a large business in Navajo rugs, pottery, and relics of all kinds. When the exposition was over, the company gave the exhibit to the city of Charleston.

When preparations began for another exposition in St. Louis, in 1904, I determined that New Mexico should do its part to make the affair a success. For a hundred years, Missourians had been following the Santa Fe Trail to New Mexico, and the business, which had sprung up between the two regions, ran into thousands of dollars every year. Missouri had, possibly, contributed more of her sons and daughters to New Mexico than any other state in the American Union. There were so many of them in the territory that they organized a club. I, myself, a native of St. Louis, had received a part of my education there.

Accordingly, I presented the matter to the thirty-fourth legislative assembly, and urged that an appropriation be made for a New Mexico exhibit at the St. Louis exposition. The assembly responded by appropriating thirty thousand dollars for the purpose, and creating a territorial board of managers for the exposition. Both Senators A. B. Fall and W. A. Hawkins were greatly opposed to this appropriation and did all in their power to defeat it. Their objections were entirely personal. I had vetoed their pet measure, the Hawkins Bill, and they simply wanted to get even with me. They thought their fight on this measure would embarrass me, and it would have done so if they had succeeded. The main fight on the bill took place during the night session of the council, several attempts being made by both Fall and Hawkins to adjourn. I remember quite well when Senator Fall made his last speech on the subject. Mrs. Otero and several ladies were seated in the gallery of the council room. Turning and pointing to them, he said: "The governor has even seen fit to bring women here tonight for the purpose of assisting him in the passage of this extravagant bill, aiming to pilfer thirty thousand dollars of the taxpayers' money for a social spree in St. Louis, ..." However, his oratorical venom had little effect, and the bill passed.

I appointed the board of managers for the exposition in May, 1901, and reconstituted it two years later. The board was assisted by a woman's auxiliary committee, of which Mrs. Otero was elected chairman. She and I not only entertained the board of managers, but also spent several days in Las Vegas and Albuquerque in arousing public interest in the exposition. The people responded readily, and our visits in both places were delightful.

The New Mexico building at the exposition was an attractive structure in the mission style. The exhibit was designed to attract the attention of home-seekers and capitalists. In addition to Navajo blankets, Indian baskets, and pueblo pottery, there were samples of the apples, cotton, and wool raised in the territory. The collection of minerals was very comprehensive, turquoise being especially conspicuous. Ours was the only exhibit of this gem at the exposition.

Another unique part of our exhibit was the "Maria-

Josefa" bell, the oldest bell in America. This had been cast in Spain in the year 1355, and had been taken from one of the seven cities of Cibola to Gran Quivira, and thence to Algodones, in Sandoval County, New Mexico. As I am one of the owners of the bell, I may be pardoned if I digress to tell something of the history of this ancient relic. I shall give it just as it was told to me by the Rev. Father J. M. Coudert, in my office in Santa Fe, during the early days of my administration.

A short time after my inauguration, this dear old friend, for many years a parish priest in Las Vegas, was transferred to Bernalillo, the county seat of Sandoval County, which was only a few miles south of Algodones. Here the old bell had been in constant use ever since the arrival of Francisco Vasquez de Coronado, in the year 1540, except for the time it had been placed in the belfry of the old church at Gran Quivira, from whence it had been returned to Tiguex, now Algondones.

Father Coudert's story, as related to me at the time, was taken down by my stenographer, and is as follows:

Dear Governor Otero:

The Catholic Church in my diocese at Algondones is just now completing the building of a new parochial school for the children of that locality, and we have placed an order for a new bell for the schoolhouse belfry. Our community is very poor, and we must raise some money to pay for it.

It occurs to me that the only use we now have for the old Maria-Josefa bell is in its well-known antiquity; it has no other value. The bell was brought to this country by Francisco Vasquez de Coronado, in 1540, and was placed in the care of Father Juan de Padilla, one of the Franciscan fathers who accompanied Coronado to New Mexico; it being first hung in one of the mission churches established in one of the "Seven Cities of Cibola." From there it was taken to the Gran Quivira where it was hung in the church, of which the ruins are still visible. From Gran Quivira it was returned to Tiguex where it was hung in the parish church and has remained there until this time. (Father Padilla was killed by his guides while on the way from Gran Quivira to Tiguex Algodones.) The bell weighs exactly 198 pounds. It was baptized "Maria-Josefa" and was cast in Spain, in 1355, according to the inscription cast in the bell. The "F" in the word Josefa is inverted and the letters "S" and "E" are transposed, the error evidently having been made in the mold. The bell is supposed to contain considerable gold, silver, and jewels, as it was customary in olden times for the devouts to cast gold, silver, and ornaments into the melted copper just as it was being poured into the mold.

My Nine Years as Governor 307

Tiguex was the winter camp of Coronado on the Rio Grande, and was the final location of the bell, as it was his headquarters. It was from this point that Coronado made all his invasions into the northern, eastern, and western sections of this unexplored country for conquests and to study his surroundings. Anyone may inform himself of these facts by reading the history of the Coronado expedition.

The old church, which was built by the Spaniards here in Tiguex, just where the present settlement of Algodones is located, had the old Maria-Josefa bell hanging in its belfry where it remained as long as the church remained standing, and when it crumbled to the earth the old bell was placed in the belfry of a new edifice, and so on down to the present time. In late years, it has hung in a schoolhouse.

I have taken great pains in tracing the origin of this old bell, through the knowledge of the oldest settlers living in the Rio Grande Valley, and they would relate legendary stories to me of the traditions handed down from generation to generation regarding this old bell, and I can assure you I am giving you this information just as it was given to me by those old residents, and what I have read regarding the Francisco Vasquez de Coronado Expedition, in 1540.

On account of all this historical value connected with the old Maria-Josefa bell, I thought perhaps you, as our governor, rightfully ought to have it. I am not offering it to any one else. Both Mr. Hovey, our teacher at Algodones, who accompanies me here and who is greatly interested in seeing our new schoolhouse have a new bell, and myself considered it our duty to first place this proposition to you, so that is what brought us here. We are not asking any extravagant price; it is simply our wish that you should have the bell, so we will gladly let you have it, if you will pay the bill for the cost of the new bell we have ordered for the new schoolhouse belfry.

Before Father Coudert began his interesting story, I invited my friend, Hon. Arthur Seligman, to be present, as I knew that he was greatly interested in antiquities. When the good father had finished, I decided to take the bell, and gave him a check for the amount of the bill for the new one. After Father Coudert and Mr. Hovey had gone, Mr. Seligman asked if I would permit him to take a half interest in my purchase. I, of course, had no objection, so he gave me his check for one-half the amount I had given Father Coudert.

As Mr. Seligman was on the board of managers for the Louisiana Purchase Exposition, he asked if he might take the bell to St. Louis. Of course, I told him to take it, and it was placed in the New Mexico building on exhibition all during the exposition. Naturally, a bell 550 years old— antedating the discovery of America by 137 years—

attracted a great deal of attention. Two different parties offered to purchase it for five thousand dollars, but Mr. Seligman told them it was not for sale. Some years later, it was hung in the belfry of the archaeology building at Santa Fe, and was rung as a signal for the services, attending the dedication of the building, to begin.

To get back to the exposition, "New Mexico Day" was the big moment of the whole show, as far as the territory was concerned. This was originally planned for my birthday, but it was later found necessary to change it to November 18, 1904. Five days before this, my family and I left for St. Louis, where we took rooms at the Washington Hotel, near the fair grounds. Mrs. James W. Raynolds, Mrs. A. M. Bergere and her son, Manuel B. Otero, went with us and stayed at the same hotel.

Our big day at the exposition was described by a St. Louis paper as follows:

> Friday, November 18th, 1904, was a typical sunshiny New Mexico day at the Louisiana Purchase Exposition in more than one sense. The sun never shone brighter, nor was weather ever fairer in the World's Fair City, according to former Governor David R. Francis, of Missouri, president of the Exposition. "The New Mexico visitors brought New Mexico sunshine with them," he said later in the day in his address. It was the last of the state days and as many said: "Excepting, perhaps, the New York Day celebration, it was the most successful event of its kind during the Exposition." The arrangements were without a flaw and the exercises of the day were not only interesting but productive of much favorable comment and enthusiasm from many hundreds of visitors.
>
> It was after 10 o'clock in the forenoon when the New Mexico party in elegant equipages, drove to the Administration Building in the grounds of the Exposition and paid its respects to Governor Francis, whose cordiality and western breeziness immediately won all hearts. After the formal introductions, he led the way, together with Governor Otero, down the wide stone steps to their carriages. Adjutant-General Whiteman, of New Mexico, Brigadier-General Edmund Rice with the silk standard of the Louisiana Purchase Exposition, as well as the other carriages followed. The vehicles were preceded by the Filipino band of eighty-six pieces, several companies of Filipino troops, the Exposition band, and the United States troops, commanded by Colonel Cecil, the procession making the rounds of the entire grounds. Upon the arrival of the cavalcade at the avenue of states, the carriages turned toward the New Mexico building, while the bands and military marched around the square and were reviewed in front of the New Mexico building, which stands just opposite the Montana building, by Governor Otero and Former Governor Francis, of Missouri.

Major Johnson, in charge of the scouts and band; Captain Archibald Campbell, of the Sixth U. S. Infantry; and Lieutenant Clark, of the Jefferson Guards, were also military representatives at the ceremonies.

Herbert J. Hagerman, of the New Mexico board of managers, presided over the day's festivities. With tactful and eloquent words he introduced each speaker, first of whom was former Governor David R. Francis, whose felicitous remarks were much appreciated and much praised. His address was pronounced one of his finest efforts and his reputation as an orator is more than local. His encomiums of New Mexico, its exhibits, and the energy of its people were evidently heartfelt.

Governor Otero followed, and his address was so well received that many requests have been made for a copy of it by St. Louis people as well as by others who heard him. Unfortunately, the one copy of this is not available for this article, since it is in the hands of Judge Matthew G. Reynolds, whose illness prevented his participation in the exercises.

After introductory remarks, in which he thanked the management of the Exposition in behalf of the people of New Mexico for the honor conferred upon them by setting apart a day dedicated to the Sunshine Territory, and after paying his compliments to former Governor David R. Francis, of Missouri, for participating and assisting in making the day a memorable one, and his kindliness and hospitality towards the visitors, Governor Otero pointed out the close historic relations of New Mexico with the Louisiana Purchase Territory. As long ago as 1529, Cabeza de Vaca reached the Mississippi River. His boat was capsized in the Mississippi and most of his party was captured by the Indians, only de Vaca and two negroes surviving. The lonely trio turned their faces toward the setting sun and set foot across the pathless wilderness. It was near the Rio Grande that it fell in with a party of Spanish horsemen and returned with them to New Spain. Then came the peaceful conquest of New Mexico by Coronado, who, in 1540, invaded the Southwest with a comparatively large force. The occupation continued until the Pueblo Rebellion, when a Pueblo Indian was elected governor and the Christian Indians were marched to the river and there had to wash off with amole, the spiritual stains of their baptism. It was in 1692 that De Vargas reconquered New Mexico, and from that time until the peaceful conquest by the Missouri troops, in 1846, the territory remained under the domination of Spain and later Mexico. Governor Otero touched graphically upon the heroism of the Conquistadores and dwelt upon the noble efforts of the devoted Friars on behalf of civilization and Christianity. Continuing, he pointed out that New Mexico owes much to Missouri. Its present laws are modeled and copied from the Missouri Code and it was Willis P. Hall, later an honored member of Congress from Missouri, who did most of the work of compiling the Kearny Code. As General Kearny reported to President Polk, it was General Doniphan's command that accomplished the peaceful conquest of New Mexico, and General Doniphan was a Missourian. Later, the ties that bound New Mexico to Missouri grew even stronger. All business of the Southwest that poured over the historic Santa Fe Trail wended its way from Missouri, particularly St. Louis, and many of New Mexico's foremost sons were educated in the metropolis of that state.

After telling in detail of the intimate commercial, social, and other ties that linked both commonwealths in those early pioneer days, Governor Otero said that it is not so much of past history that he desired to speak as the present progress and achievements of the territory. Its educational advancement, its industrial growth, its wonderful resources, its excellent laws, its perfect climate, and its energetic people, were each in turn, dilated upon. The fact that its farm products in ten years increased in value from $2,000,000 to $10,000,000, that its mines have thus far produced $18,000,000 in gold alone, that its prospected coal fields cover ten thousand square miles, upon which ten billion tons of coal are in sight and accessible, that its public domain includes over 50,000,000 acres that in the past four years almost three million acres were taken up under the homestead and desert land acts, was emphasized.

He spoke of the wealth concentrated in New Mexico's stock interests, its six million sheep, its million and a quarter of cattle, many of them high grades, its thousands of goats, hogs, and horses. Nor did he omit to mention that New Mexico maintains a score of territorial institutions, that it pays annually over three quarter million dollars for educational purposes, and that the value of its property outside of land holdings is $2,000,000, or one-twentieth of its assessed valuation. The excellent financial condition of the territory and the further facts that it pays its bills, dollar for dollar, that it is reducing its comparatively small bonded indebtedness year by year, that its thrifty banks are flourishing, that in the past four years, 750 companies incorporated with a capitalization of $500,000,000 to do business in New Mexico, were used as arguments to demonstrate the territory's fitness and readiness to assume the responsibilities of a state government.

Governor Otero concluded with a direct appeal to the states of the Louisiana Purchase to assist the territory to attain the dignity of a state as there is no sound reason why, after its long and patient probation and after repeated demonstrations of its loyalty, its patriotism, its fitness, its anxiety for the boon, its financial and intellectual ability to manage its own political affairs, it should now be admitted with its present boundaries intact and under its present name, as one of the sisterhood of states, a commonwealth of which its neighbors have every reason to be proud.

Those who heard the address highly complimented Governor Otero upon it, for it was not only a fine oratorical effect, but also a cogent historical and statistical presentation of the facts which entitle this territory to recognition and assure its growth, stability, and prosperity in the future.

Judge John R. McFie was the orator of the day and made a splendid oration dwelling in detail upon many of the points that had been touched on by Governor Otero.

Upon the conclusion of these ceremonies, the New Mexico party drove to the Hotel Washington for luncheon, returning to the New Mexico building at two o'clock in the afternoon for a reception which lasted until five o'clock, over two thousand people paying their respects. An orchestra rendered fine music and delicious refreshments were served. Many members of the most prominent and oldest families in St. Louis, who not only remembered Governor Otero as a school boy, but also his father and mother, who had been great favorites in the social circles of the Mound City, were present, as well as many distinguished visitors from elsewhere, in addition to an unusually large number of people from the territory, including many representatives of its native population. Governor and Mrs. Toole and child, of Montana, were among the guests, as well as a niece of General Doniphan, who thanked Governor Otero personally for his kind allusion to the celebrated Mexican War soldier.

In the evening a sumptuous dinner was served at the German building, the party being guests of Hon. Herbert J. Hagerman, of Roswell, and Hon. Arthur Seligman, of Santa Fe, to both of whom much of the success of the day's celebration was due. Quite an amusing little incident happened at the dinner. The band had been playing several Spanish pieces in my honor, and I stood up and bowed to the leader of the band and, calling a waiter, handed him a ten dollar bill, with a note of thanks to the band. The waiter took it and started through the crowd for the staircase leading to the balcony where the band was located, at the rear end of the dining room. While on the way he exchanged the ten dollar bill with a two dollar bill and handed the note attached to the two dollar bill to the leader of the band, who, supposing something was wrong, sent back a note by another waiter, thanking me for the two dollars. I had not noticed the waiter who took the ten dollar bill, but my son, Miguel, left his seat and hunted for the man and soon located him and told the headwaiter, who brought him to our table. The band leader came down and delivered the two dollar bill to the waiter in exchange for the ten dollar bill he had stolen. The waiter's apron was pulled off by the headwaiter and he was immediately fired. He would never have been found had it not been for the boy, who proved himself to be quite a detective. The poor fellow cried and told a story about a large family on the verge of starvation, but got very little sympathy.

The ladies in the receiving party made a very favorable impression upon the guests, and it was universally remarked that next to the reception line on "New York Day," at the Empire State building, the New Mexico ladies were superior in looks, grace, charming manners, and elegant gowns to any others at state receptions, and compared very favorably with those who represented the greatest state in the Union....

Many congratulations were extended to the ladies in the receiving line by those who were present at the reception, and it was voted the most beautiful receiving line from any state or territory at the exposition. I strongly approved of the vote, as the ladies in their handsome gowns and jewels were a perfect picture, the like of which I never expect to see again.

Unfortunately, this reception was the cause of considerable bad feelings between Mrs. Otero and Mrs. Charles Spiess. The great Chicago fire is said to have been caused by a cow kicking over a lamp. Well, this rumpus between the ladies was also caused by a cow. I had appointed Charles A. Spiess as district attorney in San Miguel County, and he was preparing to move all of his effects to Las Vegas. However, he had a Jersey cow, which he did not think he could drive overland to his new home, so he gave it to Mrs. Otero. Later, I got Superintendent Hurley to furnish a freight car, free of charge, to accommodate the Spiess family. When the car arrived, Mrs. Spiess said that there was plenty of room for the cow, and that Charlie had no business giving *her* cow to Mrs. Otero, and she wanted it back. Mrs. Otero returned it, of course, but she did not like the way Mrs. Spiess acted and felt rather hurt. As she was the one to select the ladies who would assist her at the reception, she decided to leave Mrs. Spiess out of it. As he was president of the board of managers, Charlie wanted his wife in the line, and I believe that he was right. However, the full board backed Mrs. Otero and politely asked me not to interfere with her arrangements. Spiess came over from Las Vegas and asked Mr. Seligman, who was his personal friend, to see me and intercede in his wife's behalf. This Seligman agreed to do, although he had been the principal one to side with Mrs. Otero at the meeting. He told Charlie to wait at his house, while he went to see me. He came down toward my home, but he never came near me, and did not see me at all. However, he returned and told Spiess that he had been talking with me for an hour, but that I was determined to keep Mrs. Spiess from standing in that line. When

Charlie told me this, I offered to go with him and see Mr. Seligman. However, he replied that he had some other business with Seligman, and that this might interfere, so he would take my word for it and let it drop, which he did.

The reception was a huge success in spite of this unfortunate rumpus. The register of the New Mexico building showed that there were far more than two thousand people in attendance.

Mrs. Otero and I greatly enjoyed our visit to St. Louis, where we received many social attentions from leading citizens and officials as well as old friends. We came back by Chicago, spending a day in that city.

About a week after our return to Santa Fe, I received the following telegram from the president of the Exposition:

St. Louis, Mo., Nov. 27th, 1904.

Governor Miguel A. Otero
Santa Fe, New Mexico

The president's visit to the Exposition yesterday was greatly enjoyed by himself and appreciated by the Exposition management and the people who welcomed him in large numbers. He saw and admired the New Mexico building and expressed great gratification at the participation of your territory in the World's Fair.

(Signed) David R. Francis, President.

Naturally, this message made me feel pretty good. It was proof positive that I had been right in urging the appropriation for the New Mexico exhibit at the Exposition. Time would show that we had invested our money and time well.

Chapter XXIII

THEODORE ROOSEVELT AS I KNEW HIM

RALPH E. TWITCHELL in *The Leading Facts of New Mexican History*, volume ii, page 525, refers to "the well known personal relations existing between the President (McKinley) and Governor Otero, which were of the most friendly and intimate character." He then adds:

Governor Otero's power and influence at the White House continued during the two terms of President Roosevelt's incumbency and was occasioned largely through the assistance rendered by the governor in the organization of the New Mexican troops which became a part of Colonel Roosevelt's Rough Riders regiment during the Spanish-American war, and the unsought endorsement of his administration of New Mexican affairs by ex-officers of that famous regiment, many of whom the governor saw fit to appoint to more or less lucrative or honorary offices within the patronage of the executive.

My relations with Theodore Roosevelt were tempered somewhat by my services in recruiting men for his regiment. A year after the war, when he was governor of New York, in a telegram to me which was read at the banquet given in my honor by the officers of the New Mexico Squadron, he referred to his great pride in the Rough Riders, and had said: "To you, more than any other man, we owe the getting up of the regiment." However, Roosevelt's enthusiasms came and went, and what was said on impulse today was forgotten tomorrow. I believe that he always did keep a warm spot in his heart for the men who had served with him in Cuba. But, far from showing any special consideration for me, he, at times, showed himself very inconsiderate.

Theodore Roosevelt lacked the kind thoughtfulness for others which always characterized William McKinley. The English ambassador, Sir Cecil Spring-Rice, whom I met on several occasions in Washington, once remarked: "After all, we must remember that the President is only six." The Englishman certainly hit the nail on the head. Roosevelt never outgrew the selfishness and love of self-display charac-

My Nine Years as Governor 315

teristic of children. These qualities were apparent to the discriminating observer on the occasion of Roosevelt's first visit to New Mexico during the Rough Riders' reunion in Las Vegas, in June, 1899, which I have already described. However, these little things did not keep him from being very popular with the crowds.

Many of the Rough Riders from New Mexico took an active interest in politics, and it is not surprising that they gave early support to the political ambitions of their former colonel. The *Chicago Tribune* for September 2, 1901, said:

> Governor Miguel A. Otero, of New Mexico, says the territory of which he is the head, is enthusiastic in its support of Vice-President Roosevelt for the presidency in 1904. In the opinion of Governor Otero, Vice-President Roosevelt, even at this early date, can feel reasonably sure that the united vote of the New Mexico delegation will be given to him when his name comes up in the next Republican convention.

The assassination of President McKinley startled the whole nation. Doubtless, however, some of the citizens of New Mexico were easily reconciled to the change in administration, being hopeful that the former colonel of Rough Riders and "the friend of the West" might not only do something for them personally, but would also induce Congress to admit New Mexico to statehood. Some, like Major Llewellyn and Captain Frederick Muller, did receive political preferment, but that was all. The territorial editors generally expected Roosevelt to carry out the promise made at Las Vegas, but they did not know how easily our self-appointed champion made promises or how soon he broke them.

I, certainly, was not inclined to think of the change with any pleasant anticipation. Besides having lost my best friend in President McKinley, I saw, almost immediately, that his successor was a man of very uncertain temper. This was shown very decidedly at a dinner party which President Roosevelt gave in Canton, Ohio, the evening before the McKinley funeral.

As I have already told, I journeyed to Canton in company with Senators Carter, Fairbanks, and Hansborough. After luncheon, we all took a little walk, going to the old offices formerly occupied by President McKinley when he was practicing law. After our return to the hotel, a young man entered the lobby and asked for me. Senator Carter pointed me out and the messenger came over to where I was sitting. He informed me that I was invited to a dinner which President Roosevelt was giving that evening, at the residence of Mrs. Elizabeth Harter, where he was making his headquarters. I thanked him and he checked my name on a slip of paper he was carrying. He then asked me if I knew Senators Carter, Fairbanks, and Hansborough and I pointed them out. A funny little incident happened when he addressed Senator Carter. The senator remarked that he had come to attend a funeral and not a dinner party, and had not brought his dinner clothes with him. The messenger said: "I suppose you understand that an invitation from the President is an order." Senator Carter looked at the young man and said: "Yes, I knew that before you were born." We all laughed and the young man blushed and backed away.

It was raining pretty hard that night when the three senators and I drove over to the dinner party. As we passed the McKinley home we could see the coffin in the room and the mourners sitting around and the guards passing the windows with rain dripping from their rain coats. We all bowed our heads and remained silent, without a doubt the same thought was shared by all—why this dinner at this time? It seemed but a very short distance until we reached the residence of Mrs. Harter. As we entered the front door, we encountered Honorable E. A. Hitchcock, secretary of the interior, leaving the house and I stopped to shake hands with him. He seemed greatly annoyed over something. He stopped a moment to speak to me, and said: "Governor Otero, I am so glad you came here to attend the funeral of our dear friend who lies dead at his residence, not a block away. I think this dinner is a sacrilege and an outrage as well. I quite understand you must attend but as for me, *never*, no matter what the result may be, and I am leaving this dinner party right now." Senator Mark Hanna, who heard every word of this, immediately called me into a private room behind the staircase. Honorable Elihu Root was with him and they implored me not to allow the conversation I had had with the secretary to get out, as the newspapers would make a big item of it, and a rumpus would certainly follow. This might mean the retirement of Secretary Hitchcock from the cabinet, which would be most unfortunate.

On taking the oath of office in the Wilcox home in Buffalo, Roosevelt had stated that he would continue "absolutely and without variance" the policies of his predecessor. Everyone, especially the politicians, interpreted this to mean that he would make no changes in the appointments made by the late President, which, of course, included the cabinet officers. Naturally, I promised the senators that I would remain mum, and I did so until all parties concerned were dead and buried, with the exception of myself. I saw, at the time, that Senators Hanna and Root were both greatly worried, as it was generally known that Theodore Roosevelt was rather erratic when aroused, and had an ungovernable temper. He was domineering, self-conscious, self-conceited and, at times, a regular "bully," so the fears of the senators were well founded.

Senator Root evidently told President Roosevelt that Secretary Hitchcock had left the house, and some of his reasons for so doing, as the President went into a terrible rage and decided that he would not put in an appearance at the dinner.

Senators Carter, Fairbanks, and Hansborough, and I thought it our duty to pay our respects to the President so we went upstairs to his room. We found the door to his room slightly ajar and, as we looked in, we saw the President in his shirt sleeves and travelling pants, evidently in the act of dressing for dinner, when Senator Root came up and told him what had happened. The senator did not tell him of our conversation, but merely told him that the secretary had left the house and would not stay for dinner.

As we appeared at the door, President Roosevelt was cursing Secretary Hitchcock from A to Z, and what he said would have put a drunken sailor to shame, for the sailor never could have used all the profane language we were forced to hear at the partially opened door. Finally, Senator Root came out in the passage way and told us: "You better not go in, unless you want to see a crazy man. He is simply red-hot at Secretary Hitchcock and there is no stopping him. I will tell him, when he calms down, that you gentlemen called to pay your respects, so let it go at that." We were very thankful to Senator Root for his kindness, and we all went down to the dinner. The food was fine and perfectly served. There were two large tables, the army, navy, and marine officers were in full-dress uniforms, the other guests being senators, members of the House of Representatives and governors. The occasion was much like a death watch and everyone seemed to be uneasy. However, everything passed off quietly, but the affair did nothing to add to our respect for the new President.

I have already described the way in which Roosevelt's accession to the presidency encouraged all of my enemies to renew their attacks upon me. The new President was a man of very independent character. Had he been more in earnest about carrying out McKinley's policies in reality, instead of carrying them out and burying them, he might have acted on his predecessor's endorsement of me, and sent my name to the Senate without much ado. But, no, he had to go into all of the charges very fully before he reappointed me. I did not especially appreciate this at the time, since it put me to the expense of going to Washington to defend myself. However, beyond a little annoyance and

My Nine Years as Governor

some expense, it did me no harm. In fact, it gave me a clean record. I can always point to the fact that all of the charges against me were thoroughly sifted by two presidents, as well as by the Senate.

When Roosevelt reappointed me in the fall of 1901, and I had been confirmed by the Senate, I returned to New Mexico, well satisfied that my troubles were at an end. However, I had hardly got to Santa Fe, when I received a letter signed by George B. Cortelyou, private secretary to the President, which said: "The President wishes you to return to Washington at once to satisfy him in regard to a certain matter of great importance." I immediately telegraphed the secretary of the interior for a leave of absence and started once more for Washington. On my arrival, I started at once for the White House, joining a party consisting of Senators Bard, of California, and Carter, of Montana, and Congressman Mark A. Smith, of Arizona, who were all going there to meet appointments with the President. We all went in together. On entering the reception room, we took seats together in the northeast corner. There was quite a crowd there, and it was twenty minutes before the President entered with much noise and bluster. The first man he encountered was a congressman from one of the southern states. The President jumped all over this gentleman in a gross and ungentlemanly manner. The congressman looked at him for a moment, turned deathly pale and without another word started to walk towards the door. Before reaching it, he swung around sharply and took a step toward the President. We all thought something serious was going to happen, but he stopped for a second, then turned and walked out. Roosevelt then advanced toward a group of four men from New York and started to jump all over them. Finally he shoved his clenched fist in the face of a rather stout smooth faced man and said, loud enough to be heard all over the room: "I don't give a damn." The man he addressed shoved his clenched fist in the face of the President, and answered, "And I don't give a damn either." They all turned and walked out, showing considerable feeling. The President appeared to be in a very bad humor. He came over to our group and picked out Senator Bard, of California, and said: "Senator, I want to see you regarding the matter you wrote me about. I wish you would step into the cabinet room, and I will return there in a moment." Then turning to Senator Carter, he said: "Yes, Senator, I sent for you so we might go over some matters pertaining to the Louisiana Purchase Exposition which I wish ironed out, but I am very busy today, suppose you come tomorrow." This seemed to satisfy Senator Carter, and the President switched to Congressman Marcus A. Smith, but he had forgotten what he called him for, and said he would write him. Then turning to me he said, "Well, Governor Otero, I thought you were out in your territory. What brings you here?" I answered: "The very day I reached Santa Fe I received a letter from you ordering me back to Washington at once, as you wished to see me. I cannot say for what purpose, I am merely obeying your order to come here at once." His answer was: "I never wrote you such a letter; it certainly is a mistake. I know nothing whatever about it. Did I sign the letter?" I said, "No, but Mr. Cortelyou did, and he is standing right there." He then turned and called to Cortelyou. "Did I instruct you to write to Governor Otero to come here?" The secretary answered: "Yes, sir, you certainly did." He then inquired what it was all about. Mr. Cortelyou said: "It was about that letter you received from Manuel C. de Baca, of Las Vegas." "Oh, yes, I remember now." Then, turning on me again, he said: "Don't you know where your proper department is? It is the interior department, and there is where you should go, and not come to the White House." I answered: "I know the department very well, but your letter said you wanted to see me here, so I came here." He showed much temper all during the conversation, and finally said: "Well, the interior department is where you belong and you must report there." This conversation took place in the presence of Senator Carter and Congressman Smith, and, of course, was very embarrassing to me. We all walked out together, and went over to the Arlington Hotel for a little scotch and soda, for we all had been through a "fearful ordeal" and needed something to brace us up. The two gentlemen said to me: "Governor, if either of us were in your shoes, we would tell him to go to hell with his office and resign then and there." "But," I explained, "that is just what the 'gang' in New Mexico are wishing for, and I'll see them all in hell before I'll do it." I went down to see Secretary Hitchcock and he merely laughed, and said: "I don't know what he means. I have nothing to see you about as all your matters have been thrashed out most thoroughly. It is certainly too bad that you had to make this expensive trip, but most anything is liable to happen. You have my permission to return to Santa Fe at once and should a similar demand come to you from the White House, wire me fully before you start and perhaps I may be able to save you an unnecessary trip." I left for Santa Fe the same night.

Roosevelt's enthusiasm for the admission of New Mexico to the Union vanished when his friend, Senator Beveridge, reported to him on his slumming expedition to the territory. However, in the spring of 1903, the President decided to visit New Mexico himself while on an extensive western tour.

In anticipation of this visit, I appointed a territorial reception committee, with Major Llewellyn as chairman, and R. L. Baca, vice-chairman. William Loeb, the secretary of the President, was the first of the party to arrive. Owing to illness, he had left the others in St. Louis, and planned to rejoin them here. On May 2, everything in Santa Fe was on the move and everybody on the *qui vive* with anticipation. Two days later, Major Llewellyn and I left for Trinidad, Colorado, to meet the expected guests.

The "Roosevelt train" arrived in Santa Fe on May 5. The committee was at the depot with carriages, and the party was driven to the capitol building where a large crowd had assembled. The speakers' stand was arranged on the steps on the west side. The territorial regimental cavalry band was playing "Hail to the Chief." When the party had been seated, I delivered the address of welcome as follows:

> Mr. President, it is with great pleasure that I welcome you on behalf of the people of New Mexico to this territory and to its ancient and historic capital, for our people recognize in you one who sympathizes with them and understands the many difficulties under which they labor, and the hardships and trials they endure, as no one else can, unless he himself has lived upon the frontier and has known the mountains and the plains in their varying moods.
>
> The members of your regiment who went from this territory, and who formed the New Mexico Squadron (many of whom are present here today) learned from personal contact and observation your great worth as a citizen, an officer, and a leader, and there is not one of them who would not cheerfully lay down his life for you, not as President of the United States alone, but as the loved colonel of the most famous regiment since the Civil War.
>
> We welcome you to our territory not only as the President of the greatest republic in the world, but also as a friend, to whose care was committed many of our citizens as soldiers, and we have found the trust well executed.
>
> In your long journey from sea to sea, from the barren desolateness of the arid plains, to the ever green hills and valleys of California, you will meet many people, see many finer buildings, and many larger cities than you see here, but, Mr. President, I assure you that nowhere will you find more devoted, truer, and more loyal friends to yourself and the great nation you represent than in this territory.
>
> I will now take great pleasure in introducing our citizens here assembled.
>
> Fellow citizens, ladies and gentlemen, I have the honor of introducing you to the President of the United States.

Many people from all over the territory were present to meet the President and hear what he had to say about statehood. I was a little fearful as to just what he might say, so I had my stenographers take his speech down. It was as follows:

> Governor, ladies and gentlemen, and more especially, Mr. Mayor as the chief executive of this ancient and historic city:
>
> It is with a peculiar feeling of pleasure that I come here to New Mexico, from which territory one-half and, if my memory serves me correctly, a little more than one-half of the members of my regiment came. The man is but a poor American wherever he may have been born, to whom one part

My Nine Years as Governor 323

of this country is not exactly as dear as another, and I would count myself wholly unworthy of the office I hold if I did not strive to represent the people of the mountains and the plains exactly as much as those of the Mississippi Valley or either coast, the Atlantic or the Pacific. I do know your people, Governor, and I need not say how fond I am of them, for you know yourself. How can I help being fond of people with whom I have worked, with whom I labored and marched to battle? And there are no men here excepting the veterans of the Civil War, to whom I would doff my hat quicker than to my comrades in the late war, and you know what comradeship in war means. It has always seemed to me, Governor, that in this respect my regiment was a typical American regiment. Its people came from the West chiefly, some from the East, and from the South, and some from the North, so that every section was represented in it. They varied in wealth, place of birth, and creed. Some were born on this side of the water, and some on the other side. Some had come to New Mexico, as did your ancestors, Governor, at a time when not one English speaking community existed on the Atlantic seaboard. Some were the descendants of men whose forefathers were among the early Puritans and Pilgrims, some of the descendants of those whose forefathers had settled by the banks of the James even before the Pilgrims and Puritans came to this country, but after your people came. There were many in that regiment who were born, or whose parents were born, in England, Ireland, Germany, and France, but there was not a man in that regiment, no matter what his creed or nationality, who was not an American and nothing else. We had, in that regiment, representatives of the real, original, native American. There was in the regiment but one kind of rivalry among those men and that was a rivalry of each man to see if he could not do his duty a little better than any other man, and short would have been the shift of any man in that regiment who did not do his whole duty. We had serving in the ranks, men of wealth, and men who all their lives have earned each day's bread by that day's labor, and they stood on a footing of exact equality. It would have been impossible for a feeling of jealousy or envy to have existed.

I do appreciate to the full, Governor, all the difficulties under which you labor, and I think that your progress has been astonishing. I congratulate you on all that has been done and I am certain that the future will far more than make good the past. More, I believe we have come upon an era of the fullest development for New Mexico. That development must, of course, take place through foresight, thrift, and industry of the citizens of New Mexico, but the government can help somewhat and the government will help somewhat.

This is a great grazing state and this is one of its greatest industries in it. I wish to bespeak your support of the forest reserves of the state. Its forest reserves are created and are kept up in the interests of the home-makers. In many of them there is much natural pasturage. Where that is the case, the object is to have that pasturage used by the settler, used by the people of the territory, not eaten out so that nobody will have any benefit after three years. I do not want the land skinned. I want to see it preserved and kept for the benefit of the man who wants to see it used for the benefit of his children and children's children. That is the way to use the resources of the land. I build no small hope upon the aid that under the wise law of Congress, will ultimately be extended to this as to other states and territories, in the way of reservoir aid to irrigation. Irrigation is to be in the future the most potent factor in the development of this territory and one of the factors which will do most towards fitting it and towards bringing it up to statehood. Nothing will help more than development of that kind in bringing the territory in as a state. That is the kind of development in which I am most interested here. It is the development that means permanent growth and is the proper transformation of the land to help to build up farms in these regions and to benefit the home-makers. In such a manner shall this territory of the present and this state of the future become a great state in the American Union.

I take keen pleasure in being with you this morning, in being in this part of the country, which, laying aside for a moment the rival claims of St. Augustine, represents the earliest portion of what is now the United States and what was brought within the circles of civilization in the modern sense of the word, I take peculiar pleasure in being here, not only for historic reasons, not only because of my belief in what your soil will in the future produce, but primarily because I believe in that which is the best product of any region. I believe in your men and women. I greet you all. I am glad to be here. I am glad to be in this territory, Governor, I am glad to be in this city, Mr. Mayor. In greeting you, I wish to say that my heart goes out to the men of my own regiment, to the men who are bound to me by ties that are closer than any ties that could possibly knit me to any future time in my life. Good-bye.

When the President had finished speaking, he greeted Mrs. Otero, Mrs. Laughlin, Mrs. Sparks, Mrs. Frost, Mrs. Bergere, and shook hands with them and a number of other ladies of the party on the steps.

The events of the day which followed were thus described by the *New Mexican:*

Then commenced the drive over the city. A stop was made at ancient San Miguel Church where the President spent ten minutes viewing the interior of the historic building. The next stop was made at the cathedral. Here the infant son of Mr. and Mrs. George W. Armijo was baptised, President Roosevelt and Governor Otero acting as witnesses to the baptismal ceremony which was performed by the Vicar-General, the Rt. Rev. Anthony Fourchegu. The child, which was born April 9, was christened Theodore Roosevelt Manderfield Armijo. At the conclusion of the ceremony the party moved on to Fort Marcy, where Mayor Sparks presented the President with a beautiful little book containing the history of Santa Fe, and he also presented the keys of the city.

The parade then moved back to the city and, on turning south on Washington Avenue, as the President's carriage passed under the arch in front of the executive mansion, Estella Bergere, dressed as the Goddess of Liberty, dropped a wreath of roses which the President caught. Rising in the carriage he doffed his hat to the little lady amid a shower of roses. At the executive mansion, the President alighted and the party entered the gubernatorial residence, where an informal reception was held and several bottles of cold champagne were served to cool the parched throats of the party. This was not on the program, but as there was time enough for it, the President expressed a wish to meet some of the citizens and ladies of the city. The following ladies assisted Mrs. Otero: Mrs. James W. Raynolds, Mrs. John R. McFie, Mrs. Daniel H. McMillan, Mrs. James S. Duncan, Mrs. Murray, Mrs. F. O.

Blood, Mrs. Frost, Mrs. Sparks, Mrs. J. L. Seligman, Mrs. George W. Knaebel, Mrs. A. B. Renehan, Mrs. John H. Sloan and the Misses Baum of Omaha, Miss Margaret Burns, Miss Nina Otero, and Miss Jane LaRue.

After leaving the governor's mansion, the party was driven to the depot and departed for Albuquerque. On the special invitation of President Roosevelt, Governor Otero, Colonel William H. H. Llewellyn, Major Frederick Muller, Colonel George W. Knaebel, Secretary J. W. Raynolds, Surveyor-General Morgan O. Llewellyn, Colonel R. W. Twitchell, George W. Armijo, and some others accompanied him to Albuquerque, where they met Governor Alexander O. Brodie, of Arizona. Here, according to arrangements, Governor Otero turned President Roosevelt and his party over to the Governor of Arizona, just as the Governor of Colorado had done when he had received the party at Trinidad, Colorado.

Before the President left for Arizona, I presented him with a handsome Navajo blanket. He said he would always keep it as a memento of his wonderful trip to Santa Fe. I also presented him with the rifle, formerly belonging to Tom Ketchum (Black Jack), the train robber and killer.

The impressions of the President's visit to Santa Fe were summed up by the *New Mexican* for May 5, as follows:

> The governor did not say too much to the President, but everything connected with the President's reception proves that he said just enough and that the citizens of Santa Fe did their best to make every word of Governor Otero's cordial and sincere introduction come true.
>
> From personal expressions by President Roosevelt and the gentlemen in the presidential party, it is absolutely certain Mr. Roosevelt and the members of the party were greatly pleased with Santa Fe and had a very pleasant time here. Indeed, the President somewhat regretted that a longer space of time was not allotted during which he might have remained in this city and enjoyed the very pleasant surroundings and cordial greeting he received here. The President found that the welcome extended him by Governor Otero, in introducing him to the citizens of Santa Fe, was carried out with genuine cordiality and deeply felt sentiment by the citizens of the Capital of New Mexico.

Once joint statehood for Arizona and New Mexico had been suggested, President Roosevelt favored it as a happy compromise which might satisfy the territories without running the risk of disturbing the balance of power in the Senate. The joint statehood bill became an administration measure, and the only thing which saved New Mexico from being yoked to Arizona for all time was the adverse vote of the citizens of Arizona in November, 1906. I, of course, continued to oppose joint statehood to the end.

Nor did I approve of President Roosevelt's policy with respect to appointments and removals. He paid scant attention to recommendations of those who knew the territory. Within less than a week, a request came to me for my endorsement in a post office appointment at Clayton, New Mexico. The usual request was from the Republican county committee, and as a rule we followed it unless the committee was divided. After all the papers in the case had been examined, we gave our regular endorsement and sent it in to the fourth assistant postmaster general at Washington. However, a Rough Rider from New Mexico, a Democrat, who had no endorsements from the county or town of Clayton, except those of the Democratic Party, received the appointment. The fact of his having been with Roosevelt in Cuba was all he needed. Without any explanation or even giving the territorial committee a chance to withdraw its endorsement and arrange the appointment in accordance with his wishes, the President embarrassed all his Republican friends and ordered the Rough Rider appointed. Needless to say, I never made another request nor signed another endorsement of any kind during the remainder of my term as governor.

President Roosevelt made several removals in New Mexico which I considered arbitrary and unjust. Thus, in June, 1903, I was notified from Washington that President Roosevelt had removed a member of the territorial bench on charges of general immorality. I do not hesitate to say, I think the charges were absolutely untrue and that the action of the President was unjust and unkind, for it cast a serious stigma on the character of a respectable gentleman with a wife and family. I was greatly surprised at the action of the President and decided to give the matter a personal investigation and then go to Washington and see Secretary Elihu Root, who was a warm personal friend of the judge and had been responsible for his appointment.

As Secretary Reynolds and I were returning from our

sheep ranch, I went to Lincoln County to investigate these charges which had been made against Judge McMillan by an attorney who disliked him because of a court decision. I learned that a preacher who looked very much like the judge, and who was dressed like him in a Prince Albert and a high hat, had been visiting one of his "sisters" at her home at a late hour of the night. As they forgot to lower the curtain at the front window, a passerby thought that he saw the judge and the woman in a rather affectionate position. He hastened to tell the attorney, and after the two had gone to the window for another look, they made an affidavit against the judge. Other disgruntled enemies of the judge endorsed the charges, and the result was the removal of Judge McMillan by President Roosevelt.

After securing the real facts behind the complaint, I went to Washington, convinced that I had a clear case. I first saw Secretary Root and went over the whole matter with him. He was most happy and asked me to go at once to the White House and tell the President all I had told him. I did so. When President Roosevelt came out, I noticed he was in a wild frenzy. When I told him what I had told Secretary Root, he became infuriated, just why, I never could understand. He acted so strangely, I did not like his attitude one bit. Taking a pencil and a piece of paper, he wrote out a telegram to one of the informants. Turning to me, he said: "I want you to sign this telegram. Have you some telegraph stamps to pay for it?" I answered, "Yes," and handed him a book and he pulled out two stamps, called a secretary to copy the telegram on a regular blank, had me sign it, and passed the telegram back to the secretary and the two stamps, and ordered him to send it at once. I did not want to sign the telegram, for I well knew what the answer would be. It simply meant to strengthen the position taken by the President, and no consideration was given poor Judge McMillan. I went back to Secretary Root and told him all that had happened, and I could see that he was angry and disgusted. But he said nothing, merely shrugging his shoulders. I knew that a great injustice was done Judge McMillan, but I could do no more than I had already done. The President, I thought, had acted hastily, and wanted to be sustained. At one time I felt as though he was going to take it out on me.

The press reported, in the summer of 1903, that Judge McMillan would ask the United States Senate to review the evidence in his case, but I do not believe that this was ever done. The Denver *Rocky Mountain News* gave a statement from the judge regarding his removal. He expressed surprise at the outcome, as he said that he believed that he had established a complete vindication, having answered every charge against him. He bitterly attacked the character of some of the witnesses against him, and declared that the charges were due to disappointed ambition. He stated that he did not doubt the desire of Attorney-General Knox to be fair and just, but the assistants in the department were prejudiced against him. He said that he would not permit the reflection on his character to remain, but would ask the Senate to send for the record and pass upon the question whether or not it contained anything to justify the President's decision. However, I do not believe the Senate ever reviewed the case. I have always thought that Roosevelt treated Judge McMillan shamefully.

Without doubt the President had more ground for his removal of Judge B. S. Baker on December 10, 1904. The charges against the latter were quite serious, yet nine days later the President weakened his position by revoking his order of removal and allowing Baker to tender his resignation which was immediately accepted.

The ouster of Governor Hagerman from his office as governor of New Mexico occurred over a year after I retired to private life. However, it was so characteristic of Roosevelt that I cannot refrain from saying a word about it here. That Theodore Roosevelt should appoint a man to a responsible executive office and then remove him in a little over a year was not altogether surprising when one considers his previous record. Hagerman's ouster really amounted to a removal, since he was ordered to resign. Personally, I thought that it was a great outrage and a disgraceful piece of injustice and absolutely unworthy of a fair and just man. In 1912, Colonel Roosevelt asked me what I thought of this removal. I answered: "Colonel, that matter has been passed. I do not think you should ask me." He struck his clenched fist on the table at which we were sitting, and said: "Governor Otero, I insist on your telling me." I then said: "Well, Colonel, I think you made a mistake. Hagerman was honest. He may have made a blunder. I think perhaps he did, but it was an honest one, and I do not believe you should have listened to the men who wanted his scalp."

President Roosevelt was not satisfied to use his own power of removal in rather arbitrary fashion. After my reappointment as governor, he insisted that I make several changes among the territorial officials who held office by my appointment. Secretary Hitchcock of the department of the interior made this suggestion to me, informing me that it came from the President. He explained that Catron and Fiske and the rest of the gang had made such serious charges against John S. Clark, James D. Hughes, Max Frost, George W. Prichard, and Charles A. Spiess, that the President thought that I had better appoint new men to the positions then held by them. I explained that, so far as Max Frost was concerned, he had never held an appointive office under me, although I considered him fully qualified, and a man who had supported my administration strongly and fearlessly from the first day I had taken office. As for his integrity, honesty, and loyalty, he was far superior to the men who opposed him. Catron and Fiske merely picked him out because they thought their opposition to him would hurt me. It was quite true that the non-partisan bureau of immigration had selected Mr. Frost as its secretary owing to his qualifications and superior knowledge of conditions in the territory, and not for political reasons. However, it was "any port in a storm" with such men as Catron and Fiske, and they stopped at nothing when they thought it might injure me.

I argued the point in behalf of all the men mentioned, but only succeeded in getting George W. Prichard eliminated from their list of objectionable officers. This action on the part of President Roosevelt quite naturally played into the hands of Catron and Fiske, giving them exactly what they wanted. They began at once sowing the seeds of discord in the shallow environments belonging to both John S. Clark and Charles A. Spiess. The latter, together with Chief Justice William J. Mills, became convinced that I was losing out with the Roosevelt administration, and quietly joined with Frank and Charlie Springer in opposing my administration. I had previously got the enmity of the latter through my action in the matter of the New Mexico Normal University at Las Vegas. Having ousted Dr. Edgar L. Hewett and the faculty, I had forced Frank Springer to resign as president of the board of regents and appointed Dr. W. R. Tipton in his place.

The results of President Roosevelt's unwarranted interference with my officials were as might have been expected. This San Miguel County trinity, Mills, Spiess, and Clark, like water seeking its level, soon began a silent movement into the ranks of Thomas B. Catron, my arch-enemy. Spiess received his reward from Frank Springer through the Maxwell Land Grant; Mills was made the last territorial governor, while Clark tumbled over, body and soul, into the ranks of his devoted friend, Catron, and had the pleasure of voting for Catron as one of the first United States senators from New Mexico.

Gratitude was an unknown quality in those days and I attribute this lack solely to my poor judgment in the selection of officials, who proved themselves experts in the art of playing both ends to the middle.

I have said enough to show that, while I cherished a very warm friendship for President McKinley, I was altogether lacking in enthusiasm for the personality and policies of his successor. However, he consulted me sometimes regarding appointments, and we got along somehow. And when 1904 rolled around, I was on the notification committee appointed by the Republican national convention to notify Theodore Roosevelt that he had been chosen to run for the presidency that year. Hon. Joe Cannon, chairman of the committee, called the committee to meet at the Waldorf-Astoria Hotel in New York on July 27. From there we went to Oyster Bay where we found carriages waiting to take us to Sagamore Hill. The notification ceremony was followed by an elegant lunch. The President's daughter, Alice, performed with a snake, allowing it to circle around her bare arm, much to the delight of her audience. A group photograph was taken, and we then returned to New York, with the assurance that the country would have to endure four more years of Theodore Roosevelt.

Chapter XXIV

I WIND UP MY ADMINISTRATION

As I WAS a business man and a banker prior to becoming governor, I prided myself on giving New Mexico a business-like administration. I was always greatly pleased when my successes along this line were recognized. Thus I was highly gratified while in Washington, in January, 1903, on receiving a copy of the *United States Journal for Investors* which was published in Boston. On the first page was a full-page picture of myself and a brief but very complimentary sketch of my life and career. The sketch particularly praised the ability with which I had handled the financial affairs of the territory.

Another article along the same line appeared in the *New Mexican* for June 4, 1904. It was headed "The Financial Record of the Otero Administration." The piece attracted particular attention as it gave facts to refute the charges made by Democratic newspapers and by Catron and Fiske and other enemies. It was plainly written and its facts and figures can at any time be fully substantiated by the books and accounts of the auditor and treasurer of the territory. It showed that the credit of New Mexico was of the very best. Only a few weeks before this, refunding bonds to the amount of $101,000, bearing 4 per cent interest, had been sold at par. The proceeds were being used to take up and refund bonds for the same amount bearing 5 per cent interest. This little transaction alone would save the taxpayers $1,000 per annum in interest. As the bonds had ten years to run, that would mean $10,000 in time. The article pointed out that under former administrations refunding was never considered. Deficits and the issuing of bonds for current expenses were the order of the day. It stated, however, that under my administration deficits were unknown and a reduction of the territorial debt was the rule.

These facts spoke for themselves, and fair-minded and intelligent citizens could judge accordingly. In conclusion, the editor called attention to the fact that territorial debts of over half a million dollars left by the Prince administration and by the Democrats had been reduced under my administration by $352,900, and he predicted that the balance would soon be taken up.

The *Rio Grande Republican* also endorsed my financial record. It said, on June 10:

> The Democratic sheets of the territory that have so much to say about higher taxes under Governor Otero's administration do not tell their readers that under the same administration the territorial institutions have become the best in the Union. That the small increase in taxes represents more and better territorial schools, normals and hospitals, nor do they tell them that since the present governor took office not a warrant has been drawn, nor a bonds presented that was not promptly paid in full. Is it better to have these institutions, the pride of New Mexico and our credit at the best, or to pay a few measly dollars less taxes and bring dishonor and disgrace upon us? The taxpayers of New Mexico may rest assured that the public funds are safe and its institutions growing and prosperous under the Otero administration.

A few days later the *New Mexican* said:

> Governor Otero is today receiving congratulations upon beginning the eighth year of his administration as governor of the territory of New Mexico. The past seven years have been indeed auspicious and prosperous for the territory, to which result Governor Otero contributed no small share.

In speaking of the territorial Republican convention of 1904, I have already pointed out that Ralph E. Twitchell was strongly opposed to me politically. As a politician and as a friend of Rodey, he did not like the way in which I secured the nomination of Andrews for delegate to Congress. However, as a historian, he praised my administration so fully that one might suspect him of being a partisan supporter of mine. In *The Leading Facts of New Mexican History*, volume II, page 524, he says.

> The political policies and methods advocated and pursued by Governor Otero are susceptible to adverse criticism. This cannot be said of his administration so far as the business interests of New Mexico were involved.

Calling to his aid in the conduct of his office the business methods with which he was familiar and in which he had received a thorough education, he accomplished much for the welfare of New Mexico. At the time of his retirement from the governorship, New Mexico was never in a more prosperous condition. In all lines of industry there was great activity. The territorial finances were in most excellent condition. From the first year of his incumbency, Governor Otero labored for a reduction of the bonded debt of the territory. In this he was successful. The end of each fiscal year during his administration found a balance of respectable proportions in the treasury of New Mexico.

Governor Otero was not an applicant for reappointment. He had filled the executive chair for a greater continuous period than any other governor, Mexican or American.

Colonel Twitchell would probably not have given me such a strong endorsement in 1904 or 1905, but other political leaders of the territory did. Thus, Honorable Thomas D. Burns, of Rio Arriba County, was in Santa Fe in October, 1905, and boosted me for still another reappointment.

The *New Mexican* for October 26 quoted an interview with him as follows:

We feel that we owe our prosperity to the Republican administration. We are also grateful to the administration for the appointment of Governor Otero. I have known every governor of New Mexico, who has been our chief executive during the past forty-three years. I honestly believe that Governor Otero is the strongest and brainiest man who has held the position during this period. He is independent and fearless. A man after the President's own heart. The people of the northern counties sincerely hope that he will receive a much deserved reappointment.

The *Washington Post*, which was always interested in and well informed regarding the territories, referred to the likelihood of another term in office for me. The *Post* said on October 17:

The territory of New Mexico has a thoroughly business executive in the person of Honorable Miguel A. Otero, who was seen at the New Willard. Governor Otero is now nearing the end of his second term and it is considered probable that he will be again chosen for the office. During his administration the public debt of New Mexico has been materially decreased, the credit of the territory strengthened, and many reforms have been established. The governor is one of the most extensive sheep breeders in the Southwest and his flocks in Guadalupe County aggregate 65,000 head. He is a native of the territory, a scion of one of its oldest families, and speaks Spanish and English with equal fluency.

Some time before this, as early as the preceding March, strange rumors had begun to leak out in the legislative assembly that I had forwarded my resignation to President Roosevelt, and that he had agreed to appoint Fritz Muller as my successor as governor of New Mexico. Of course, this was simply "bull" gotten up by Catron and Fiske in the hopes that the assembly would endorse their man Fritz for the position and forward recommendations to Washington. It was simply another scheme of the "gang." I thought that they had run out of ammunition, but, being members of the "Die-Hard Club," they never missed an opportunity where I was concerned. My term of office was to expire the following January and some of my friends were asking for my reappointment. This naturally alarmed the whole outfit—Catron, Fiske, Muller, Berger, Prince, Vorhees, Vance, and others—as they did not know what I intended to do.

As a matter of fact, I decided about this time that I had had enough of politics for awhile. Having served nine years continuously I felt that I deserved a vacation. For some time, I had dreamed of going to Europe, and now that Miguel would soon pass his fourteenth birthday, it seemed an opportune moment to gratify my wanderlust. Accordingly, I decided that I was through with politics—for a while—and that my son and I would celebrate my freedom by going on a European tour.

I saw no reason to give publicity to my plans immediately. I certainly wanted to keep my enemies guessing as to what I would do. And, of course, many of my friends were very anxious that I should serve another term. Consequently, while in Washington early in October, 1905, I called on President Roosevelt and told him of my plans for the future. I said that I was in no sense a candidate for reappointment, although the best people in New Mexico wanted me to continue to administer the territory. I added that I had told them that, while I was not a candidate, if the President saw fit to reappoint me, I would accept. Mr. Roosevelt said that he regretted very much that he had not known my attitude before, but that he had promised

Secretary Hitchcock that he would appoint Mr. Herbert J. Hagerman. He added that, if he had known what I had just told him, he would not have considered appointing anyone else. However, he said that things had gone too far and that under the circumstances he would have to keep his promise to Secretary Hitchcock. I then told him of my proposed trip to Europe, and asked him to make a public announcement of his intention to appoint Hagerman.

The President took no action immediately but, on November 21, the Associated Press announced that he had told a delegation from Chaves and Eddy counties that he intended to appoint Hagerman governor of New Mexico upon the expiration of my term, on January 22, 1906. On November 24, President Roosevelt made a formal announcement through the press that he would appoint Hagerman. This was welcome news to me.

On the day following this announcement, the *New Mexican* said:

> Governor Otero will retire from office with the consciousness of having done his duty, and of having given the territory a highly creditable and beneficial administration. He had opposition to be sure, but this is one of the phases incident to New Mexico politics. There has not been a governor of this territory, during the past thirty years, who has not had the same condition to confront. The splendid Republican victories of 1898, 1900, 1902, and 1904, while he was executive of the territory, prove what the *New Mexican* says concerning Governor Otero's record.

One of the numerous friends who were interested in the possibility that I might be appointed for another term was Levi A. Hughes, who later became president of the First National Bank of Santa Fe. As an expert on finance, he was in a position to speak with authority regarding certain phases of my administration. Hence I shall include the splendid letter which he wrote to President Roosevelt in my behalf. Here it is:

My Nine Years as Governor

Santa Fe, N. M., November 20, 1905

To the President
White House,
Washington, D. C.

Sir:

Permit me as a citizen of New Mexico, and one who is vitally interested in its welfare and zealous for its progress, to write a few words to emphasize the advancement made under the administration of Honorable Miguel A. Otero as governor.

I feel well able and competent to write you fully, inasmuch as I was at one time secretary of the Republican organization of this territory and was collector of internal revenue under President Harrison's administration. In recent years, my business has been such as to prevent me from taking an active part in politics. I have been asked to accept the nomination for Congress on the Republican ticket, and have been offered positions under Governor Otero's administration, all of which I have declined to accept.

It was less than nine years ago when Governor Otero was appointed that this territory was financially in a moribund condition. Its securities were below par, even at a high rate of interest; the current revenues again and again failed to meet current expenditures; "graft was boldly rearing its head," capital and enterprise were discouraged, and for a time it seemed as if New Mexico was retrograding both in population and wealth. A striking change has taken place since then; a change that did not come suddenly but surely and without interruption, until today New Mexico's lowest interest securities command premiums; until the revenues exceed the demands of the many educational, philanthropic, and other public institutions created by the territory during the past eight years, and every just demand upon the public treasury is promptly met. The public debt of the territory has been reduced over 50 per cent; there is a surplus in the territorial treasury and has been for a number of years, while funds are accumulating in the sinking funds to pay off all bonded indebtedness when due. The number of banks has doubled, new manufacturing and other industrial enterprises have sprung into existence; there has been a remarkable absence of labor troubles and lawlessness, and on every side there are undeniable signs of confidence, of prosperity, and of progress, for which, in a great measure, thanks are due to the able and firm administration of territorial affairs under the present chief executive. But even more gratifying than the financial prosperity is the change for the better in the manner of the administration of the public business; the triumphs that have been won over graft and grafters against great odds; the better spirit exemplified by the strict observance of the Sunday laws; the restriction of gambling and the beginning that has been made toward its eventual suppression as a public institution; the economy and honesty in the administration, not only of territorial but of county and municipal affairs. Let me assure you, the New Mexico of today is quite a different New Mexico from that of nine years ago, when anyone who would have predicted the present admirable status would have been derided as a visionary.

Governor Otero began over eight years ago what you are so strongly advocating today, the "doing away of bosses." It is a well known fact that New Mexico for years and years had been dominated by the worst sort of boss rule, under the lead of the old "Santa Fe Ring," headed by Thomas B. Catron and others. The inside workings were disgraceful, and all sorts of crimes and illegalities were charged to it. No governor seemed able to cope with it until Otero was appointed. He promptly set about in a fearless and determined manner to crush this serpent, and his success has been marvelous, as well as beneficial.

He found it impossible to administer proper doses in the second judicial district, of which Albuquerque is the headquarters, so long as the judiciary of that district was linked to the grafters. But, after the removal of Judge Baker and the appointment of Judge Abbott, Governor Otero entered once more with determination into the cleaning out of the Bernalillo County grafters and bosses. It is a well known fact that all these bosses and their satellites are doing everything they possibly can to get rid of Otero, because they cannot run him. We, of New Mexico, are proud of him "for the enemies he has made" and the very men who are opposing him should be a sufficient guarantee of his fitness for the position, and although I have never heard him state that he is a candidate or cared for reappointment, at the same time I can truthfully say that it will be a great loss to the territory if he is not retained in the position at this particular stage of the game. Governor Otero is too good a man to be allowed to surrender his office under the fight that is being made against him by the unscrupulous and dishonest element that is opposing him.

Our prosperity under his administration only goes to show what one conscientious man clothed with the necessary power and influence, and backed by a strong national administration, can do to redeem a commonwealth from untoward conditions.

Hand in hand with all these improvements went the growth of the public school system, the awakening of civic pride, the optimism that goes with advancement in every direction. But let it be understood that this has not been achieved without virulent opposition, an opposition that even at this day boasts that it will again come to its own the moment that Governor Otero lays down the responsibilities of chief executive of this territory. This opposition has never let up in harassing him. Yet he has never wavered; he has always kept in mind, first, last, and all the time, the weal of the commonwealth and the high trust reposed in him. His friends, and the best people of this territory, love him for his fearlessness and courage. There was a time when even his friends thought and said that these enemies were invincible and so strongly intrenched that it was impossible to compel them to observe the laws; but Governor Otero was no respecter of person and insisted upon what he deemed right, no matter how strong the opposition.

Much more I might add to this tribute, but the achievements of the past eight years are public record, and they are a chapter in New Mexico's history of which the people and the National administration have every reason to be proud as time passes.

I might tell of the days when the fires of patriotism leaped high from coast to coast, when Governor Otero took the lead in the effort to send to the front, to Cuba, a worthy and full representation of New Mexico's sons; the pride it brought to him to hear that New Mexico had acquitted itself well before Santiago. I might dwell upon the many admirable personal qualities of Governor Otero; I might detail many incidents of his public career that reflect great credit upon the qualities of his mind and heart; I might tell of the friends he has made for New Mexico; the noble example he has set to young men who love civic righteousness for its own sake. But I merely desire to conclude with a prayer that Governor Otero be given an opportunity to push to its logical completion the great work for the territory that he has not only begun, but has prosecuted with such vigor. Even those who at first misunderstood, are now comprehending that one of the greatest blessings that nine years of Republican supremacy have brought to New Mexico, is the administration of Governor Otero. It would be a misfortune to the territory and its people, and a setback to the cause of civic righteousness, if Governor Otero, at this time, were to be superceded by any one less experienced in the guidance of the ship of state. It would cause undesirable elements, once dominant to the detriment of the territory, to lift their heads again, to point to the relinquishment of official duties by Governor Otero as a victory for them; it would negative results only recently achieved in the very stronghold of corruption and would make further progress difficult, for the present at least; certainty would for a period give way to uncertainty; confidence to doubt; the good work begun, if not undone, would receive a check that only time and another administration like that of the past eight years could redeem. There is still heavy work to be accomplished before New Mexico takes its place among the sovereign states, and I believe implicity that Governor Otero is the ablest, the best, the very man to do it. In my humble opinion, if the public welfare is the first consideration, Governor Otero will certainly be reappointed upon the expiration of his present term, which I understand will be January 22nd.

I feel authorized to make above statements to you for I am deeply interested in the welfare of New Mexico. I am not a candidate for any political office, but have large financial interests in the territory, and am a large taxpayer.

I have the honor to be, Sir,
Your very obedient servant,
(Signed) Levi A. Hughes.

An excellent summary of my achievements as governor of New Mexico appeared in the *Fort Sumner Review* ten years after I left office. The issue for October 21, 1916, said:

He came into office to find an empty treasury, a large territorial debt, bonds selling at a low figure and hundreds of thousands of dollars in unpaid accounts. When he went out of office the territory's credit was on a cash basis, the debt had been reduced to $60,000 a year, accounts due had been paid in full and there was several thousand dollars in the treasury. He established the offices of traveling auditor, insurance commissioner, and game warden, vetoed the infamous Hawkins Bill, prevented the building of the international dam at El Paso instead of at Elephant Butte, pocket vetoed many graft bills, removed the Hubbells from office in Bernalillo County, helped secure 1,500 soldiers in New Mexico for the Spanish War, and secured legislative appropriations for state institutions.

The Republican Party of the territory did not endorse me as an organization, but nine out of ten members of the territorial central committee and twenty-four out of twenty-five county Republican organizations did strongly endorse me for reappointment.

After President Roosevelt had made his announcement the *Santa Fe New Mexican* had this to say:

> Governor Otero will be the first to welcome Mr. Hagerman. The governor feels that he is right in doing so, that he has served his people for nine long years to the best of his ability, and for the upbuilding of the moral, political, and material interests of the territory. He is perfectly ready to retire from his official duties as governor, as he had only consented to allow his name to be used as a receptive candidate upon the very urgent and most strenuous solicitations of his friends who have aided him so much in making his administration so successful, and also because they constitute the best people in New Mexico, both in business and social circles, and to whose wishes and desires he could not conscientiously and considerately say "Nay."
>
> The governor will retire from office on January 22nd, 1906, according to the report, and the verdict of the people will be: "Well done, thou good and faithful servant."
>
> The fact that he is the only governor of New Mexico who has served two terms and over in the executive office, is more than sufficient to prove fully and satisfactorily that his administration has been acceptable to two Presidents, to four legislative assemblies of the territory, and to the people as a whole. A representative of the press called on Governor Otero this afternoon at the executive office, when the governor was very busy. He was shown the telegrams quoting President Roosevelt referred to above, and while reading it, a very good-natured smile spread over his features. He was asked what his opinion was. Very pleasantly, and not a bit excited or flurried, he said: "I suppose your correspondent is reliable, as soon as the report is confirmed, I shall congratulate Mr. Hagerman, I have nothing to say in the matter except that I have a very high regard for Mr. Hagerman, whom I have known quite well for several years, and who, in my opinion, is a fine young man of ability, education, and of the highest standing in the community. When relieved from duty as governor of this territory, I shall, without regret and with the kindliest of feeling, retire to private life, feeling that I have done my duty to the very best of my ability, and have always acted, as far as man can, for the best interests and the good name of our people."

Personally, I had no regrets whatever on leaving office, as I very much doubted my ability to satisfy Mr. Roosevelt, and I had very little confidence in his statements or in his actions. He was too egotistical and overbearing. He was always seeking to get in the spotlight, and would sacrifice anyone in his way, even though it be a friend. I clashed with him several times, and in place of seeking a reappointment under him, I always considered myself lucky to be able to serve out my term.

Mr. Hagerman arrived in Santa Fe on December 20. He announced: "Whatever is done in the matter of my inauguration, will depend, to some extent, upon the views held by Governor Otero, and I shall discuss the matter with him this afternoon."

In this conference we easily disposed of the question of his inauguration, and he was duly installed in the office which I had held for nine years, on January 22. Fortunately, neither he nor I could foresee that he would be ousted within a year and a half. That, of course, was an outrage for which Theodore Roosevelt was to blame. At the time of his taking over the administration, he impressed all as a brilliant and promising young man, although, perhaps, a little inexperienced in the ways of territorial politics.

At any rate, he made a couple of statements which impressed me as quite sensible. I remember he told me that Eugene A. Fiske had called on him just after his arrival in Santa Fe to tell him how glad he was that I would soon be out, and that he wished to assure the new governor of his loyalty and willingness to assist in every way. Mr. Hagerman added that this was very amusing to him, as he knew Fiske quite well and also his general reputation. He concluded: "I did not tell him, but my mind is made up to avoid Fiske and his satellites."

Three days before he assumed office he gave out an interview to the press in which he said: "The debt of New Mexico is not high. There has been a gratifying decrease during the administration of Governor Otero, and for this and other things he deserves great credit."

On the last New Year's Day on which I was in office, the *New Mexican,* which had always supported me loyally, said:

> *A happy New Year* to Governor Otero. He retires from office having done his duty for nine years faithfully and well. *A happy New Year* to the new governor. The people of New Mexico, especially of Santa Fe, have received him cordially and well. He must mark out his own destiny and his own record. The *New Mexican* believes this will be of the right kind. *A happy New Year* to him.

I was forty-seven years old when I handed over my office to Hagerman. I did not know it then, but there were still many years in which to mark out my destiny. I have lived to make my long cherished European tour, to play again a decisive part in territorial politics, and to hold an important office in the Panama Canal Zone. All of which I hope to describe in my concluding volume.

APPENDIX

Chapter I

LETTER FROM JOHN S. CLARK

East Las Vegas, N. Mex., June 2nd, 1897.

Hon. M. A. Otero,
Washington, D. C.
My dear Gillie:

Just a line in addition to our joint message this noon. I am too happy to attempt to write much and will simply content myself by offering my unselfish congratulations. No man in all New Mexico rejoices as I do in your triumph. As I look back over the rough and rugged political path you have trod for the last six or eight years and myself a good part of the time with you, sharing in your misfortunes and tribulations, I have often thought what fools we were, and, but for your foresight, wisdom, and perseverance, I would have abandoned the inviting field of politics ere this, but as your services have at last been recognized, I feel able to endure double what I have endured to bring about this result, yes, to have the satisfaction of seeing you triumph over the gang of would be patronage distributors that hang out in a certain town not far from Las Vegas. Men you had every reason to believe your friends after making promises to aid you, when it came to a show-down used all the means at their command to destroy you politically. To come out more than a victor against such a combination is glory enough for one day.

It is an old saying, "That one should be magnanimous in victory," but I cannot help rejoicing in the rout of Frost, Bartlett, Catron and company, and all others of their kind.

Your appointment is received here with almost universal satisfaction, and a plan is being arranged to give you a rousing reception on your home coming, which I hope will be soon, but have no idea that you will leave Washington until after your confirmation. Be sure and keep me advised as to your movements when you start for home, etc.

Sol Luna came up yesterday morning and along with about ninety per cent of Las Vegas citizens, thought you would be appointed secretary. He seemed pleased at the idea and said he thought in that event you would support him for marshal. I laughingly said you would be appointed governor. He treated it as a joke, but today, when your appointment became a certainty, his manner was entirely different. He remarked that, "outside of Pedro Perea, he preferred you to any one else." He also joined Twitchell and myself in a telegram, but he left the impression upon my mind, by the tone of his conversation and manner, that he was anything but pleased, and I may add that he impressed both Twitchell and Spiess the same way. I do not want to do him an injury, and it is possible that I misjudged him, but this is the impression he left upon me.

Spiess asked me to say to you in confidence that he would be an appli-

cant for judge of the first judicial district. It is useless for me to say more as you can judge the rest I suppose by the time this reaches you. You will be deluged with letters and telegrams asking favors, as there are more *original Otero men* in Las Vegas than there are voters, and I suppose this will be true of the entire territory. I forgot to say that Spiess and Catron are at outs, in fact Charlie gave him and Mrs. Catron the devil today in my presence. I suppose it is a row between their wives. Well I started out to offer additional congratulations, but here I am at the bottom of the fourth page scratching out a harangue that possibly will not interest you. Well, Old Boy, good-night. If I could only see you for just a few hours and shake your hand it would afford me much pleasure, but as that cannot be tonight, I can only repeat, accept hearty congratulations upon your deserved success, from
Your unselfish friend,
(Signed) John S. Clark.

Chapter II
LETTER TO JOHN SHERMAN
Santa Fe, New Mexico,
Sept. 27, 1897.

Hon. John Sherman,
Secretary of State,
Washington, D. C.
Dear Sir:—

As governor of the territory of New Mexico, and in defense of what I believe to be the highest rights of her people, I desire to enter an earnest protest against the execution of the treaty between the United States and the Republic of Mexico, whereby the Republic of Mexico asserts, and seeks to obtain, joint control of the waters of the Rio Grande and other rivers flowing through the territory of New Mexico, and to prevent the construction of systems of storage and irrigation along said streams in said territory. A draft of such treaty, as I have been reliably informed, has been prepared by the representative of the Mexican government and is now pending for consideration by your department. In support of this protest I beg to submit the following facts and reasons why such treaty should not be entered into by the government of the United States:

1. The Rio Grande enters the territory of New Mexico at a point near the town of Antonito, in the state of Colorado, flows through the central portion of the territory a distance of about five hundred miles, emerging therefrom near the city of El Paso, in the state of Texas, and is the most important river of said territory.

2. The Rio Grande is really a small stream of water. It flows rapidly through the mountains of northern New Mexico, through the valley of the central and southern portions of the territory. It passes through many fertile valleys in the northern part of the territory, and from the central part to the southern boundary; it flows practically through one continuous broad and fertile valley.

3. The most thickly settled portion of the territory of New Mexico is the Rio Grande Valley. For many years almost the entire population of the territory was congregated along this stream, and the wealth of the territory, as represented by its agriculture, horticulture, and mining industry, is found in this valley and tributary to it, with this exception, that the Pecos and Gila valleys, within the last few years, have been developed very rapidly and are fast becoming rivals of the Rio Grande.

4. The Rio Grande is not a navigable stream in any part of the territory of New Mexico, and never has been, nor has it ever been used for any beneficial purpose other than for agriculture, horticulture, mining, and stock raising. From a residence in the territory of New Mexico of more than eighteen years, I am very familiar with the stream, and from this knowledge I can say that it is absurd to claim that the Rio Grande is, or ever has been, a navigable stream. Indeed, the nature of the river in the central and southern portions of the territory makes it impossible that it shall ever be a navigable stream. In those portions of the territory the banks are almost entirely sand, the banks being constantly cut away until the stream has become so wide that it has a depth of but a few inches. Large sand bars form every few miles in the stream rising near and sometimes above the surface of the water, so that, unless during the flood time in the spring, even logs could not be floated upon its waters, and so far as I am aware no such attempt has been made. This river goes perfectly dry during the cropping season, and I have known it to be entirely without water for a distance of 230 miles from the southern line of the territory. Within the last ten years the Rio Grande has been dry for a distance of 150 miles above the city of El Paso, one-half of the time during the cropping season, and during those years said river has been entirely dry from the city of El Paso, Texas, to the Concho, a distance of 200 miles below. There is a time during the spring of each year, usually during the months of May and June, when a large quantity of flood water passes down this stream from the rains and melting snows in the mountains of Colorado and New Mexico, and during this period there is sufficient water for all of the lands now under cultivation along said river in said territory, and indeed much more than is necessary for such purpose; but after the flood waters have passed, or have ceased to flow, it is an exceptional year when there is sufficient water for the lands now under cultivation.

5. The people of New Mexico have been using the waters of the Rio Grande for many years for the purposes of irrigation, and have constructed systems of irrigation suitable to the necessities of the different valleys along the banks of that stream. Large areas of fertile lands are now under cultivation, and great quantities of grain, fruits, and forage are raised by the people of the territory by means of irrigation from this stream; and, indeed, it is impossible to raise crops in the territory of New Mexico, especially in the Rio Grande Valley, without artificial irrigation. Water rights have been obtained in the ditches constructed by the people at great expense, and to prevent the use of the waters of the Rio Grande for the purpose of irrigation would practically destroy New Mexico and make it what it once was—a

portion of the Great American Desert, ruining thousands of people settled along this stream, and destroying vast amounts of valuable property.

6. The system of storage reservoirs along the Rio Grande is, in my judgment, absolutely essential to the growth and prosperity of the people and the territory, for the reason that there are large quantities of the most fertile lands lying in their arid condition even along the banks of said river, because they cannot be irrigated from the present supply of water and the ditches now existing; and yet, during the time the flood waters are passing and during the winter months, sufficient water passes by unused to irrigate every foot of irrigable land in the valley along said stream. If these waters could be stored in reservoirs, sufficient water could be obtained to guarantee a permanent supply of water during the cropping season of each year and every year, and thus furnish homes and fields for cultivation of crops for a largely increased population. To concede the claim of the Republic of Mexico to the use of the waters of the Rio Grande within the territory of New Mexico would be destructive of the rights of the people of the territory, for the reason that it would prevent the storage of water, which is essential to the further development and prosperity of that territory; in that it would prevent the erection of dams and reservoirs for the storage of waters for irrigation and other purposes, not only as to the waters of the Rio Grande, but also as to the waters of the Pecos; and I submit that when the United States obtained the lands embraced in said territory under and by virtue of the treaty of Guadalupe Hidalgo and the Gadsden Purchase, it obtained, also, the waters of the streams within the limits of said territory, for the use and benefit of the people settling upon said lands now embraced in the territory of New Mexico, and that there is nothing in the treaties ceding said lands to the United States that gives the Republic of Mexico any claim or right whatever in the waters of the Rio Grande flowing within the limits of the territory of New Mexico.

I believe it to be a fact susceptible of abundant proof that the Rio Grande River is not a navigable stream for a distance of 1,000 miles below the city of El Paso; that the waters of the Rio Grande flowing through the territory of New Mexico never reach any navigable portion of said stream during the cropping season. On the contrary, I believe it to be a fact that said waters cease to exist between the city of El Paso and the mouth of the Concho River, about 200 miles below, almost every year during the summer season, and I submit the navigable portion of said river, which, I understand exists near the mouth of said stream, is not affected in any way by the waters flowing through the territory of New Mexico.

I desire to call your attention to the lack of good faith of those who are setting up the rights of the Mexican government to demand that the waters of the Rio Grande shall be allowed to flow through the territory of New Mexico to the boundary line between Mexico and the United States, and from thence on to the sea, on the ground that the use of these waters for irrigation in New Mexico is depleting the navigable extent of this river, especially in view of the fact that the citizens of Mexico themselves have, I am reliably informed, diverted, and are now using nearly all the water of the Concho River, which flows northward through the northern states of Mexico and empties into the Rio Grande, and which, it has long been understood in this country, is the largest confluent of the Rio Grande and contributes most to its navigable character. It is a fact well known in this country that the irrigation plants and systems of the citizens of Mexico on the Concho River have been very greatly increased within the last few years and subsequent to the time when the large canal systems had been built on the Rio Grande in New Mexico and Colorado. This is also true, I am informed, of every other stream which lies within the Republic of Mexico and which is confluent of the Rio Grande.

I am of the opinion that the desire for this treaty originated in the interest of, or has become part of, a movement for the erection of what is to be known as an "International Dam," to be located near the city of El Paso, Texas, and from information I have received I am impressed with the thought that this movement is mainly promoted by individuals residing in the city of El Paso, and Ciudad Juarez, on the opposite bank of the river, who own and control large bodies of land sought to be irrigated by this international dam, hence it is intended to prevent the storage of the waters of the Rio Grande in New Mexico, in order that they may flow unobstructed to this international dam. Now, it is certain that the construction of this international dam will not benefit a single citizen of the territory of New Mexico. The dam, if constructed, being below the southern boundary of said territory, the waters impounded by said international dam would flow back upon and submerge some of the cultivated land of New Mexico. Therefore, the construction of the international dam cannot in any way benefit the people of the territory of New Mexico, but, on the contrary, it would be decidedly injurious. It is a fact, however, that during the winter months of each year large quantities of water flow unused to any great extent by the people along this river, and I am fully satisfied that sufficient water flows down the Rio Grande during the winter months and the flood waters of the stream, to fill many large reservoirs in New Mexico, as well as the international dam, if constructed, at El Paso; consequently, there appears to be no good reason why people of the territory of New Mexico should not be allowed to provide for their own prosperity by the construction of reservoirs in the Rio Grande Valley, notwithstanding the erection of the international dam, but I must earnestly protest against the execution of a treaty which shall deprive the people of New Mexico of the right of impounding the waters which belong to them alone, but at the same time award the right of impounding the water by others, and especially citizens of a foreign country.

Yours very obediently,
(Signed) Miguel A. Otero,
Governor of the Territory of New Mexico.

RESOLUTIONS

WHEREAS, The Valley of the Rio Grande and its tributaries contains over 1,000,000 acres of bottom lands in New Mexico (only a portion of which is under cultivation), which lands are capable of the highest state of cultivation and the largest yield per acre in the United States, and will support over 100,000 families by the use of the waters of the said river under a judicious system of irrigation, and

WHEREAS, The population of New Mexico is being rapidly increased by immigration from the states and from the old world, and capital is being invested from abroad, the immigration and capital being induced to come here on account of the cultivation of the soil, which can only be accomplished by means of irrigation, and

WHEREAS, The great hope for any considerable prosperity in New Mexico lies in the use of the waters of the Rio Grande and its tributaries for cultivation, mining, and stock raising, and

WHEREAS, A bill has been introduced in the Congress of the United States, House Resolution No. 9710, entitled a bill to provide for equitable distribution of the waters of the Rio Grande between the United States of America and the Republic of Mexico, and for the purpose of building an international dam and reservoir on said river at El Paso, Texas, which bill was introduced in Congress by Mr. Stephens, of Texas, and is now pending before the committee on foreign affairs, and

WHEREAS, The enactment of said bill into a law will paralyze all the industries of New Mexico, dwarf her prosperity, and prevent any future growth or development therein, Therefore, be it

RESOLVED, By this convention of delegates representing the entire people of New Mexico, called together by the governor of this territory for the purpose of considering and expressing their opinion in regard to the merits of said bill, that we earnestly and emphatically object and protest against the enactment by the Congress of the United States of House Bill No. 9710 into a law, as being destructive of nearly every interest of the people of New Mexico, injurious to the welfare and prosperity of all of her inhabitants, and is calculated to stop the growth of her population and the increase of her wealth, that no such law as is contemplated by said bill is necessary, the reservoir provided for by it will hold more than twelve times the amount of water sufficient to irrigate all the lands which have ever been irrigated by the waters of the Rio Grande in the states of Texas and New Mexico, it will, therefore, be an extravagant waste of the waters of said river, and will, consequently, leave several millions of acres of land in New Mexico unused and unoccupied, which otherwise in the very near future would be cultivated and occupied by enterprising citizens of the United States and furnish homes and a livelihood for more than a million people.

RESOLVED FURTHER, That the governor of the territory be requested to appoint a committee of twelve citizens, residents of this territory, to aid our delegate in Congress in opposing and preventing the enactment of said bill into a law, that a copy of these resolutions be forwarded by the secretary of this convention to said delegate to be placed by him before said committee and the Congress of the United States, and that a copy thereof be also sent to each member of Congress, that every effort be made by every member of this convention and the people of this territory to defeat the passage of said bill, so as to prevent it from becoming a law, and that the agitation of the matters contemplated by the said bill and the treaty mentioned therein, may be stopped and buried, a continuance of which agitation intimidates capitalists and prevents investments in New Mexico.

I SPEAK BEFORE THE SENATE COMMITTEE

Mr. Chairman and Gentlemen of the Committee:

I appear before you representing the two hundred thousand people in the territory of New Mexico as well as the material interests of that great territory, which are vitally affected by Senate Bill No. 3794, now under consideration. This bill is identically the same as introduced in the House by Mr. Stephens, of Texas, and against the passage of which the people of New Mexico, in their legislature, and in various political conventions, have entered their earnest protests. The same bill now appears, introduced by the honorable senator from the state of Texas, and has been favorably reported by the committee on foreign relations of that body, without any consultation with the people of New Mexico, or any attempt to get their views upon the subject, and, indeed, without their knowledge, until the report of the committee was made public on the 19th of last month.

New Mexico has, for fifty years, been the ward of this government and, supposed to be, by treaty stipulations and the relations existing between guardians and wards, entitled to the fostering care of this great nation. But this bill, introduced in the Senate and recommended for passage, is calculated to deprive the territory of its chief source of income, and its main dependence for existence. Irrigation has been practiced in that territory successfully for the last three hundred years. It was the first part of North America to be irrigated, and while the methods were crude, and the results, most of them, small, in the aggregate, they have made the valley of the Rio Grande a succession of vineyards and alfalfa fields for more than 200 miles along its borders.

This committee will observe that the Senate committee recommends in the fifth paragraph, under the head of recommendations, found at page 5 of the report which is before you, "that in the proposed treaty for the final settlement of all questions regarding the distribution of the waters of the Rio Grande, some way shall be provided with which to prevent the construction of any large reservoirs on the Rio Grande in the territory of New Mexico, or, in lieu thereof, if that be impracticable, restrain any such reservoirs hereafter constructed from the use of any waters to which the citizens of the El Paso Valley, either in Mexico or the United States, have the right by prior appropriations."

It will be observed in this report that nothing is said in regard to the construction of such reservoirs in the state of Colorado, although in a previous portion of the report it is shown that a much larger amount of water is taken by that state than by the territory of New Mexico. Thus it is proposed to absolutely prohibit any irrigation enterprises in the territory of New Mexico, at a time when this government is being urged by the representatives from Colorado to appropriate $12,000,000 for the construction of reservoirs in certain states named, this bill not including the territory of New Mexico. *With New Mexico a state,* as of right it ought to be, no such proposition as this would for an instant be entertained by any one, and I most respectfully submit that our very helplessness in the national councils should be a most potent argument for the national Congress to see that our present rights are not infringed upon or curtailed for the benefit or to the advantage of the great state of Texas, or our sister republic on the south. Under the treaty of Guadalupe Hidalgo, our citizens were forever guaranteed their rights of property as they existed at that time, May 30, 1848, and to the enjoyment of all the rights of citizens of the United States, according to the principles of the constitution.

This report of the joint commission, which is made a part of the report of the Senate committee on this bill, was made November 26, 1896, and upon a wrongful assumption of the facts. After that date, the United States instituted a suit against the Rio Grande Dam and Irrigation Company to restrain it from constructing or maintaining a dam across the Rio Grande at a point about one hundred miles north of the city of El Paso, Texas, where the boundary line between the United States and Mexico is the center of that stream. The defendants below demurred to the bill, the demurrer was sustained in the district court, the United States took it to the supreme court of the territory, which, on the 5th of January, 1898, sustained the district court. It was then taken by the government to the Supreme Court of the United States, where, on the 22d day of May, 1899, the case was reversed and remanded, with instructions to set aside the decree of dismissal, and to order an inquiry into the question whether the intended act of the defendants in the construction of the dam and in appropriating waters of the Rio Grande will substantially diminish the navigability, and if so, to enter a decree restraining those acts to the extent that they will so diminish. This case is reported in 174, United States, at page 690, in which Judge Brewer delivering the opinion, says, at page 699: "I am not, therefore, disposed to question the conclusion reached by the trial court and the supreme court of the territory that the Rio Grande, within the limits of New Mexico, is not navigable; neither is it necessary to consider the treaty stipulations between this country and Mexico." In accordance with the mandate of the Supreme Court of the United States, testimony was taken for several weeks before Judge Parker, of Las Cruces, near the Mexican border, and a large number of witnesses were examined with reference to the fact whether such a dam would substantially diminish the navigability of the Rio Grande within the limits of present navigability. All of this testimony was to the effect that such a dam as was contemplated would not have any effect in that direction, and the court so found. From this judgment of the district court the United States took an appeal to the supreme court of the territory, which affirmed the judgment of the court below. Thereupon the United States again appealed to the Supreme Court of the United States, where it is now pending, and will not be reached for argument at the present term; and I submit to this committee that, until the decision of that court, it would be highly improper for a coördinate branch of

My Nine Years as Governor

the government, i. e., the legislative, to act in such a way as is contemplated by the bill in question while the matter is *sub judice*.

The transcript of the record in that case contains an enormous amount of testimony from reliable parties upon the subject in controversy, to which I would invite the attention of the committee, as my time is too limited to read even a portion of it.

It will be observed that this "joint commission" earnestly recommends the construction of a dam across the Rio Grande at El Paso, at an expense of $2,317,133.30, and the ceding by the United States to Mexico to a portion of the territory of New Mexico, and that the Senate committee agrees in these recommendations in its report on this bill, while the United States, by *its law department*, has, for more than three years past, been endeavoring *to prohibit the construction of a similar dam one hundred miles north* of El Paso, upon the ground that it would materially impair the navigability of that river at a point between 800 and 900 miles below El Paso, thus violating the provisions of the treaty of Guadalupe Hidalgo and impairing the contract entered into by that treaty between us and the Republic of Mexico. Just how the distinguished gentlemen on the commission and on the Senate committee arrived at the conclusion that an international dam at El Paso is demanded by the treaty of Guadalupe Hidalgo and will result in great benefit to both nations by the expenditure of more than $2,300,000, while the same dam, constructed by private parties without expense to either government, one hundred miles above the point, is a gross violation of treaty obligations, and will seriously impair the navigability of the stream, is something about which I am not advised, and I desire, and earnestly urge, this committee to grant our people time in which to solve this problem and fully present arguments and facts to show the ruinous effect which the passage of this bill would have upon the industries of our people.

As I have stated before, the legislature of New Mexico and its people in conventions have most earnestly protested, in the name of justice and right, against the passage of the so-called Stephens bill, which is identical with the one under consideration. The legislature of that territory assembles on the 21st inst., and, immediately after its convening, one of the first acts will be to authorize the appointment of a non-political committee to visit Washington at the expense of the territory for the purpose of presenting arguments and facts against the passage of this bill. Before 1850, New Mexico had been an outlying province of the Kingdom of Spain and the Republic of Mexico, neglected and uncared for by either government, compelled to depend upon herself and her own resources, to contend against an arid climate and the savage Indians within her borders. Since that time, she has had little from the national government, but has conducted her own internal affairs, erected a capitol building, a penitentiary, university, agricultural college, school of mines, and normal schools, entirely at her own expense, until, in 1898, Congress gave to her certain donations of land for various public institutions, and sections 16 and 36 for the benefit of our public schools, which are now being utilized as rapidly as conditions will permit. Persistent endeavors to be admitted to the sisterhood of states have been ignored; both political parties, and every legislature for the last twelve years, have made the application in vain, notwithstanding we have more wealth and population than any of the recently admitted states of the union. We bow with submission to this will of Congress, but we cannot find words sufficiently strong with which to protest against this bill, now pending before you, which deliberately proposes to cede a portion of our territory, to prohibit the construction of reservoirs upon our principal stream, and deprive our people of using even the limited means at our command for purposes of agriculture. While we admit that Congress has the power to do all these things, as the guardian has the disposal of his ward's property, yet we protest against the right to exercise it, as taking away our property, not only without compensation, but actually inflicting an irreparable injury in addition to its loss.

∞

Chapter IV

SPEECH BY WILLIAM H. H. LLEWELLYN

Governor Otero, there has been assigned to me by the officers of the New Mexican Squadron of the First United States Volunteer Cavalry, the pleasing duty of delivering at this time to you a short address.

On the 22nd day of last April, a peace extending over a period of thirty-three years in our beloved country was broken and the American people were confronted with a war with Spain. From the time of the sinking of the Maine in the harbor of Havana to the 22nd day of April, that peerless statesman, that greatest of living Americans, William McKinley, the President of the United States, had stood like a wall of adamant against the restless, seething clamor of an excited American people, who would have plunged our country into a war for which we were illy prepared indeed. Never before in the history of nations has been presented a spectacle of a more sublime character during the above period and weary days of anxious waiting, but during this time our navy was being strengthened and our armies equipped to face the relentless front of battle.

How wisely our President wrought will be told in history until time shall be no more. The country sprang to arms and an object lesson of what a united, free American people could do in the hour of a great and exacting emergency was presented. You, sir, as chief executive of this territory and commander-in-chief of its forces, were called upon by our President to furnish the quota of troops assigned to this territory.

On May 6th and 7th, 1898, there were mustered under your orders and instructions, troops E, F, G and H of what, under Divine Providence, was destined to make an imperishable name in history and reflect the luster of fame upon yourself, as well as upon the patriotic people of New Mexico, who so promptly furnished this contingent of the now world-famous regiment—Roosevelt's Rough Riders. It was my good fortune to receive from your excellency a captain's commission, and to be placed in command of Troop G, and I see before me here, tonight, Captains Luna, Curry, and Muller, who commanded the other three troops, as well as a number of the lieutenants and many troopers of the New Mexico Squadron. These officers, without exception, selected by your excellency from among our people, were as gallant a set of men as ever went forth from any state to do battle and, if necessary, offer up their lives upon the altar of their country.

But what words can I find to do justice to the men in the ranks who bore unflinchingly every duty imposed on them. I cannot describe them in more fitting language than by narrating an anecdote told by President McKinley to Major Maximillian Luna and myself at the White House after our regiment was mustered out. He said, "I have made up a little story about Governor Otero's soldiers of this regiment, that when they landed at Daquiri they went ashore in squads of fifteen and twenty and really needed no officers, as they just inquired for the trail to the Spanish stronghold of Santiago de Cuba, and never stopped until they reached that place and captured it." History will record the fact that on that terrible march through the tropical jungles over a trail barely made wide enough for two men marching abreast, a distance of fifteen miles under the glare of a sun, whose fatal rays struck down hundreds of the regular troops, who marched ahead of us and whom we passed on each side of the trail in groups of three, four, and five, prostrated by the heat and compelled to rest from exhaustion, and yet not a single soldier of the New Mexico Squadron was left behind, and by 8 o'clock that night our regiment had passed more than 8,000 regular troops and bivouacked at Siboney with nothing between us and the enemy but the outposts of the Twenty-second United States infantry. Before landing from our transports, each trooper had been requested to give us the address of his nearest relative or friend, so that they might be notified should any be killed in action. In my troop quite a number gave the same directions as did Trooper George Roland, of Grant County, the wounded hero of Guasimas, who when I asked him for the address, simply replied, "You can just send word to Governor Otero that I have been killed, doing my duty, as I promised him in Santa Fe I would do." The soldiers of our command reposed that trust and confidence in you which was inspired by your untiring efforts in their behalf.

In the war between the states, there was developed a number of men who have a lasting place in history as "war governors." Fairchild, of Wisconsin; Morton, of Indiana; Wise, of Virginia; Fletcher, of Missouri; and Yates, of Illinois, are among the names of our great war governors in the irrepressible conflict, and tonight, your excellency, we lay this tribute at your feet and place upon your brow the immortal title of the "War Governor of New Mexico," to which you are so justly entitled for the celerity with which you met every demand of the national government and dispatched to the front, under the several calls for troops, more than New Mexico's quota. After the war was ended and your troops returned to camp at Montauk Point, you were there visiting the hospitals and seeing in person that your fever-stricken and wounded soldiers needed nothing that money could purchase to alleviate their sufferings.

Sir, I have not the command of language to properly express my thoughts upon the subject, but when I tell you I have seen fever-stricken and emaciated New Mexico soldier boys bow their heads after your visit to Montauk Point and reverently say, "God bless Governor Otero," my sentiments and their relation to yourself are more clearly portrayed than any words I might utter.

White winged peace has spread its mantle over the land, and the soldiers of yesterday are the citizens of today, pursuing the pathways of life in the different channels of industry and employment, and while you, as the governor of New Mexico, will be forever enshrined in our hearts, we have thought that it would be fitting to present to you, as a mark of our respect and esteem, some small token which might be handed down to all future generations of your family, and ever be a silent witness of the affection and respect in which you are held by your officers and men. I therefore, in the name of the officers of the New Mexico Squadron of the First United States Volunteer Cavalry, present you with this medal.

MY RESPONSE

Major Llewellyn, officers, and members of the New Mexico Squadron of the Rough Riders regiment. Gentlemen: When, not long ago, I learned that the officers of the Roosevelt Rough Riders belonging to this territory were to give a banquet, I had no intimation that it was to be other than a mere reunion of fellow-soldiers, to renew the friendships and recall the incidents of the memorable campaign before Santiago, in which they had taken so prominent a part. Although it was vaguely hinted that something further might be done, I had no idea that the presentation of a medal to me was on the program, and although afterwards informed of what was in store for me here, I am, nevertheless, greatly at a loss as to how to express myself on this occasion and show, in fitting terms, my appreciation of a compliment so flattering, knowing as I do how slight are the causes by which you claim to justify your action.

You are pleased to declare it to be in recognition of the value and importance of something I was enabled to do, in connection with the raising, organizing, and forwarding of New Mexico's quota of volunteers for service in the recent war with Spain, so admirably conducted and gallantly fought, and so gloriously ended; a war in which we won a place second to none among the nations of the earth, and in which, by once again bringing together in intimate association the patriotic soldiery of the long-estranged north and south, to battle side by side in a common cause, equally dear to both, we have, at last, happily been enabled to dispel, and I trust forever, the sectional prejudices and animosities mutually engendered by the fratricidal war formerly waged between the northern and southern states; prejudices and animosities long fondly nurtured by the fierce non-combatants of either section, but rarely indulged in by any who had periled their lives in the cause they espoused, a desideratum never until now fully realized, and sufficient in itself to compensate for all the treasure expended and the precious lives lost in this righteous war with Spain; and it is especially gratifying to know that the existing evidences of goodwill toward each other are mainly, if not wholly, due to the patriotism and magnanimity of the soldiery of our Union, and each of you must personally glory in the fact that none contributed more by precept and

My Nine Years as Governor 355

example so desirable a result than your own brave Colonel Wood, and his worthy successor, Colonel Roosevelt, from the north, and your Commander of Cavalry, the ever glorious veteran, Major General Joe Wheeler, the pride of the south.

That, in common with all the people of the territory, I took great interest in the organization of your now famous regiment, and having great pride in its personnel, that I felt personally interested in the welfare of every man who joined from the territory, is true, and if I was so situated officially as to be able to have rendered you individually or collectively any special service (and I protest that I can recall none worthy of notice), I am already more than repaid in the glory reflected on the territory by your conduct in the field.

It became my official duty, as well as a valued privilege, to employ the means necessary to meet as speedily as possible every call that should be made upon the territory for troops, and happily the patriotism of our people was so universally and thoroughly aroused, that no difficulty was found in promptly enlisting, organizing, and sending forward the number required under each call made by the President of the United States. In fact, on each occasion the number of volunteers offering was in excess of the number called for. No merit, therefore, can justly be claimed by any of the officials engaged, beyond that of having promptly and to the best of their ability, discharged the duties devolving upon them, but I can bear witness to the commendable zeal and ability displayed by all officially engaged with me in this undertaking and, particularly, to that manifested by each member of the staff and regimental officers of the National Guard of the territory.

Our task, not proving difficult, all at once became imbued with the desire to maintain as far as possible, the splendid record made by the territory during the war between the states, when she sent to the field in the cause of the Union almost 10 per cent not merely of her entire population (Indians excluded), a record never before equalled in the history of any country, and this although more than 90 per cent of the people of the territory at that time, had been born citizens of the Republic of Mexico, and had enjoyed the privileges and advantages of our government for less than a score of years, thus exhibiting a devotion to the country to which they had so recently transferred their allegiance, worthy of perpetual remembrance, and I allude to this matter here because, whenever the territory has applied for admission as a state into the Union, it has been and still is objected by many people of the East, that the population of Mexican descent, who have ever comprised a majority of the inhabitants of the territory, are not qualified for self-government, by reason of their ignorance of our government and institutions, and of their general illiteracy, forgetful of the fact that nine-tenths at least of the class thus unjustly and unblushingly decried, are born citizens of the United States, and not only entitled by birth, to all the rights and privileges of such citizenship, but have lived their whole lives under our government, that in education and intelligence they need not fear comparison with any others of similar stations and vocations, and unmindful also of the further fact that Congress has, as yet, never spent a dollar to assist them in acquiring the education which is now demanded as a prerequisite to admission into the Union, while millions almost have been spent in supporting in indolence the brutal savages of the territory, and in futile efforts to civilize and educate them. Had one-tenth of the money thus uselessly expended on these miscalled "wards of the nation" been applied in aid of common schools in the territory, our diverse population would long ago have been thoroughly assimilated and as familiar here as elsewhere with the language common to the people of the several states, in which our laws are enacted, our public records kept, and all judicial proceedings in the higher courts conducted.

As in the war between the states, so in that with Spain, New Mexico not only furnished more troops in proportion to her population than any state or territory of the United States (thus maintaining her former precedent), but in addition to this she has the enviable distinction of having supplied the now famous Roosevelt Rough Riders with more men and officers than any other territory or state, and also more of the men and officers of that regiment who participated with such conspicuous gallantry in the terrible battles before Santiago, as to add unfading lustre to the fame of our American soldiery.

I will not attempt to narrate to the gentlemen Rough Riders here present, what they undertook and accomplished in these memorable battles, as they know a thousand times more about it than I and doubtless think less of it than others do, suffice it to say that as raw troops with but little training, and never before under fire, they behaved with all the coolness and steadiness of veterans, always to be found at the front in every advance, acting almost without concert with the other forces engaged, every trooper seeming to feel all the responsibility of an officer, and every officer sharing in all the arduous duties required of the men, each intent only on inflicting the greatest loss on the enemy and reaching the position sought for at the time, by the most direct line and in the shortest time possible (and it seems that they never failed to accomplish whatever they undertook), they so distinguished themselves individually and collectively, by their dash and gallantry, as to make themselves conspicuous among all the brave soldiers who participated in those desperate conflicts.

Now, I might ask, what could have redounded more to the credit of New Mexico than the share she had in sending this famous regiment to the field—a regiment whose fame is already world-wide? Has she not emulated almost her former and most remarkable record? But this is not all we did during this war. We sent, in addition, 440 equally brave men, under the second call of the President, who were not able to get to the front before hostilities were suspended, who, no doubt, would have given an equally good account of themselves had the opportunity offered, for, as was remarked by some one in my hearing not long ago, while speaking of the gallantry of the Rough Riders "New Mexicans are all built that way."

And right here I wish to say that I have again and again congratulated myself on my fortunate appointments of officers for the troops we furnished to the Rough Riders. By the meritorious conduct of each in every position assigned him, and by your distinguished gallantry in the field on every opportunity afforded, you clearly show that no better selections could have been made. Each and every one of you has more than fulfilled my highest expectations, and I take especial pleasure in so declaring to you here.

And let me assure you that I am not alone in this opinion of your military merits and standing. I have received letters from both General Wood and Colonel Roosevelt, your first colonel and lieutenant-colonel were eye-witnesses of your behavior in the battles before Santiago, and each expressed the highest admiration of the conduct of every officer from this territory. And praise from either of these distinguished officers is high praise indeed.

I accept the beautiful medal which you have here presented me, not, believe me, as a memento merited by anything done by me officially or otherwise during the recent war, but rather (and what I can and ever will highly prize) as a flattering token of your personal friendship and regard.

☙

Chapter V

I ACCEPT NEW CAPITOL BUILDING FOR NEW MEXICO

Mr. President, Ladies, and Gentlemen:

I congratulate you, and the people of the whole territory of New Mexico upon this auspicious occasion when the new capitol building is turned over by the committee to whom was intrusted its re-construction to the territorial authorities, for the use of its legislatures and officers.

I also congratulate you and the territory upon the character and construction of this building, and the comparatively small amount of money which has been expended thereon, it being in all respects more desirable and better adapted for the purpose than its predecessor upon these grounds which was destroyed by fire eight years ago. That was a beautiful building and cost the territory $250,000. After its loss the territorial officers were obliged to find quarters where they might, in different parts of the city, and the legislature was housed temporarily during their sessions in different buildings.

The legislature of 1895 passed a bill providing for the rebuilding and refurnishing of the territorial capitol, and authorized the issuance of bonds to the amount of $75,000 for that purpose, and a capitol rebuilding board was directed to be appointed for the purpose of rebuilding the destroyed capitol. This board consisted of five well-known citizens of high character and distinguished ability from different parts of the territory, and has conducted its arduous and responsible duties in the most satisfactory manner. There have only been two changes since the original appointment, caused by the resignation of Hon. Solomon Luna and Hon. A. Staab from the board.

During the five years of its appointment, this board, as assembled, has met at the capital many times each year, for the purpose of making contracts, auditing bills, and carrying on all the routine work essential and necessary to the proper expenditure of the money at its disposal, and without any compensation whatever.

It was soon ascertained that this appropriation was altogether inadequate for the purposes named, in order to insure a building which would be a permanent credit to the territory, and the last legislature was asked to authorized an additional issue of $60,000 in 4 per cent bonds for the completion and furnishing of the building. This act was cheerfully passed by the legislature early in its session. Congress at once ratified the action of the legislature and these 4 per cent bonds were sold for $1.03 (above par), and were used in bringing this building to the state of perfection in which it now stands before you.

Too much credit cannot be given, Mr. President, to the earnest and untiring efforts of the board, its secretary and clerk in conjunction with the supervising architect, Mr. I. H. Rapp, for providing the territory with such a building as we now have, at an expense in bonds of only $135,000. Solidity, convenience, and safety have been the three cardinal principles upon which this building was constructed, and each of these has been attained by the architect, under the direction of the rebuilding board, and I accept the building and its keys from you with pride in your work and the congratulations of the people on its consummation.

It is moot and proper that we should assemble here today for the purpose of suitably dedicating to the public service this grand structure, designed not only for the use of the territory, its legislature, and officials but also to stand as a permanent evidence of the progressive spirit of our people, and the modern ideas which prevail among them.

The taxes necessary to be levied for its construction and the one which was destroyed have been promptly and cheerfully met by our people. The territorial treasure has last month purchased and retired $20,000 of the original capitol building bonds. The two issues of capitol building bonds make the total amount issued for capitol building purposes $385,000. The oppropriation for the present capitol building has been $135,000. And I venture to say that nowhere else in the United States can the duplicate of this present building be erected for that amount. We see before us a capitol building, completely finished and furnished, admirably adapted for its purpose at present and for many years to come, which, under any ordinary methods of construction would have cost at least $400,000. In my report to the honorable secretary of the interior, I shall refer with pride to this building, its manner of construction, and the gentlemen under whose call and direction it has been erected.

While this is a new and modern building, supplied with all the latest conveniences and accessories, it is situated in the second oldest capital city in the new world.

The original capitol building of this province, or New Spain, is on the other side of the river, where it was erected by the Spanish viceroy in 1598. It has been occupied from that time down to the present by the chief executives of this territory under Spain, Mexico, and the United States, until this day, when I, as governor, formally abandoned the same, and took up my quarters here, and for the last time the old palace in Santa Fe has sheltered the chief executive of this great territory, but its historic associations will always remain.

It was in that building that the viceroys, captains-general, and governors of Spain and Mexico issued their edicts and governed the people, levied war upon the Indians and sent out expeditions in search of new lands to conquer. It was there that the Taos Indians' governor, for a brief period, assumed to act as governor until he was shot in the plaza by order of Governor Armijo, the last of the Mexican governors. There Colonel Zebulon Pike was confined as a prisoner of war on his expedition into northern New Mexico (now Colorado), when he discovered the peak which bears his name. The New Mexico legislature, after the conquest, sat within its historic walls for many years, and the Supreme Court had its room in the west end of the buildings for a number of sessions.

This old historic building, full of memories and associations of the past, is now the property of the territory, by donation from Congress, and in the glory of the new we should not forget the old. The legislature should deal kindly with this old building by keeping it in proper repair and preservation, as one of the most interesting landmarks of this ancient city of the holy faith.

The rebuilding board and the supervising architect have builded well and upon you, gentlemen of the capital custodian committee, now devolves the duty and responsibility of caring for and preserving this public property. In the discharge of your duties you should be guided by nothing, in the selection of employees and assistants, except capacity and fidelity, as the responsibility is too great to be trusted to any except those who are honest, sober, and capable.

With perfect confidence in your ability and desire to preserve this beautiful structure in the same condition that it has come to you, I, as governor of New Mexico, on behalf of its people, who have reared this beautiful edifice, turn it over to your care and keeping and deliver you its keys as guardians of this monument to the liberal and progressive spirit of our people.

Chapter VI

GOVERNOR'S MESSAGE, JANUARY 16, 1899

Gentlemen of the Council and House of Representatives of the Thirty-third Legislative Assembly of the Territory of New Mexico:

I heartily congratulate you upon the happy auspices under which you are now assembled for the performance of the highest duty known to civilization —that of making the laws by which we and our fellow citizens shall be governed in the future.

Since the last legislative assembly in this place, prosperity has returned to our country and our territory. All industries and branches of business have revived, and particularly in New Mexico. Sheep and cattle raising has been prosperous beyond experience for many years previous. Mining also, for all the precious metals, coal, and copper, has been resumed with renewed vigor, and a large amount of capital has been invested in mining plants and machinery. More miles of railroad have been constructed in the territory during the last two years than ever before in its history, with the exception of 1879 and 1880.

The beet sugar factory at Eddy continues in successful and prosperous operation and other similar plants are being contemplated for erection, at an early date, in other parts of the territory.

Within the past year, the United States, for the first time in a generation, was compelled to wage war, which lasted barely three months, and resulted in a series of victories by land and sea, without parallel in the annals of warfare, gaining for us honor, respect, and admiration abroad and at home, uniting our people from all sections of the country in a devotion to the national flag, which has not existed since 1860. In these grand achievements of the nation, New Mexico bore no unimportant part: her sons responded to the President's call for volunteers with an alacrity not equalled in any other section of the country, and more than our quota was promptly furnished; nearly one-half of the world famous "Rough Riders" was enlisted from here, and the conduct of our officers and men, both in the field and camp, was admirable, eliciting compliments from the highest officers in the army. The territorial regiment of infantry, for which New Mexico furnished four full companies, did not have an opportunity to engage in active warfare, but its conduct, discipline, and drill was such as to excite the admiration of regular army officers, and we may well feel proud of our share in its organization.

The question of our admission as a state is again before Congress, bills for that purpose having been introduced in both the Senate and House and, while they may not become laws at the short session of the present Congress, there is good ground for belief that the new Congress will pass an enabling act for our admission.

The act of June 21st, 1898, donating public lands to territorial institutions, and for the benefit of the common schools, was found, upon examination, to be practically inoperative on account of the very large amount of money required to be paid by the territory as land office fees under the rulings, and construction given to the act by the interior department. A bill is now pending in Congress for the purpose of correcting the act in this particular, and it is hoped that early in the future, we will be able to avail ourselves of the donation made by Congress.

For the first time in many years, the legislature of this territory is in political harmony and accord with the executive of the territory, and the President and Congress of the United States. There is practically no political opposition in your body; this fact carries with it grave duties and responsibilities; not only will you, and each of you, be responsible, held so by your constituents, but your actions in this body will reflect credit, or the reverse upon the party to which you belong, and upon whose platform you were elected; and your deliberations at this session and the result of your actions, are fraught with more than ordinary responsibilities to other than yourselves. Custom has ordained that, at the opening of the legislature, the executive should advise it officially of the condition of the territory during the previous two years and suggest for its consideration such measures as he may deem expedient or necessary.

The reports of the various territorial officers, boards, and territorial institutions are transmitted herewith, as a part of this message.

These reports will give to your body, in detail, the operations of the several officers, boards, and institutions, and it will be necessary to give them most careful attention through your proper committees, so that you may act wisely and prudently in dealing with them in the future, something which, I believe, has not been done so carefully as it ought by previous legislatures, a neglect which has resulted in unnecessary and conflicting legislation.

While these reports give in detail many matters of interest and information, I deem it my duty to call your attention especially to some of them, which seem to me of vital importance.

The financial condition of the territory demands your earnest attention; the preservation of our credit by the prompt payment of the interest due upon our territorial and municipal debt, is of the first and greatest importance. Second to that is the payment of the current expenses of the territory. Whether our debts were wisely created or not, is a question with which we have no concern; we have issued our solemn obligations, which have gone into the markets of the world, and have been bought by persons relying upon the faith and credit of the territory, which was pledged for their payment as much as upon the tangible property upon which the bonds were based. It is a notorious and lamentable fact that the total assessed value for taxation in the territory is far below what it should be, and that even upon this reduced valuation, and consequent high rate of taxation, the collection of taxes has been most unsatisfactory, resulting in a deficit reported to the legislature at every session, which has to be provided for. It is a mathematical proposition that a levy of a given amount should produce a given amount of money upon a given amount of taxable property, but experience has demonstrated that the actual result is anywhere from 25 per cent to 40 per cent less than the mathematical. This is unjust to the creditors of the territory and unfair to the counties which collect a larger amount. In one county of the territory, the commissioners have assumed, during the past two years, to "abate and rebate" territorial taxes to the amount of $30,000, without any pretense of authority, or law for so doing, besides in the same manner "abating and rebating" taxes due to their county of an annual amount many times greater. Suit has been instituted by the solicitor general to recover from the county commissioners and the sureties on their bonds, this amount due to the territory, but to avoid the recurrence of such acts in the future, and the delay and expense connected with such suits, there should be a stringent law prohibiting, under severe penalties, any attempt on the part of county boards to interfere with the adjustment and collection of taxes, either terriorial or county, and, while it is not believed that the present law gives them such authority, yet, they assume to exercise it with the above results.

Also, the power to compromise the taxes, given to district attorneys in conjunction with the auditor after suit is brought, should be taken away. Persons who think themselves aggrieved in any manner in the assessment or levy of taxes, already have ample and complete remedy in a meritorious case before the board of county commissioners and the territorial board of equalization.

During the past twelve years, the expenditures of the territory have exceeded the receipts from the usual and customary sources of revenue. Of the present bonded debt of the territory, $553,800 represents this excess up to the close of 1892, as follows:

Current expense bonds	$150,000
Provisional indebtedness bonds	200,000
Casual deficit bonds	101,800
Refunding bonds	102,000
	$553,800

To the above must be added, to get a correct statement of this excess of expenditure over receipts, the unpaid accounts of the years 1893, 1894, 1895, and 1896, for which a special tax was laid by the last legislature, to provide for the payment of about $70,000 of these accounts, leaving without such provision at least $25,000 of the claims of the same years, and there must also be added the deficits of 1897 and 1898, which are about 30 per cent of the appropriations for those years, or say, $60,000 for 1897, and $50,000 for 1898; in addition to which must be added a large sum to bring up the interest fund to completion at the close of the present fiscal year, in March, 1899. Adding these various amounts to the present bonded debt as listed above, and we have, as a total for the twelve years, that is to say, from 1886, as the refunding bonds represent a portion of the expenses of 1886 and 1887 of about $730,000 or an annual average shortage of over $60,000. On the bonded debt covering the funded portion of this excess, the territory is paying now, and will continue to pay for many years, an annual interest charge of over $32,000, or about half the present annual interest charge of the territory. The question arises, in view of these facts, what can be done to remove this increasing annual deficit? It can be remedied only by a decrease of expenditure, or by an increase of annual revenue. Can there be any decrease of annual expenditure, and if so, to what extent, and in what specific direction? To consider this question, let us take up the annual appropriation bills to see what expenditures, if any, can be eliminated without serious injury. The interest fund must stand, as it simply covers the actual interest on the bonded indebtedness, and at the close of the present fiscal year, first Monday of March, 1899, the deficit in this fund will be $55,000, which must be provided for to meet this deficit, and I recommend an issue of ten years' 6 per cent bonds, redeemable at any time after one year, with a provision for a sinking fund sufficient to pay all the bonds at the expiration of ten years; this rate of interest is necessary by reason of the very short time the bonds have to run.

It appears from the report of the *capitol rebuilding board,* that for the proper completion and furnishing of that building $60,000 will be necessary, notwithstanding that the board has exercised the utmost care and economy in all its expenditures. The result is open for inspection, and it is confidently believed that no public building in the country comparable with it has ever been erected for so small an expenditure. The former capitol building cost the territory $200,000, while the present structure, with this issue of $60,000 in bonds, will only represent $135,000; and it is much larger, more substantial, in every way better adapted for the purpose, than its predecessor. To authorize your body to make such an issue of bonds, an act of Congress will be necessary, and a bill for that purpose has been introduced in Congress at the suggestion of the rebuilding board in order that, in case you should take favorable action upon this suggestion, there may not be any delay in obtaining such an act of Congress—thus making the proceeds of such bonds immediately available for the purpose so that the work may proceed to a speedy completion and I earnestly recommend that you authorize the issue of this amount of additional bonds on the same terms and conditions, and to be expended under the same commission as was the original $75,000.

The penitentiary fund cannot be reduced, neither can the salary nor supreme court fund; but in the miscellaneous fund, there seems to me room for great retrenchment, during the next two years at least. I refer to the private, charitable, and educational institutions, for which there was appropriated by the last legislature, $17,500 annually. I am aware that local interests over the territory will strenuously object to this action by your body, but while these are all meritorious institutions, and if our financial conditions would justify the expenditure, should be maintained; yet, the fact remains, that we are not financially able, and, like an individual, must retrench in all matters of expenditure which are not actually necessary in maintaining the public credit in conducting public business.

The large appropriations made to the different territorial educational institutions in the past should be carefully curtailed, and only such sums as are absolutely necessary for the maintenance of said institutions should be appropriated, at least for the time being, or until we can place the territory upon a sound basis. While retrenchment in this direction may seem a hardship to those sections immediately affected, it is, nevertheless, necessary for the good name and financial standing of the territory. I do not care to particularize in this matter, but consign it as a whole to the sound judgment of the assembly.

For the insane asylum and the school for the deaf, dumb, and blind, adequate provision must be made, as this class of unfortunates have a peculiar and special claim for the protection and assistance of the territory, and the appropriation for these institutions can be easily increased to an adequate sum by lopping off some of the other institutions, whose necessities are not so great. The above suggestions exhaust the possible sources of retrenchment and we should now consider the possibility of increasing the annual revenue without any increase of the rate of taxation. This, in theory, is very simple, but in practice it is shown that the mill of taxation six years ago on practically the present assessed value produced net cash to the treasury, after deducting cost for assessment and collection, over $30,000; while the mill of taxation since has dwindled to a net cash product of about $20,000. The arithmetical product of a tax rate, and the actual cash product six years ago, was less than 30 per cent, while since that time, and for the past four years, they have differed by 50 per cent. A seven mill tax on $40,000,000 assessment should produce $280,000. Deducting from this the cost of collection and normal delinquencies would leave a net cash result of $210,000; but the seven mill tax of the last two years has only produced about 70 per cent of the appropriations payable of the tax. These results show a lax assessment and collection of the late years, as there is nothing in general conditions to warrant this great dropping off, and there is no good reason for this failure to collect nearly one-half of the taxes as assessed. Twenty-five per cent is a liberal allowance for the average uncollected and uncollectable taxes, and when the percentage goes above that figure, in the absence of great financial depression or misfortune, there is something radically wrong in the machinery for the assessment and collection of taxes, or in its operation, and I believe this difficulty and danger is in the lax execution of our present laws by the persons charged with their enforcement, not only by the county commissioners in assuming to "abate and rebate" taxes that have been duly levied and equalized but by the assessors and collectors, the former, as a rule, taking the list as handed them, without any personal examination of property returned, or inquiry in regard to its value, as required by law. It is a matter of public notoriety that the number of cattle and sheep returned and assessed is grossly inadequate. There are at least 3,000,000 sheep, and 500,000 cattle, which are not returned and escape taxation, when, under the present conditions, they are the class of property of all others in the territory which can best afford to pay their proportionate share of the burdens of the government. The proper assessment of these animals would add at least $5,000,000 to our taxable value. The present exemption of $200 to heads of families should be repealed. This would not only add another $5,000,000 to our assessed value, but would give the small taxpayer a personal interest in the administration of the affairs, which he does not possess under the present system, and the individual burden would be so slight as to be hardly appreciable, and instead of being a benefit to the small taxpayer, as was evidently the intention of the law, it is in reality a hardship, for the reason that it has reduced the revenues of the different counties to such an extent as to prevent the holding of courts, thereby depriving witnesses and jurors of the small fees and allowances which otherwise they would receive; it is taken advantage of by persons who possess much more property and are amply able to pay their taxes; the practice has become common for heads of families to dispose of their property in amounts of $200 to others, for the sole purpose of taking advantage of this exemption, while really they possess the property themselves, thus bringing the law into disrepute and contempt, besides depriving the territory of the legitimate revenue, and not accomplishing any good result.

The fiscal year should be changed to some other date than the first Monday in March, which is a most awkward season. I would suggest the first of August as its beginning, as at that time the taxes of the previous year will all have been accounted for, and the legislation for the current year have been completed. At present the fiscal year comes during the middle of the session of the legislature, which may change all the arrangements of the fiscal officers.

The insurance business has grown so in this territory, and the legislation upon that subject has been such, as in my opinion, to call for the creation of a commissioner of insurance. The duties of the auditor are sufficiently onerous without adding those of insurance commissioners. This office need not be a

My Nine Years as Governor 365

source of expense to the territory, and an intelligent administration of it would result in great good. I believe that a traveling auditor for the territory, whose duty should be to personally examine the assessment rolls, tax books, collector's and treasurer's accounts, at stated or irregular intervals, would cause an immense saving to both the territory and the several counties.

Such officer should be given full power to examine into the fiscal affairs and administration of each county, suggest and enforce improved and exact methods of transacting the business, and seeing that the accounts and reports are accurately and uniformly made. The salary of such an officer, I am satisfied, would be much more than saved by the resulting benefits. Such an officer is generally provided for by the laws of the states and their work has always proved beneficial.

The several counties of the territory should be required to care for their own poor and infirm, and for that purpose should be authorized to establish poor farms and hospitals in connection therewith, and maintain the same by the levying of a tax, as is now provided by law for the construction of bridges.

The governor should be given power by explicit statute to summarily remove, or cause to be removed, upon proper proceedings, and after hearing, any territorial officer, or county commissioner, or other county officer for the neglect of duty, malfeasance, or nonfeasance in office.

The present provisions for the removal of the county or precinct officers are altogether inadequate to be of any practical service requiring trial by jury, resulting in delays, where expedition is the main object sought.

Educational

The educational interests of the territory have, for the last ten years, had the special attention of the various legislative assemblies, and it seems that each assembly vied with the one immediately preceding it in providing for the firm establishment of the schools in the territory.

In 1891, there was a comprehensive act passed, known as "The common school law," and under this law with the funds it furnishes our public schools in every precinct and hamlet throughout the territory are maintained in a flourishing and satisfactory condition. Innovations upon this law with a view to materially altering its benign features would be dangerous. Reports from all parts of the territory show that outside of the cities and towns of the territory during this year 511 schools were conducted, employing 541 school teachers; in these schools, there was an enrollment of 23,061 pupils, whose average daily attendance was 14,388. Reports from the cities and towns show even more flattering conditions; at least 5,000 pupils were enrolled in these schools during the year 1898. Magnificent school buildings have been erected in most of our cities for the accommodation of our school children, and successful graded schools under the management of competent and experienced tutors are conducted therein.

The existing laws were compiled in one volume under the act for that purpose passed by the last legislature, the English and Spanish editions being separately bound, making a compact and handsome volume of a very convenient size. This compilation was regularly approved and promulgated, and has given general satisfaction. The report of the solicitor general upon this compilation shows in detail the omissions therefrom, which should be added by legislation and suggested additions, changes, and repeals, to which I would invite your special attention.

I desire to call attention once more to the act of June 21st, 1898, donating public lands to the territory. Under that act of Congress granting these lands to the territory, it was provided in section 10, "that the lands used for university purposes, including all saline lands and sections sixteen and thirty-six reserved for public schools, may be leased under such laws and regulations, as may be hereafter prescribed by the legislative assembly of said territory; but until the meeting of the next legislature of said territory, the governor, secretary of the territory, and the solicitor general shall constitute a board for the leasing of the said lands." Under this section of the act of Congress, it will be necessary for your body to pass suitable legislation to carry into effect this donation under the restrictions and limitations provided for in said act, and any amendments that may be made thereto during the present session of Congress. Your attention is invited to the act itself, which was approved the 21st day of June, 1898, and will be found in the statutes at large of the second session of the Fifty-fifth Congress.

Rewards

The former provisions of the law authorizing the governor in proper cases to issue rewards for the apprehension of persons accused or suspected of crime, were repealed at your last session, leaving the executive without any authority to proclaim rewards for the detention or punishment of criminals. The former statutes, or similar ones on this subject, should be reënacted, as in no instance do I know of the power being abused, and in many cases it has resulted in great good.

Equalization of Taxes

I desire to direct your attention especially to the report of the board of equalization as many recommendations are contained therein, which if possible to carry out, would be of great benefit to the territory.

There may be matters requiring your attention, which I have omitted to specifiy, but which, if necessary, I will bring to your notice later in a special communication.

In conclusion, the time of your session is limited to sixty days. Your duties are arduous and responsibilities great, and I believe the former will be discharged, not by enacting a great number of hastily prepared new laws, but by a fewer number which have been carefully considered, and in taking stringent measures to enforce the laws which we already have, or repeal them wholly if they are not to be enforced.

VETO MESSAGE NO. 4

March 11th, 1903.

To the Speaker and Members of the House of Representatives of the Thirty-fifth Legislative Assembly of New Mexico:

Gentlemen: —I return herewith to your body, being the house in which it

My Nine Years as Governor

originated, House Bill No. 155, entitled "An act establishing the law and procedure in certain cases," without my approval.

My objections to this bill are that it makes an entirely new and untried innovation upon our practice, one which has never been tried in any other jurisdiction, and I can see no possible advantage to be gained by its passage here as an experiment. It makes a radical innovation on legal practice and procedure everywhere in not allowing the plaintiff the right to select the court in which he litigates. He is compelled to go into a court selected by his adversary, where he is bound without any right of appeal from any judgment that may be rendered against him.

Under the provisions of this act there is a practical injunction against the plaintiff bringing a suit in the jurisdiction which he selects and a mandamus compelling him to bring his action in the jurisdiction desired by the defendant.

There is no need in this territory for such an act for there is no right that cannot be enforced and no wrong that may not be redressed under our present laws; and this act is very drastic and its constitutionality very doubtful. It attempts to exercise our writ of mandamus in other jurisdictions to not only compel the commencement of actions here, but also to compel the courts of such jurisdictions not to take jurisdiction in certain instances, as well as to prohibit the doing of something that is already accomplished.

This act would create great criticism of our people, and I believe is not for the best interests of the territory, and after very careful consideration I have deemed that I cannot give it my official approval.

Very respectfully,
(Signed) Miguel A. Otero, Governor of New Mexico.

GOVERNOR'S RECOMMENDATIONS IN MESSAGE OF JANUARY 16, 1905

A good, comprehensive primary election law. A strong and forcible corrupt practice law, embodying publicity of election expenses; publicity of all public offices and a severe punishment for falsifying any required publication, or for malfeasance in office. Severe penalty for bribery. Revision of registration. Grammar and high schools for rural districts. Straight salaries for county officials or, at least, a limitation of the total fees lawful to retain, the balance to go to the public school fund. That collectors of public funds account for 100 per cent of the money to be collected by them, and deficiency, unless specifically exonerated, to be collected from their bondsmen. Exclusion of professional lobbyists from the floor of the assembly. A territorial investigation board. That territorial and county depositories, as well as all territorial and county officials, give guaranty companies bonds. That greater powers be granted to the board of equalization and to the traveling auditor. That collectors and ex-officio treasurers be compelled to deposit public funds in authorized banks to draw not less than 3 per cent interest. Law to compel artesian well owners to place caps on wells when not in use. A libel law. Law regulating the sale of patent medicines. Revision of road laws. Appropriation to complete scenic road. Recession of the Old Palace to the federal government. Law requiring druggists to keep register of poisons sold. Liberal appropriation for Historical Society. That portraits of former governors be placed in capitol rotunda and halls. Continuance of boards and managers of the Louisiana Purchase Exposition until final settlement of accounts. That territorial officials be in their offices during business hours on week days, unless given leave of absence not to exceed thirty days in any one year. An appropriation, not to exceed $2,500, for apprehension of the assassins of Colonel J. Francisco Chaves. Reduction of auditor's bond from $100,000 to $25,000. That the treasurer of the New Mexico Military Institute be required to give bond. Triplicate system of receipts for taxes and licenses to be consecutively numbered and signed by the traveling auditor who is to issue them. That permanent school income fund derived from public lands be placed in banks on interest. Jail penalties for violation of game laws. Repeal of amendment of three minor sections of the existing statutes. Permanent and high grade teachers certificates. Financial support of territorial institutions. Close collection of poll tax. Consolidation of office of commissioner of public lands and clerk of the United States Land Commission. That the following new offices be created: Insurance commissioner, irrigation engineer, assistant superintendent of public instruction, assistant traveling auditor, force of rangers.

I urge at once the following: Revision of assessment and taxation laws. Passage of new jury law. Equal enforcement of Sunday law in every locality and its amendment to meet wishes of the majority of the people. Curfew legislation. Prohibition of saloons in precincts of less than 500 inhabitants and within five miles of a military reservation used for sanatorium purposes. Rigid investigation of every territorial office and board. Restriction in number of legislative employees. Better salary for adjutant-general. Straight salary of $2,500 for the superintendent of public instruction. That no new laws go into effect until thirty days after the adjournment of legislature unless absolutely necessary. Appropriation for flood sufferers of last fall. A memorial urging settlement of Texas-New Mexico boundary differences as well as of the Colorado-New Mexico boundary differences.

I also request a law making disfranchisement the penalty for deserters from the national guard during active service. A memorial on statehood.

Greater care should be taken in drafting bills creating new counties, and I admonish you against creating new counties with insufficient wealth and against the desires of the people affected. I would like to be given authority by your honorable bodies, to remove officials who fail to make annual reports in due time, and also to remove summarily county officials accepting illegal fees, or county commissioners granting such illegal fees. Also of county officials guilty of nonfeasance, misfeasance, or malfeasance in office. To offer rewards for apprehension of criminals. I further believe in equalization of taxes, honesty in elections, uniform fairness and impartiality on the part of all state, county, or municipal officials, towards all citizens of the state or territory, equally for *all,* special privileges for *none;* equal justness and fairness in all disputes arising between Capital and Labor, and a strict enforcement of every law.

My Nine Years as Governor

Chapter IX

THE NEW MEXICAN DESCRIBES A NOMINATING CONVENTION

The convention was called to order by Honorable John S. Clark, chairman, who announced that the committee had selected Honorable George W. Prichard as temporary chairman, and a committee of three was appointed to escort Colonel Prichard to the chair, and after a splendid address, the different committees were named.

The committee on permanent organization named Honorable Frank A. Hubbell as permanent chairman.

On motion of I. H. Elliott, of Chaves County, seconded by Benjamin M. Reed, of Santa Fe County, an invitation was extended to Governor Otero, "who has given the territory such an excellent, clean, and efficient administration, which has added greatly to the importance and dignity of the territory thereby" to attend the afternoon session of the convention. The chairman named as committee to notify the governor and escort him to the convention hall, I. H. Elliott, P. F. Garrett, Elfego Baca, Margarito Romero, and L. Bradford Prince.

During a discussion Governor Otero was ushered into the convention hall, and was greeted with thunderous applause. President Frank A. Hubbell, in presenting Governor Otero to the convention, paid him the high compliment of being "the best governor the territory of New Mexico has ever had." Governor Otero, with great feeling and much appreciation, thanked the convention for the high honor paid him. He paid a glowing tribute to President McKinley, and urged the election of the nominee for delegate to Congress, Hon. B. S. Rodey. Governor Otero spoke as follows:

"Republicans and fellow citizens: I desire to thank you for your welcome at this time, and especially to thank the territorial convention for its expressions of indorsement of my course as governor of this territory for more than three years past. I do not take this expression of approval altogether to myself, but as an additional evidence of your respect for the confidence in that great statesman and patriot, William McKinley.

"For the first time since it has been in the control of the territory this beautiful building is used by the people as their own, and its first use is for a most noble purpose—to place before the electors of New Mexico a candidate for the Congress of the United States, who will represent our loyalty to sound money, to the American doctrine of protection to American products and labor, and above all to that flag which floats above us, and whose azure, scarlet, and white folds surround us in this room, emblematic of the blue vault which covers all, of the red sunset which presages the coming day, and the white dawn of the morrow, which rises now for our country in the west, toward which this noble building faces, as if in greeting to that new east where this flag has been set in glory and honor, and from which it shall never be removed so long as Americans are on guard and the principles of the fathers and the honor and love of our country prevail. From the presidio to Honolulu, to Luzon, and the islands of the sea—to the forbidden city itself —it has been carried by brave Americans in the line of duty, to shelter and protect the weak and oppressed, and thence it shall not return, but remair forever as a benison and promise from the new West to the ancient East—a symbol at once of power and justice, of commerce and christianity.

"I congratulate the Republicans of New Mexico upon their platform. It gives no uncertain utterance upon the fundamental principles that must always guide the nation if it would continue in the prosperous and onward course, which these principles have given us in the past. They are all attacked by the common enemy. Every one of the measures which the Republicans have advocated, and which the experience of four years has shown to be full of good results for the whole people, is denounced by the Democratic nominees, press, and orators. The war with Spain, for which they were most clamorous, is denounced, the peace which followed is assailed. Nothing that has been done for the past four years has any merit to them. Four years ago they made direful prophecy of calamities that would come if McKinley were elected; none of them has come to pass. On the contrary, plenty and prosperity, a full treasury and a full dinner pail have resulted. And now they fill the air with wails about imperialism, and militarism, and the dangers of 100,000 soldiers to our population of 80,000,000. They sympathize deeply with Aguinaldo and his dusky minions, whose consent to be governed has not been had, while in the southern states they conceive and execute constitutional amendments that will deprive the dusky citizen there of any right to vote, or any chance to say how or by whom he shall be governed. Abroad they are full of sympathy for the disfranchised Tagal, while at home they devise ingenious methods to prevent the native colored man from voting, and if he persists they appeal to the shotgun and the stake.

"I heartily endorse the platform of 1900 and the nominee of the convention. That he is your nominee is sufficient to guarantee his election, and with that I can confidently predict statehood at the coming session of Congress. The East has come to know us better during the past four years, and much of the prejudice against us has been dispelled. We have the personal promise of Governor Theodore Roosevelt that he will help us to that condition, and there is no doubt that he will be elected and in a position to make his assistance a most potent one for our welfare. The conditions of the internal affairs of the territory and the conduct of the various territorial institutions during the past four years under the wise and prudent laws passed by the last legislature has greatly improved, and will be a strong argument not only for the election of our nominee for delegate, but for members of the legislature and the various county officers. Fifty thousand dollars of our territorial debt, bearing 6 per cent interest has been cancelled, our rate of interest has been reduced not only for the territory, but for many of the counties, to 4 per cent, taxes are more promptly paid and collections are larger than ever before, and the coming legislature, instead of facing a large deficit will meet the pleasing novelty of a surplus, which it will doubtless apply to further reduction of the public debt. This has not come to pass by accident or the nature of things, but by Republican officials. We have seen the good results of Republican administration in the nation and at home, and it is no idle theory, but cold and satisfactory fact, to which we as an organization point with pride. Then why should we not continue in this path that we have trod, which leads us to safe high ground, instead of following after glowing exhalations of rhetoric, which lead we know not where, but from experience in the past, we are sure to find, terminate in the bogs and swamps of repudiation, hard times, idleness, and treason itself."

Chapter X

FRITZ MULLER'S AFFIDAVIT — AFFIDAVIT OF EUGENE A. FISKE

Territory of New Mexico } ss.
County of Santa Fe

I, Fred Muller, being duly sworn on my oath, say that I am and for the past twenty years have been a resident of the territory of New Mexico, and am now holding the office of collector of the county of Santa Fe, territory of New Mexico, to which I was duly elected.

I am well acquainted with the people of New Mexico and its political situation and the manner in which the affairs of New Mexico have been conducted under the administration of Miguel A. Otero as governor of said territory. Under his administration the affairs of that territory have since his appointment as governor been steadily going from bad to worse. *He has debauched the legislature* by appointments of its leading members or their relatives to office within his gift and by such has procured the passage of laws which he approved as governor, increasing his own and other salaries and otherwise squandering the money collected in taxes from our citizens. The general effect of his administration has been to *depreciate all property values and destroy business confidence and increase the rate of taxes*. Since the commencement of his administration taxes for territorial purposes have increased from 7.75 mills to 14.79 mills, or nearly double, and there has been a steady falling off in the assessed values of property in New Mexico, notwithstanding our staple products of wool and sheep are now higher than when he was appointed, and railroad properties have been added to since then. In 1891, such assessed values aggregated $45,329,560, while for this year, 1901, such assessed values are $38,227,878, a decrease of nearly $7,000,000, and this too, although the past four years have been years of great prosperity for all of our surrounding states and territories. In Arizona, which is reported to be in a prosperous condition and which I believe to be quite as expensive to run properly as a territory as New Mexico, the annual salary list paid by the territory of Arizona, as published, was but $13,638 in 1900, while for the same year the like salary list in New Mexico was $41,423, or nearly three times as great. In 1901, the New Mexico salary list was $44,550, which does not include about $10,000 paid to penitentiary officers *out of the earnings of that institution,* and some $3,000 appropriated as contingent expenses, *but used for and which really should be charged to salary account.* This increased expenditure is largely due to *bad laws,* fostered and approved by Otero as above stated, either for his own personal benefit or for the benefit of *the gang of boodling henchmen who surround and control him,* among whom is a *fugitive from justice from the state of Tennessee,* who is now coal oil inspector by Otero's appointment; the clerk of the penitentiary, who is an ex-convict, who served a term of imprisonment in the penitentiary of which he is now clerk, as well as friend and confident of the governor; and the editor of his official organ, who was found guilty by a jury of a United States offense, *and is regarded as personally one of the most corrupt men in New Mexico.* Otero is both *weak* and *vain,* and in my judgment and as I believe, in the opinion of the greater part of the *respectable people of the territory,* is practically powerless in the hands of this *boodling irresponsible element of our territory.* I can state positively: *that the general reputation of Otero and this gang that controls him, is very bad in New Mexico,* and it is generally believed there that both he and they *are corrupt beyond anything ever previously known in that territory.* A general crookedness permeates all parts of Otero's administration, and reaches even the *administration of justice.* Our *jury commissioners* are appointed by the respective *judges* and such commissioners select the juries for each term, and it is *within my personal knowledge that such commissioners are expected to select only known Otero men for jurymen.* I was appointed one of the three jury commissioners to select jurors in the spring of 1901, and I selected my share of them, *with the sole idea of getting good, honest, and reliable men on the jury.* When I submitted my list to the other commissioners, *one of them, who is a rank Otero man,* looked it over and turned to me with a *surprised and troubled expression,* and the remark: *"What does this mean? There are no Otero men on your list."* With a careful exclusion of all but Otero men from our juries, and *prosecuting attorneys, all friends and appointees of Otero,* it is not difficult to see how hopeless it is to try to investigate in *our courts, the acts of this governor and his henchmen,* and how impossible it is to protect life, liberty, and property in New Mexico if the governor *and his advisors, seek to punish any of his enemies.* In fact, the conditions now existing in New Mexico are *un-American and tyranny,* and we do not *now have a republican form of government,* and, in *my opinion,* this *deplorable condition* will continue to exist there, so long as Otero is the governor, *for just so long he will be controlled by the criminals and otherwise bad element of advisors with which he has surrounded himself,* and which he is too *weak* and too *bound* to rid himself of if he should try that experiment, an experiment he has thus far shown no disposition to attempt. I am credibly informed that when he was given his recess appointment, in June, 1901, he was informed by the present secretary of the interior that he must rid himself of the bad element by which he was surrounded, but thus far *he has not rid himself of a single one of this element,* who, then as now, easily manage him for their evil purposes to the great injury of the territory. *Nine-tenths* of the wealth, business, and professional capacity and enterprise, and of all other ingredients that tend to assist and forward *progress along the best American lines in New Mexico,* is *with the emigrants to that territory from other states and their descendants, and its governor should, therefore, be a man in sympathy with and capable and strong enough to fully comprehend the wishes of and, if necessary, lead that element of our citizens.*

(Signed)   Fred Muller.

Sworn and subscribed to before me this 10th day of January, 1902.

(Seal)   (Signed)   Ernest A. Johnston, Notary Public.

District of Columbia } ss.
City of Washington

I, Eugene A. Fiske, being duly sworn on my oath, say that I am a resident of the city and county of Santa Fe, territory of New Mexico; that I am well acquainted with Fred Muller, lately captain of the Rough Riders Regiment during the Spanish war, and who was, in December, 1901, appointed and confirmed as receiver of the U. S. Land Office at Santa Fe, New Mexico, and who on the tenth day of January, 1902, signed and made oath to the truth of the foregoing and attached affidavit before E. A. Johnston, a notary public of said Santa Fe County; that I know said Johnston was at the date of the taking of said affidavit a notary public duly qualified under the laws of New Mexico to administer and certify to the taking of such oaths, and *that I personally saw said Fred Muller sign the foregoing affidavit with his genuine signature and heard him make oath thereto before said Johnston IN MY OFFICE of said Santa Fe and saw said Johnston certify thereto in manner and form as the signature and certificate appears on said above affidavit.*

(Signed) Eugene A. Fiske.
Sworn and subscribed to before me this 20th day of January, 1902.
(Signed) James D. Maher, Notary Public.

CATRON WRITES TO THE PRESIDENT

Santa Fe, New Mexico, October 28, 1901.
To Theodore Roosevelt,
President of the United States,
Dear Sir:

[1] Some months since several residents of the city of Santa Fe, together with myself, addressed a communication to the President of the United States protesting against the reappointment of Miguel A. Otero as governor of the territory of New Mexico. That communication, I understand, was filed with the secretary of the interior, being signed by me and others.

[2] In order that you may have some slight idea as to who I am, I inform you that I have resided in this territory more than thirty-five years; that I have held several offices under the territorial government; was for more than six years U. S. attorney for this territory, and was the delegate in Congress from this territory at the fifty-fourth Congress. If you desire to know more about me and my antecedents I refer you to Senator Elkins, who was a classmate of mine in college, and also a law partner of mine in this territory.

[3] I wish to call your attention again to the facts stated in the communication filed with the secretary of the interior why Governor Otero should not be reappointed as governor of this territory.

[4] His administration ever since his first appointment has been extravagant, impure, oppressive, tyrannical, partial, and has been run by rings and cliques, nor has it been for the welfare of the people, but has been injurious to their prosperity, and the harmony of the Republican Party. It does not represent the wishes of the majority of the Republican Party in this territory. It has been prosecuted in the interest of office-holders under him and of persons who receive some kind of benefit from him and his administration.

[5] Before his appointment as governor, he was discharged as cashier of the San Miguel National Bank of East Las Vegas on account of alleged mal-administration of the bank.

[6] In 1888, he was probate clerk of San Miguel County, N. M. Chief Justice O'Brien was then appointed to our supreme court, and as such judge of the fourth judicial district court of this territory, including San Miguel

County, Otero sought from him the appointment as clerk of that district court. At his solicitation many Republicans recommended him therefor on the promise that if appointed he would resign the office of probate clerk so that another might be appointed to the same. He received the appointment but refused to resign the probate clerkship, and continued to hold both offices in violation of his promises. As probate clerk, he was ex-officio clerk of the board of county commissioners of that county, during which time it was necessary to issue a large amount of bonds to pay current expenses. More bonds were issued than was necessary. Patricio Sandoval, one of the members of the board, has made affidavit and forwarded it to the secretary of the interior showing that various monies of the county were at that time paid out on fictitious or bogus accounts to one Baltazar Vermudez and that there was no such party in the county; that Otero received the moneys on these accounts in whole or in part. It is also alleged and proven, as I am informed, that other bogus accounts were made up, and paid out of those moneys, particularly one in a fictitious name of Joe Bowers; that the warrant for these accounts were signed by Otero as clerk, and that he knew of the fraud which was being practiced upon the county. In this way, it is claimed that during the time he was clerk of the probate court and of said board, the said county was defrauded of many thousands of dollars.

[7] His support for reappointment as governor comes mainly from those to whom he has been indebted, and from those who expect favors from him officially, and not from the people at large who are interested in good government and economy of the territory. Many persons have signed petitions for his reappointment, a great many of whom are Democrats, among them the late chairman and the late secretary of the Democratic Central Committee in this territory, both of whom have openly declared that they and the other Democrats who recommended such reappointment did so because they believed that the reappointment of Otero would either bring the administration into such disgrace, or create such dissension in the Republican ranks here as would enable the Democrats by means thereof to triumph at the next election.

[8] The people here protest against any such subterfuge or the permitting of any such possibility. Others who are Republicans, who signed such petitions, did so because the office-holders, both county and territorial, and those belonging to the clique or ring of the governor urged and insisted upon their doing so, and they had not stamina sufficient to refuse the request, it being much easier to the large body of people to sign petitions than to say no.

[9] Governor Otero has outraged and compromised the best interests of the Republican Party in New Mexico. He and his ring have outraged and scandalized the best Republicans of the territory and compromised the welfare of the party.

[10] By means of official patronage and favoritism with the aid of his ringsters he has undertaken to control and shape the party and its policy as if it belonged to him. The party had, two years before his appointment, regained power in the territory. He has, however, ignored, overridden, and attempted to break down every man of prominence in it who manifests a spirit of independence, or who will not do his bidding, or aid him to manipulate politics in the interest of himself or clique or ring. In Santa Fe County, where the capital of the territory is situated, he has encouraged the worse element, advised and aided them to foment dissensions in the Republican Party and in its conventions and at the polls. He aided and advised the

My Nine Years as Governor

putting up of an Independent Republican ticket at the last election in said county against the ticket regularly nominated by the *party*. At the last convention of the party in said county, to nominate county officers, office-holders owing their appointment or position to him headed a bolt from the convention because they could not have the convention organized their way; they appointed a committee styling themselves "Regular Republicans," and by his advice and assistance when he was present, nominated an independent ticket, calling it "Regular Republican Ticket." This was done with closed doors, he being present and taking part. D. M. White was placed on that ticket of bolters. He is the locating agent of public lands donated to the territory for educational and other institutions. He owes his position to Governor Otero's influence; a single word from Otero would have kept White off that ticket; he was placed on it, as a candidate for the legislative council, the undersigned T. B. Catron being the nominee of the Republican Party at the convention from which the bolt had taken place. White canvassed the county, and told the voters openly and publicly that he was Otero's candidate for the office of legislative councilman and that Governor Otero was backing him. He received 284 votes; T. B. Catron, the nominee of the Republican convention, received 1,283 as counted; Charles F. Easley, the Democrat, received 1,300, nominally electing Easley, Democrat, by 17 plurality. White stated that this was the result Governor Otero wished to accomplish. Governor Otero could have prevented the election of a Democrat; he refused to do so, although requested to interfere. His refusal was as currently reported and stated that he did not wish T. B. Catron, the Republican candidate, to be in the legislature, because he would prevent the passage of many laws which was desired to be enacted, creating new offices, increasing salaries, and making extra appropriations.

[11] All the Republican ticket not endorsed by the bolters was defeated; the county was practically turned over to the Democrats, although there is a Republican majority of more than two hundred and fifty. The committee which made the nominations for the bolters was composed of E. L. Bartlett, solicitor general, appointed by Governor Otero; D. M. White, locating agent of public lands, appointed at the instance of Governor Otero; Max Frost, who controls and manages Governor Otero and was the secretary of the board of immigration, appointed by the board, which was appointed by Governor Otero; J. D. Hughes, public printer, appointed by Governor Otero; R. L. Baca, then an employee of Max Frost, a forger and counterfeiter, was the secretary, Bartlett was chairman; others holding office or receiving favors from the governor were either members of the committee or placed on the ticket. Governor Otero and his adjutant-general, W. H. Whiteman, were both present at the meeting of the Bolters Committee when they made the nominations, and advised in regard to the same. At the Republican convention last fall, when a candidate for delegate to Congress was to be nominated, several of Governor Otero's appointees who were members thereof were informed by him if they supported either L. Bradford Prince, J. Francisco Chaves, or *T. B. Catron* as candidate for such delegate, they would not be reappointed by him.

[12] At the primary convention held in Santa Fe in the spring of 1900 to select delegates for the convention to send delegates to the national convention of the Republican Party, Solicitor-General Bartlett, Governor Otero's appointee, publicly advised that armed deputy sheriffs take charge of the convention halls, and admit only a majority of persons who favored Gov-

ernor Otero and his supporters as delegates to the national convention. This was done. Every person favoring Otero was admitted, and numbers who opposed him were excluded. Some were ejected by force. The undersigned attended one of such primaries, and saw the sheriff and his deputies close doors, they being armed, and admit only such as they saw proper, excluding as many as fifty or more from the hall, all of whom were Republicans and entitled to participate in the meeting, and all of whom were opposed to Governor Otero and were sufficient in number to have reversed the action of that meeting, together with those inside who were opposed to Governor Otero. In this manner all four precincts of the city of Santa Fe were carried in the interest of Governor Otero and his supporters, although the majority of the people were two to one against them.

[13] Under a decision of the supreme court of New Mexico, it has been held that when the governor commissions a person to an office, it is to be presumed that a vacancy exists, which authorized the issuance of the commission, and that the appointment was regular and that the commissioned person was thereby installed in the office, and the one elected by the people ejected, although the governor may have acted wrongfully and contrary to law in giving such commission, and although there may not have been any such vacancy. The last session of the legislature of New Mexico was entirely manipulated and controlled by a clique and ring of strikers and manipulators, who used Governor Otero for their purposes. It passed a law authorizing the governor to fill all vacancies in county offices. Under this law, and the decision of the supreme court above referred to, the governor can remove any county officer or any district or territorial officer by the mere issuance of the commission to some one else, although the law does not confer such power on him, but only authorizes him to fill all vacancies occurring in county offices, and vacancies occurring in territorial offices by reason of death or resignation. This law was enacted at the instance of Governor Otero and his supporters to give the control of the county officers to him and enable his ringsters who control him to secure themselves and manipulate the counties and territory officially, financially, and politically. Since its enactment, the governor has notified several county officers that if they oppose him he will commission others to take their places. This law has enabled him and his clique by means of threats, promises, and bulldozing, to so terrorize and overawe every officeholder and the people generally of the territory that he and they can do so as they will. The decision of the supreme court above referred to overruled a half dozen others announcing the contrary rule. By such means, the governor and his ringsters and clique, many of whom are of the worst element of the Republican Party, and many of whom are active political workers, are forcing, persuading, and inducing the people throughout the territory to come to his support for a re-nomination as governor, even though they do not wish it, thus securing many Democratic signatures in his behalf in Democratic counties. Petitions were circulated among the members of the legislature recommending his reappointment as governor, as also the appointment of other parties to other offices where they wish to get the spoils, and oust some one who did not affiliate with them. The members of the legislature, while in session, were given to understand if they refused to sign they would be ignored by the governor; on the contrary, they could have whatever they wished; thus he obtained almost their unanimous endorsement, many of them being radically opposed to him. In the same way, D. M. White, who was the Bolters candidate for the legislative council, was recommended for

surveyor-general. They give out that all who oppose Otero, or them politically, or otherwise, cannot be appointed, or elected to any office, if they can prevent it. Also, that as soon as Otero shall be reappointed governor and confirmed, they will get even with all who opposed them. He and his gang have strangled freedom of thought and political action in the territory, so far as office-holders and those depending upon him, or desiring favors from him are concerned. This has operated very radically where a majority of the people are of Mexican or Spanish origin, they being of a timid disposition, and very obedient to law, having a high regard for official authority, submit to it, and those holding authority implicitly, whether right or wrong, under all circumstances. Whenever he has not been able to control the nominating conventions he and his supporters have encouraged bolts and dissensions, have recommended independent tickets with candidates who were his tools. Whenever he has been unable to control persons of prominence in the party, he and his ringites have studiously and industriously, Iago-like, invented and circulated falsehoods and slanderous statements about them from one individual to another, and thus brought about trouble, enmity, and discord between them, and thereby made much bad blood in the party. He is known to be mendacious in the highest degree; he will not scruple to make and circulate false statements and misrepresentations as coming from one person about another, so as to put them against each other. With some exceptions, he has surrounded himself with disreputable characters, or rather allowed himself to be surrounded and controlled by such characters. He has been largely under the manipulation and control of Max Frost, a political libertine and free lance, who during the last legislature boasted that no one could be appointed to office by the governor unless he, Frost, was first seen about it. He also boasted after the adjournment that he had notified certain persons who wished to be appointed to office that they must see him; that they had failed to see him in regard to their appointment, and therefore failed to get the office. Frost is the same person who, when register of the land office at Santa Fe some years since, was indicted for demanding illegal fees and for conspiracy on the United States side of the court. He was tried on one indictment, found guilty and sentenced to the penitentiary, and secured a new trial because one of the jurors had failed to state that he had a prejudice against Frost when he was examined as to his qualification to serve as a juror in the case. After the new trial was granted, although he stated that he could do justice in the case, the indictment and all other indictments against, him, amounting to six or seven which had not been dismissed by the U. S. attorney, disappeared from the files, and have never since been found. In the meantime, the statutes of limitation had run against the crime. This man, Max Frost, is generally known and regarded by the people as being venal in all of his actions and doings. He makes no pretense to being honest. His influences are of the worst kind. He is full of political trickery, and shrewd in manipulation. He is the editor of the *New Mexican* newspaper, claims to be a Republican. Whenever the Democrats are in power, he turns his paper over to them; when the Republicans are in power, he gets it back.

[14] Governor Otero has appointed J. Francisco Chaves, the superintendent of public schools. This action is evidently the outcome of a deal based upon the proposition that the undersigned, T. B. Catron, who claimed to be elected to the legislature or legislative council, but did not receive the certification yet contested for the seat against the Democrat, who succeeded in getting the certificate mainly because Governor Otero's special pet,

D. M. White, was induced to run independent for the office by Otero, was to be kept out of the legislature and not to be allowed a hearing, it being understood that Chaves, who was the president of the legislative council, would appoint such committee on elections as would be hostile to Catron, and that they would make no report on his contest. This was done, and Catron could get no hearing, and was kept out of the legislature. The purpose of keeping Catron out of the legislature was because it was feared and known that he would oppose all extravagance, increase of salaries, extraordinary appropriation, or the making of new offices, and the employment of extra officers, who were prohibited by Congress. The Democrat kept his seat, voted and worked with Otero's clique, and did their bidding in everything. Chaves was appointed to the office of superintendent of the public schools. He is the same person who had been designated by the superintendent of the census as census supervisor in the territory in the last census. At that time, Chaves and Otero were not working together politically. Charges were preferred against Chaves by Otero and his ringsters, alleging that Chaves was dishonest, corrupt, a drunkard, a man of bad habits, and that he had received a bribe while a member of the legislature four or five years since to vote against the division of Grant County. It is alleged they furnished proof of the matter of bribery by affidavits, one being by a member of the council at the same time, who, it is said, had the disposition of the money to be paid to Chaves and other members to defeat said measure, the amount given him being $2,500. Chaves was not appointed supervisor of the census, and learning of the charges and that Otero had instigated them, he became very hostile to Otero, but his attitude was changed by receiving the appointment.

[15] The legislature in which, it is alleged, Chaves was bribed was held in 1897. Joe Sheridan, who was then editor and publisher of a Republican paper at Silver City, wrote and published a long and open article in his paper, charging Chaves with having received the bribe while a member of the legislature, to vote against the division of Grant County. This article was extensively circulated and made use of by the governor to prevent Chaves' appointment as supervisor of the census, yet Otero subsequently knowing these facts appointed him school superintendent. Joe Sheridan is now holding the office of coal mine inspector in this territory; he was appointed to that office on the recommendation of Governor Otero. The appointment of Chaves as school superintendent is generally regarded as being vicious, made from bad motives, and of a quasi corrupt character. It has created much dissatisfaction among the people interested in education.

[16] The people and especially the Republicans in New Mexico believe that Governor Otero's administration is not conducive to the welfare of the territory. That it is run by rings and cliques; that it is dishonest and corrupt; that it is oppressive and overbearing, unfair and dangerous; they are not satisfied; they wish some one else for governor.

[17] Governor Otero appointed W. E. Martin to interpret into Spanish the laws of the last legislature, a place of great trust and confidence, yet he detected Martin in the embezzlement of school funds, which he had collected as coal oil inspector while holding that office under Governor Otero. He compelled Martin to resign, but has since allowed him to remain, contrary to law, at the penitentiary as an employee boarding there at the public expense with his family, he being paid a salary out of convict earnings. Martin is an ex-penitentiary convict: he was sentenced there for murder and pardoned after a long term by a Democratic governor, and this Otero knew when he

My Nine Years as Governor 379

appointed him coal oil inspector [I never appointed Martin coal oil inspector, and Catron knew it. He was appointed before I became governor. I requested and received his resignation.] Suit has been brought against Martin and his bondsmen to recover the embezzled school funds, which is still pending. There is a law in the territory which prohibits any person who has received and collected public moneys and not turned them in, from holding office until he has so turned them in to the proper officer. There is another law which makes it the duty of the governor to summarily remove every officer who may have collected school funds and not turned them over according to law. On Martin's resignation of coal oil inspector, the governor appointed *John S. Clark* to that place. Clark, next to Max Frost, has most influence over Governor Otero. Clark, like Max Frost, has also been indicted, but in the state of Tennessee for the crime of *murder;* he absconded, came here. When his whereabouts were ascertained, and a warrant for his arrest was sought to be issued, as in Max Frost's case, it was found the indictment against him had disappeared and has never since been found; that the sheet of the record showing the presentment of the indictment had also disappeared.

Martin's embezzlement of school funds consisted in retaining of the amounts collected by him as coal oil inspector everything in excess of two thousand dollars, which was his salary, the balance he was required to turn over to the school fund. Clark, his successor, held the office for about ten months before the end of the next legislative assembly. He collected about $2,600 in excess of his salary, and has never turned it over to the school fund, yet, notwithstanding the laws before referred to requiring the governor to remove persons who collect and do not turn over to school funds, and also disqualifying them from holding office, still Governor Otero has twice since then reappointed Clark to the same office, well knowing the provisions of the law and Clark's defalcation. Clark by mere sham has attempted to evade the law by depositing with the territorial treasurer a check on a bank, signed by himself and endorsed that it is not to be collected until the suit on the bond of M. S. Hart, a former coal oil inspector, who also embezzled the excess due the school fund, should be decided by the courts adversely to the defendant, and also the suit on Martin's bond. Clark is one of the bondsmen of said Hart. He does not deny that he collected the moneys and has not paid them over, but he now claims that the law under which he collected them was illegal and void, that the taxes were improperly collected; that he had a right to retain them all to himself. Of these facts Governor Otero is well aware. These three defaulting coal oil inspectors now owe the school fund of the territory with interest over thirteen thousand dollars, and yet complaint is made that our schools have not sufficient funds. John S. Clark is also an ex-gambler and saloon keeper at Las Vegas. He is a partner with Governor Otero in sheep and ranch business; became such since his appointment of coal oil inspector. It is alleged that Governor Otero is largely indebted to him and many insinuate that the indebtedness has been cancelled by Clark's appointment. Two years ago, Clark by the aid of Governor Otero and others of the clique manipulated the legislature so as to change the coal oil inspection law in order that the total amount of collection should go to Clark and none to the school fund. This gave him an income therefrom of about $7,000 a year for which he did less than ten days' work each year. Very little coal oil was inspected. In most instances the inspector's brand was placed on the oil tanks at Florence, Colorado, more than a hundred miles outside of the territory without inspection. There is no authority to appoint deputies or inspectors to act outside of the territory. Governor Otero is well aware of all these facts. Instead of removing Clark as required by law for his defalcation Governor Otero has twice reappointed him to the office during the time he was a defaulter.

[18] Governor Otero has appointed as his adjutant-general at a salary of one thousand dollars per annum, W. H. Whiteman, who was appointed by President Harrison, associate justice of the supreme court of New Mexico, and failed of confirmation in the Senate because he embezzled money he had collected for some Swiss clients as their attorney in this territory. The Swiss minister or consul-general at New York preferred charges against Whiteman when he was appointed, for the embezzlement. The matter was investigated, found true, and Whiteman was either rejected or his name withdrawn. Governor Otero knew of these facts, yet thereafter appointed him to said office.

[19] During Governor Otero's administration, the assessed valuation of property for taxation in the territory has gone down over four millions of dollars when it should have been increased from eight millions to ten millions under the general boom caused by the tariff legislation at the commencement of President McKinley's term. There has been an increase of the number of sheep from three million to five million, and in value from sevent-five cents per head to two dollars per head; on sheep alone there has been an increase in value of six millions of dollars more; cattle, horses, and other livestock have increased in like proportion—probably to the amount of three millions of dollars more. The wool crop has tripled in value; it was four cents before the present tariff, it is now about 13 cents per pound, making an increase of about a million dollars per year. From wool, sheep, and cattle alone there has been an increase in value of over twelve millions of dollars. This has been offset, however, by the great increase in the rate of tax levy during Otero's administration. That rate has been nearly doubled, so that the value of all property except livestock has been correspondingly reduced. For example; property in Santa Fe County has gone down from two million, eight hundred thousand to about one million six hundred thousand. The tax levy not counting the amount to pay interest on the debt of the county is about six and one-tenth mills, while the court has issued mandamuses compelling the board to levy an additional tax or taxes of about 9 per cent to pay interest on the county debt, which covers a period of about six years, but when properly distributed will raise the annual tax levy to fully 8 per cent, a greater amount than can be realized by loaning money. Before Governor Otero's administration the tax levy in Santa Fe County did not exceed 4 per cent.

[20] Governor Otero, although recommending economy, has persistently urged the legislature to create offices with large salaries to be filled by his appointees without regard to their importance, or the interest of the tax payers. In many instances, he has favored the increase of salaries and compensations when they were already too large. He has approved every bill enacted, increasing salaries, creating new offices or office-holders, and making expenses beyond what previously existed without objection to a single one. When the act was passed to give John S. Clark all the money collected as coal oil inspector and take it away from the schools, it passed by a vote of seven-five in the council, the undersigned being a member and voting against it. Governor Otero's veto would have killed the bill. He approved it because his friend Clark had to be provided for. By an act of Congress, May 25th,

1896, Vol. 29, page 161, it is provided that no other officer of either house of the legislative assembly in New Mexico, than those provided for therein should be elected or appointed, or paid out of any moneys appropriated by Congress, or by the legislature of New Mexico, except an interpreter and a translator. Notwithstanding this last law, the legislature appointed about one hundred extra officers beyond those provided for in that act, and appropriated the money to pay them for "interpreters, translators, and incidental expenses" without specifying expenses, it being known that the appropriation was to pay these extra officers, the act of Congress not allowing more than one interpreter and one translator for both houses. The appropriation amounted to $18,000 and was made by three joint resolutions, two of which provided that the money should be paid to the president of the council and speaker of the house and disbursed as directed by the legislative assembly, the third not stating anything about the disbursement; no provision was made as to who or how many interpreters and translators there should be or their salaries, or what incidental expenses were, or how many extra officers were to be employed or what they were to be. No provision was made for any receipts or vouchers or accounting for the money. The $18,000 were taken out of any funds in the treasury not collected to pay interest on the public debt regardless of the object for which they had been collected. Eleven thousand dollars were in like manner appropriated two years prior thereto. Governor Otero approved the resolution appropriating the money, although he knew they were positively prohibited by said act of Congress.

[21] The Organic Act of this territory, September 9, 1850, Sec. 3, speaking of the powers of the governor says: "He shall take care that the laws be faithfully executed." With that injunction over him, he allowed without objection $29,000 collected and appropriated for other purposes to be paid to officers of the legislature contrary to the act of Congress, Sec. 1888 R. S. of U. S. provides that no legislative assembly of the territory shall in any instance on any pretext exceed the amount appropriated by Congress for its annual expense. This alone ought to have prevented those appropriations. The act of May 28th, 1896, forbids them in turn. Sec. 1887 provides: "Hereafter no expense for printing exceeding $4,000 including printing laws, journals, bills, and necessary printing of the same nature shall be incurred by any session of the legislature of any of the territories." This law was a prohibition on the legislature of this territory. There is another act of Congress which provides that the laws, journals, and bills shall be printed in the English language. This is also a limitation on the power of the legislature, yet the last session of the legislature appropriated from eight to ten thousand dollars in a loose manner to be used without any safeguards or restrictions in paying for printing laws, journals, bills, governor's message, and reports of various territorial officers, in the Spanish language, and for their translation. The territorial law, if valid, provides that such expenditures shall not cost more than 25 per cent in excess of the amount paid by Congress for the same work. Yet these appropriations have more than doubled the rate to be paid without so specifying, and this in the face of the acts of Congress prohibiting all of it. Governor Otero, with full knowledge of the facts, approved these appropriations.

[22] One of the extra officers, who was illegally employed by the legislature last session and paid a large salary per diem, was Page B. Otero, brother of the governor, who at the same time was drawing a salary of $1,200

per annum as clerk of the board of land commissioners, all of which was known to the governor.

[23] Sec. 1855 R. S. of U. S. prohibits territorial legislatures from enacting or enforcing any law by which the governor of the territory shall be paid any compensation beyond that provided by the United States. Congress appropriates $500 for executive expenses of the territory. The last legislature appropriated $3,000 to pay expenses of the governor's office, which is otherwise fully provided for in the capitol building; it also appropriated $1,200 to pay his private secretary; he approved both of these acts without protest. He lobbied with the members to secure their passage, and when the provision appropriating $3,000 for expenses of his office was under consideration by the committee having it in charge, he saw members of the committee, as it is reliably stated, and urged them to pass the act, but to strike out a provision which required him to furnish vouchers, stating the objects for which he expended the money, the amount of each disbursement, giving as a reason, as stated by a member of the committee, that it was beneath the dignity of the governor to return vouchers or take receipts for his disbursements. That it was a reflection on his honor and integrity. This money will be expended, no one will know how or where it will go.

[24] Congress appropriates $3,000 for the governor's salary; $500 for executive expenses; $500 to pay an interpreter, making $4,000. The territory $4,200 to pay expenses of the governor's office and a private secretary, making $8,200 per annum. The governor occupies free of rent a fine building belonging to Fort Marcy Military Reservation, worth fully $500 more per annum, giving him an income of about $8,700, out of which he is to pay his private secretary, if he has one, and his interpreter, if he has one.

[25] The person employed as interpreter and his man to work upon and influence the people of Mexican or Spanish origin is Antonio Alarid, who was one of the bolters at the county convention in 1900 before referred to.

[26] At the outbreak of the late war with Spain this man Alarid and one Adolfo Hill got up a company and swore every man of them not to enlist to go to war unless Governor Otero would appoint them as officers of the company. They thereby prevented every one of those men, all of them good men, from enlisting. This fact was reported to Governor Otero in detail by the undersigned, still thereafter he kept said Antonio Alarid in said position and has continued to do so uptodate, when there are plenty of other competent persons who would be glad of the place. Another company was gotten up by one R. L. Baca and in like manner swore to not enlist unless the governor would appoint Baca an officer of the company. This fact was also reported to the governor and was well known to him. All of those men were thus prevented from enlisting. Baca is the same man who was secretary of the bolting Republican committee which nominated the bolting Republican ticket at the last election. He has since been employed by Governor Otero to translate his message and other documents under an act of the legislature at its last session authorizing him to employ some one to do such translating at the expense of the territory. Baca is the same man who at the last election in Santa Fe County was appointed by the board of election officers of the county as a register of voters in precinct No. 18 and after he and the other members of the board of registers had registered and posted a list of the voters, which was a finality, took down the list and erased from it over forty names, all straight Republicans, and left their names off of the list which was furnished to the judges of election, the same being erased by scratching

them off of the list; he, Baca, being also one of the judges of election, refused to allow any of those parties to vote, although they had been legally registered and although the list furnished still showed enough to make out the names of some of them. In this manner, the Republican Party in Santa Fe County was deprived of forty votes or more, which if cast would have resulted in giving a majority to T. B. Catron, the undersigned, for the legislative council on the face of the returns. It was boasted that this was done to defeat the election of Catron, and prevent him from being a member of the legislative assembly, as it was feared that his presence in the council would seriously interfere with many of the schemes which were intended to be carried through by Governor Otero and his ring, increasing salaries, making new offices, appropriating money for the use of the governor's office and his private secretary, and the payment of a large amount of extra officers for the legislature, who were not permitted by law. This man, R. L. Baca, has openly boasted on the streets of Santa Fe that he cannot be indicted by a grand jury for anything whatever he may do, and if he should be indicted and convicted for anything, Governor Otero would grant him a pardon. Whether he had any reason for making such statements I do not know, but it is sufficient to know that he is working and training with the governor's clique; that he is a mere tool for Max Frost, the governor's boss manager, and that an attempt has been made twice to indict him for an open, notorious, and flagrant forgery committed by him in connection with Narciso Mondragon, in making out and signing the name of P. Carrick Shannon to a receipt for $500 in favor of said Mondragon after the death of said Shannon, Baca being the administrator. Such attempts in both instances failed although it is stated that the proofs were clear, unequivocal, and undoubted.

[27] During the present administration of Governor Otero counting from his first appointment more than four years ago, the affairs of this territory, political and financial, have gone wrong. Politics have in a great measure been run and controlled by rings and cliques in the interest of the governor. His office and the influences of his office have been used to control and manage the people and particularly men of influence in different counties, to get up delegates and candidates to conventions under her office to work directly in the interest of Governor Otero, promote the schemes of himself and those who control and influence him, and to work upon and deplete the treasury of the territory, and of the various counties.

[28] It seems that the door to fraud and wrong doing has been thrown wide open. The people believe that the present status of the territory should not exist longer; that under it the territory will not prosper.

[29] New Mexico is now applying to be admitted to statehood; she has ample population, intelligence, and wealth to justify making a state of her. She should be made a Republican state, and if so, the Republican Party should be kept clean and pure so that we will have a state worthy to be counted as such. The Republican Party should try to benefit the territory and people, and not tolerate and encourage wrong and plunder. Should matters go on as they are, and New Mexico be made a state, it is possible that she would come in as such under Democratic management and control, unless a better administration can be placed in charge of the territory. Our people believe that a strong, honest, and systematic administration should be inaugurated here, who will establish order, bring about harmony, see that honest elections are had, extravagance cut off, taxes reduced, valuations increased, and such things done as will help rather than injure.

[30] Since Governor Otero's reappointment by President McKinley, an attempt has been made to overcome the charges preferred against him; that during his administration the assessed valuation of property was reduced four millions of dollars; it has been said that President McKinley and the secretary of the interior insisted that the facts in regard to that charge should be made to appear in the future differently. In order to make such change, the territorial board of equalization, appointed by Governor Otero, and mainly under his influence and control, at their last session, undertook to make a horizontal raise in the valuation of all property in the territory of about 15 per cent, which would make an increase in the total valuation in the territory of about six millions of dollars and thereby apparently overcome the decrease in valuation during his administration. It is insisted that arbitrary action like that is not justified by law, right or anything else; no statute of the territory permits it in the opinion of the best lawyers. It is insisted that although some parties may have undervalued their property, other parties correctly valued theirs, and an arbitrary raise of 15 per cent without notice or an appeal being taken is unjust to every property owner, who made a fair and honest return. Such action is deemed outrageous and arbitrary and oppressive. It is calculated to bring the administration into disrepute; to create a want of confidence and injure the Republican Party, which being in power must bear the responsibility of all such acts.

[31] Being thoroughly acquainted with a large number of the people of the territory, having traveled all over it constantly for the last 35 years, practicing my profession as an attorney-at-law, and coming in contact with all the representative people of the territory, I can confidently say that I believe I am well informed as to the opinions and wishes of the masses of our people, especially those belonging to the Republican Party, and it is almost the unanimous desire of the Republicans in this territory, outside of those holding office, or receiving favors, directly or indirectly, from Governor Otero's administration, that there should be a change in the office of governor of this territory; that it is not believed that the present administration is working for the best interest of the territory or the Republican Party, on the contrary that the finances of the territory are being badly managed, extravagance in legislation is being encouraged, taxation has been increased and the values of property decreased, so that the administration as it now exists amounts to an oppression and wrong. The people therefore hope that you will look into their affairs and remedy the wrongs which have been committed and prevent them for the future by giving us some good, honest, true, and faithful Republican for governor, who will help to purify the ballot box, correct the financial errors and irregularities, put down crime, place better men in the offices, and give us such an administration as will inspire confidence, promote immigration and increase the value of property and lower the rate of the tax levy.

Hoping that you may do such, I remain,
    Yours respectfully,
      (Signed) Thomas B. Catron,
   Ex-Delegate in Fifty-fourth Congress from New Mexico.

District of Columbia } ss.
City of Washington

Thomas B. Catron being duly sworn upon his oath says: He was the delegate in the Fifty-fourth Congress from New Mexico; that the foregoing communication signed by him is a true copy of the original thereof which was

My Nine Years as Governor

duly verified and transmitted to the President of the United States through the hands of Capt. Fritz Muller, that the facts set forth in said communication are true to his knowledge except such of them as are stated on information and as to those he has the best reasons to believe and does believe them to be true.

(Signed) Thomas B. Catron.

Subscribed and sworn to before me this January 7th, 1902.

(Signed) Aaron Russell, Notary Public, District of Columbia.

∞

Chapter XI

INAUGURAL ADDRESS

Fellow citizens: For the second time I have before Almighty God and in your presence taken the oath of the high office to which I have been called, and for the first time in more than half a century of our existence as a territory, has its governor been reappointed. I would be more than human did I not feel proud and honored by the exception thus made in my favor, but I recognize in it less a personal compliment to myself and to my past administration than a compliance with the express will of the people of New Mexico who, with hardly an exception, were in favor of my reappointment. The President of the United States heard this voice of the people and recognized its force, so that I feel as though my present position were almost the result of a popular election and that I am indeed the choice of the people as well as that of our Chief Magistrate in Washington. I have been and shall strive to be in the future, governor of the people of New Mexico without regard to race, creed, or party.

Four years ago, I took the same oath I have this day assumed. Then I was new and untried and with scant preparation for the duties of the office I then assumed, but I entered upon them with the firm determination to abide by my obligation and to administer the office to the best of my ability and give to it my whole time and my best endeavors for the good and welfare of the territory. In this effort I was seconded by the best men in the territory and the result is before you. Two legislatures have come and gone during my administration, and while it was not always in accord with me nor I with it, the result has been that the laws enacted by the thirty-third and thirty-fourth legislative assemblies compare favorably with those of any previous sessions, and some of them have proved of the greatest public good. Among these are the Duncan tax law, the Bursum refunding bill, and the Springer school law, together with many others that will occur to you.

It has been charged that under my administration the tax rate has been increased and capital has been driven out of the territory. While it is true that in some counties the tax rate has been increased, this has been caused by purely local conditions such as decreased assessments or the payment of bonded debt, as in Santa Fe County, with which the territory had absolutely nothing to do and was not in any manner responsible; while, as a matter of fact, the rate of tax for territorial purposes has diminished and the collections have been larger and better for the last year than ever before. It is an unfortunate and lamentable fact that the assessed valuation of the territory has decreased during the past two years about four million dollars. There is no excuse for this; conditions as we know them to exist do not justify it and it has resulted in a higher rate of taxation for territorial and county purpose than is necessary. I called the attention of the last legislative assembly to this and asked it to devise a remedy, which was not done. We know that the total valuation of this territory for taxation should be nearer one hundred million than forty, and I shall use all my authority during my term of office to bring up this valuation to its proper figure. This is necessary, not only to reduce our rate of taxation, but to show to the government at Washington, and the people of the United States, something of what our real valuation is, and that we are ready and willing to pay our share of the public burden by taxing ourselves upon it; the present practice is about as sensible as it would be to reduce our census returns of population in order to evade a poll tax, and so far as I can do so I shall endeavor to stop this unbusinesslike, misleading, and illegal practice in the efficient assessment of property. At the end of the fiscal year, for the first time in the history of New Mexico, there was a surplus in the treasury instead of a deficit, and this notwithstanding the purchase and retirement of $69,000 of territorial bonds and certificates of indebtedness and the collection of a sinking fund to meet outstanding bonds becoming due. The total tax levy for all territorial purposes for the present fiscal year is less than for the past, although the rate was slightly increased for the support of territorial institutions and the payment of maturing obligations. Our credit has been strengthened so that our 4 per cent bonds sold at a premium two years ago, while before that our 6 and 7 per cent bonds had to be disposed of at a discount. The only bonds issued under my administration were $60,000 4 per cent for the completion of the capitol, and certificates of indebtedness to take up deficiencies created under former administrations. The administration of the land grant by Congress, under boards of which I have the honor to be a member, has resulted, up to this time, in producing the following amounts in cash to the credit of the various institutions:

Common School Income Fund	$14,401.92
Normal School, Silver City	10,830.61
Normal University, Las Vegas	10,830.62
School of Mines	13,368.46
Penitentiary	14,519.45
Military Institute	6,512.14
Blind Asylum	3,032.14
Deaf and Dumb Asylum	12,686.71
	$86,182.05

Besides 187,735,950 acres of land yet undisposed of, and 3,140,000 acres of school lands not leased.

In regard to capital having been driven out of the territory by reason of the high taxes and generally lax administration of affairs, it is a fact well known to all of you that there has been more railroad construction in the territory during the past four years than since 1879 and 1880. During the last fiscal year there were 730 miles projected, upon which construction is progressing, and even now the great Rock Island is srtetching across our county towards El Paso at the rate of a mile every day. The records of the secretary's office show that during the past four years there were 652 articles of incorporation filed for mining and industrial companies authorizing them to do business in the territory, and from January 1st, 1901, to June 15th, 1901, 116 filings were made with more than fifty million dollars capital, while for the four years previous there were only 565 of such articles, and for the four years preceding this last period 525. The capital stock of these corporations varies from a few thousand to several millions each, but every one represents money invested in the development of our territory, while I do not know of a single monied corporation that has withdrawn from the territory, or corporation that has ceased to do business during the past four years. The investment of foreign capital in railroads, mining, and other industrial pursuits is what we most need for the development and increase of our wonderful natural resources of soil and mine. Our sheep and cattle interests will take care of themselves, but our vast deposits of iron, coal, gold, silver, copper, and lead require large capital and expert management to develop and make them tangible assets. Already our laws are most liberal for all enterprises of this character and my policy will be, as in the past, to afford every facility for companies or individuals to do business in the territory which will tend to give our vast natural resources a commercial and market value.

During my term of office I have not heard of a single act of misfeasance, nonfeasance, or malfeasance on the part of any officer appointed by me. The revenues have been carefully collected and honestly disposed of. This magnificent building was constructed and furnished by a committee of your citizens at a ridiculously low sum of $135,000 without one dollar of expense for administration or supervision. The board of public lands has collected and turned over for the benefit of the territory more than $100,000 cash without a cent of expense except the salary of the commissioner of public lands and his office expenses. Our penitentiary and other public institutions are models of their kind and are better equipped for their respective purposes than ever before. Justice has been administered by our courts more promptly and surely than was formerly the case, and our public schools are in better condition and have more revenue than since the present system was adopted ten years ago.

There are always croakers and those who look on the dark side of everything. They are either ignorant or willfully blind who see nothing in the condition of our territory that does not promise brightly for our future. The books and records in this building will corroborate my statements and they are open to the inspection of any one who wishes to know the truth about our condition. Each year shows a decided improvement and advance; and under the oath I have just taken and my obligation as a citizen, it will be my duty and my pride to assist in that advancement and improvement so far as in me lies. Fellow Citizens, I do not expect to complete my four years term of office. Before that time expires I firmly believe that my term will be ended by our admission as a sovereign *state* of this grand union and that another white star will be added to that glorious constellation that floats on the azure field above us, whose luster will not be dimmed nor its glory diminished by any of those which have been placed there before, for New Mexico in war or in peace, at Valverde, Las Guasimas, or Luzon, in Chicago, Paris, or St. Louis, has always been progressive, aggressive, and more than loyal to the United States and its flag under whose protecting folds it came fifty-one years ago.

HON WILLIAM E. MARTIN'S ADDRESS

Governor Otero, ladies, gentlemen, and dear fellow citizens: We have met here with the greatest joy and pleasure from different portions of the territory to tender our sincerest and warmest welcome and congratulations to the man whom the whole people of New Mexico idolize and esteem, Miguel Antonio Otero, and to welcome him, not, however, fully as he deserves, nor even as is his merit, but as a slight token of our affection and as a mark of the high esteem in which he is held by the people whose wise executive he has been for the last four years.

The electric wires wafted the joyful news of his reappointment as our governor on the 15th day of June last by his Excellency, the President, re-echoing the gladsome tidings not alone to the very center of the arches of this most magnificent edifice, but also continuing and concluding its vibrations in the deepest and most hidden depths of the hearts of the New Mexicans. This was to have been expected because of his wise, economical, just, and impartial administration during the last four years manifested as much, notwithstanding that there were envenomed fulminations thrust at random against him. These, however, fell harmless at his feet, failing in their aim as straws driven by the winds. And not only this much, my dearly beloved fellow citizens. They, who exploded these fulminations, have fallen supinely at his feet, humbled, defeated, and beaten in the most shameful and abject humiliation.

The solemn pledges of the National Republican platform have been completely carried out, and the President has not only given us home rule, but he has done more, having given us a native-born executive for a second time; a native in whom we find the possession of all these qualities necessary for the making of a true statesman, capacity, honesty, firmness, and amiability, giving us to understand, not alone that the present administration is perfectly cognizant that we are capable of self-government, but assuring us of the fact that no long time will elapse ere our territory will be admitted to the sisterhood of states. And when this shall have come to pass, the people of New Mexico will prove to the President that he has not made the slightest mistake in having appointed the man for governor who is our first choice, for she will encircle his brow with the senatorial laurel of the new state.

Kindly permit me, Governor Otero, to offer you this small garland of flowers in the name of the New Mexican people. They are as white as the driven snow, symbols of the character of our governor. And permit me, also, to present to you this other garland on behalf of the inhabitants of the great county of Socorro, to which I have the honor to belong; it is composed of pinks, pattern of purity, and a token of the most fervent love which we profess for you.

Your excellency, please accept my hand, with which I tender you my most sincere congratulations. It is not a strong hand, but it is that of a faithful admirer and of a true friend, and it will ever be ready to join yours in the defense and advancement of the best and dearest interests of New Mexico.

COLONEL J. FRANCISCO CHAVES' ADDRESS OF WELCOME

Governor Otero, ladies and gentlemen, and citizens of New Mexico: We appear today to greet the arrival in our midst of the Honorable Miguel A. Otero, our late governor, and with the grace of God, and by the reappointment of our great Republican President, William McKinley, the governor of New Mexico for the next ensuing four years.

Welcome, Sir, thrice welcome to our beautiful territory, to our mountains and plains, to our health giving climate, to our cities and hamlets, to our mining and grazing camps. Welcome, Sir, to our homes, where the hand of fellowship and friendship stretches out to grasp yours with genuine affection and love. Welcome, Sir, to the bosom of our families, who are ready to receive you with open arms as their governor, friend, and champion. And last but not least by far, I welcome you in the name of all the ladies of New Mexico, and more especially of the good and handsome ladies of Santa Fe, whose beautiful faces and bright eyes are directed upon you, and in whose happy appearing countenances you see pictured the fullness and cordiality of their welcome. God bless them all.

Welcome, Sir, to us as the representative of Republican principles in our territory. Welcome, Sir, as the first choice of the better Democratic element of the territory of New Mexico, alike welcome to the rich and to the lowly and poor, the banker, the merchant, the manufacturer, the cowpuncher, the shepherd, and the farmer. Welcome, Sir, to those important and delicate duties incumbent upon you as the executive of the territory, coming now amongst us anew with a mind and heart single only to the performance of those duties as the representative of law, and with a view and firm resolve that such performance may redound to the best interests of all the people of New Mexico, irrespective of party, creed, race, or condition. Sir, I have the honor to welcome you in the name of all the people of New Mexico to its capital in the city of Santa Fe. Welcome, Sir, to the budding state of New Mexico, hoping that the bud will ere long burst and blossom into full maturity, during and before the expiration of your present beginning of the four years as governor of the good old territory of New Mexico, and that its future star whose glimmer can at present be barely distinguished, will in time grow in size and brilliancy into a star of the first magnitude, lighting with its effulgence the firmament of heaven, and second to no other in the glorious constellation of the American Union.

Sir, you have had a struggle, and but for some disagreeable features attending it, a struggle that under our form of government cannot be avoided; indeed, it is questionable whether it is not preferable that such struggles for honorable positions should continue. In fact, it is my humble opinion that such competitive struggles for place and honorable position should be the rule, rather than exception. In that struggle you have come out victorious; you have attained the honorable position sought in spite of severe competition; in spite of slander and detraction. You have reached the goal of your ambition first, and have distanced all of your competitors. You have been vindicated fully and completely, both by your superior and by your equals and fellow citizens. Doubtless you are satisfied. The people of New Mexico are satisfied, the Republican party of New Mexico is satisfied. Welcome, then; thrice welcome, greets you from the north and from the south, and from the east, from the west, and from the center of New Mexico, irrespective of party. And now, my fellow citizens, the battle is over, and the skies are clear. Let us bend all our undivided energies for the best interests of our beloved territory of New Mexico. Divided we are weak, but united we are strong. This is our home, and it is to our best interest so to labor that when the many attacks come we will find a solid front and no weak spot in our ranks to assail. Let Statehood be our slogan from this day; let it continue day and night, and, with the help of God, we will achieve the victory which will bring New Mexico into the Union as a sovereign state. God bless you all. I thank you.

Chapter XV
I SPEAK ON STATEHOOD

Fellow citizens: It is with pride and pleasure that I greet you on this occasion when for the 21st year the metropolis of New Mexico celebrates her territorial fair.

This occasion is one of unusual significance and importance to you and the whole territory, as upon your action today will largely depend the action of Congress in regard to that question of supreme importance to our future, our admission as a state of the Union.

My own views upon this subject are too well known to need repetition here; in each message to the legislature, and in every report to the secretary of the interior, I have urged the passage of an enabling act and set out in full the reasons and arguments for it. I have issued the proclamation calling this meeting of the people that they might express themselves directly instead of through their legislature or governors.

For more than half a century we have been of, yet not one of, the United States; during all that period we have been true and loyal to the laws and flag of that glorious Union of which we hope to become a part, and have freely given of our blood and treasure to maintain its supremacy and glory. During that time we have seen fifteen states admitted, one of them taken largely from within our borders, and a territory created out of one of our counties; each of these states save one, when admitted had less population and taxable property than we now possess, and none was in any respect better equipped for self government than we.

As early as June, 1850, a constitution was adopted by our people for the formation of a state which prohibited slavery in New Mexico, showing at that early day that our people were fully alive to the dangers that threatened the republic, and the only course it could pursue to carry out the great future which these United States have wrought in proclaiming liberty throughout the world and to the peoples thereof. Under this constitution, two United States senators and a member of Congress were elected, who were not recognized by Congress. But it did in September of that year create us into a territory by the organic act which is still our fundamental law.

Nothing further was done of a public nature towards our admission until 1874, when a bill for that purpose was introduced by Honorable S. B. Elkins, our delegate. This was defeated but the effort was renewed at the next and each succeeding Congress. With every renewed effort and additional reasons for our admission the opposition has grown the stronger, until the conclusion is irresistible that some strong personal and financial interests are arrayed against us for selfish aggrandisement. One evidence of this is the Elephant Butte dam; and another the segregation of large areas of public domain for so-called forest reserves, and the effort being made for a government lease law. As a territory, we cannot combat these schemes; we have no voice in the disposition of that land that we have struggled so long to maintain as a part of our territory, while, as a state, we would be able to assert and retain our rights.

In 1889, as distinguished a body of men assembled for the purpose of framing a constitution for the new state of New Mexico as had ever gathered for a similar purpose, and after deliberating for nearly a month, formulated a constitution which is the peer of any similar document in the Union. It is so fair, so liberal, and so comprehensive that I caused it to be published in my last report as the strongest showing that could be made upon our capacity for self government. Owing to an unfortunate combination of circumstances, this most admirable constitution was rejected by the people at the election held in 1890, but it will stand as a monument to the wisdom and statesmanship of is framers.

I believe that the time is now ripe for the fruition of our hopes; that

Congress knows the merit of our claims and will not longer deny us the privilege we have sought so long, and that the action of this assemblage of representative citizens of the territory will prove a potent help toward that end.

I do not, on an occasion like this, wish to speak of disagreeable facts, but it is well that we should realize and face them and then apply the remedy.

Our ridiculously low assessment for taxation is constantly spoken of and reflected upon. The present assessed value of the territory is less than forty millions, while it is a notorious fact recognized by all who know anything about the subject that it ought to at least be three times that amount. The figures show that we have dropped from forty-five millions, in 1890, to less than thirty-eight million, in 1901, and the reduction still goes on, until, as a means of self preservation, in order to protect our credit and pay the actual expense of the government, the territory board of equalization last month made a raise on the returned value of all the property it could reach. This, my fellow citizens, is a lamentable state of affairs and one that must be remedied by you. You must see to it that proper men are elected to assess the property and equalize its value, so that we may appear to the world that we are in fact, as to our wealth and ability, able to pay our obligations.

This I believe to be the principal objection to our immediate admission, and if at this meeting you will adopt suitable resolutions upon this most important and vital subject and determine to see them carried out, you will have taken a long step toward the object for which we are here assembled.

I understand that some timorous people are afraid of the expense and responsibility attached to our becoming a state, but such fears are unworthy of American manhood; if they were to prevail in the ordinary affairs of life no one would exercise his rights of citizenship, or incur the duties and responsibilities of family life. The history of every newly admitted state is one of growth, advance, and prosperity, and we would be no exception to this rule, but, on the contrary, by our location midway of the oceans which bound the nation, with our natural wealth of mineral, timber, and lands, and the railroad connections we already have, New Mexico will at once assume a commanding position in the sisterhood of states, and the present motto, "Crescit Eundo" on our seal will assume added meaning and signfiicance from the date of our admission.

MY SPEECH AT STATEHOOD CONVENTION

Mr. Chairman, ladies, and gentlemen:

I have to thank you most sincerely for the warm and cordial welcome you have given me in this beautiful and prosperous city of Phoenix, the seat of government of the territory of Arizona, and I can assure you it is a great pleasure to me to be here on this occasion, which is of so much importance for your future: the question of your admission to the sisterhood of states in our glorious Union.

New Mexico greets you and wishes you every success in your endeavors, and promises as well her most loyal support. The same reasons given by New Mexico why she is entitled to statehood are applicable to you: population, wealth, education, and superior class of American citizens.

Prior to the organization of your territory, every reason advanced by New Mexico up to that date, applies also to Arizona, and since that time you have made even greater advancement than we have, in proportion to the population at the time you were created into a territory. In 1863, by proclamation of President Abraham Lincoln, Arizona was taken from New Mexico. In the words of your distinguished executive, made during his last visit to our territory: "God's best gift to man was carved from the rib of man, and as the small part taken to make the woman had ever since been the best and most beautiful part of man, so the part taken from New Mexico to make Arizona had ever since remained the best and most beautiful part of the grand domain that originally constituted the territory of New Mexico."

I do not propose on this occasion to take issue with Governor Murphy upon the point so aptly made by him, on the contrary, I desire to express the pleasure I have felt in traveling over your beautiful territory and witnessing the marvelous growth of your cities and towns, the rapid development of your various industries, and the evidences of your prosperity I have seen upon every hand. I may add, however, that man accepts the gift of God as his companion, and together as man and wife, New Mexico and Arizona stand today. Let us, therefore, unite at once on this most important question of statehood and work as a happy family to accomplish that which means so much for our future happiness. Our industries are the same; we each find our principal wealth in the bowels of the earth, in the cattle and sheep that graze on our vast grass-covered plains, in the rewards that follow the toil, and in the various business pursuits of our people. Our aspirations are the same. We desire to be participants in the best form of government of which we have any knowledge, and we believe that such a government can only be found within the union of states which makes up the great United States of America.

It is this identity of interest and unity of feeling and aspirations that justifies my presence here today within the borders of your territory, to speak briefly to you upon the subject of statehood for Arizona and New Mexico, and in this connection I desire to acknowledge the indebtedness of New Mexico to your governor for his eloquent and masterly presentation of the cause of statehood made in the city of Albuquerque ten days ago, and his effort in that behalf will long be remembered by our people. During the past four or five years, I had the pleasure of meeting Governor Murphy many times and in many places, and I cheerfully bear testimony to the fact that statehood for Arizona has been his constant theme, and that he has presented it with marked ability upon all occasions.

In presenting this question to the people of Arizona, it seems to me to be unnecessary to go at length into the many arguments advanced in favor of our admission. This is no new question, it has been before you for years, you have studied the different phases of it, and should know by this time upon which side lie your interests. But with those people who have not the good fortune to reside in either of our territories, I have often thought that the actual conditions of things in the two territories is less understood, or, I may say, more persistently misunderstood, than any other question that has disturbed the minds of the people within the memory of man. In New Mexico each year we have thousands of eastern tourists who stop for a day or two and delude themselves with the idea that they are making a study of the people and existing conditions. Few of them learn anything of value about the people or conditions as they actually exist. They are attracted by that which is novel and abnormal. They press the button upon every burro they meet. They are delighted to catch the features of a worthless old Indian. They photograph the oldest adobe building erected over three hundred years ago, and they re-

My Nine Years as Governor

turn to their homes fully convinced and satisfied in their own minds that they know all about New Mexico, and that we are unfitted for statehood.

How few of them take note of the countless herds upon our plains, of the vast treasures within our mountains, of the stately and magnificent buildings, public and private, that may be seen on every hand, of our hundreds of school houses and of the modern methods of education that prevail throughout the territory. Do they take note of the thousands of intelligent men and women they meet on every side, men and women who in intelligence, honesty, integrity, virtue, and all that goes to make up character, are equals of the men and women of the most favored state in the land? I have known of the invalids coming to our health-giving climate, who return to their eastern homes, forgetting that their lives were prolonged or saved in the *"Land of Sunshine,"* and who immediately feel called upon to criticize our conditions in a shameful manner. They will begin by speaking of the disloyalty of the native people. I resent such talk, because I am one myself.

Is it not a fact that, at the signing of the Treaty of Guadalupe-Hidalgo, February 2nd, 1848, the Mexican citizens, residing in the territories acquired by the United States, were given the right to retain their property and remain citizens of Mexico, but that they were under obligations to make their election within one year from that date as to whether they would remain Mexican citizens or become citizens of the United States, and if, at the end of the year, they failed to declare themselves Mexicans, they should be considered to have elected to become American citizens; and it is a fact, well known, that very, very few took advantage of the Mexican side. And this was done notwithstanding the fact that at that time our territories were under a military government, our very worst form of government.

Later the Mexican government made provisions for the removal of those who were unable to do so themselves, and who desired to return to Mexico, and I am unable to learn of any who took advantage of this offer. Again, during the Civil War, while Arizona was still a part of New Mexico, we furnished 6,561 soldiers in defense of the Union out of a population of 80,567 and about 97 per cent of these men were native born citizens of Mexico. Once more, during the Spanish-American War, New Mexico and Arizona not only sent more troops to the front, in proportion to the population, than any other state or territory in the Union, but also furnished more than one-half of the grandest regiment organized during the war, "Roosevelt's Rough Riders." I thank you for your kind attention. Let us have statehood.

∞

Chapter XIV
MORE HISTORICAL INFORMATION

Thomas B. Catron's letter addressed to President Theodore Roosevelt, dated October 18, 1901, and copied verbatim in Appendix, pp.. 373-385, herein, shows him to be unworthy of consideration. As a whole his letter could be answered as follows: 1 per cent truth and 99 per cent political chicanery.

Sometime before I was appointed governor, it was a notorious fact that one of the lowest "gangs" of murderers was located in Santa Fe and was known as the "Button Gang," controlled in politics by the Republican faction opposed to me. Such men as Hipolito Vigil, Francisco Gonzales y Borrego, and many others of the very lowest type of manhood made up the "gang" membership. It was this same "Button Gang" who allegedly assassinated Sheriff J. Francisco Chaves and many others. These men were identified by a copper button worn on the lapel of their coats, given them by their recognized leader, who actually took pride in his organization and seemed proud to wear the "button" himself. This "Button Gang" was a flourishing society; only a few Anglos belonged and these were known as "stool pigeons" for the leader. Frequently men of the opposition would disappear and it would be difficult to trace the many murders committed in Santa Fe County, attributed to the "Button Gang." This society continued to do "business" all through the administration of Governor L. Bradford Prince, but did not last long under the able administration of Governor W. T. Thornton. An attempt was made to revive it after I became governor, but it soon blew up, believe me.

Many valuable and highly interesting historical facts can be gathered by reading New Mexico Reports, Volume No. 8, in the following cases:

In Re Petition for Disbarment vs. Thomas B. Catron and Charles A. Spiess.

In the matter of Contempt vs. Thomas Hughes and W. T. McCreight.

Francisco Gonzales y Borrego et al., Plaintiffs in Error, vs. Territory of New Mexico, Defendant in Error.

INDEX

INDEX

Abbott, A. J., 235, 238
Abbott, E. C., 224, 260
Abbott, Ira A., 244, 262, 263
Abeyta, A., 297
Adams, Alva S., attended re-union, 62-63; mentioned, 234, 288
Ainsworth, F. C., 203
Alarid, Antonio, 382
Albright, George F., 258
Albuquerque American, quoted, 205-206
Albuquerque Citizen, quoted, 107, 141-142, 156-167, 169, 204, 219, 226, 265
Albuquerque Journal, quoted, 204, 219
Alger, R. A., letter, 38; mentioned, 39
Andrews, William H., mentioned, 216, 220, 226, 229-235, 237-239, 262; on statehood committee, 211
Antonio, Joseph, 12
Archuleta, Don Diego, death, 68
Arizona Gazette, mentioned, 211
Arizona Republican, quoted, 20
Armijo, Don Jacinto, 48, 247
Armijo, Felipe, killed, 110
Armijo, George W., 324-325
Armijo, Governor, 359
Armijo, Justo R., 139, 242, 244
Armijo, Mrs. George W., 324
Armijo, Perfecto, 242, 244
Armijo, Theodore Roosevelt Manderfield, christened, 324
Atkins, Beatrice, 250, 268
Atkins, Dr., 268
Austen, E. Goodwin, 11, 268, 270
Austen, Mrs. E. Goodwin, 268

Axtel, S. B., vetoed Jesuit School Bill, 88; mentioned, 103
Baca, Doña Jose Albino, 264
Baca, Elfego, 369
Baca, Jose Albino, 264
Baca, Jose A., Jr., 264
Baca, R. L., 204, 237, 321, 375, 382-383
Baker, B. S., 213, 228, 259, 338
Bailey, N. E., 46
Baldwin, Frank D., 258
Ballard, Lieutenant, 42
Bandera Americana, La., mentioned, 244
Bantz, Gideon D., opinion given, 29; mentioned, 106
Bard, Senator, 319, 320
Barnes, R. P., 254, 283, 285
Bartlett, E. L., appointed solicitor general, 15-17; mentioned, 2, 78, 105, 119, 236, 248, 259, 375
Bascom, F. H., 48
Baum, Misses, 325
Beardsley, Sam, 180
Bergere, Alfred M., 136, 224, 235, 251, 259, 260, 261, 263, 275
Bergere, Estella, 324
Bergere, Mrs. A. M., social life, 18, 65, 215, 251, 253, 256, 260, 298, 301, 308, 324
Berger, William M., 148, 160, 183-185, 238, 335
Bergmann, E. H., mentioned, 13; revealed conspiracy, 94-96; superintendent of penitentiary, 17
Beveridge, Albert J., 184, 185, 212, 214, 215, 220, 221
"Billy the Kid," 227
Birdsall, B. P., 87
Black, John C., 258
Bliss, C. N., 6, 54

Blood, Mrs. F. O., 324-325
Borrego case, 90
Borrodaile, John, 46, 206, 265, 288
Bourgade, Peter, archbishop, 72, 186, 252, 253
Bowen, George W., 259
Bowers, Joe, 374
Boyd, Nathan, syndicate head, 28; mentioned, 184
Brady, Thomas J., 194
Brevier, David J., 32
Brodie, Alexander, governor of Arizona, 217; mentioned, 325; presented Colonel Roosevelt, 63
Broncho Bill, *see* Walter, William; in charge of "Robbers' Roost," 112; left Black Jack, 114
Brown, C. T., 303
Brunswick, Marcus, 266
Bryan, John D., 92
Bull, Thomas J., 247
Bullard, E. D., 158
Bunker, William B., 123, 127
Burke, Dennis, 210
Burke, Edmund, 184
Burkhart, S., 30
Burns, Margaret, 325
Burns, Thomas D., 137, 334
Bursum, Holm O., appointed superintendent of penitentiary, 98; killed prisoner, 110; mentioned, 102, 109, 158, 159, 166, 183, 204, 215, 216, 219, 221, 232-234, 260, 261, 263
Bursum, Mrs. Holm O., 109

Cackley, fireman, 112
Campbell, Archibald, 309
Cannon, Joe, 331
Cantrell, J. D., 117
Capital Removing Bill, 69, 70

397

Carlsbad Argus, quoted, 141
Carper, Frank, 110
Carr, Clark, 18
Carruth, J. A., 158
Carter, Thomas H., 177, 185, 316-317, 319-321
Carver, Will, alias G. W. Franks, alias Harvey Logan, 111
Castillo, Marcos, 237
Catron, Mrs. T. B., 344
Catron, Thomas B., affidavit, 384-385; defeated, 140-152; letter to Roosevelt, 373-384; made speech, 36; mentioned, 7, 12, 30, 43, 46, 75, 77-81, 90, 92, 158, 172, 181, 183, 184, 189, 190-198, 201, 223, 224, 237, 254, 282-285, 287, 329, 330, 332, 335, 337; poison plot, 94-99; urged capitol rebuilding, 67-68
Chama Tribune, quoted, 138, 155
Chamberlain, L. H., 46
Chandler, senator from New Hampshire, 287
Chapell, Delos A., 259
Chaves, Amado, mentioned, 204, 224, 258, 263; read resolutions, 37
Chaves, Frank, 143
Chaves, J. Francisco, address, 288; mentioned, 77, 167, 168, 207, 208, 231, 258, 368, 375, 377; murdered, 99-101; on statehood committee, 211
Chavez y Chavez, Jose, sentence commuted, 106, 107
Chicago Journal, mentioned, 254
Chicago Times-Herald, mentioned, 65
Chicago Tribune, quoted, 298, 315
Childers, Mrs. William B., social life, 134, 250, 254, 257, 278
Childers, William B., 77, 92, 134, 145, 183-185,

213, 250, 252, 257, 275, 278
Clancy, Frank W., mentioned, 101, 171, 240, 241, 261, 275, 287; reported irregularity, 227-228
Clark, C. D., 203
Clark, John S., appointed coal oil inspector, 17; letter, 343-344; mentioned, 2, 3, 10, 89, 260, 261, 270, 330, 369, 379, 380
Clark, William A., 290
Clayton Enterprise, quoted, 199, 203
Cleveland, Grover, 286
Closson, Charles, headed posse, 101; mentioned, 280
Cochran, Irad, first death in New Mexico Squadron, 51
Coleman, Lieut., Troop E, 42
Collier, T. W., 106, 147
Conway, John V., 224, 268
Cook, Dave, 97
Cook, John W., investigated poison plot, 97-98
Cooper, Capt. Charles L., examined men, 44; mustering officer, 40; reported, 45
Cooper, Rev. W. A., 186, 248
Cordova, Perfecto, 115, 128, 129
Coronado, Francisco Vasquez de, expedition, 307, 309; mentioned, 76
Cortelyou, George B., 172, 173, 175, 319, 320
Coudert, Father J. M., 306, 307
Crist, J. H., 105
Crowfoot, engineer, 112
Cruickshank, C. G., 46
Crumpacker, J. W., chief justice, 275; mentioned, 204, 254
Culberson and Stevens Bill, 33

Culberson, Senator, introduced bill, 31; mentioned, 32
Cunningham, J. M., 157-158
Curry, George, captain, Troop H., 42; mentioned, 12, 52-53, 65, 270, 300

Dalies, Carl A., 89, 260
Dame, W. E., 41
Daniels, Henry, sentence commuted, 106
Dargan, Marion, foreword, viii
Davies, Charles G., 521
Davis, Mrs. Stephen B., Jr., 260
Davis, Stephen B., married, 258
Davis, Webster, 295
De Baca, appointed superintendent of public instruction, 17; mentioned, 18, 320
DeBois, Mr., miner, mentioned, 278, 279; mine, 278-279
De Luna, Doña Isabel B., 65
Deming Headlight, quoted, 20
Denver News, quoted, 296
Denver Republican, quoted, 21, 165
Dewey, Admiral, defeated enemy, 45
Dillingham, William P., 212, 213
Dobson, E. W., 11, 204, 270
Doña Ana County Republican, mentioned, 14; quoted, 199, 211
Dorsey, S. W., 194
Drew, Scotty, ordered to open safe, 112; mentioned, 119, 124
Duncan, James S., 139, 228, 258, 270
Duncan, Mrs. James S., social life, 270, 324

Easley, Charles F., elected, 140; mentioned, 132, 141, 196, 375

My Nine Years as Governor

Eddy, C. B., 30, 269-271, 277
Eldodt, Samuel, mentioned, 13, 77, 78; retained, 17
Elephant Butte, dam construction started, 28; mentioned, 339
Elizabeth Town Miner, quoted, 295
Elkins, Stephen B., 7, 33, 218, 219, 287, 373
Elliott, J. H., mentioned, 369; on statehood committee, 211
El Paso Times, quoted, 286-287
Elwood, John A., 302
Emerson, H. J., 265
Emmett, Lafayette, 3, 191, 192
Enriquez, Alfonso, 37
Errett, H. H., 127
Estabrook, H. D., 253
Etter, W. K., 41
Eustis, E. L., 185

Fairbanks, Charles W., 177, 316, 317
Fall, Albert B., appointed captain, 46-48; mentioned, 12-14, 16, 30, 46, 154, 181, 182, 201, 216, 258, 292, 305; on statehood committee, 211; received letter, 15; removed from office, 15
Fall, Mrs. A. B., 16
Farr, Edward, 115, 116, 127-129
Fergusson Act, 291
Fergusson, Harvey B., introduced act, 69; mentioned, 9, 30, 70, 133, 225, 291; on statehood committee, 211
Fiske, Eugene A., and Fritz Muller affidavit, 371-373; mentioned, 15, 155, 158, 172, 173, 183, 184, 189, 192, 194, 198, 238, 285, 287, 329, 330, 332, 335, 341
Fletcher, S. O., 158

Folsom, S. M., 171
Foraker, Creighton M., 5
Foraker, Joseph B., 5, 183, 221, 299
Fort, Lewis C., in charge of execution, 125-126; mentioned, 10
Fort Sumner Review, quoted, 339
Foster, A. G., 203
Fountain, Albert J., mentioned, 279; murdered, 90-92
Fourchegu, Anthony, 324
Francis, David R., 308, 309, 313
Franks, G. W. ("Will"), holdup, 112-118; *see* Carver, Will
Franks, Sam, in holdup, 112-113
Freeman, A. A., 30, 287
Freeman, H. B., 32, 184, 300
Freeman, Julia, social life, 257, 277, 300
Frost, Max, editor, *Santa Fe New Mexican,* 2; mentioned, 189, 194, 261, 263, 329, 375, 379
Frost, Mrs. Max, social life, 255-257, 260, 261, 280, 281, 303, 321, 325, 383
Fuller, Thomas C., 250, 252
Funston, Fred, 276

Gallegos, Desederio, received New Year's pardon, 105
Garcia, Emeterio, received New Year's pardon, 105
Garcia, Marcelino, mentioned, 16; retained, 17
Garcia, Sheriff, performed execution, 126
Garner, W. H., alias C. H. Schultz, 98
Garrett, Pat F., 48, 92, 93, 277, 369
Gavin, C. J., 208
Gay, Father J. L., benediction, 72

Gildersleeve, Charles H., 154
Gilliland, James, resisted arrest, 92
Givens, J. Crockett, 267
Goff, Nathan, 159-161
Gortner, Mrs. W. E., 4
Gortner, Robert C., mentioned, 96, 99, 105; received evidence, 95
Gortner, W. E., 4
Gould, George T., 51
Grayson, Charles F., business man, 282; "Moody Merrill," 283-285
Grayson, Mrs. Charles F., 283
Green, Lieutenant, Troop E, 42
Griffin, Lieutenant, Troop E, 42
Gross, Jacob, 251, 261
Gross, Mrs. Jacob ("Sister Carrie"), 251, 268
Guilliford, Mrs. William, 270
Guyer, John R., 74-75

Hagerman, Herbert J., mentioned, 236, 261, 309, 311, 329, 340, 341; named governor, 336
Hagerman, Percy J., 261, 262
Hale, Edward Everett, 300
Hall, C. C., 264
Hall, Willis P., 309
Hamilton, Judge, 106
Hand, Prof., band leader, 4
Hanna, Mark, 5, 7, 145, 183, 297, 300, 301, 317, 318
Hanna, Mrs. Mark, 301
Hansborough, Henry C., 177, 316, 317
Harrington, Frank, conductor, 112; mentioned, 114, 115, 121, 125; reported robbery, 113; shot Ketchum, 120; testified, 124
Harris, A. W., on statehood committee, 211
Harrison, G. W., 213

Harrison, President, 6
Harter, Elizabeth, 316
Hathaway, W. L., 204
Hawkins Bill, mentioned, 87, 305, 339; passed, 86
Hawkins, W. A., 30, 216, 258, 305
Heath, Perry, 177
Heinz, F. Augustus, 290, 291
Heitfield, Henry, 212
Henshaw, S. A., 213
Herman, Binger, 203, 292
Hersey, H. B., appointed adjutant general, 11; mentioned, 42, 56, 57; presented flag, 44
Hewett, Edgar L., 158, 330
Hightower, William M., 105
Hill, Adolfo, 382
Hitchcock, E. A., 158-160, 179, 188, 260, 284, 300, 316-318, 321, 329, 336
Hobbs, A. L., 248
Hole, L. B., 283, 284
Holt, Herbert B., clerk of council, 12; mentioned, 260
Holzman, Sadie, 268
Hopewell, Willard S., mentioned, 259, 260; on statehood committee, 211
Hopkins, Albert, 70
Hoskins, Daniel T., 158
Hubbell, Frank A., mentioned, 83, 107, 139, 216, 229, 233, 240-245, 265, 297, 369; on statehood committee, 211
Hubbell, Thomas S., 30, 208, 227-229, 232, 233, 240-244, 275
Hudson, Richard, 144
Hughes, J. D., 224, 329, 375
Hughes, Levi A., 260, 261, 281, 336; signature, 339
Hughes, Thomas, 258
Hurley, J. E., 3, 41, 43, 214, 266, 281, 296, 312

Inter Ocean, quoted, 202

Independente, mentioned, 20

Jacobs, Hannah, 166
James, Capt., 288
James, Mr., 122
Jaramillo, Venceslao, 11, 258, 265, 268-270, 276
Jesuit School Bill, passed over veto and annulled, 88
Johnson, Ernest A., notary public, 372, 373
Johnson, Gus R., 224
Johnson, Major, at Louisiana Purchase Exposition, 309
Johnson, prisoner, testifies, 92-93
Jones, A. A., 107
Jordan, C. T., 158
Joseph, Anthony, on statehood committee, 211
Joseph, Antonio, mentioned, 143; president of council, 12

Kearney, Mr., fired upon, 92
Keen, A. A., 204, 252, 258, 260
Keen, Mrs. A. A., 257
Kelly, Harry W., 261
Kelly, Lieutenant, Troop H., 42
Ketchum, Berry, visited brother, 112
Ketchum (Tom), Black Jack, alias Stevens, 120; arrested, 120; body exhumed, 127; brought to justice, 93-94; execution, 126-127; established rendezvous, 111; gang, 108; held up train, 112-113, 118, 120; loses arm, 121; mentioned, 111, 116, 122, 123, 325
Ketchum, Sam, member Black Jack gang, 111, 113, 114, 122
Kibbey, Joseph H., 220
Kilburn, E. P., 127
King, N. L., 288
Kirchgraber, engineer, mentioned, 119; testified, 124
Klock, George S., 232
Knaebel, George W., 168, 325
Knaebel, John H., 260
Knaebel, Mrs. George W., 325
Knapp, Dr., 109, 110
Kneeland, H. F., 56-57
Knox, W. S., letter to, 69; mentioned, 328
Kohlsaat, H. H., 65

LaRue, Jane, social life, 258, 325
LaRue, Jeannette, 256
LaRue, Mary, social life, 166, 249, 250, 257, 268, 293, 296
LaRue, Miss, 187
LaRue, Mrs. J. A., 258
Las Vegas Daily Optic, mentioned, 82-83; quoted, 14, 16, 19
Las Vegas Examiner, quoted, 4
Las Vegas Record, mentioned, 157; quoted, 25-226
Las Vegas Republican, quoted, 140
Laughlin, Mrs., 324
Laughlin, Napoleon B., associate justice, 3; mentioned, 5, 105, 259
Lawton, Henry W., 65
Lay, Ezra, alias William H. McGinnis, *see* McGinnis, William H.
Leading Facts of New Mexican History, quoted, 34, 142-143, 333
Leahy, David J., 219, 235
Leahy, Jeremiah, 123, 124, 127
Lee, Oliver, resisted arrest, 92
Leeson, J. J., 251
Lincoln, Abraham, 24
Linton, Moses, 251
Llewellyn, Morgan O., 260, 261, 263, 325
Llewellyn, Mrs. Morgan O., 261
Llewellyn, Mrs. William H. H., 279

My Nine Years as Governor 401

Llewellyn, William H. H., letter from Santiago, 52; mentioned, 22, 30, 42, 65, 177, 184, 216. 232, 235, 265, 279, 321, 325; presented medal, 60; ruins picture, 63; sick, 58; speaker of the house, 12; speech by, 352-354
Loeb, William, 321
Logan, Harvey, see Carver, W.
Lohman, Martin, 48, 279
Lopez, Celso, 237
Lopez, Jose L., 18
Lopez, Lorenzo, 190
Lopez, Miguel, 115, 128
Lordsburg Liberal, quoted, 19, 157
Los Angeles Times, quoted, 165
Louisiana Purchase Exposition, 307-309, 320, 368
Love, H. N., killed, 116; mentioned, 115, 127, 129
Luna, Maximiliano, captain, Troop F, 42; mentioned, 52, 65, 77, 79, 134, 251; reported killed, 65-66
Luna, Mrs. Maximiliano, 251
Luna, Mrs. Soloman, 260
Luna, Solomon, mentioned, 5, 6, 18, 134, 136, 144, 166, 191, 203, 215, 216, 218, 219, 221 258, 260, 261, 270, 278, 287, 288, 297, 343, 357; on statehood committee, 211
Luntzel, A., 46

Mack, Norman E., 302
Maher, James D., notary public, 373
Maine, U. S. Battleship, blown up, 35
Mann, Edward A., 262, 263
Manning, J. F., 238, 239
Manzanares, Francisco A., delivered keys of capitol, 72; on statehood committee, 211
Maria Josefa bell, 306-307
Marron, O. N., mentioned, 30, 204, 206, 213, 268; on statehood committee, 211
Martin, James, 102
Martin, T. P., 234
Martin, William E., mentioned, 13, 14, 102, 104, 136, 137, 166, 168, 192, 225, 378, 379, 387; resigned, 17
Martinez, Clofas, 268
Martinez, Felix, 10
Martinez, Malaquias, 258
Massie, James A., 43
Matthews, T. J., 288
McArthur, Arthur, 276
McCord, Myron H., 45, 46
McCrea, Louis A., 46
McFie, Mrs. John R., 258, 261, 324
McFie, Ralph, soldier, 52
McGinnis, William H., guarded horses, 112; mentioned, 114, 118, 204; pardoned, 108; 131; quelled mutiny, 131; see Lay, Ezra; sentenced, 130; trial, 127-129; wounded, 116, 117
McKenna, Joseph, 8
McKinley, Abner, 54-55
McKinley County Republican, quoted, 163
McKinley, Mrs. William, 174, 175, 292, 293
McKinley, William, President, call for volunteers, 39; died, 175; eulogy, 178; issued order, 58; mentioned, vii, 1, 2, 4, 6, 7, 9, 13, 21, 33, 34, 36, 45, 69, 142-146 148-150, 157-159, 161, 164, 170-173, 176, 177, 179, 189, 197, 288, 289, 292-295, 297-299, 314-316, 318, 331, 380, 384, 388
McMillan, Daniel H., 324
McMillan, Judge, 327, 328
McNair, Lilburn G., 302
McNary, James G., 261
Medler, E. L., 261
Meek, Sam Cary, poem by, 37-38
Mennet, J. P. S., 46
Merrill, O. L., 99
Miller, Lorian, acting governor, 12; mentioned, 14, 17, 77
Mills, Anson, mentioned, 33, 187; favored treaty, 31-32
Mills, Byron T., 190
Mills, Mrs. Anson, 186
Mills, Mrs. William, 268
Mills, William J., made speech, 36; mentioned, 8, 9, 18, 72, 123, 125, 139, 249, 253, 254, 259, 261, 262, 266, 268, 270, 275, 277, 282, 289, 330
Mitchell, D. D., made lieutenant-colonel, 46; mustering officer, 45
Mitchell, James P., 19
Mondragon, Narciso, 383
Money, G. P., 236, 238
Money, Hernando de Soto, 185
Montoya, Nestor, 244
Moore, O. J., 185
Morgan, James H., mentioned, 115; testified, 128, 129
Morgan, John T., 180 185, 186
Morrison, Alexander L., made speech, 36; mentioned, 6
Morrison, W. O., 46
Morton, Paul, 62
Moule, Mrs. Ed., 267, 268
Muller, Frederick, affidavit, 371-373; captain, Troop E., 42; mentioned, 44, 56, 65, 146, 147, 151, 154, 155, 172, 179, 184, 189, 192, 198, 238, 285, 315, 325, 335; signed letter, 153
Murphy, Governor of Arizona, 205-207, 209-211, 216, 217

My Nine Years as Governor

Murphy, Mrs., 209-210
Murphy, N. O., attended reunion, 62-63; mentioned, 92, 93, 203
Murray, Mrs., 324
Murray, W. M., 250, 252

National Guard (New Mexico), drilling, 36; mentioned, 51; ordered to recruit full strength, 38
Nelson, Knute, 216
Newcomb, S. B., 30
N. M. Squadron, 314, 322, 352-354
New York World, quoted, 35

O'Brien, Gus, 193
O'Bryan, Harry J., 174, 190, 298, 373
O'Bryan, Mrs. Harry J., 166, 257
Ogborne, Senator, 213
Olsen, Clara H., mentioned, 258, 277; private secretary, 206
Osgood, J. S., 259
Osgood, Mrs. J. S., 259
Otero, Don Miguel A., father of governor, 56
Otero, Eduardo, 277
Otero, F. J., 261
Otero, Manuel B., 308
Otero, Manuel Rito, 6, 224, 277
Otero, Mariano S., 204
Otero, Miguel A. (governor), appointed Fall captain, 48; appointed governor, vii; charges against, 152-154; commended, 105-106; congratulated, 134; inaugurated governor, 168, 169, 171, 173-176; letter to Fall, 15; letter to *World*, 36; report, 199; mentioned, 1, 2, 4, 5, 7, 8, 10, 14, 16, 19, 21, 30, 37, 43, 50, 53, 83, 84, 107, 132, 135, 138-142, 149, 155-157, 160-167, 181, 182, 186-188, 201-204, 206-211, 216, 219-221, 224-226, 234, 238, 243, 245, 247, 254, 256, 258- 260, 262, 265, 293, 295-298, 303, 306, 308-210, 313-316, 320, 325, 329, 333, 334, 336-341, 353, 369, 371-384, 387, 388; offers Spanish-speaking cavalry, 38; receives medal, 60; resolution, 81; success as war governor, 40; veto messages, 85-86, 366; vetoed bill, 89; second trip to Washington, 33; signed letter, 347; thanked, 104
Otero, Miguel A., Jr., kidnap threat, 101; mentioned, 3, 4, 92, 93, 134, 173, 174, 187, 252, 268, 275, 276, 289, 292, 293, 295, 296, 298, 300, 302, 311; pleads for Black Jack, 121
Otero, Mrs. Miguel A., social life, 3, 4, 18, 24, 61, 92, 93, 134, 144, 166, 167, 173-176, 186, 187, 214, 215, 249-260, 264, 268, 271, 275-278, 280, 289, 293, 295, 296, 298-302, 305, 312, 313, 324
Otero, Page B., 46, 191, 192, 251, 260, 280, 281, 288, 292, 381

Perez y Ovante, Mariana, 91
Padilla, Eleuterio, received New Years pardon, 105
Padilla, Father Juan de, 306
Palen, Mrs. Rufus J., social life, 256, 257, 261, 263, 270
Palen, Rufus J., 259-262
Pardons, holiday, established, 102, 103
Parker, Frank W., 8, 9, 18, 166, 197, 254, 260, 262, 270, 278, 279, 287, 350
Parker, O., 265

Patterson, Thomas J., 186
Peace Jubilee, the, 293
Peck, George R., 203
Pecos Valley Stockman, mentioned, 223
Pendaries, John, 264
Pendaries, Marguerite, 264
Pendaries, Mrs. John, 264
Perea, Pedro, 144, 343
Pierce, Mrs. Fred H., 258
Pike, Zebulon, 359
Pinard, Saturnino, 123
Platt, Tom, 143
Pope, William H., advised auditor, 16; became Republican, 15; mentioned, 154, 184, 259, 260, 262, 263; on statehood committee, 211
Porter, John A., 1, 2
Porter, Mrs. John A., 294-295
Prescott Journal Miner, mentioned, 211; quoted, 208
Prescott Mining Courier, quoted, 210
Prichard, George W., mentioned, 183-185, 241, 262, 329, 369; on statehood committee, 211; recommended pardon, 105
Prichard, Mrs. George W., 261, 262
Prince, L. Bradford, 72, 137, 148, 152, 153, 160, 179, 186, 248, 251, 253, 256, 256, 335, 369, 375
Prince, Mrs. L. Bradford, social life, 180, 186, 251, 254, 270, 271

Quay, Matt, 143

Rankin, R. C., 51
Ransom, Bonnie, 289
Rapp, I. H., commends prisoners, 109; mentioned, 71, 72, 358
Rapp, W. M., 71
Raton Range, quoted, 50
Raynolds, E. D., 261
Raynolds, Jefferson W., 21-23, 77, 158, 159, 172,

173, 176, 183, 187, 215, 256, 258, 259, 261, 263, 325
Raynolds, Joshua S., 61, 247, 268
Raynolds, Mrs. E. D., 258
Raynolds, Mrs. James W., 258-260, 308, 324
Raynolds, Mrs. Joshua S., social life, 61, 172, 268
Reed, Benjamin M., mentioned, 75, 369; sponsored bill, 76
Reed, Joseph R., 250
Reed, Tom, 143
Reeder, James H., 288
Reeder, Mrs. James H., 288
Reid, W. C., clerk of house, 12; mentioned, 46, 292
Renehan, A. B., 132, 166, 263
Renehan, Mrs. A. B., 166, 325
Reno, W. H., investigated robbery, 113; mentioned, 115
Reymond, Nuna, 47, 200
Reynolds, F. A., 21
Reynolds, Matthew G., 154, 184, 281, 308, 309
Rice, Otto L., 158
Richardson, G. A., mentioned, 78-79; on statehood committee, 211
Rievera, Carlos E., pardoned, 103
Riley, John H., letter, 47-48
Rio Grande Dam and Irrigation Co., suit against, 29
Rio Grande Republican, quoted, 333
"Robbers' Roost," 112
Roberts, John, 172
Rocky Mountain News, mentioned, 328; quoted, 246
Rodey, Bernard S., mentioned, 137, 139-141, 184, 201, 211-213, 215, 216, 218, 224-226, 228-230, 232, 233, 237-239,

300, 333, 369; delegate to Congress, 136
Roland, George, 353
Romero, Eugenio, 139
Romero, Secundo, 18, 297
Roosevelt, Mrs. Theodore, 297, 299, 300
Roosevelt, Theodore, mentioned, 39, 41, 57, 58, 146, 151, 154, 155, 177, 179-182, 188, 189, 197, 198, 300, 301, 314-319, 321, 322, 324-333, 335, 336, 340, 341, 355, 357, 370, 373; opposed to statehood, 215-218, 223; received rifle, 123; Rough Riders, 268; speech, 64; telegram from, 60-61; visited New Mexico, 62-64
Root, Elihu, 255, 317, 318, 326, 327
Rothberg, Blanche, 258
Rothchild, L. G., "the Baron," 212, 213
Rough Riders (Roosevelt's), first encounter, 51, 52; honor Governor Otero, 56-58; mentioned, 42, 45, 59, 60, 146, 155, 179, 180, 189, 268, 294, 295, 314, 315, 326, 352, 354, 356, 360, 372, 393; received silk flag, 44; reunion, 61-65
Roux, Father John, 268
Ruffner, J. F., 246
Ruiz, Jose D., murderer, 107
Russell, Aaron, notary public, 385
Ryan, Thomas, 207

Safford, Charles V., traveling auditor, 88; mentioned, 260
Salazar, Manuel M., 248
Sanchez, Pedro, 74-75
Sanders, Frederick W., 276
Sandoval, Patricio, 374
Sandoval, Pedro, 130
Sandoval, Placido, mentioned, 13, 14, 89; resigned, 17

Santa Fe Capitol, mentioned, 148, 184
Santa Fe New Mexican, mentioned, 39, 121, 136, 250, 332, 377; quoted, 19, 30, 33, 40, 82-87, 89, 104-106, 141, 155, 160-162, 164, 166-169, 175, 186, 199-200, 202, 207, 211, 219, 225, 234, 236, 243, 247, 256, 259-263, 324-325, 333, 334, 336, 340, 369
"Santa Fe Ring," 197, 337
Sargent, William G., 260
Savage, W. H., 201
Schley, Mrs. W. S., 58
Schley, W. S., 58
Schnepple, William C., soldier, 52
Schultz, C. H., *see* Garner, W. H., 98
Scott, Homel, 114
Seeds, Edward P., 154, 184
Seligman, Arthur, 132, 260, 302, 307, 308, 311, 313
Seligman, James L., 260
Seligman, Mrs. Arthur, 256, 260
Seligman, Mrs. J. L., 325
Sena, Elisio, pardoned, 109
Sena, Jose D., 168, 224, 234, 260
Sena, Vicente, pardoned, 109
Shannon, P. Carrick, 383
Sheridan, J. J., 244, 378
Sherman, John, letter to, 344-345; mentioned, 29
Shoup, George L., 2, 70, 203
Simon, R. C., 213
Sloan, J. H., 122, 205, 275
Sluss, Henry C., 250
Smith, Edna Scott, 260
Smith, H. M., 46
Smith, Mark A., 319-321
Smith, Thomas, 154, 184, 185
Smith, W. Scott, 220, 239, 260, 303
Snyder, Karl A., 287

Somborn, E. K., 298
Sparks, Mayor, 300
Sparks, Mrs., 324, 325
Spies, Charles, mentioned, 143, 150, 232, 251, 312, 329, 330, 343, 344; law partner of T. B. Catron, 12; on statehood committee, 211; sustains veto, 87
Spiess, Mrs. Charles A., 251
Springer, Charles, 184, 330
Springer, Frank, 4, 30, 63, 158,, 330
Springer Sentinel, 166
Spring-Rice, Sir Cecil, quoted, 314
Staab, Abraham, 144, 258-260, 357
Star Route Frauds, 194
Stephenson, George, 110
Stevens Bill, mentioned, 31, 351; protest against, 30
Stevens, John S., introduced bill, 30
Stewart, M. Cicero, 117
Stone, Wilbur F., 250, 288
Stover, E. S., letter to press, 50-51
Stover, William, 46, 292
Stroup, Andrew B., 242
Sturgis, W. S., 220

Tafoya, Jesús María, examined, 213
Taft, William H., 15, 239
Taylor, R. W., 148
Thacker, Capt., 115
Thomas, Rufus, 117
Thompson, A. W., 126

Thornton, Governor W. T., mentioned, 246; resigned, 12, 90; returned to territory, 22
Tipton, Mrs. W. R., 268
Tipton, William R., 208, 268, 330
Traen, G. W. T., 259
Tubbs, engineer, 114
Twitchell, Ralph E., mentioned, 11, 44, 203, 254, 270, 287, 325, 333, 334, 343; quoted in *The Leading Facts of New Mexican History*, 34, 142-143, 226, 232, 239, 314

United States Journal for Investors, mentioned, 332

Valdez, Marcial, 270, 274, 279
Vance, Quinby, 148, 159, 160, 172, 179, 239, 287, 335
Van Patten, Eugene, appointment of, opposed, 47; mentioned, 270
Vaughn, J. H., territorial treasurer, 78; mentioned, 260
Vermudez, Baltazar, 374
Victory, J. P., 105
Vigil, Eslavio, 214, 240, 242, 243, 245
Villegos, Francisco, pardoned, 103-105
Vincent, William A., 302
Voorhees, A. C., 147, 238, 335

Wade, Walter, pardoned, 105
Waldo, Henry S., mentioned, 14, 15, 87; revealed kidnap plan, 101
Walker, William A., 90
Wallace, George H., 4, 21-24, 72, 153, 239
Wallace, Lew, 180, 181, 182
Walsh, Thomas F., 301
Walter, Paul A. F., 65
Walter, William (Broncho Bill), 111
Walton, William B., 74
Ward, C. W., 204
Washington Post, mentioned, 160, 293; quoted, 289, 298, 334
Washington Star, quoted, 202-203
Weakley, Lieutenant, Troop F, 42
Webster, George H., 236
Wheeler, Joe, letter, 59-60; mentioned, 55, 57, 355
Whigman, Harry, 11
White, David M., 196, 224, 231, 375, 378
Whiteman, W. H., 47, 48, 208, 230, 270, 276, 277, 295, 308, 375, 380
Wilkinson, Thomas N., 204
Wood, Leonard, letter, 44; mentioned, 39, 43

Young, Lafe, 65

Zollars, John W., 268
Zollars, Mrs. John W., 268

www.ingramcontent.com/pod-product-compliance
Lightning Source LLC
Chambersburg PA
CBHW021140240426
43661CB00075B/1596